The International Development Dictionary

THE INTERNATIONAL DEVELOPMENT DICTIONARY

Gerald W. Fry
Galen R. Martin
University of Oregon

ABC-CLIO

Santa Barbara, California
Denver, Colorado
Oxford, England

Library of Congress Cataloging-in-Publication Data

Fry, Gerald.
    The international development dictionary / Gerald W. Fry, Galen R. Martin.
      p. cm.—(Clio dictionaries in political science)
    Includes bibliographical references and index.
    1. International economic relations—Dictionaries. 2. Economic development—International cooperation—Dictionaries. 3. Developing countries—Foreign economic relations—Dictionaries. I. Martin, Galen R., 1957– . II. Title. III. Series.
    HF1359.F79 1991   338.9'1'03—dc20   91-18707

ISBN 0-87436-545-7

98 97 96 95 94 93 92 91   10 9 8 7 6 5 4 3 2 1

ABC-CLIO, Inc.
130 Cremona Drive, P.O. Box 1911
Santa Barbara, California 93116-1911

This book is Smyth-sewn and printed on acid-free paper ∞ .
Manufactured in the United States of America

*In memory of Clarence E. Thurber
and his life-long commitment to
international development and understanding*

Clio Dictionaries in Political Science

SERIES STATEMENT

Language precision is the primary tool of every scientific discipline. That aphorism serves as the guideline for this series of political dictionaries. Although each book in the series relates to a specific topical or regional area in the discipline of political science, entries in the dictionaries also emphasize history, geography, economics, sociology, philosophy, and religion.

This dictionary series incorporates special features designed to help the reader overcome any language barriers that may impede a full understanding of the subject matter. For example, the concepts included in each volume were selected to complement the subject matter found in existing texts and other books. All but one volume utilize a subject-matter chapter arrangement that is most useful for classroom and study purposes.

Entries in all volumes include an up-to-date definition plus a paragraph of *Significance* in which the authors discuss and analyze the term's historical and current relevance. Most entries are also cross-referenced, providing the reader an opportunity to seek additional information related to the subject of inquiry. A comprehensive index, found in both hardcover and paperback editions, allows the reader to locate major entries and other concepts, events, and institutions discussed within these entries.

The political and social sciences suffer more than most disciplines from semantic confusion. This is attributable, *inter alia*, to the popularization of the language, and to the focus on many diverse foreign political and social systems. This dictionary series is dedicated to overcoming some of this confusion through careful writing of thorough, accurate definitions for the central concepts, institutions, and events that comprise the basic knowledge of each of the subject fields. New titles in the series will be issued periodically, including some in related social science disciplines.

—Jack C. Plano
Series Editor

CONTENTS

A NOTE ON HOW TO USE THIS BOOK

The International Development Dictionary is organized so that entries and supplementary data can be located in several ways. Items are arranged alphabetically within subject-matter chapters. The term *foreign aid*, for example, is found under the analytical category "development assistance and technology transfer" in the chapter titled "Basic Development Concepts." An "Alphabetic List of Entries" as well as an index are provided to further facilitate the reader's access. Entry numbers for terms appear in the index in bold type; subsidiary concepts discussed within entries can be found in the index identified by entry numbers in regular type. A "Glossary of Acronyms" is also provided.

The reader can also more fully explore a topic by using the extensive cross-references provided in most entries. These may lead to entries in the same chapter or may refer to the subject matter of other chapters. Entry numbers have been included in all cross-references for the convenience of the reader. In addition, the dictionary includes a comprehensive bibliography of works cited to aid further research.

The authors have designed the format of this book to offer the user a variety of useful applications in the quest for information. These include its uses as (1) a *dictionary* and *reference guide* to the language of the international development field; (2) a *study guide* for introductory courses in development studies and international relations; (3) a supplement to the *textbook* or to a group of paperback monographs adopted for use in international development or international relations courses; (4) a *source of review material* for the student enrolled in advanced courses; and (5) a *social science aid* for use in cognate fields in such courses as international economics, development education, world or comparative politics, and development administration.

PREFACE

The objective of this volume is to provide a basic reference work for the field of international development. Our interdisciplinary approach includes perspectives from such diverse disciplines as economics, political science, sociology, demography, geography, psychology, history, anthropology, and the humanities. We have also attempted to make the work as international as possible by drawing upon examples and development thinking from all regions of the world. Finally, our approach is intellectually pluralistic, including a wide range of ideological perspectives on international development.

Gunnar Myrdal, in his important but neglected volume, *Objectivity in Social Research,* emphasizes that social science is not value-free and that authors should make explicit their underlying value premises. In this volume we attempt to present all major development perspectives fairly, but our own normative assumptions do underlie our perspectives on development. We firmly believe that the fundamental end of development is the improvement of the *human* condition, not the increase in material wealth per se. We are deeply concerned about the need to promote sustainable development in ways consistent with the carrying capacity of the earth and compatible with the preservation of the earth's magnificent biological and cultural diversity. We also consider the distributional and social justice aspects of development as fundamentally important. For this reason, in chapter 3, for example, we provide a number of entries related to the measurement of inequality, inequity, and injustice.

This reference work has clear limitations. First, it is not comprehensive. A truly comprehensive reference work on international development would run thousands of pages. For example, we have provided only a sampling of the better known development practitioners. There are many able, quiet, and unknown development workers around the world committed to their international work.

They often work in remote areas, rather removed from communication and scholarly channels. Similarly, there are thousands of organizations involved in development work, particularly nongovernmental organizations (NGOs) and private voluntary organizations (PVOs). Included in this volume are only some of the more significant and prominent ones. The chapters on conceptual and analytical frameworks of development tend to be more comprehensive, though even in these chapters it is not feasible to cover every concept or analytical framework of development.

Our volume is organized into four chapters. Each chapter is subsequently divided into analytical categories. For example, the first chapter is broken into two analytical categories: development thinkers/theorists, and development leaders and practitioners. While these categories are helpful, in some instances they overlap. For example, a number of individuals have been prominent as both development theorists and practitioners. In such cases, we have included individuals under the category in which we believe they have attained the greatest prominence and made the greatest contribution. Other chapters are similarly subdivided into analytical categories.

In compiling this reference work, a number of sources have been particularly valuable. Among these are Gerald Meier's and Dudley Seer's *Pioneers in Development* (1984); Charles K. Wilber, ed., *The Political Economy of Development and Underdevelopment* (1988); Gerald Fry's and Clarence Thurber's *The International Education of Development Consultants: Communicating with Peasants and Princes* (1989); Mark Blaug's *Who's Who in Economics: A Biographical Dictionary of Economists 1799–1986* (1986); and Michael Todaro's *Economic Development in the Third World* (1985). The *Christian Science Monitor* and *South* magazine also have provided valuable information related to extremely current or contemporary entries.

In compiling this work, both authors owe important intellectual debts to a number of individuals. The volume is dedicated to Clarence E. Thurber, the late director of International Studies at the University of Oregon, who encouraged and inspired our interest in international development and development studies. Gerald Fry would also like to acknowledge the intellectual influence of mentors such as Paul Baran, Sir Arthur Lewis, Fred Harbison, Marion Levy, Hans Weiler, Martin Carnoy, and Robert Textor. Fry's thinking on development was also strongly influenced by the Thai scholars/thinkers Buddhadasa Bhikku, Sippanondha Ketudat, and Sulak Sivaraksa. Galen Martin would like to acknowledge the influence of Denis Goulet and E. F. Schumacher as well as numerous development practicioners and Third World citizens who have shared with him their direct experience and observations.

Preface

We would also like to thank a number of individuals for their help in completing this work. For research assistance we thank Sarah Shafer, Kanya Worawichawong, Rebecca Murphy, Lisa Johnson, Tatsanee Setboonsarng, Aila Lehtonen, and Li Zhang. We also thank several of our colleagues at the University of Oregon who reviewed a number of our entries. Among these individuals were Anita Weiss, John Foster, William Mitchell, Barry Siegel, Deanna Robinson, Aletta Biersack, Christina Kreps, Irene Diamond, and Roger Durham. We also benefited from the extemely helpful and careful editing of Professor Jack Plano and Richard Bass. Despite all such help and influences, we remain solely responsible for any weaknesses or limitations in the work.

—Gerald W. Fry
—Galen R. Martin

ALPHABETIC LIST OF ENTRIES

Please note that numbers in the following are entry numbers and not page numbers.

GLOSSARY OF ACRONYMS

ACFOA	Australian Council for Overseas Aid
ACFOD	Asian Cultural Forum on Development
ACP	African, Caribbean, and Pacific States
ACVAFS	American Council of Voluntary Agencies for Foreign Service
ADAA	Australian Development Assistance Agency
ADAB	Australian Development Assistance Bureau
AED	Academy for Educational Development
AFSC	American Friends Service Committee
AID	U.S. Agency for International Development
AIDAB	Australian International Development Assistance Bureau
AIDS	Acquired Immune Deficiency Syndrome
AIT	Asian Institute of Technology
AP	Associated Press
APPEAL	Asia-Pacific Program of Education for All
AT	Appropriate Technology
AWID	Association of Women In Development
BAPA	Buenos Aires Plan of Action for Promoting and Implementing Technical Co-operation among Developing Countries
BBC	British Broadcasting Corporation
CAD	Computer Assisted Design
CAM	Computer Assisted Manufacturing
CBC	Christian Base Community
CBI	Caribbean Basin Initiative
CCID	Community Colleges for International Development
CD	Community Development
CDC	Center for Development Communities
CELAM	General Conference of the Latin American Episcopacy
CEPAL	Commissión Económica para América Latina (UN Economic Commission for Latin America, ECLA)
CFTC	Commonwealth Fund for Technical Cooperation

CGIAR	Consultative Group on International Agricultural Research
CIA	Central Intelligence Agency
CIAT	Centro Internacional de Agricultura Tropical (International Center for Tropical Agriculture)
CIDA	Canadian International Development Agency
CIDE	Research and Educational Development Center
CIDOC	Center for Intercultural Documentation (Mexico)
CIMMYT	Centro Internacional de Mejoramiento de Maíz y Traigo (International Center for Improvement of Maize and Wheat)
CIP	Centro Internacional de la Papa (International Potato Center)
CODEL	Coordination in Development
CODESRIA	Council for the Development of Economic and Social Research in Africa
CRS	Catholic Relief Services
CUAVES	Self-Managed Urban Community of Villa El Salvador
DA	Development Assistance
DAC	Development Assistance Committee
DAG	Development Assistance Group
DANIDA	Danish International Development Agency
DAWN	Development Alternatives with Women for a New Era
ECDC	Economic Cooperation Among Developing Countries
ECLA	UN Economic Commission for Latin America
ECOSOC	Economic and Social Council
EEC	European Economic Community
EEZ	Exclusive Economic Zone
ESCAP	Economic and Social Commission for Asia and the Pacific
ESF	Economic Support Fund
EVI	Ex-Volunteers International
FAO	Food and Agricultural Organization
FINNIDA	Finnish International Development Agency
FSR	Farming Systems Research
GATT	General Agreement on Tariffs and Trade
GCC	Gulf Cooperation Council
GDP	Gross Domestic Product
GNP	Gross National Product
HDI	Human Development Index
HIID	Harvard Institute for International Development
HYV	High Yield Variety
IADS	International Agricultural Development Service
IBPGR	International Board for Plant Genetic Resources
IBRD	International Bank for Reconstruction and Development
ICARDA	International Center for Agriculture Research in Dry Areas
ICDS	Institutional Cooperation and Development Service
ICOR	Incremental Capital Output Ratio

ICRISAT	International Crop Research Institute for the Semi-Arid Tropics
ICVA	International Council of Voluntary Agencies
IDA	International Development Association
IDB	Inter-American Development Bank
IDC	International Development Conference
IDCA	International Development Cooperation Agency
IDRC	International Development Research Centre
IDS	Institute for Development Studies
IESC	International Executive Service Corps
IFAD	International Fund for Agricultural Development
IFC	International Finance Corporation
IFPRI	International Food Policy Research Institute
IGGI	Inter-Governmental Group of Indonesia
IIEP	International Institute for Educational Planning
IIR	Institute for International Research
IITA	International Institute for Tropical Agriculture
ILCA	International Livestock Centre for Africa
ILO	International Labor Organization
ILRAD	International Laboratory for Research on Animal Diseases
IMF	International Monetary Fund
INGO	International (or Indigenous) Non-governmental Organization
INRA	Institute for Natural Resources in Africa
INRES-South	Information Network Referral Service
INSTRAW	United Nations International Research and Training Institute for the Advancement of Women
INTECH	Institute for New Technologies
IPPF	International Planned Parenthood Federation
IPS	Industrial Promotion Services
IPVO	International (or Indigenous) Private Voluntary Organization
IRD	Integrated Rural Development
IRRI	International Rice Research Institute
ISA	International Seabed Authority
ISNAR	International Service for National Agricultural Research
ISP	Index of Social Progress
ITDG	Intermediate Technology Development Group
ITK	Indigenous Technical Knowledge
JAIDO	Japan International Development Organization
JICA	Japan International Cooperation Agency
JOCV	Japan Overseas Cooperation Volunteers
LDC	Less or Least Developed Country
LIC	Low Intensity Conflict
LORCS	League of Red Cross Societies
MCC	Mennonite Central Committee
MDC	More Developed Country

MNC	Multinational Corporation
NAM	Non-Aligned Movement
NDP	Net Domestic Product
NGO	Nongovernmental Organization
NIAC	Newly Industrialized Agro-based Countries
NIC	Newly Industrialized Countries
NIEO	New International Economic Order
NIIO	New International Information Order
NRDC	Natural Resources Defense Council
NRR	Net Reproduction Rate
NWICO	New World Information and Communication Order
OAS	Organization of American States
OAU	Organization of African Unity
ODA	Official Development Assistance
ODA	(British) Overseas Development Agency
ODC	Overseas Development Council
OECD	Organization for Economic Co-operation and Development
OFDA	Office of Foreign Disaster Assistance
OPEC	Organization of Petroleum Exporting Countries
ORS	Oral Rehydration Salts
ORT	Oral Rehydration Therapy
OXFAM	Oxford Committee on Famine Relief
PACT	Private Agencies Collaborating Together
PAID	Pan African Institute for Development
PC	Population Council
PL	Public Law
PQLI	Physical Quality of Life Index
PVO	Private Voluntary Organization
RCCDC	Research Centre for Cooperation with Developing Countries
RF	Rockefeller Foundation
RIO	Reshaping the International Order
RRA	Rapid Rural Appraisal
SAP	Social Action Party (Thailand)
SAREC	Swedish Agency for Research Cooperation with Developing Countries
SDR	Special Drawing Rights
SEAMEO	Southeast Asian Ministers of Education Organization
SEZ	Special Economic Zone
SIA	Social Impact Analysis
SID	Society for International Development
SIDA	Swedish International Development Authority
SIPRI	Swedish International Peace Research Institute
SSP	Small-Scale Producer
STABEX	Export Revenue Stabilization Scheme
TCDC	Technical Cooperation among Developing Countries
TFR	Total Fertility Rate

TNC	Transnational Corporation
TUP	Trickle Up Program
UN	United Nations
UNCTAD	United Nations Conference on Trade and Development
UNDP	United Nations Development Program
UNEP	United Nations Environmental Program
UNESCO	United Nations Educational, Scientific and Cultural Organization
UNFPA	United Nations Fund for Population Activity
UNICEF	United Nations International Children's (Emergency) Fund
UNIDO	United Nations Industrial Development Organization
UNU	United Nations University
UPI	United Press International
USAID	U.S. Agency for International Development
WARDA	West African Rice Development Association
WCED	World Commission on Environment and Development
WEP	World Employment Programme
WHO	World Health Organization
WID	Women In Development
WIDER	World Institute for Development Economics Research
WIPO	World International Property Organization
WRI	World Resources Institute

The International Development Dictionary

1. Development Thinkers/Theorists, Leaders, and Practitioners

A. Development Thinkers/Theorists

Achebe, Chinua (1)

A Nigerian novelist, poet, and essayist who is Black Africa's best known writer of fiction. Achebe's first novel, *Things Fall Apart* (1958), was a landmark publication in African fiction, making Achebe one of the first internationally renowned African novelists. In his first work and in the two to follow, *No Longer at Ease* (1960) and *Arrow of God*, for which he won the 1965 New Statesman Award, Achebe offers a particular African perspective on the tragic consequences of the African encounter with Europe and the ambiguities resulting from the colonial experience. The publication of his fourth novel, *A Man of the People* (1966), a tale that ends with the military takeover of a corrupt civilian government, coincided with the Nigerian coup of that same year. Following the Nigerian civil war, Achebe was a professor of English at the University of Massachusetts and became founding editor of the African Writers Series to promote other African writers. He continued to write works of poetry and nonfiction, including *Christmas in Biafra, and Other Poems* (1973) and *The Trouble with Nigeria* (1983). However, he did not publish another novel until *Anthills of the Savanah* (1987). The long-awaited novel was well received. In 1989, Achebe became chairman, publisher, and columnist of a unique periodical, *African Commentary: A Journal of People of African Descent.*

Significance   As author of *Things Fall Apart* and founder of the African Writers Series, Achebe helped pave the way for the emergence of a rich body of African literature. These works are vital resources for those seeking to understand African perspectives on colonialism,

3

independence, and development. They also serve as aids in the process of "decolonizing the mind" of former colonial societies. Achebe's books are widely read in Africa, Europe, and North America. They are highly critical of European involvement in Africa, but equally harsh on the shortcomings of Nigerian society. Perhaps more importantly, Achebe uses fiction as a tool for reasserting African dignity and identity through insightful writing and vivid characters. He does so not with propagandistic or romanticized accounts, but rather through honest, creative, and thoughtful works of fiction that focus on Africans but are accessible to non-Africans.

Adelman, Irma (2)
A development economist who has focused on the equity and distributional aspects of economic development. Adelman's initial interest in economics was motivated by her desire to work on problems of global poverty. Among her many publications are *Economic Growth and Social Equity in Developing Countries* (1973) and *Society, Politics and Economic Development: A Quantitative Approach* (1967) (both with C. T. Morris). Techniques and problems associated with economic planning have also been a major interest of Adelman. Born in Romania, she has been a professor of economics at the University of California, Berkeley since 1979. *See also* DEVELOPMENT METHODOLOGY, 319.

Significance Collaborating with Professor Cynthia Taft Morris, Adelman pioneered the use of multivariate techniques to quantify interactions among economic, social, and political forces in economic development. Her work has contributed to the movement to refocus development policy on issues of income distribution and basic needs. In addressing problems of global poverty and income distribution, Adelman has been impressive in her use of multiple research methods and approaches. Adelman's work demonstrates the practical value of rigorous quantitative economic research when applied to important development problems.

Amin, Samir (3)
An Egyptian economist often noted for his articulate presentation of a radical perspective on development and a leading exponent of the dependency school of development. Amin is currently with the Council for the Development of Economic and Social Research in Africa (CODESRIA) in Dakar, Senegal. For many years he directed the United Nations African Institute for Economic Development and Planning. He is part of the Forum du Tiers Monde in Senegal. He

taught development economics at the universities of Poitiers, Paris, and Dakar, and was a development adviser in Mali from 1960 to 1963. Among his many books and writings are *Accumulation on a World Scale* (1974), *Unequal Development* (1976), *The Law of Value and Historical Materialism* (1978), "Self-Reliance and the New International Economic Order" (1984), *La faillité du developpement en Afrique et dans le Tiers Monde: Une analyse politique* (1989), and *Eurocentrism* (1989). *See also* DEPENDENCY THEORY, 106.

Significance   Amin is one of the leading radical thinkers on development who has adapted both dependency theory and Marxism to apply to current global economic conditions. Central to Amin's thinking is the notion of peripheral capitalism, in which the dominant center (Western industrial countries) dominates the dependent Third World in a system of growing global inequalities. Amin calls for the liberation of the periphery and development beyond capitalism. He argues for the needs for more self-reliant development and for rejection of the rules of profitability. He is also highly critical of international specialization, which produces unequal development. Amin's development theory derives primarily from African and Latin American experiences and seems less relevant in explaining development patterns in many parts of the Pacific Basin.

Arevalo, Juan José (1904–1990)   (4)
Guatemalan intellectual, writer, politician, and former president of Guatemala (1945–1951) famous for his critical and satirical views describing U.S. political and economic domination of Latin America. Arevalo's successor as president, Jacobo Arbenz (1951–1954), backed policies that threatened the interests of the United States, and was overthrown by a CIA-supported coup d'état. This led to Arevalo's eventual exile from Guatemala and his bitterness toward the U.S. government and its role in Latin America. A prolific writer, Arevalo has authored 12 books, the most famous of which is *The Shark and the Sardines* (1961). Using allegory and satire, Arevalo presents a sharply critical view of how the shark (the United States) dominates the sardines (the smaller Latin American countries). Arevalo denounces the Pan-American system of diplomacy as an instrument of imperialism. He presents a conspiracy theory of domination which involves collaboration among the U.S. State Department, U.S. monopoly capital, "the big press" in Latin America, Latin American military dictators, and other influential local individuals who have prostituted themselves to Yankee dollars. According to Arevalo, U.S. monopoly capital's main interest in Latin America is to obtain cheap

resources, such as Guatemalan bananas and Chilean copper, and profits from investments and markets in Latin America. Arevalo is particularly critical of a U.S. foreign policy that denounces as communists all those working toward greater social justice and equity. While president, Arevalo claims to have been committed to programs improving the economic and political conditions of the indigenous Indians, who constitute the vast majority of Guatemala's population. Among his other books are *Anti-Kommunism in Latin America* and *Escritos Politicos y Filosoficos* (Political Writings and Presidential Speeches).

Significance   Though Arevalo's writing is highly polemical and journalistic, it reflects many sentiments and views that have become the underlying intellectual framework for dependency theory. As early as 1956, when *The Shark and the Sardines* was first published in Spanish, Arevalo was using the terminology, North-South, which was later to attain popularity in the 1970s. Though he did not use the current term, countertrade, Arevalo argued for this type of barter to reduce Latin American economic dependency on the United States. Arevalo's famous fable of the shark and the sardines also shows remarkable prescience in anticipating the basic principles set forth in the Law of the Sea Treaty and its attempt to legislate internationally more equitable access to the sea for all nations so as to prevent the domination of the sea by a few superpowers. As Arevalo would have predicted, "the shark" has refused to sign the Law of the Sea agreement, the development of which represented remarkable collaboration and consensus building among North and South nations.

Baran, Paul (1910–1964)   (5)

An influential thinker who applied Marxist thought to the problems of developing areas. Baran was originally from the Soviet Union and later migrated to Germany and then to the United States, where he taught comparative economics at Stanford University until his death in 1964. Baran's basic theme is that the conventional capitalist economic system with its links to imperialist external forces blocks the potential for genuine development. Baran is particularly critical of the institution of private property, wasteful nonessential consumption stimulated by advertising, and the production of goods and services adverse to the human condition (e.g., prostitution and armaments). As a result of such phenomena integral to capitalist economic systems, developing countries are unable to achieve their potential economic surplus and thus their economic growth is dramatically inhibited. Among Baran's most important writings were

The Political Economy of Growth (1957), *Monopoly Capital* (1966), and *The Longer View* (1970). *See also* DEPENDENCY THEORY, 106.

Significance   Baran was, in his early years, one of the few Marxists teaching at a major U.S. university. Though *The Political Economy of Growth* was written more than 30 years ago, it is still widely used as a seminal work that reflects a radical approach to development. Perhaps the Chinese economy under Mao best reflects an example of the practical application of Baran's development theories and ideas. As long as serious poverty and inequality persist in both the world system and individual nations, Baran's ideas will continue to be highly salient, hotly debated, and inspiring to those committed to revolution as the only means to bring about fundamental political and economic transformations. Baran's thinking also has important methodological implications; an example is his critique of conventional economists as preoccupied with elegant methods instead of concerned with the critical substantive issues related to the enhancement of the global human condition.

Bauer, Lord (P. T.)   (6)

A development thinker who emphasizes classical development paths and the adverse effects of comprehensive planning and excessive government intervention. Bauer's development thinking derives primarily from extensive field experience in the 1940s and 1950s in West Africa (Ghana) and Southeast Asia (Malaya, now Malaysia). Bauer emphasizes the important role of small-scale traders, farmers, and entrepreneurs and advocates a market theory of development. Based primarily on his field experiences and related research, his work noted "pronounced differences in economic performance among different cultural groups" (Bauer 1984b:33). In Bauer's view, economists tend to ignore such differences because of conventional taboos. Bauer makes no attempt to formulate a theory of development and finds the variables used in conventional economic growth models to be unimportant. Originally from Hungary, Bauer has been articulating such perspectives as a professor at the London School of Economics since 1960. Among his most important publications are *The Economics of Under-Developed Countries* (1957), *Dissent on Development* (1972), and *Reality and Rhetoric: Studies in the Economics of Development* (1984).

Significance   Lord Bauer has displayed intellectual courage in challenging more conventional and popular views of development. Bauer admits, however, that in his earlier writings he failed to appreciate

The International Development Dictionary

the "pervasive significance of the politicization of economic life in LDCs [least developed countries]" and related biases against productive ethnic minorities. Bauer has also been criticized for overgeneralizing from his experiences in West Africa and Southeast Asia. Conditions in a country such as Bangladesh differ dramatically from those in Malaysia, for example, and many would question the applicability of development paths based on free markets in the former. Bauer's efforts to compare the economic performances of different cultural and ethnic groups not only violate conventional intellectual taboos, but also make him vulnerable to charges of racism and ethnocentrism. Despite these criticisms of Lord Bauer's development thinking, his critique of the tendency to aggregate all LDCs into one category reflects the stark reality of differential development performance among the nations of the South.

Berger, Peter (7)
Noted writer on the sociology of religion and critic of much development theory and practice. Berger was born in Vienna in 1929 and received his Ph.D. from the New School for Social Research in 1954. He has held numerous teaching posts throughout the eastern United States and early on established a reputation as a humanist sociologist. His book, *The Sacred Canopy* (1967), was widely acclaimed and remains as one of the most important writings on the sociology of religion. In 1969, the focus of Berger's study and writings shifted to the Third World following a trip to Mexico at the invitation of Ivan Illich. He began to explore how sociological insights could contribute to more compassionate political and economic development strategies. These themes were first explored in *The Homeless Mind: Modernization and Consciousness* (1973), which focused on technology and civilization. Berger's best known book on development, *Pyramids of Sacrifice* (1975), addressed political ethics, social change, and Third World development. As reflected in *Pyramids*, Berger is a staunch critic of both capitalist and socialist theories of development and change. He claims that the two major paradigms of development are constructed "without due regard for the sacredness of persons, traditional securities, and human suffering." Recent works include *The Capitalist Revolution: Fifty Propositions* (1986) and *Capitalism and Equality in the Third World* (1987). *See also* CULTURAL DEVELOPMENT, 219.

Significance Berger offers a provocative and humbling critique of the Western notion of means of achieving "progress." He reminds us that the high social cost of development cannot be easily discounted as a necessary, though regrettable cost. In *Pyramids of Sacrifice*, he calls

8

to accountability the powerful and the intellectuals who guide and legitimize the development process, and those willing to sacrifice silent individuals, even whole generations, to the insatiable gods of development. He calls into question the missionary zeal and arrogance of both revolutionary and orthodox thinkers who purport to "speak for the people." We must, he argues, show "cognitive respect" for all people. Pessimistically, Berger contends that as much suffering has resulted from "good intentions" as from unabashed exploitation. The implication is a hands-off approach that presents its own set of problems not fully considered by Berger. Nevertheless, his critique deserves serious consideration as an alternative humanistic approach to development problems.

Boserup, Ester Talke (8)

Danish development researcher, consultant, and pioneer in the field of women in development. After ten years with the Research Division of the United Nations Economic Committee for Europe she began her long association with the Third World in 1957. Until 1965 she worked as a freelance writer and development consultant in India and Senegal. From 1971 to 1980, Boserup was a member of the UN Committee of Development Planning and for two years served on the board of the Scandinavian Institute of Asian Studies. In 1979, she joined the staff of the United Nations International Research and Training Institute for the Advancement of Women (INSTRAW). Boserup's publications include *The Conditions of Agricultural Growth* (1965), *Woman's Role in Economic Development* (1970), and *Population and Technical Change* (1981). *See also* WOMEN IN DEVELOPMENT, 256.

Significance Boserup's research on women's roles in changing economies, as reflected in her 1970 publication, helped serve as a catalyst for the emergence of women in development (WID) as a vital new field in development studies. Of particular concern in her initial studies were the problems facing women as Third World economies have undergone transformation in the colonial and postcolonial periods. She has remained central to WID since that time with further publications and her work with the Committee of Development Planning and INSTRAW. In her earlier study, *The Conditions of Agricultural Growth*, she developed a controversial model of intensification of land use in which "population density is a precondition for the adoption of intensive techniques of land use." She proposes that even though intensive agricultural techniques yield more per acre than extensive techniques, extensive techniques have a higher production-to-unit labor ratio. Further, Boserup examines the differences in male- and female-dominant farming systems.

Boulding, Kenneth (9)

Prolific writer and creative thinker whose works are an eclectic and ambitious attempt to explain the modern world as an interdependent system. Born in 1910 in Liverpool, England, Boulding was trained in economics at Oxford and the University of Chicago. Though he has never taken his doctoral degree, he taught at many universities in England, Japan, and the United States. Currently the distinguished professor of economics emeritus at the University of Colorado, Boulding is the recipient of more than 30 honorary degrees. He has written more than 40 books whose titles reflect his broad range of interests. These include *Economic Analysis* (1941, a well-received textbook), *Human Betterment* (1985), *The Meaning of the Twentieth Century* (1964), *Beyond Economics: Essays on Society, Religion, and Ethics* (1968), *Economics of Peace* (1945), *Ecodynamics: A New Theory of Societal Evolution* (1978), and his latest major work, *The World as a Total System* (1985). In the most recent work, Boulding attempts to show how international economics and communications have brought the world to the brink of becoming a "single social system." This system, he explains, is comprised of three major subsystems: threat, exchange, and integrative systems. Boulding's interest in integrative theory dates back to the 1950s when he and others formed the Society for General Systems Theory. Their goals were to unify the sciences and to counter reductionism. Though systems theory fell out of vogue, Boulding continued his tireless search for some form of Ockham epiphany—the apprehension of a single principle that unites diverse phenomena. A devout Quaker, Boulding also helped start publication of *The Journal of Conflict Resolution,* to which he is a frequent contributor.

Significance   Boulding's writings represent a substantial contribution to the areas of alternative economics, peace studies, and world development. His works form a creative quest for understanding human betterment and reflect ideas that transcend national and disciplinary borders. He has contributed to the insight that development cannot be addressed by any single discipline. The interconnectedness of the world, which Boulding has always stressed, is now becoming more evident in international economic and global environmental problems. Boulding creatively draws from all branches of knowledge in his attempt to understand the development of the world as a total system.

Carnoy, Martin (10)

An economist of education at Stanford noted for his critical analyses of the role of education and schooling in development. Originally from Poland, Carnoy has been a professor at Stanford's International Development Education Center since 1969. While carrying out a cost-benefit analysis of education in Kenya for the World Bank, Carnoy became skeptical about the value of the human capital approach to analyzing education in developing countries. A prolific scholar, Carnoy has produced a number of important books and studies for organizations such as the World Bank, UNESCO, the International Labor Organization (ILO), and the International Institute for Educational Planning. In his important volume, *Education as Cultural Imperialism* (1974), Carnoy questions the conventional views of the role of schooling and sees it as a mechanism for reproducing existing social structures and systems of stratification. Carnoy also emphasizes the correspondence principle, which postulates a close association between educational experiences and later employment situations. With respect to development thinking, Carnoy is highly critical of modernization theory, emphasizes liberation from dependency, and calls for economic democracy. Among Carnoy's other books are *Economic Democracy* (1980), *The State and Political Theory* (1984), and *Schooling and Work in the Democratic State* (1985). *See also* ECONOMIC DEMOCRACY, 141.

Significance   Much of Carnoy's thinking has focused on the development problems of Latin America and he is best known among radical intellectuals in that region. In fact, he has personally trained a number of prominent Latin American development educators, economists, and thinkers, who are occasionally referred to as *Carnoyistas.* Carnoy's thinking has mellowed since he wrote *Education as Cultural Imperialism.* He now recognizes that public education can be both a force for greater social equity and a conflicting pressure for social reproduction and preservation of an inequitable status quo. Carnoy is a major figure in the field of education and economic/political development and an extremely articulate advocate of greater economic democracy in all societies, both rich and poor.

Chambers, Robert (11)

British economist of rural development, particularly known for his criticism of conventional approaches to researching conditions in rural areas. Chambers is a fellow of the Institute of Development Studies (IDS) at the University of Sussex in England. Chambers has

11

served as a rural development consultant in such countries as Botswana, Burundi, Ghana, India, Kenya, Sri Lanka, and Zambia. He also served with the Ford Foundation in India as a consultant on irrigation in rural development and was an evaluative officer of the United Nations High Commission for Refugees. Chambers is highly critical of both "quick and dirty" (e.g., quick trips during times when conditions are most favorable) and "long and dirty" (e.g., extensive and esoteric scholarly fieldwork) approaches to understanding rural development. He is the father and advocate of an alternative method-ology known as rapid rural appraisal, a highly cost-effective and cul-turally sensitive approach to learning about genuine rural conditions in ways relevant to action and practical policy. Among Chambers's publications based on his extensive research are *Managing Rural Development* (1974), "Rural Poverty Unperceived" (1980), *Rapid Rural Appraisal* (1980), *Seasonal Dimensions to Rural Poverty* (1981) (coeditor), and *Farmer First: Farmer Innovation and Agricultural Research* (1989) (coeditor). *See also* RAPID RURAL APPRAISAL, 185; DEVELOPMENT METHODOLOGY, 319.

Significance   Chambers is at the cutting edge of new approaches to rural development methodology. His critical World Bank paper, "Rural Poverty Unperceived," propelled him into a prominent posi-tion in the international development field. Chambers is identified with a number of important development concepts that became pop-ular in the 1980s. Among these are rural development tourism, tropi-cal seasonality, indigenous technical knowledge, optimal ignorance, and proportional accuracy. Chambers is one of few Western scholars who show a genuine appreciation of the importance of indigenous technical knowledge and the need to learn from rural people. One of his most perspicacious insights is that most development disasters have resulted from failing to learn from rural people.

Clark, Colin   **(12)**
A British development scholar well known for his thinking about the evolution of economic structures, agricultural productivity, and de-mographic change. His career has been divided between practice and scholarly research and also divided geographically between Britain and Australia. His major developmental experiences occurred in India. After teaching at Cambridge, he held high-level government positions in Australia from 1938 to 1952. From 1953 to 1969, he was director of the Institute for Research in Agricultural Economics at Oxford. Since 1969, he has been at the University of Queensland in Australia. Among his best known works are *The Conditions of Economic*

Progress (1940), *Population Growth and Land Use* (1967), and *Poverty before Politics* (1977).

Significance   Colin Clark has made several important contributions to development economics. Based on his reading of Sir William Petty (circa 1691), Clark presented a basic "law" of the evolution of economic structure:

> As time goes on and communities become more economically advanced, the numbers engaged in agriculture tend to decline relative to the numbers in manufacture, which in turn decline relative to the numbers engaged in services. (*The Conditions of Economic Progress*, 3rd edition) (cited in Pyatt 1984:79).

Clark also is well known for questioning the view that capital accumulation was a necessary and *sufficient* condition for economic progress. Another important research interest is the international comparison of national incomes; he pioneered the concept now known as purchasing power parity, which takes into account the dramatic differences in the cost of living from country to country. With respect to population growth, Clark has challenged conventional views for ignoring possible beneficial effects of population growth and the importance of achieving minimal population densities. Finally Clark has argued that improvements in agricultural productivity are a prior condition for successful development.

Critchfield, Richard   (13)

International journalist with nearly two decades of firsthand experience in various developing countries. Critchfield writes insightful and sympathetic accounts of villagers and village life with special focus on the culture of changing rural communities. He presents an optimistic picture of the rural poor. In addition to numerous newspaper and journal articles, Critchfield has written two books on comparative village culture, *The Golden Bowl Be Broken* (1973) and *Villages* (1981), as well as books on Vietnam, Egypt, and India. *See also* DEVELOPMENT JOURNALIST, 225; VILLAGES, 191.

Significance   Critchfield has long appreciated that which is worth preserving in village cultures throughout the world. Unlike many journalists who sweep into areas for quick stories, Critchfield has spent considerable time living among and working with villagers in an attempt to understand their perspectives on their lives. The extensive range of his travels and stays in Bangladesh, Brazil, Egypt, India, Indonesia, Iran, Mauritius, Mexico, Morocco, Nepal, the Philippines, and Vietnam lends breadth to his work and forms the basis for comparative reflection. The amount of time spent in the villages enhances the depth of his understanding. In many cases he has returned to villages after many years to note changes over time. Such follow-up visits give his work a dynamic dimension that is frequently lacking in village studies rooted in a single or limited time frame.

Fanon, Frantz (1925–1961) (14)

A radical thinker, originally from Martinique, noted primarily for his books on the Algerian revolution and the anticolonial and antineocolonial movements. Fanon died at the age of 36 from leukemia. His most famous work was *The Wretched of the Earth* (1965), a devastating critique of colonialism and neocolonialism and a call for violence in the struggles for decolonization and against injustice and domination. Fanon was particularly critical of the members of the national bourgeoisie who are "bribed" by the former colonial powers in the period after independence to facilitate the continuation of colonial type economic relations, which exploit developing nations. Fanon was completely opposed to the notion of Africa imitating Europe as it seeks development. Finally, Fanon felt a strong affinity for both the peasant and the urban lumpen proletariat in slums and saw them as potentially powerful forces in fighting to achieve decolonization. *See also* DECOLONIZATION, 200.

Significance   Fanon's thinking was particularly influential in the French-speaking world, the Arab world, and in Africa. The legitimization and near idealization of violence as necessary represents another of Fanon's significant political legacies. His belief in the revolutionary efficacy of exploited peasants is also of considerable historical value. The successes of the insurgent peasants of Vietnam, the rebels of Afghanistan, and the Khmer Rouge in nationalistic and revolutionary rebellions illustrate dramatically the relevance of Fanon's thinking. Had the Americans in Vietnam and the Russians in Afghanistan really comprehended Fanon's messages, thousands of lives might have been saved. Though Fanon died nearly 30 years ago, his ideas remain powerful and relevant in a number of contemporary colonial and neocolonial contexts. While Fanon perceptively noted the revolutionary potential of oppressed peasant groups, he may have exaggerated the political efficacy of the urban lumpen proletariat.

Frank, Andre Gunder (15)

A key proponent of dependency theory. Frank argues that the conditions in poor countries were systematically created by colonial exploitation and preserved by the structures of modern international capitalism, a process that he calls "the development of underdevelopment." According to Frank, this system, with its roots in European expansion and colonialism, continues today under the guise of international trade, foreign investment, and development assistance as carried out by Northern-based institutions. Frank's original thesis was based on his studies of Brazil, Chile, Mexico, and Cuba, though his analysis has been applied to much of the Third World.

Frank was born in Berlin, Germany, in 1929 and received his economics training at the University of Chicago. He moved to Brazil in 1962, and in 1966 published his first major article, "The Development of Underdevelopment" (*Monthly Review* 18). In this and later works, Frank articulated his critique of orthodox development and economic theory, which he claimed fails to explain the structures and development of the international capitalist system and fails "to account for its simultaneous generation of underdevelopment in some parts and of economic development in others." Traditional societies may have been undeveloped, but they were not underdeveloped. He demonstrated that the areas of Latin America most drawn into the colonial system, because of the colonial powers' need for natural resources and cheap labor, are today underdeveloped, while those regions that were not suitable for plantations, mines, or other modes of economic exploitation are today more prosperous and developed. In addition to his own research, Frank draws from Marx, Baran, and Prebisch, among others, to construct his theoretical framework, which is cast in terms of the historical relationship between metropoles (economic centers) and satellites (economic outposts). Under the colonial and capitalist system, the metropoles develop at the expense of the satellites by removing economic surplus to the economic centers. This holds true at both national and international levels, so that what is a metropole at one level may be a satellite in the larger system. Thus, Frank attempts to explain persistent inequality at the local level in Latin America and in the world capitalist system. The only way to break away from this chain of capitalist underdevelopment, he suggests, is through class struggle whereby the national bourgeoisie, who are the allies of international capitalist interests, are removed. Only then will underdeveloped nations be free to pursue their own development interests. *See also* DEPENDENCY THEORY, 106.

Significance   The importance of Andre Gunder Frank's thesis is best illustrated by the extensive writing and discussion it stimulated in both the South and the North. His writing helped pioneer what has become known as dependency theory, a major challenge to capitalist development theory that offers considerable explanatory power for the persistence of poverty and inequality in Latin America and elsewhere in the Third World. Frank's early works served as a catalyst for a dynamic period of development literature. Both supporters and detractors felt compelled to respond to his sweeping and provocative interpretation of the world economic system, even while some questioned its degree of originality and its reductionist tendencies. In his writings, Frank directly attacked the conventional wisdom on development, economic assistance, and especially the role of the United States in Latin America. He was even critical of other progressive Latin American writers such as Pablo Gonzalez Casanova and Celso Furtado. Frank himself categorized his critics into three camps: the conservative right, the traditional Marxists, and the new left. He revised his thinking in the process of responding to all of them. For example, Samir Amin charged that Frank ignored the world outside Latin America. In response, Frank developed an analysis of the capitalist system on a global scale, which both influenced and was influenced by the world systems theory of Immanuel Wallerstein.

Freire, Paulo (16)
A Brazilian educator noted for his innovative and political approach to teaching adult literacy. Growing up in Recife, in the center of the extremely impoverished area of Brazil called the Northeast, Freire early on became highly conscious of the special problems of the poor and illiterate. Freire developed his ideas about teaching literacy at the University of Recife. His approach became popular among radical Catholics, who spread his approach throughout the Northeast. Freire's methodology emphasizes *conscientização*, which "refers to learning to perceive social, political, and economic contradictions, and to take action against the oppressive elements of reality" (Freire 1972:19). In teaching literacy, key words with relevance for the poor are used, such as *land reform, justice, liberation,* and *oppression.* With its emphasis on critical thinking, the methodology can be quite threatening to conservative elements. After a military coup in Brazil in 1964, Freire was arrested, then exiled. He moved to Chile to continue his work from 1964 to 1969 with UNESCO and the Chilean Institute for Agrarian Reform. Since leaving Chile, he has worked with both Harvard University and the World Council of Churches in Geneva. Among Freire's many important publications are *Pedagogy of the Oppressed* (1972) and *Educação como Prática da Liberdade* (1967).

Significance   Freire is one of the world's most influential educators. His thinking reflects an optimistic belief in the untapped potential of all human beings to be literate and critical, and to affect their political, cultural, and environmental surroundings. With a strong belief in unconditional love, Freire maintains that change can be both good and progressive. He strongly objects to the "banking" concept of education, which treats students and participants not as candles to be lit, but as vessels to be filled with often irrelevant and innocuous information. Freire's thinking has had global impact on various educational systems, particularly in areas such as Nicaragua and among staff members of Thailand's Department of Nonformal Education. Freire's ideas represent the educational dimension of the participative approach to development. Perhaps of greatest interest is his call to empower people "to speak their word."

Furtado, Celso   **(17)**
Brilliant development economist best known for his penetrating and insightful analyses of Latin American and Brazilian development problems and issues. Before achieving international renown, Furtado was minister of planning in Brazil (1963–1964) and head of the Development Agency for Northeast Brazil (1958–1959). He became a research fellow at Yale (1964–1965) after a military coup in Brazil and currently is director of research, École de Hautes Etudes en Sciences Sociales, at the University of Paris. Furtado's books on development have been translated into eight languages, including Japanese, Polish, and Swedish. Among his most significant books are *The Economic Growth of Brazil* (1963), *Economic Development of Latin America* (1976), *A Nova Dependencia* (1982), and *Accumulation and Development* (1983).

Significance   Furtado's understanding of development represents a combination of rigorous academic training and extensive, direct experience in the Latin American development process. Unlike some dependency theorists, Furtado avoids polemics and presents both highly analytical and empirical analyses of the Latin American development situation. His later work is, however, more qualitative and philosophical. *Accumulation and Development* presents a genuinely interdisciplinary approach to development, "linking theory of accumulation with theory of social stratification and theory of power." In this work, he showed remarkable insight and prescience in analyzing Chinese development prospects, and accurately predicted the type of

17

political turmoil and instability that was experienced in June 1989. Furtado, reflecting the critical spirit typical of many Latin American scholars, condemns pollution, the squandering of nonrenewable resources, the loss of cultural heritage, and Western consumerism and its transmission to developing countries. Furtado also documented the social distortions created by the rapid economic growth Brazil experienced in the 1970s. The development outcomes that Furtado emphasizes transcend those of most economists. He sees the opportunity to be both creative and free as the essence of humanity.

Galtung, Johan (18)

Norwegian scholar/philosopher known for his broad, holistic thinking about the complex interrelationships among environment, development, peace, and military activity. While working with the United Nations in Europe, the Geneva International Peace Research Institute, and the International Peace Research Association in Oslo, Galtung has devoted special attention to the goals, processes, and indicators of development. Teaching in Chile in the 1960s acquainted Galtung with the realities of development issues and became a highly formative exerience. Galtung played a key role in alerting the Chileans to Project Camelot, a counterinsurgency research project of the U.S. Department of Defense. Galtung (1982:20) defines the goal of development as the

> adequate and sustainable satisfaction and further development of human needs—material and nonmaterial—and the process of development includes building institutions for production of basic needs, with priority for those most in need, in an equitable and self-reliant structure, consistent with ecological balance, culture and development of others.

Galtung divides development into two dimensions: human and social. Four basic needs constitute the essence of human development, namely, survival needs (such as realizing the biologically potential lifespan), well-being needs (such as shelter, food, health, and schooling), identity needs, and freedom needs. Galtung identifies the negation of these needs as violence, misery, alienation, and repression. Key elements of Galtung's definition of social development include (1) broad-based *production* related to basic needs, (2) *distribution* with an emphasis on social justice and equality, (3) *institutions* to implement such goals, (4) *structure* that stresses equity and self-reliance, (5) *culture* with an emphasis on the consistency of development with indigenous culture, and (6) *nature* focusing on the need for sustainable ecosystems. With this perspective, Galtung is a major advocate of ecodevelopment, the exploration of the interface between environment and development. Among his extensive publications is *Environment, Development and Military Activity,* which outlines his development theory.

Significance   Galtung is among the most humanistic and holistic of Western development thinkers. He recognizes both the material and nonmaterial dimensions of development. He also draws upon the critical philosophical distinction developed by Erich Fromm of having versus being. In his thinking about development, Galtung reflects a Buddhist, middle-way orientation. He fears contexts in which either the state or markets (large corporations) dominate. Similarly, in the political realm he would seek to avoid excessive centralization or extreme decentralization. Thus, Galtung stresses both plan and market, national and local. Apart from his important place in the humanistic, holistic approach to development, Galtung's greatest contribution has been to demonstrate the critical link between peace and development and the crucial obstacle to development posed by militarism.

Geertz, Clifford   (19)

Cultural anthropologist noted for his penetrating and insightful interdisciplinary analyses of cultural phenomena in developmental contexts. Geertz, a student of Talcott Parsons and for many years at the Institute for Advanced Study at Princeton, became initially known with his study of urbanization in Indonesia, *Peddlers and Princes* (1963), which compared a Javanese and a Balinese town. Geertz, utilizing a cultural ecology approach focusing on the complex relations between individuals and their environment, also introduced the concept of agricultural involution to explain Java's rural rice economy and its relation to Indonesia's colonial history. In that study, *Agricultural Involution* (1963), Geertz demonstrated his comparative style by drawing important distinctions between Inner and Outer Indonesia and between Java and Japan, and explored the former's failure to develop. He has also done important work comparing Islam in Morocco and Indonesia in *Islam Observed* (1968). Geertz strongly rejects reductionist or deterministic approaches that see individual behavior as determined by physical environment or rational considerations of utility maximization. From Geertz's perspective culture is never external, but at the core of individuals' values and behavior.

Significance   Geertz has contributed to the field of culture and development a number of important concepts such as agricultural involution, the theater state, thick description, and local knowledge. He has rigorously assessed the relationship between culture and development and rejects overly simplistic perspectives such as culture-as-obstacle, culture-as-stimulus, culture-as-mystifying ideology, and culture-as-forceless trapping. Instead culture is central to any society and must be understood in its own terms, rather than with respect to external norms. In this sense, Geertz is the leader in the field known as interpretive anthropology, which focuses on understanding "the natives' point of view," their modes of expression, and their symbol systems. The key is to capture somehow the essence of natives' inner lives, "to give a sense of what life really seemed like in these places for the people that actually lived them." Over time, Geertz has become increasingly disillusioned with the idea of anthropology as a science. His most recent book, *Works and Lives: The Anthropologist as Author* (1988), emphasizes great ethnographic writing and the importance of the narrative, and clearly places anthropology more in the domain of the humanities. Geertz could well be the cultural anthropologist who has contributed most to our understanding of the cultural contexts of development.

George, Henry (1839–1897)   **(20)**
Former mayor of San Francisco and journalist who popularized the concept of a single tax, a tax on land. George's thinking drew heavily on Ricardo's concept of economic rent. "Site value taxation" of land is the essence of Georgism, the ideas of which are synthesized in his major book, *Progress and Poverty* (1879). Other books presenting his ideas on land taxation include *The Land Question* (1881) and *The Science of Political Economy* (1897). George is not taken seriously by most conventional economists because they perceive his approach to economics to be overly normative and simplistic. For example, Marshall and Fawcett in Britain rejected George and his views.

Significance   Despite the unconventional nature of George's thinking, there is a network of intellectuals, scholars, and policy researchers who appreciate George and his work. The Henry George Foundation in Washington, D.C., was established to promote and disseminate George's thinking, and *The American Journal of Economics and Sociology* provides a scholarly outlet for articles relevant to his ideas. In addition, several countries, including the People's Republic of China, Hong Kong, and Taiwan, have land policies or land taxation patterns relevant to George's concepts. His ideas are particularly popular in Australia and New Zealand. While George's notion of a single tax is certainly unfeasible in most if not all societies, the policy of placing higher taxes on land to encourage its productive use and to discourage profiteering from land speculation is highly relevant to both developing and developed countries.

Goulet, Denis   (21)
A pioneer in interdisciplinary and humanistic approaches to development. Goulet is the University of Notre Dame's first O'Neill Professor of Education for Justice in the Department of Economics and a faculty fellow in the Kellogg Institute for International Studies. His writings, in English, Spanish, Portuguese, and French, build on his extensive experience in developing areas and cover topics including development ethics, appropriate technology, and development assistance. Goulet has authored seven books, among them *The Cruel Choice: A New Concept in the Theory of Development* (1971), and has helped introduce a number of new dimensions and considerations in the discussion of development, a field traditionally dominated by economics and political science. Goulet begins his seminal book on humanistic development by presenting development as liberation as opposed to material production and accumulation. His ethical approach implies that *how* development is achieved should not be secondary to *what* is accomplished. He stresses the provision of life-sustaining goods, the creation of conditions that enhance esteem and dignity, and freedom from servitude. These should serve as the core values for development efforts, he believes. *See also* LIBERATION, 113; DEVELOPMENT, 107.

Significance   *The Cruel Choice* and subsequent writings challenged many assumptions and effectively broadened the concept and discussion of development. Goulet's consideration of development ethics and his emphasis on cultural values has helped humanize development studies. Ultimately, however, Goulet is not just engaged in a philosophical debate. His perspective contributes to more practical, humane, respectful, and effective efforts to alleviate human suffering.

Gramsci, Antonio (1891–1937)   (22)
An Italian political philosopher, a leader and organizer of the workers' struggle in Turin during World War I, and a founder of the Italian Communist party. Gramsci was born and grew up in a poor family in Sardinia. He had to work hard as a youth and his socialist thought was born out of his anger against his bitter childhood. The development of his thought began in 1910 during his study in Turin under

a scholarship. He devoted himself to studying the writings of Marx, Engels, and Lenin, and believed that Marxism is the ideal philosophy to bring about "a new total integral civilization." He desired to build a society where the working class ruled, since capitalism had failed to bring prosperity to the society. Before World War I ended, he became involved in the working-class movement and was elected secretary of Socialist Section in Turin. By the end of the war, he was put in prison as the first Italian Marxist. Inspired by the 1917 Soviet Revolution, Gramsci became a leader of the Factory Councils movement. The councils were a powerful weapon of the industrial working class at the time. As an organ of this movement, he founded a newspaper, *Ordine Nuovo*, in 1919, which supported the working-class movement and presented socialist perspectives or principles. Although the struggle of the councils was successful for only a short period of time and the newspaper was forced to cease publication in 1922, it provided Gramsci with the experience upon which he built his theory of Italian revolution. The formation of the Italian Communist party in 1921 also was an outgrowth of the Ordine Nuovo group. Gramsci was elected secretary of the Communist party in 1924. He was one of only a few Communists elected to the Parliament in 1924 when the fascism of Mussolini was predominant in Italy. Gramsci was arrested when he began to unite the force of industrial workers in the North and peasants in the South. During his years in prison, he wrote an enormous series of notes, which were published after his death, 1941–1951. The major volumes were the *Lettere dal Carcere* (*Letters from Prison*) and the six volumes of the *Quaderni del Carcere* (*Prison Notebooks*).

Significance   Except for the great protagonists of the Soviet Revolution, there are no other figures in the history of workers' movements of these last fifty years whose works and personality have aroused inspiration of workers' leaders worldwide greater than Gramsci's (Bobbio 1977:viii). His prison volumes are considered one of the most original contributions of the last half century to a Marxist analysis of Italian and European society as well as philosophical reflection on some crucial concepts in the struggle for the development of a new society. His concept of hegemony continues to be influential among dependency and other more radical development thinkers. He is thought of as one of the most original Communist thinkers of the twentieth century in Western Europe.

Hagen, Everett   **(23)**
Economist and political scientist best known for his emphasis on the noneconomic factors that explain economic growth. His detailed

analysis of the noneconomic dimensions of economic growth are elaborated in great detail in his best known work, *On the Theory of Social Change: How Economic Growth Begins* (1962). As a basis for this analysis, Hagen developed an impressive command of relevant anthropological, sociological, and psychological literature, and was particularly influenced by Erik Erikson's stress on the impact of childhood on society. Motivated by his dissatisfaction with solely economic theories of growth, Hagen's analysis involved systems analysis, the integration of various social science theories, and the relationship of childhood to history. Hagen's thinking on development was perhaps heavily influenced by three years (1951–1953) he spent as an economic adviser in Burma. Hagen saw the presence of creative and innovative individuals as a key to economic growth and viewed immigrant groups as an important source of technological innovation. *See also* MODERNIZATION THEORY, 114.

Significance   Along with individuals such as David McClelland, Alex Inkeles, Daniel Lerner, and Marion Levy, Everett Hagen is one of the prominent scholars stressing an individualistic, personality approach to development. Unfortunately, such an approach suffers from many of the same problems associated with the overgeneralizations of national character studies in fashion at the time of Hagen's major work. Critics also argue that such personality approaches give inadequate attention to macrostructural and international obstacles to development that transcend individual traits and behavior. In addition to his work on the noneconomic causes of economic growth, Hagen later made contributions in three areas: (1) arguments showing the irrelevance of the theory of a low-income population trap, (2) support for the need for protection of manufacturing industries to enhance chances for economic growth, and (3) the relevance of the theory of technological disemployment. By the latter, Hagen refers to technological progress not associated with import substitution or export expansion. In such cases, technological advance leads to increased inequality of income distribution as disemployed workers shift to jobs with lower productivity and less remuneration.

Harrington, Michael (1928–1989)   **(24)**
Prolific writer and lecturer whose book *The Other America: Poverty in the United States* (1962) sparked the War on Poverty in the early 1960s. Harrington was the United States's leading proponent of the socialist ideal, along with Norman Thomas. His views were shaped by his firsthand knowledge of the poor, experience he gained as a social worker in St. Louis, associate editor of the *Catholic Worker*,

organization secretary for the Worker's Defense League, and social researcher. In *The Other America* he argued that large-scale poverty existed in the United States, but was ignored by the government and U.S. society in general. He demonstrated that tens of millions of Americans formed an underclass whose members, even when employed, lived well below the poverty line. President John F. Kennedy was profoundly moved by the book and took immediate steps toward poverty alleviation. These efforts were solidified under the Johnson administration. Appointed as a leading consultant to the antipoverty program, Harrington became increasingly frustrated with the funds being diverted to support the growing war in Vietnam. From 1960 to 1968 Harrington was a member of the national executive board of the Socialist party. He chaired the Democratic Socialists of America throughout the 1980s. From 1972 until his death in 1989, he taught political science at Queens College, Flushing, New York, while maintaining a demanding lecture schedule. Harrington was always eager to share his vision of a human social order based on popular control of the resources and production, economic planning, equitable distribution, feminism, and racial equality. In *The Vast Majority: A Journey to the World's Poor* (1977), Harrington applied his ideas forcefully to the problem of global poverty. *See also* UNEVEN DEVELOPMENT, 173.

Significance   Few books have had the impact upon a nation of *The Other America*. Harrington brought the plight of the poor to the attention of the government and the American public. In broader terms, he stimulated an awareness of need amid prosperity and growth. Recognition of poverty in the United States raised further questions about the suggestion by some development theorists that issues of justice and equality are secondary to concerns for economic growth. Perhaps more importantly, Harrington's work demonstrates the need to look beyond macroaggregate data to subnational and subregional economic conditions in all countries, both developed and less developed.

Hill, Polly (25)

A British economic anthropologist who is highly critical of conventional development economics. As a student of both Joan Robinson and Meyer Fortes, Hill has been exposed to both rigorous economics and anthropology. She argues that the traditional study of rural life by development economists is flawed by ethnocentrism, faulty conceptualization, naive acceptance of official statistics, and misperceptions of the realities of rural life. Hill's critique derives primarily from her own field research in West Africa and South Asia. Hill's major criticisms are presented in *Development Economics on Trial: The Anthropological Case for a Prosecution* (1986). Hill has also published volumes on rural conditions in Ghana, Nigeria, and India. *See also* DE-VELOPMENT METHODOLOGY, 319.

Significance   Hill is bold and courageous in her attack against development economics, since this branch of the social sciences is normally considered to be most rigorous and scientific. Two of Hill's most compelling criticisms relate to the neglect of the role of women in development and misconceptions concerning migration. Her quarrels concerning terminology such as *peasant* are understandable but seem less compelling and even somewhat pedantic. Another criticism of her work relates to the fruitfulness of cross-disciplinary "battles." It is also easy for economists to attack anthropologists for using samples of N = 1 and being preoccupied with descriptive ethnographic detail. Though Hill's work may contribute to acrimony between economists and anthropologists, it does raise fundamental questions concerning many conventional research approaches to rural development problems. Like the work of Robert Chambers at Sussex, Hill's critique may inspire future students of rural development to be more careful and culturally sensitive in their thinking and their development of research designs.

Hirschman, Albert O. (26)

A leading thinker in the field of development economics, noted for his advocacy of unbalanced growth. Originally from Germany, from 1946 to 1952 he worked with the Federal Reserve Bank dealing with economic reconstruction in France and Italy and with various schemes for European economic integration. Thus, he became intimately acquainted with the inner workings of the Marshall Plan. From 1952 to 1956 Hirschman had a pivotal experience working as an economic adviser in Colombia. He then taught development economics at Yale, Columbia, and Harvard universities. Since 1974 he has been a scholar at the Institute for Advanced Study at Princeton. Among his most influential and pioneering works in the development field are *The Strategy of Economic Development* (1958), *Journeys toward Progress* (1963), *Development Projects Observed* (1967), and *A Bias for Hope: Essays on Development and Latin America* (1971).

Significance   Hirschman challenged the conventional and popular paradigm of balanced growth. His challenge grew out of his practical experience working on the Marshall Plan and his four years as an economic adviser in Colombia. His book, *Strategy of Economic Development,* was the first to articulate the concept of unbalanced growth, though at the same time Paul Streeten was independently developing essentially the same concept, which appeared in an article, "Unbalanced Growth," in *Oxford Economic Papers* (June 1959). Hirschman saw shortages, bottlenecks, and other unbalanced growth sequences in the course of development as having possible hidden rationality. He deserves considerable credit for his willingness to challenge conventional paradigms about development but also to try to understand development processes from the inside. While many development economists criticized countries such as Colombia for their economic "irrationality" and lack of "proper" balanced planning, Hirschman was more empathetic and willing to learn from their experiences. In this sense, he is clearly an inductive development thinker. Hirschman also was the first to develop the important concept of linkages, which is now an integral part of development theory. He argued for the support of those industries that have both strong forward and backward linkages. The relevance of Hirschman's ideas today is that they allow for nonlinear development and the skipping of traditional stages of development, thus giving developing nations more options and choices in their development strategies. A common misinterpretation of Hirschman's concept of unbalanced growth is the view that political development can lag behind economic development as a way to justify political repression and military dictatorships.

Horowitz, Irving Louis   **(27)**
A sociologist of development who popularized the term *the Third World* with the publication of *Three Worlds of Development* in 1965. Horowitz's three worlds were: "the First World of the United States and its Western Allies, the Second World of the Soviet Union and its Eastern Bloc Allies, and the Third World of nonaligned, but variously committed nations of Latin America, Asia, and Africa." In 1972, in the second edition of his *Three Worlds of Development,* Horowitz upheld the basic theoretical structure of his earlier volume. He views the three worlds of development as a condition of unstable disequilibrium with the Third World "incapable of preserving its goals and functions apart from either of the major power centers." In his revised volume, he also elaborates on his controversial concept of overdevelopment and recognizes the presence of Third World impulses within "the very heartland of the American Empire." Horowitz has been one of the most productive scholars of the sociology of development. Among his many books are *Taking Lives: Genocide and State Power* (1982), *Beyond Empire and Revolution: Militarization and Consolidation in the Third World* (1982), *Masses in Latin America* (1970), and

Latin American Radicals (1969). Horowitz has also been a leading figure behind the critical interdisciplinary journal, *Transaction*.

Significance   Horowitz was one of the most influential social scientists dealing with development questions in the postwar period. His work has stimulated extensive debate about fundamental development issues and questions. His work also documented and dramatized the nature of international economic, political, and social stratification. His *Rise and Fall of Project Camelot* (1967) reflects his strong moral stance against the abuse of social science by power structures. Despite the controversy surrounding the term *Third World*, Horowitz remains a powerful intellectual figure in the development field who has inspired critical thinking and research on the most fundamental of development questions dealing with social justice and exploitation. Horowitz's three worlds of development have undergone many changes, particularly the Second World where, in the 1980s and 1990s, political and economic changes have dramatically altered Soviet and East European approaches to development.

Huntington, Samuel P. (28)

Widely read political scientist whose writings focus on political order and change in developing societies. Huntington is best known for his theory of political development and decay. His early works compared the political development of Europe and the United States. In his best known book, the controversial *Political Order in Changing Societies* (1968), he extended his inquiry, based on a structural-functional analysis, to the Third World. His thesis is that the forces of modernization undermine traditional political institutions, causing political decay manifested in instability, corruption, authoritarianism, and violence. For development to occur, the building of new political institutions must not lag behind social and economic change. Huntington sees the institutionalization of politics, especially the creation of strong political parties, as the key to political and national development. He views the nature of the mobilization of peasants as the key to differential development outcomes. *See also* POLITICAL DEVELOPMENT, 211.

Significance   Huntington's theory of political development and decay has generated considerable debate. His analysis provided a framework for discussion of the role of political change in the broader development process. He stresses the importance of widespread participation in all aspects of development, especially in politics. In retrospect, his conclusions often appear much too sweeping in scope, given the diversity of political experiences within the developing countries. At the same time Huntington is rightly criticized for his somewhat narrow, Eurocentric concept of political development with its emphasis on party politics and political stability. Nevertheless, his writings stand as an important, if debatable, contribution to the broader discussion of Third World politics and the interplay of political, economic, and social development.

Illich, Ivan (29)

Austrian-born radical thinker residing in Mexico who is highly critical of the Western model of development and modernization. After formal training as a Catholic theologian, his work as a priest brought him to Latin America. He is perhaps best known for his critique of modern schooling, *Deschooling Society* (1971). He is also highly critical of modern medicine and the modern consumer society. Illich's *Tools for Conviviality* (1973) provides a critical assessment of various modern technologies. While he finds that the telephone is a convivial tool, for example, he is extremely critical of the automobile. Illich also criticized technical assistance. He feels that Americans should not teach the Third World, but come to learn from it. *See also* TECHNICAL ASSISTANCE, 305.

Significance   Illich's ideas clearly depart from the development mainstream. Despite the extreme nature of his writings, Illich's critiques of modern institutions deserve careful attention. Illich's thinking has inspired developing countries to view more critically the importation of Western culture, values, institutions, and technologies. His Center for Intercultural Documentation (CIDOC) training center, in Cuernavaca, Mexico, has influenced many young people from industrial countries to think critically about cultural and technological change and has brought them into direct contact with radical Latin American thought. Illich's critique of modern schooling has also had an impact on educators around the world and has contributed to a greater emphasis on informal and nonformal education, particularly in developing countries.

Kuznets, Simon (1901–1985) (30)

A Russian-born economist who won the 1971 Nobel Prize in economics for originating the concept of gross national product as a measure of national income and economic growth. Kuznets and his family immigrated to the United States after World War I. He obtained his doctorate in economics from Columbia University in 1926. He also served as a fellow with the Social Science Research Council at the time. During his long and productive career, he taught at the University of Pennsylvania, Johns Hopkins University, and Harvard University. He also worked for the National Bureau of Economic Research in Washington, D.C., where most of his studies were conducted.

Kuznets, influenced by Wesley Clair Mitchell, his mentor and professor at Columbia, believed that economics could be transformed from an ideology to a science by careful measurement and quantitative analysis. To put this theory into practice, he initiated a program for estimating and analyzing the national income of the United States, including the sum of earning flows such as wages, interests, profits, and rents, then refined his statistical data for measuring the nation's economic growth. He defined the national product, which includes expenditures on consumer goods and services, and the national income, which is the sum of wages, rents, interests, and profits generated in creating the national product. His system for determining growth eventually became the basis for the concept now called the gross national product (GNP), which records the actual output of a nation's goods and services and is one of the standard international indices of wealth. After World War II, hoping to establish guidelines for the successful economic growth of developing countries, Kuznets initiated a comparative study to determine the factors that lead some nations into prosperity and others into depression and decline. Among his major works are the extensive two-volume study, *National Income and Its Composition 1919–38* (1941), and *Economic Growth of Nations: Total Output and Production Structure* (1971). *See also* KUZNETS INDEX, 331.

Significance   Apart from developing the gross national product approach to measuring national income and economic growth, Kuznets is also known for his theory of the inverted U curve, presented in his 1955 presidential address to the American Economics Association. The curve illustrates the relationship between the level of per capita GNP and inequality in the distribution of income. As per capita income rises, inequality may initially rise, reach a maximum at an intermediate level of income, and then decline as income levels characteristic of an industrial country are reached. His insight was proved correct in later years when data published by the World Bank, covering more than 50 countries, revealed that during the period 1965–1982 inequality in those countries first rose, then fell as the pace of development continued. Kuznets's empirical study of patterns of development and economic growth, through an analysis of data on the gross national product and the structure of that product for various nations around the world and through time, has proven to be one of the most prominent thoughts in modern economic science.

Langoni, Carlos Geraldo (31)

An influential Brazilian economist who served as the president of Brazil's Central Bank until resigning in 1983. At present, he is the director of the Getulio Vargas Foundation, the leading Brazilian economic research center. He has written extensively about economic development.

Significance Langoni is well known for his new approach to development strategy. Paul Volcker notes that Langoni has a "unique ability to make intelligent analysis of the international debt crisis accessible to a large readership" (Langoni 1987:xi) through various publications. In his book *The Development Crisis: Blueprint for Change* (1987), which was written in English, he suggests that the debt crisis in Third World countries, especially in Latin America, has revealed the failure of "the older approach of development characterized by heavy governmental intervention in the economy, widespread subsidies and protectionism, all supported by large borrowings." (Langoni 1987:xii) He maintains that "Latin American governments, American leaders, banks of other industrialized nations, multilateral economic institutions, and others—all contributed to the problem" (Langoni 1987:1) and believes that "the long-term economic growth can occur only in an atmosphere of greater political and economic freedom." (Langoni 1987:3) In addition, the state should act as an agent for change on behalf of the public rather than as an endogenous contributor to internal imbalances. The private sector should be provided with more opportunity in the development arena, Langoni believes. Recent political events in Eastern Europe, Latin America, and Africa confirm the apparently universal appeal of the political and economic freedom emphasized by Langoni.

Lappé, Frances Moore (32)

Well-known researcher and speaker on international food policy. She has written extensively on food and food aid, challenging conventional wisdom on such topics while posing the basic question: why does hunger persist in a world of plenty? Lappé is the cofounder of the San Francisco–based Institute for Food and Development Policy. Lappé's first book, *Diet for a Small Planet* (1971), has sold over three million copies and been translated into six languages. In it she draws connections between Northern consumerism and Third World poverty, and suggests diets more sensitive to global needs. Also well received was her second study, with Joseph Collins, *Food First: Beyond the Myth of Scarcity* (1977). Lappé and Collins are highly critical of economic policies and political arrangements such as those that encourage agriculture for export in countries with high incidence of malnutrition and hunger. As Lappé suggests in the subtitle, the cause of hunger is not a shortage of food, but misplaced priorities in production and distribution. Her subsequent books, *World Hunger: Ten Myths* (1979) and *Aid as Obstacle* (1980), also coauthored with Collins, continue the attempt to expose the "myths" of hunger and offer a strong critique of bilateral and multilateral aid programs, especially the policies of the World Bank and U.S. AID. More recently Lappé has assessed the agrarian reforms of Nicaragua and Cuba following their revolutions. *See also* BILATERAL AID, 277; GREEN REVOLUTION, 180.

Significance   Lappé's work has served to popularize and generate considerable discussion about world hunger issues. Her work has had a marked impact in public, academic, and development circles. In addition to books, she has written numerous articles for a wide range of publications, in keeping with her commitment to raising general public consciousness regarding international food and agriculture systems. In 1987, Lappé and the institute received the Right Livelihood Award, Sweden's "alternative Nobel Prize."

Lewis, Sir W. Arthur   (33)
A Nobel laureate in development economics originally from Saint Lucia in the British West Indies. He currently occupies the James Madison Chair of Political Economy at Princeton where he has taught development economics since 1963. Lewis has had extensive experience as a development practitioner. Among his practical roles have been UN economic adviser to Ghana and Nkrumah, deputy managing director of the UN Special Fund, vice-chancellor of the University of the West Indies, and president of the Caribbean Development Bank.

Significance   Lewis's receipt of the Nobel Prize in development economics in 1979 reflects his many contributions to the field. Two of his most influential works are *The Theory of Economic Growth* (1955) and "Economic Development with Unlimited Supplies of Labor," which appeared in the *Manchester School of Economics and Social Studies.* Lewis's scholarship benefits enormously from his practical experience in developmental contexts and his keen perceptions of *lebenswelt,* the world as it is actually lived. Though Lewis is considered mainstream, he is often highly critical of governmental policies that foster the persistence of underdevelopment. Major ideas stressed in Lewis's writings are the need for human resource development, balanced growth with adequate attention devoted to improving agricultural productivity, diversification of exports, development of local industry, and improved financing for development. While Lewis sees dependency theory as relevant to understanding development during the second half of the nineteenth century, he does not view it as helpful in understanding economic phenomena during the second half of the twentieth century when many governments are much more politically independent.

Lubis, Mochtar (34)

Indonesian journalist noted for his critical commentary on Indonesian life and society. Born the son of a district commissioner on March 7, 1922, in Padang, Sumatra, he attended the School of Economics, Kayutanam, Indonesia. Lubis joined the Indonesian Antara News Agency in 1945. During 1946–1961, he was a publisher and editor of the daily *Indonesian Raya*. He also published and edited the *Times* of Indonesia. In 1975, he was arrested by Indonesian military police for publishing editorials critical of the government and army, and imprisoned without trial for several weeks. On his release he was placed under house arrest on undisclosed charges. During the earlier Sukarno period, he was imprisoned for more than four years and under house arrest for another four and a half years. Lubis has won several awards including the Indonesian National Award for the Novel in 1954, a prize from the Press Foundation of Asia, and the Magsaysay Award for journalism and literature in 1958. Among his works that have been translated into various languages are *Twilight in Djakarta* (1963), *A Road with No End* (1952), and *The Indonesian Dilemma* (1983).

Significance   Through his powerful writing, Lubis provides an in-depth view of an Indonesia in cultural and social transition. His *Twilight in Djakarta* presents in vivid detail and powerful imagery the glaring inequalities in modern Djakarta and accounts of Indonesian rural migrants caught in cultural collisions between urbanized Djarkata and their rural roots. Lubis's nonfiction work, *The Indonesian Dilemma*, is the Indonesian equivalent of *The Ugly American* or *Japan Unmasked*. In this volume, Lubis is highly critical of an Indonesia in which he sees individuals, particularly the elite, as being overly status-oriented, materialistic, hypocritical, and concerned with preserving privilege. Lubis shares much with other radical Southeast Asian intellectuals such as Sulak of Thailand and Constantino of the Philippines in his often biting criticisms of contemporary "development" in Indonesia.

Marx, Karl (1818–1883) (35)

German philosopher whose works helped shape modern social science and world politics and continue to permeate these fields. Marx wrote extensively on a number of subjects, but concerned himself primarily with the rise and fall of the capitalist system. Drawing from Hegel, he depicted history as being driven by a dialectic process, which was played out in class conflict. In economic, social, and political terms, this process meant the transformation of society through stages of feudalism, capitalism, and socialism to the final stage, a communist order. Marx pointed out the inherent contradictions and exploitive tendencies within capitalism, characteristics that he predicted would lead to its destruction. These contradictions have to do with ownership of the means of production and the impoverishment of the working class even amidst greater productivity. The alienation of exploited workers is also an important theme in his works. Marx predicted that the proletariat would seize power and dispose of the bourgeoisie, who serve no productive purpose. His writings stand in sharp contrast to such other influential writers as Adam Smith and Max Weber who viewed capitalism as essentially beneficial. Herein lies the essence of the development debate between Marxists and capitalists: does capitalism represent the highest form of social order or is it to be destroyed and replaced with a new, more progressive order? *See also* PARADIGMS OF DEVELOPMENT, 116.

Significance   Marx is one of the most influential writers of the last two centuries. Not surprisingly, references to and innumerable interpretations of his ideas permeate development literature of all types, both in support of and in opposition to his interpretation of history and progress. Since Marx wrote well before the post–World War II notions of development and the Third World emerged, it has been up to his numerous and varied supporters, such as Paul Baran, to interpret his writings as they relate to recent development history. Marxist theory serves as the basis for political economy interpretations of development such as dependency and other forms of critical theory. In the struggle for independence, many Third World intellectuals found Marxist theory much more compelling than the competing Western notions of modernization. Marxists assert that capitalism has failed in its self-proclaimed mission to develop the Third World, whose best option is to throw off its internal and foreign economic and political oppressors. What follows revolution is not so clear. Many forms of Marxist thought are more powerful as a critique of capitalism than as actual models of development, though development directions are implied. In practice, various Marxist states have followed a variety of development strategies ranging from the "soft Marxism" of Yugoslavia to the stricter manifestations found in Albania or the People's Democratic Republic of Korea (North Korea). There also are contemporary humanistic Marxists who emphasize social justice and the end of exploitation and alienation without necessarily advocating violent revolution and dictatorship by the proletariat.

Memmi, Albert (36)

A Jewish intellectual, teacher, and writer noted for his philosophical and sociological writings on colonization. His empathy for the colonialized derives primarily from his experiences of French colonialism in Tunisia and German fascism during World War II, when he was interned in a force labor camp. Growing up in Tunisia, he saw the many faces of colonialism. His broad concept of colonialization includes internal colonialism in which a racial minority is oppressed by a dominant class and gender, and the exploitation of women by men. As an example of internal colonialism, Memmi used the problems of French Canadians dominated by English Canadians. For Memmi, colonization is above all political and economic exploitation with privilege (not only economic, but psychological and cultural) at the heart of the colonial relationship. He also stresses that the entire life of the colonized is dependent and that the members of the proletariat are dependent creatures. Memmi is highly critical of the mythical portraits of the colonized perpetuated by the colonizers, in which colonial peoples are stereotyped as deficient, lazy, and weak. They are required to define themselves through the categories of the colonizers, and value their own languages and cultures the least. A final dimension of Memmi's argument is that colonization corrupts both the colonizer and the colonized. To remedy the colonial problem, Memmi presents two alternatives: assimilation and revolution. In his view, the former strategy, in which the colonized seek to imitate the colonizer, has failed. Even when individuals are "successful" in such imitation, they sacrifice their own cultural identity and meaning. The only alternative is thus to seek liberation and liberty through revolution to end the oppression and racism inherent in colonialism. Memmi's ideas are presented primarily in two major works: *The Colonizer and the Colonized* (1957) and *Dominated Man* (1968). *See also* NEOCOLONIALISM, 210; DECOLONIZATION, 200.

Significance There is debate about the originality of Memmi's thinking and its relation to the perspective of Frantz Fanon. Though both Memmi and Fanon were critical of racism and oppression associated with capitalism, they appear to have been intellectual competitors. Memmi claims that all his books were written before those of Fanon except for Fanon's *Black Skin, White Masks.* Memmi also sees his work as being more sociological, while Fanon's is phenomenological and psychiatric. Memmi's thinking related to colonialism, anomie, alienation, and exploitation clearly reflects Marxist and Leninist influences. Several of his insights show remarkable prescience. His statement that "colonization can only disfigure the colonizer" was dramatically confirmed by the French in Algeria, the French and U.S. experiences in Vietnam, and Soviet presence in Afghanistan. His concerns about internal colonialism are manifesting dramatically in the Soviet Union of the 1990s. Finally, his views anticipated the people's struggles against oppressive and exploitative rule in countries such as Nicaragua, Iran, Vietnam, and contemporary South Africa. In many other developing countries, however, such as India, Bangladesh, and Thailand, his projected revolutionary struggles have failed either to emerge or to succeed.

Myint, Hla (37)

Noted Burmese-born development economist with a focus on dualism. Myint has taught at both Oxford (1950–1965) and the London School of Economics (1965–present). Among Myint's major books are *Economic Theory and the Underdeveloped Economies* (1971), *Southeast Asia's Economic Development Policies in the 1970s* (1971), and *The Economics of the Developing Countries* (1980). His development thinking emphasizes dualism and the impact of external economic forces on internal economic organization. *See also* DUALISM, 139.

Significance Like other development scholars such as Sir Arthur Lewis, Celso Furtado, and Amartya Sen who had formative experiences in developing countries, Myint similarly benefits from knowing firsthand the economic conditions of a nation such as Burma. Myint is probably the best known Southeast Asian development economist. Of special significance are his ability to relate the history of economic thought to development studies and his application of theories of economic organization and institutions to the context of the developing nations. Given Myint's emphasis on the impact of external economic forces, he could perhaps be considered Asia's first dependency theorist.

Myrdal, Gunnar (1898–1987) (38)

A Swedish Nobel laureate in economics who wrote extensively about development problems. Myrdal was a senator, cabinet minister, and international civil servant. His most famous work was a three-volume study of development problems in Asia, *Asian Drama: An Inquiry into the Poverty of Nations* (1968), in which he stressed internal factors as the major obstacles to development. While he recognized the importance of international factors, he focused on the need for internal reforms. Myrdal's approach to development was basically qualitative with an emphasis on the human aspect. He was the first economist to write about the soft state, which fails to make tough policy decisions to deal with critical development problems. He thus had a special interest in values and institutions and their roles in development. Given Myrdal's background as a Swedish politician, it is not surprising that he also emphasized the distributional problems of development and the critical importance of finding ways to meet basic needs. *See also* SOFT STATE, 215

Significance   Myrdal diverged from conventional development economics by directing his attention to qualitative dimensions of development and stressing internal reforms. In this sense, he was a genuine political economist in the classical sense. Myrdal was also important from a methodological perspective. His important but little known book, *Objectivity in Social Research* (1969), was an insightful and remarkably open approach to research that stressed the value-laden nature of the social sciences and the need to make explicit the underlying value premises of the research. Among Myrdal's other important works are *The Challenge of World Poverty* (1970) and *Rich Lands and Poor* (1957). Though Myrdal was highly regarded as a development thinker, he does have critics. Hla Myint, for example, feels that Myrdal inappropriately denied the need for more outward-looking policies toward foreign trade and investment. The economic successes of Taiwan, Hong Kong, and Korea suggest the relevance of Myint's point. However, it is important to note that Myrdal's development thinking was derived primarily from his ten-year study of South Asia reported in *Asian Drama*.

Olson, Mancur   **(39)**
Rational choice economist who has applied public choice theory to explain the rise and decline of nations. Olson is best known for his book, *The Logic of Collective Action* (1965), a highly influential volume dealing with the complexities of the provision of public goods. In *The Rise and Decline of Nations*, published in 1982, Olson applied his ideas in the international development arena. In this important volume, he tries to explain why some nations and geographic economic areas are much more economically dynamic than others. He is particularly in-

trigued with the impressive success of economies such as Korea, Taiwan, and Hong Kong. He concludes that the presence of strong interest groups inhibits development, while the existence of an all-encompassing national interest facilitates economic dynamism. *See also* NEWLY INDUSTRIALIZED COUNTRIES, 163.

Significance   Olson's work represents an excellent example of the application of rigorous economic analysis and theoretical thinking to the practical problem of explaining relative economic dynamism. With his emphasis on interest articulation and aggregation, he creatively relates economics and politics, and reflects the growing importance of the analytical genre, political economy. While some may consider his conclusions too simplistic and not generalizable to all development contexts, his *Rise and Decline of Nations* has stimulated extensive discussion and debate. In his more recent work, Olson reveals an even broader perspective with a special interest in phenomena that go "beyond the measuring rod of money."

Prebisch, Raúl   (40)
A noted Argentinean development economist and founder of the United Nations Conference on Trade and Development (UNCTAD). From 1964 to 1969 he was secretary general of UNCTAD and from 1948 to 1962 he was the executive secretary of the UN Commission for Latin America in Santiago, Chile. Adamantly opposed to protectionism among advanced industrial countries, Prebisch was one of the early proponents of a Latin American Common Market. Without access to markets for their manufactured goods, developing countries could not develop, according to his perspective, which linked trade to development. *See also* UN CONFERENCE ON TRADE AND DEVELOPMENT, 446.

Significance   Prebisch's creation of UNCTAD represents one of his crowning achievements. His greatest intellectual contribution was his emphasis on a world economy comprised of central and peripheral countries. This framework has become one of the leading paradigms in development thinking and helped lay the groundwork for dependency theory. In 1981, Prebisch synthesized much of his development thinking in an important volume titled *Capitalismo Periferico: Crisis y Transformación* (1981). In this work, he stresses the need for a synthesis of economic and political liberalism, an integration of socialism and genuine economic liberalism. Certain elements in Prebisch's basic development thinking have been confirmed by the examples of Pacific Basin dynamism. Through industrialization, economic diversification, trade, and access to foreign markets, countries such as South Korea, Taiwan, Hong Kong, Singapore, and Thailand have experienced rapid economic development, while moving away from reliance on the export of a few primary commodities. In *Capitalismo Periferico*, Prebisch presents the argument to combine the best features of socialism and political-economic liberalism. Osvaldo Sunkel places Prebisch in a class with Schumpeter and Myrdal as one of the great contributors to the field of political economy in the twentieth century. An entire issue of *Development & South-South Cooperation* (December 1986) was devoted to Prebisch's thinking and influence; the homage includes a comprehensive bibliography of Prebisch's writing on development.

Rosenstein-Rodan, Paul N. (41)

Polish-born economist who was one of the first scholars to devote attention to the problems of developing countries. Trained in Austria in the 1920s, Rosenstein-Rodan made his initial contributions in neoclassical economic theory and was praised for his brilliance by Schumpeter. From 1930 to 1946, he taught at the University of London, and during World War II was part of a study group of the Royal Institute for International Affairs that was working on the problems of underdeveloped countries. Rosenstein-Rodan's 1943 article, "Problems of Industrialization of Eastern and South-Eastern Europe," is a classic in the development field. Sir Arthur Lewis credits this article, which presents the essence of national development programming, with introducing the concept of balanced growth. Rosenstein-Rodan's development thinking in the 1940s and 1950s led him to the theory of the big push, that is, that "there is a minimum of resources that must be devoted to a development program if it is to have any chance for success." Another important element in his development thinking was the concept of disguised unemployment in agriculture, which provided potential for increased manpower for industrialization. Rosenstein-Rodan's more recent development thinking is presented in *The New International Economic Order* (1981). *See also* BIG PUSH DOCTRINE, 126.

Significance What is perhaps most impressive about Rosenstein-Rodan is his evolution from a neoclassical economics theorist to an interventionist development thinker who realizes the need for massive structural changes at both national and international levels to achieve developmental goals. He also deserves considerable credit for directing his attention to development questions and issues long before they became a popular field of inquiry in the 1950s. His emphasis on an analysis of the disequilibrium growth process is one of his major contributions to development theory and thinking.

Rostow, W. W. (Walt Whitman) (42)

A U.S. economic historian best known for his influential volume, *The Stages of Economic Growth: A Non-Communist Manifesto* (1960). Based on a series of lectures delivered at Cambridge University, this work states that *all* countries pass through five stages of development: (1) traditional society, (2) preconditions for takeoff, (3) self-sustaining growth, (4) drive to maturity, and (5) age of high mass consumption. As the key to takeoff Rostow sees the mobilization of domestic and foreign saving to generate sufficient investment to accelerate economic growth. As an economic historian, Rostow recognizes the important noneconomic dimensions in societal performance and stresses "the crucial role of politics in the early phases of modernization." He also notes the particularly important role of private and public entrepreneurs in the development process. A high-ranking official in the Kennedy and Johnson administrations (1961–1969), Rostow is a keen observer of the evolution of U.S. policy toward developing countries. Overall, he is a strong advocate of development aid and its efficacy. In the 1970s, Rostow devoted his energies to analyzing the broad sweep of modern economic history with his volume, *The World Economy: History and Prospect* (1978). Using the concept of Kondratieff cycles to explain flows of world economic history, he postulates that the period since 1972 is a fifth cycle of high energy and commodity prices.

Significance   Rostow's development thinking is highly controversial. Some find that his fixed stages of growth deny flexible development paths and political choice. Do all societies have to manifest the high mass-consumption syndrome? Can certain stages of development be skipped or modified? Others argue that his thinking inadequately recognizes perspectives from the South and that he ignores conflicts and contradictions inherent in the capitalistic development process. Despite these criticisms, Rostow deserves credit for transcending the limitations of his discipline and, as a student of Alfred Marshall, for taking the long view and engaging in a dynamic analysis of whole societies. Rostow's major works of economic history have stimulated a healthy debate about the fundamental nature of the development process and future economic change.

Said, Edward William (43)

A major critic of Western thinking about the Middle East and Asia.

Born in Palestine, he migrated to the United States and became a citizen. He received a bachelor's degree from Princeton in 1957 and a doctorate in English from Harvard in 1964. After teaching English and comparative literature at Harvard until 1977, he went on to Columbia where he has served as a professor in English and comparative literature. He is not only a distinguished literary critic, but also an influential writer on Arab culture and politics. Among his numerous publications are *The Arabs Today: Alternatives for the Future* (1973), *U.S. Policy and the Conflict of Powers in the Middle East* (1973), *Orientalizing the Orient* (1978), *The Question of Palestine* (1979), and *Orientalism* (1978).

Significance　　The term *Orientalism*, in Said's book, refers to activities and thinking concerning the Orient and the Oriental, although the focus of Said's Orient is the Middle East. His critique applies to all academic fields such as anthropology, sociology, history, economics, philosophy, and political science. Said notes that the term *Orient* was invented by Europeans to refer to the people, places, and cultures that existed geographically east of them. In fact, the Orient and the Occident are two man-made geographic constructs that support and reflect each other. Their binary contrasting images, ideas, and experiences help identify each other. He feels that in much Western writing the Orient, especially its Islamic countries and cultures, is perceived negatively as a threat to the West. Therefore, he suggests alternative nonhostile and nonpolitical ways to gain knowledge about other countries and their cultures. The study of Orientalism should not be merely political but rather "a distribution of geopolitical awareness into aesthetic, scholarly, economic, sociological, historical, and philological texts," Said (1978:12) argues. Such a perspective necessarily must transcend narrow geographical distinctions to comprehend a whole series of interests by such means as "scholarly discovery, philological reconstruction, psychological analysis, and landscape, and sociological description" (Said 1978:12). Central to this approach is the will or intention to understand a manifestly different world on its own terms. Such discourse has no direct relationship with raw political power, but "rather is produced and exists in an uneven exchange with various kinds of power, shaped to a degree by the exchange with power political, power intellectual, power cultural, and power moral." Those trying to understand the Third World on its own terms must pay serious heed to Said's insightful critique of Western ethnocentric and misleading perceptions of the Orient.

Schultz, Theodore W. (44)

A Nobel laureate in economics (1979) from the University of Chicago who has emphasized the crucial role of human capital in the development process. Early in his writing Schultz stressed the importance of education and health in enhancing human productivity. He also recognized the critical role of agriculture in development. Among Schultz's many books are *Transforming Traditional Agriculture* (1964) and *Investing in People: The Economics of Population Quality* (1981). *See also* HUMAN CAPITAL, 247.

Significance   Schultz was one of the first modern economists to note the increasing importance of human capital and the decline in the economic importance of land. The striking success of economies such as those of Japan, South Korea, Taiwan, Singapore, Hong Kong, and Thailand suggests the critical importance of the Schultz perspective. Schultz also stresses the importance of history in understanding economic phenomena and realities, and calls for doubt and skepticism. He argues that "economics would be better if we would substitute reasoned doubts for our parochial economic doctrines" (Schultz 1986:763). Schultz is one of the key founding fathers of the human capital school in economic development theory.

Schumacher, Ernst Friedrich (E. F.) (1911–1977) (45)

The author of *Small Is Beautiful: Economics As If People Mattered* (1973), and founder of the Intermediate Technology Development Group (1966). Schumacher was born in Bonn but settled in England after studying as a Rhodes scholar in Oxford in the 1930s. Educated in mainstream economic theory and a protégé of John Maynard Keynes, he became chief editorial writer on economics for *The Times*, an economic adviser to the British Control Commission in Germany, and, for twenty years, chief economist to the National Coal Board. While working with rural development programs in Zambia, Burma, and India, Schumacher began to question conventional wisdom regarding economic development. He found that most planners advocated economic growth through labor-saving and capital-intensive technology, even though labor was abundant and capital was scarce. At the same time he took interest in the teachings of Buddhism, which stressed nonmaterialism. The ideas later articulated in *Small Is Beautiful* and *A Guide for the Perplexed* began to take shape. He suggested that India and Burma pursue an indigenous form of development stressing capital-saving, labor-intensive, intermediate technology. In the 1950s and 1960s, when economic growth and technology transfer were virtually unquestioned as key elements of development, Schumacher's ideas were dismissed as idealistic and irrelevant. These ideas were later expressed and popularized in his classic essay "Buddhist Economics" (included in *Small Is Beautiful*).

By 1966 Schumacher had gathered enough supporters to form the Intermediate Technology Development Group to disseminate information about alternative technology and self-help development. As disillusionment with unlimited economic and industrial growth models of development grew, Schumacher's ideas slowly gained recognition. *Small Is Beautiful* received little initial attention in England, but the U.S. edition, accompanied by a lecture tour, was widely acclaimed. By the time of his death in 1977, E. F. Schumacher was recognized worldwide as a pioneer in alternative development thinking. Another book, *Good Work*, published posthumously in 1979, recounts many of Schumacher's direct development experiences and related creative thinking. *See also* "SMALL IS BEAUTIFUL," 121; BUDDHIST DEVELOPMENT/ECONOMICS, 103; APPROPRIATE TECHNOLOGY, 276.

Significance   Schumacher began questioning the wisdom, sustainability, and narrowness of conventional economic development theory long before sustainability, holistic development, and basic needs became common topics of concern within the development field. He introduced and promoted the notion of intermediate or appropriate technology and indigenous models of development. He stressed the social and spiritual cost of unemployment and meaningless employment. He was one of the few people to have anticipated the energy crisis and to offer viable alternatives. As such, Schumacher and his works continue to gain respect, recognition, and admiration. After his death, *Resurgence* magazine and his family established the Schumacher Society to promote his vision of development, which emphasizes the small and the beautiful.

Schumpeter, Joseph (1883–1950)   (46)

One of the most influential twentieth-century economic thinkers who published a major work in the development field as early as 1912. A member of the Austrian school of economics, Schumpeter did his graduate work at the University of Vienna (1901–1906). Schumpeter was not only a prominent scholar but had substantial practical experience as a bank president, the finance minister of Austria in its first republican government, and a practicing lawyer and economic consultant in Egypt. Born in what is now Czechoslovakia in 1883,

Schumpeter was offered academic appointments in both Germany and Japan, but decided to pursue his academic career in Germany. Later he joined the faculty of economics at Harvard in 1932 and remained there until his death in 1950. Among Schumpeter's most important books are *Theory of Economic Development* (1912); *Capitalism, Socialism, and Democracy* (1942); *Business Cycles* (1939); and *Imperialism and Social Classes* (1951). Schumpeter emphasized innovation, entrepreneurship, and competition as central elements in the development process and as major factors explaining cyclical fluctuations of macroeconomic performance. He also stressed change as the pervasive feature of social life.

Significance   Along with individuals such as Keynes and Marx, Schumpeter was one of the most influential economic thinkers of the modern era. His genuinely great ideas transcend time, space, and narrow disciplinary boundaries. Schumpeter's perspectives on the importance of innovation, entrepreneurship, free enterprise, free trade, new ways of producing things, new products, and new markets are compatible with recent economic thinking. The aspects of the current economic performance of the Pacific Basin that are associated with strategies of free trade, economic diversification, and privatization reflect the persistence and relevance of Schumpeterian thinking. Schumpeter also anticipated the growth with equity achieved by a number of countries such as South Korea, Taiwan, and Singapore. His emphasis on both social class and ideology reflected his ability to integrate political and sociological insights with this economic thinking. He also went beyond narrow methodological perspectives, and during his 44 years of writing worked "for a combination of historical, statistical, and theoretical analysis." The reading of Schumpeter is a must for anyone seriously interested in the political economy of development.

Scott, James   **(47)**
A proponent of the moral economy in peasant society, considered one of the leading moral economists. Extensive periods spent at Wisconsin's Land Tenure Center have heavily influenced Scott's thinking about peasant societies. His theory, as presented in his major work, *The Moral Economy of the Peasant: Subsistence and Rebellion in Southeast Asia,* draws heavily on Burmese and Vietnamese experience. The economy dimension of his theory assumes that peasants are risk-aversive and seek to minimize variations in income to assure basic subsistence. The moral dimension of the theory applies to periods of crisis or economic depression, when the richer and more powerful

are morally obliged to help peasants from falling below the subsistence threshold. This moral obligation is not necessarily altruistic, but may be based on both tradition and the need for reciprocity, that is, the loyalty of peasants in exchange for help in times of need. Scott's theory goes well beyond simple economic criteria of minimum calories or income and emphasizes the peasants' perception of their economic conditions, which may be influenced by both relative and absolute deprivation. Individuals rebel primarily because of moral indignation and outrage when their basic rights to subsistence are badly abused. More recently, Scott has written *Weapons of the Weak: Everyday Forms of Peasant Resistance* (1985), which draws on Malaysian experience. In this volume Scott describes ways in which peasants are cleverly able to undermine and resist exploitation under modern agribusiness conditions. *See also* WEAPONS OF THE WEAK, 216.

Significance   Scott's work on moral economy is rather controversial. Certain political economists and rational choice theorists such as Samuel Popkin (1979) feel that Scott romanticizes premodern and precommercial Southeast Asian villages alleged to practice the moral economy. Popkin also is skeptical about Scott's assumption that peasants are risk-aversive and negative toward modern markets. Popkin argues instead that rational peasants will seek to maximize their individual utility and income. Other scholars question whether Scott's thinking can be generalized beyond Southeast Asia to other cultural and geographic areas, where indigenous peasant societies may have differed significantly. The major impact of Scott's theory has been to force scholars and development theorists to rethink their assumptions about the economic and political behavior of peasants. His theory also has considerable practical relevance. Those political leaders and policymakers at both national and local levels who ignore the peasants' moral claims to a decent life of subsistence increase the likelihood that they will face some type of peasant resistance either through direct revolt or more commonly through the subtle but effective "weapons of the weak."

Sen, Amartya   **(48)**
Indian-born economist who is noted for his focus on ethical and normative issues of economics such as poverty, famine, inequality, and social welfare. Since 1981, he has been a professor of political economy at Oxford. The range of Sen's thinking and writing is extensive. Among issues he has analytically and rigorously addressed are methods for measuring poverty, inequality, and unemployment; the causes

of poverty and famine; methods of cost-benefit analysis and related shadow pricing; the validity of rational choice theory; the choice of technology in developing countries; and problems of collective rationality. His Indian and Asian background provide him a rich comparative perspective. For example, he is knowledgeable about fourth century B.C. Indian economic thought. His familiarity with the Japanese economy lends support to his skepticism concerning rational choice theory. Among his numerous articles and books are *On Economic Inequality* (1973); *Poverty and Famine: An Essay on Entitlement and Deprivation* (1981); *Resources, Values and Development* (1984); and *On Ethics and Economics* (1987).

Significance   Of Sen's many contributions, his analysis of the problems of poverty, famine, and inequality is central to a basic-needs approach to development. Perhaps most importantly, Sen shows an ability to transcend narrow Western definitions of man as acting only in his private self-interest. Sen recognizes the universal reality that behavior can reflect a mix of both selfish and selfless acts. In his analysis of famines, Sen shows insight in recognizing that they are not caused by problems of food supply but instead by complex elements of economic interdependence. Sen also departs from mainstream economics with his strong interest in the links between economics and ethics. Both disciplines could be enriched by greater intellectual interaction. Like the British philosopher Bertrand Russell, Sen combines high levels of analytical ability with a practical human concern about fundamental issues of human life such as basic well-being. Sen's work clearly shows the artificial distinction between theory and praxis. His theoretical concerns are central to the development process.

Shiva, Vandana   **(49)**
Indian physicist, philosopher of science, and leading advocate of ecofeminist perspectives on development. She is currently the director of the Research Foundation for Science Technology and Natural Resource Policy near Delhi. The diversity of her knowledge and concerns is reflected in the breadth of topics integrated into her well-articulated views of development and maldevelopment. Her writing examines the relationships among gender, nature, and environment, and scientific/economic paradigms of progress, as implied in the title of her book, *Staying Alive: Women, Ecology, and Development* (1988). Focusing on the experience of Third World women, she links the violation of nature resulting from the maldevelopment of modernization to the violation and marginalization of women. Highly

critical of current agricultural and reproductive technologies, she strongly advocates the need for a more harmonious, inclusive, and sustainable approach to development. She points out that such an approach is already understood and practiced by many Third World women, as demonstrated in the Chipko movement. Shiva, who is from a family of women activists, is an ardent supporter of Chipko and other citizens' groups acting against environmental destruction. She also serves as a consultant to the United Nations University. *See also* ECOFEMINISM, 262; CHIPKO MOVEMENT, 358.

Significance   Ecofeminism represents an important and vital challenge to conventional development thought and practice. Drawing from her insights into the hard sciences, social sciences, the environment, and feminism, Shiva makes a compelling case for an urgent and radical shift in the general approach to development. In *Staying Alive*, Shiva creatively draws connections among patriarchy, science, and environmental destruction. Conversely, she presents the relationship among women, feminine principles, and nature, paying particular attention to feminine systems of food production. Shiva's work and writing are important contributions to the search for new and sustainable development approaches. As she points out, such approaches may not be new at all, but rather a recovery of security systems practiced in preindustrialized and precolonial cultures.

Singer, H. W. (Hans)   **(50)**
A German-born development economist best known for his work on the problem of gains from trade and investment. Singer addressed this issue in a famous article that appeared in the May 1950 issue of the *American Economic Review*. A student of both Keynes and Schumpeter, from 1947 to 1968 Singer served with the United Nations, helping strengthen its Economics Department. Since 1969 he has been with the Institute of Development Studies (IDS) at the University of Sussex in Britain. Singer's development experience took place primarily in India, Pakistan, and Brazil, with a particular interest in the special development problems of Northeast Brazil. In his research on trade, Singer's perspective is basically that of the South: that the terms of trade for developing countries have deteriorated and that the poorer LDCs have experienced the greatest deterioration. Given this trend, Singer actively advocated soft development financing and fought for the establishment of the UN Development Program and the International Development Association, the concessionary window of the World Bank.

Significance   Permeating Singer's work on international development is a concern for distributive justice or distributive efficiency,
which reflects the influence of Alfred Marshall, R. H. Tawney, and
William Beveridge. Singer's pessimism regarding terms of trade for
developing countries led him to emphasize an inward orientation
toward development focusing on import substitution rather than
export expansion. Given present development trends, Singer's perspective seems best to describe Africa and parts of Latin America, but
not the more dynamic parts of the Pacific Basin that have benefited
from outward-oriented trade and foreign investment. It should also
be noted that Singer's conclusions concerning trends in the terms of
trade have been questioned by international economists such as Bela
Balassa.

Sippanondha Ketudat   (51)

Harvard-educated president of the National Petrochemical Corporation of Thailand, which is implementing that nation's largest industrial project. In his earlier role as minister of education under Prem
Tinsulanonda, Sippanondha articulated a major reform of Thailand's educational system, which was related to his role as leader of
an important educational reform movement initiated following a student revolution in Thailand in 1973. While secretary general of
Thailand's National Education Commission, Office of the Prime Minister, during the 1970s, Sippanondha encouraged numerous policy
research studies related to the proposals of the Educational Reform
Committee. These studies documented major educational disparities
in Thailand and problems with a curriculum divorced from the realities of contemporary Thai society. The reform movement also called
for more unity in the administration of Thai education and greater
decentralization of power and authority.

Significance   Sippanondha's National Petrochemical Corporation is
a major actor in Thailand's Eastern Seaboard Project, a principal element of the nation's attempt to decentralize development away from
Bangkok. In developing the Eastern Seaboard, Sippanondha has
been deeply concerned about the need for integrated development
and planning that reflects not only industrial needs and physical infrastructure but also related social, cultural, environmental, and
educational needs. As minister of education, Sippanondha was able to
orchestrate a major administrative change to shift primary education,
which consumes approximately 10 percent of the national budget,
from the control of the Ministry of the Interior to the Ministry of

Education. Many thought that such a change, regardless of its desirability, was politically impossible. Sippanondha's remarkable accomplishments show that dedication, commitment, and inspired leadership can lead to important change, even in highly bureaucratized Third World systems of governance. His case also illustrates the importance of entrepreneurship in the development process. The presence of individuals such as Sippanondha is one factor in explaining Thailand's development success of the 1980s. *See also* INTEGRATED INDUSTRIAL DEVELOPMENT, 267.

de Soto, Hernando (52)
A Peruvian economist and businessman, increasingly recognized as an influential development thinker. The son of a diplomat who sought exile from Peru, de Soto studied in Canada, the United States, and Switzerland, earning a master's degree in international economics and law from the University of Geneva. Apart from Spanish, de Soto is fluent in English and French. Returning to Peru in 1979, he initially managed a placer gold mine, but then became deeply interested in the informal economy of Peru. He established the Institute of Liberty and Democracy where much research on the Peruvian economy has been conducted. His book, *El Otro Sendero* (1986), has been a best-seller in Latin America and has been published in English as *The Other Path* (1989).

Significance De Soto is well known for his provocative ideas on the underground or informal economy, which includes, for example, drug traffickers, smugglers, and tax evaders. Although he is not the first to have studied the informal economy, "no one has delved into it more thoroughly or heralded its possibilities more enthusiastically" (Main 1989:15). De Soto believes that the economic potential of the informal economy is enormous because it involves thousands of people who are striving for a better life. He sees the informal economy as a solution rather than a problem for a country's development. If the entrepreneurial spirit is encouraged, legalized, and nurtured rather than oppressed by regulations and bureaucracy, it will help developing countries to manage their huge external debt, raise living standards, and increase international trade. Claiming that the informal economy often adds 29 percent to the official GNP in Peru, de Soto shows that food retailing in Lima is dominated by some 90,000 illegal street vendors and that most bus and taxi transportation in the city is informal. In addition, he finds that between 1960 and 1985, $8.3 billion of informal housing went up in Lima. Other studies have revealed that the informal economy was valued at about 70 percent of the official GNP in Argentina and about 35 percent of that in Kenya. Since businesses in the informal economy are illegal, they do not have titles for their property; they cannot enforce business contracts, obtain loans, or receive insurance. They also have to stay small to avoid official attention and, as a result, are prevented from maximizing their productivity. The enormous amount that the government could receive from this economy in taxes instead goes as bribery to a select group of government officials. De Soto has encouraged reforms to legalize the informal economy through the provision of titles to property, equal rights to go into business, and ability to borrow money and enforce contracts, all of which will lead to a maximizing of economic potential. Although de Soto has been criticized for exaggerating the size and potential of the informal economy, he is praised for opening up a new way of thinking about solutions for developing economies, and his idea is increasingly recognized worldwide.

Stavrianos, Leften Stavros (L. S.) (53)

Noted historian of the Balkans area and the Third World. His book, *Global Rift: The Third World Comes of Age* (1981), is a masterful and comprehensive analysis of four centuries of Third World history. He traces the origins and growth of the colonial system and the resulting political and economic dynamics of what came to be known as the Third World. Stavrianos also makes the case that the United States is taking on characteristics of the Third World.

Significance In *Global Rift,* Stavrianos contributes to development literature the first comprehensive Third World history, though its similarities to Fernand Braudel's three-volume work, *Civilization and Capitalism: 15th–18th Century,* should not be overlooked. Stavrianos emphasizes that Third World history is everyone's history, not just a corrective to history as written by the powerful, not just an attempt to understand the perspectives of Third World nations. He suggests that the conditions and institutions associated with the Third World are present in the more developed countries as well.

Sulak Sivaraksa (54)

An internationally known Thai intellectual and social critic and a prominent member of the Asian Cultural Forum on Development (ACFOD). Sulak is a prolific Thai critic of modern Western development, which in his view, is overly materialistic and environmentally destructive. Sulak and many of his colleagues at the ACFOD see the international penetration of capital into Southeast Asia as having contributed to militarization, the violation of human rights, the disruption of cultural values, and the growth of inequality. Sulak would like to see Thailand return to its Buddhist culture to erase the dangers from modern cultural imperialism. He opposes what he calls the think-big, GNP-based approach to development because it emphasizes capital output ratios and ignores basic human dimensions of development. He calls for a Buddhist type humanistic development emphasizing popular participation, social justice, human rights, basic needs, and reverence for life in all its forms. Among his many publications are *Siamese Resurgence* (1985) and *Siam in Crisis* (1980). Sulak is also active in the Siam Society, an organization devoted to the preservation of Siamese culture. Reflecting his nostalgic reverence for Thailand's past, Sulak often dresses in traditional rural clothes and prefers the name Siam to the modern name of Thailand, which he considers ethnically biased and colonial. *See also* BUDDHIST DEVELOPMENT/ECONOMICS, 103; CULTURAL IMPERIALISM, 220; DHAMMIC SOCIALISM, 109.

Significance   In more repressive societies than Thailand throughout the Third World, many individuals like Sulak have been incarcerated or are not allowed to publish their radical, critical thinking. Though Sulak was arrested in 1984, for the most part he has been free to pursue his intellectual critique of modern development and cultural imperialism. Through his bookstore, publishing firm, teaching, extensive writings, and his active involvement in the Asian Cultural Forum on Development and the Siam Society, Sulak has challenged individuals, both in the South and North, to rethink their views on modern development and Western values.

Sunkel, Osvaldo   (55)
An influential Latin American economist who was one of the early dependency theorists. Sunkel is currently coordinator of the Development and Environment Unit at the UN Economic Commission for Latin America and the Caribbean (CEPAL). A Chilean, Sunkel was part of a team of brilliant young economists (including Raúl Prebisch and Celso Furtado) working from 1955 to 1962 at the Economic Commission of Latin America (ECLA) in Santiago, Chile. Sunkel has also worked at the Latin American Institute of Economic and Social Planning, the Institute of International Studies at the University of Chile, and the Institute of Development Studies at the University of Sussex, England. As early as April 1967, long before dependency theory was fashionable, Sunkel was writing about the problems of ex-

extreme external dependency. He was also deeply concerned that the broad masses were not benefiting from the development process. Sunkel coined the term *país succursal,* which means branch-plant country. Identifying the overcoming of dependence as the major goal of development, Sunkel emphasized the need to develop indigenous manufacturing operations to serve the needs of the rural poor. To facilitate that end, he was willing to restrict free trade and allow for extensive state economic intervention. *See also* DEPENDENCY THEORY, 106.

Significance   Sunkel is well known for his important contributions to the structural theory of inflation. He has also displayed impressive prescience in a number of other areas. For example, he discussed not only economic dependence but cultural dependence. As early as 1967, he foresaw the future debt problems of developing countries. Sunkel's concept of branch-plant countries also showed remarkable foresight, given the current trend of transnational corporations to locate manufacturing facilities offshore. Like the brilliant Indonesian planner and thinker, Soedjatmoko, Sunkel is deeply concerned about the affirmation and preservation of national personality and related indigenous values and culture. Sunkel's development thinking has been, to our knowledge, almost entirely influenced by the experiences of Latin American economies. He did not foresee the emergence of Asian NICs such as Taiwan and South Korea that would develop extensive external economic relations while achieving impressive economic diversification. Sunkel's writing and thinking has inspired an entire generation of Latin American intellectuals. His current major interests are transnationalization approaches and the environment/development question.

Tinbergen, Jan   **(56)**
Dutch Nobel laureate in economic science in 1969, best known for his important contributions to the field of development planning. Tinbergen was director of the Central Planning Bureau of the Netherlands for 11 years (1945–1955). Thus, his knowledge of planning derived from firsthand experience. From 1933 to 1973 Tinbergen was also a professor at Erasmus University. The major focus of his research and writing were the methods and practice of planning for long-term development, which he described in volumes such as *The Design of Development* (1958), *Central Planning* (1964), and *Development Planning* (1967). His approach to planning emphasized the application of the powerful quantitative tools of econometrics and linear programming to macroeconomic policy and decision making.

Tinbergen viewed differences in human capital and other differences in power as key factors in explaining inequality. He also emphasized human resource development as the longest production process and incorporated the need for educational planning into his analyses. Tinbergen made the distinction between tradable and nontradable goods, which has implications for economic planning and policy.

Significance   Tinbergen's approach emphasizes the need for both politicians and economic policymakers to take long-term perspectives. Tinbergen's thinking is also highly pragmatic. For example, he stresses that the quality of management is much more important than the type of ownership of an enterprise. An internationalist who emphasizes the need for North-South cooperation and dialogue, Tinbergen was coordinator for *RIO (Reshaping the International Order): A Report to the Club of Rome* (1976). The RIO project involved the close cooperation of representatives from the First, Second, and Third Worlds in dealing with the problem of global injustices and the need for a new international order. Though formal economic programming and planning tools have certain limitations related to basic data and underlying assumptions, Tinbergen made highly significant contributions to applying and refining such tools and relating them to practical questions of policy and long-term economic decision making.

Todaro, Michael   (57)
Development economist at New York University, known for his popular and highly valuable texts on the economics of development. Todaro's extensive development research has focused on rural-urban migration and related problems of urban unemployment. He developed the concept *Todaro's Paradox,* in reference to the growing urban unemployment associated with policies to create more urban jobs. Urban job-creation projects only make large cities in developing countries even greater magnets to attract rural migrants, further swelling a labor force already growing rapidly from natural fertility increases. Todaro's books on development economics have been translated into five languages. Among his best known works are *Development Planning: Models and Methods* (1972), *Economic Development in the Third World* (1981), and *The Struggle for Economic Development* (1983).

Significance   Todaro could be considered the Paul Samuelson of development economics. He has made both theoretical and educational contributions to the field while writing textbooks noted for their lucidity, scholarship, and comprehensiveness.

Wallerstein, Immanuel (58)

Originator of world systems theory and founder of the Fernand Braudel Center for the Study of Economics, Historical Systems and Civilizations. Wallerstein, who earned his Ph.D. at Columbia University, focused his early work on Africa and the sociology of development utilizing center-periphery theory. This led to an ongoing, ambitious, and compelling attempt to interpret the history of the world capitalist system, the findings of which are to be presented in a four-volume work, *The Modern World System*. Volumes 1 and 2, covering the period from the mid–1400s to 1750, were published in 1974 and 1980. These works focus on the transition from feudalism to capitalism and the establishment of world centers of capitalist power. Wallerstein traces the emergence of an international economic system based on a single international division of labor operating within a multicultural context. The basic institutions comprising the world system are states, classes, ethnonational status groups, and households. World systems analysis concerns itself with the roles of these groups in the numerous dynamic cycles of economic expansion and contraction inherent within a capitalist system driven by supply and demand. Wallerstein detects in this process the transfer of surplus from the peripheral, subjugated areas to the center, colonial powers such as Holland, Britain, and later the United States. Further, he examines the structural mechanisms devised by the center powers to reproduce and preserve unequal relationships or positions of dominance. He devotes less attention to the various forms of class struggle that result. Wallerstein foresees, in the next 100 to 150 years, the transition from world capitalism to world socialism. *See also* CENTER-PERIPHERY, 104; DEPENDENCY THEORY, 106.

Significance   Wallerstein, in world systems theory, offers a brilliant and intriguing synthesis of economic and political history with strong implications for understanding the present. His research has quickly gained a high measure of respect throughout the development field of the social sciences. *The Modern World System* is a momentous work and, even as yet unfinished, has stimulated extensive response and further inquiry into the meaning of the history of the world capitalist system. World systems theory is a helpful augmentation to dependency theory, expanding on its basic notions of center-periphery analysis. Any scholarly undertaking of this extent, attempting to synthesize several centuries of world history, is no doubt open to criticism. Most of Wallerstein's detractors point out his tendency to downplay or misinterpret those aspects of history that are not neatly integrated into or accounted for by the world systems analysis. Others argue that he neglects internal conditions as a development factor. Regardless of its shortcomings, world systems analysis brings attention to the need for less fragmented and narrow approaches to the study of world development and underdevelopment.

Ward, Barbara (Lady Robert Jackson) (1914–1981) (59)
A world-renowned British economist who made important contributions to the development field. Ward was a prolific scholar, producing approximately 20 books and thousands of articles. Her most important works in the development area were *The Rich Nations and the Poor Nations* (1962), *Two Views on Aid to Underdeveloped Countries* (1966), *The Widening Gap* (1971), and *Progress for a Small Planet* (1981). As the titles suggest, Ward was particularly concerned with distributional and environmental dimensions of development. During the early 1940s Ward served as an economic adviser in both India and Pakistan. This experience facilitated her developing empathy and understanding of the genuine development context. Ward also served as chairperson of the Society of International Development.

Significance   Ward's career showed a fascinating evolution from journalist, to development planner, and finally to protector of the fragile global environment. Ward worked particularly hard to increase consciousness of the need for those in the West to change their life-styles to facilitate prospects for global development and environmental preservation.

Worsley, Peter (60)
Leading British sociologist who has written extensively on the Third World. He is professor emeritus of sociology at the University of Manchester and twice served as president of the British Sociological Association. Worsley first wrote about the Third World in 1964 in *The Third World*, which focused on Africa. He updated the book three years later and was struck by the massive changes taking place in the Third World. He argued that it was not updating that was needed but "a radical reappraisal of one's whole framework and its constituent categories." This reassessment is embodied in Worsley's lifework, *The Three Worlds: Culture and World Development* (1984). *See also* CULTURAL DEVELOPMENT, 219; IRVING HOROWITZ, 27.

Significance   Worsley draws freely from many disciplines to construct a compelling analysis of the three political worlds and a synthesis of Third World history. More importantly, the discussion is placed firmly within the context of culture as a shared set of values. Of particular concern for Worsley is the relationship of ethnicity and nationalism to class, a study he finds inadequately covered in social theory, particularly Marxist materialism. *The Three Worlds* is a landmark critique of and contribution to development theory and literature, particularly because of its discussion of culture as an important, but often overlooked, constituent of development.

B. Development Leaders and Practitioners

Atatürk, Mustafa Kemal (1881–1938)   (61)

The father of modern Turkey, who headed that nation's first republican government. Atatürk's role in modernizing Turkey is often compared with that of the Meiji in Japan. Though of humble background, Atatürk rose to power through his military career and leadership during Turkey's War of Independence (1919–1922), in which the Turks defeated the Greeks and the Allies. Atatürk was known as a strong nationalist who emphasized the need for a distinct Turkish identity and homeland. Key principles underlying Atatürk's leadership were republicanism, nationalism, populism, secularism, etatism, and revolutionism. In 1922, the sultanate was abolished, paving the way for a secular, republican government under Atatürk's leadership. *See also* KEMALISM, 205.

Significance   Atatürk's importance is primarily based on his early and decisive success in creating a modern nation-state in Turkey and his related leadership to inspire key institution building. Atatürk's success in creating a secular state in a previously Muslim empire is also remarkable. Atatürk was deeply committed to a rationalist model of civilization and was open to many aspects of Western society, for example, in dress, the use of a Latin alphabet, and greater equality for women. As a testimonial to Atatürk's success, Turkey today is one of the most politically stable nations in the Middle East. With respect to basic social and economic indicators, Turkey has achieved an impressive level of development compared to other developing nations. Atatürk was an early internationalist and "peace all over the world" was the keynote of his foreign policy activity.

Borlaug, Norman   (62)

Father of the Green Revolution and the only development expert to be awarded the Nobel Peace Prize (1970). Since 1944, Borlaug has worked primarily in Mexico as an agricultural scientist under the auspices of the Rockefeller Foundation's international technical assistance program. He is most noted for his development of high-yielding and highly adaptable varieties of Mexican wheat. The dwarf wheat developed by Borlaug and his colleagues at the Centro Internacional de Majoramiento de Maize y Trigo (CIMMYT) became the cereal prototype for new rice varieties developed at the International Rice Research Institute (IRRI) in the Philippines during the mid–1960s. Borlaug is also noted for his down-to-earth personal style. He likes to get close to ordinary farmers and communicates with them in Spanish, and takes pride in working with his hands. Borlaug stresses to his trainees that "they should listen closely to what the plants themselves say" (Fry and Thurber 1989:123). Borlaug has emphasized the building of local applied agricultural research capacity and related training programs. *See also* GREEN REVOLUTION, 180; HIGH YIELD VARIETIES, 181.

Significance   Borlaug's applied research in Mexico has contributed greatly to a quadrupling of wheat production in Mexico since 1950 and a doubling of wheat output in both India and Pakistan between 1968 and 1972. The Green Revolution deriving from Borlaug's work in Mexico is, of course, highly controversial. Critics have noted that the Green Revolution contributes to growing rural inequality because of differential access to the production factors needed for growing the new seeds, such as credit and chemical fertilizers. They also charge that, following the Green Revolution, exports of U.S. chemical fertilizers to the Third World have increased dramatically. Proponents of the Green Revolution, in contrast, argue that this technological advance has bought needed years in which to stabilize population growth in developing countries. There is also debate about the impact of the new seeds on genetic variability. The high yield varieties (HYVs) developed by Borlaug and others have replaced native varieties in many locations. Borlaug argues that "more genetic variability is being put into grains now than ever before in the history of the world" (Fry and Thurber 1989:123).

Brundtland, Gro Harlem   (63)
Former prime minister of Norway and chairperson of the World Commission on Environment and Development (WCED). Brundtland, born in 1939, received her formal training in medicine and public health. She entered politics in the early 1970s as a pro-choice activist and in 1974 was appointed as Norway's environment minister.

In 1981, as head of the Labor party, she served as prime minister for eight months, a position she regained in 1986. In 1983 she was appointed chairperson of the WCED, which became known as the Brundtland Commission. The commission published its findings in 1987 in a book entitled *Our Common Future: The Report of the World Commission on Environment and Development. See also* BRUNDTLAND REPORT, 257; SUSTAINABLE DEVELOPMENT, 272.

Significance   In addition to her impact in Norway, where she has helped reshape Norwegian politics, Brundtland was instrumental in the success and influence of the WCED. The Brundtland Commission brought urgent international attention to the relationship between environment and development, and associated problems. The commission's report outlines the environmental effects of development and proposes strategies for addressing these issues. The strategies proposed have generated considerable discussion, mainly centered around the adequacy of the changes proposed for the world's wealthiest nations. Brundtland has put considerable effort into publicizing the report through interviews and participation in international conferences. She has effectively raised the issue of global responsibility in her home country and throughout the world.

Chandler, Robert (64)

Key figure in the development and promotion of high yield varieties (HYVs) of rice as part of the Green Revolution. Born in 1907, Chandler taught soil sciences at Cornell and served as dean of the School of Agriculture at the University of New Hampshire before joining the Rockefeller Foundation. As agriculture science adviser for East Asia, Chandler came to recognize the importance of developing improved strains of rice to meet the demands of Asia's growing population. In 1959 the foundation asked Chandler to establish the International Rice Research Institute (IRRI) in the Philippines. By 1965, under Chandler's direction, the IRRI had produced IR-8, the first high yield variety of rice. After 12 years at IRRI, Chandler moved to Taiwan where he became the founding director of the Asian Vegetables Research and Development Center, which focuses on improving basic vegetable crops in tropical areas. In 1986 Chandler was honored as the second recipient of the World Food Prize in recognition of his efforts to increase world food supplies. *See also* INTERNATIONAL RICE RESEARCH INSTITUTE, 423; GREEN REVOLUTION, 180; HIGH YIELD VARIETIES, 181.

Significance   Chandler was instrumental in promoting and implementing the research that has led to unprecedented growth in rice production since the mid-1960s. It has been estimated that two-thirds of the increase in Asian rice production is directly attributable to the work of the IRRI. Chandler recognized early the importance of rice and the rice farmer in meeting growing world demands for food. He pointed out and sought to counteract the urban bias prevalent in much development planning. In agreement with his counterpart in the Green Revolution, Norman Borlaug, Chandler stresses that technological improvements must be coupled with enlightened politics and population constraint if world food demands are to be met.

Chenery, Hollis (65)

Noted comparative development economist with extensive experience as a development practitioner. Chenery had high-level economic policy experience at both the U.S. Agency for International Development (1961–1965) and the World Bank (1970–1982). Since 1983, Chenery has been a professor of economics at Harvard. Among his many books are *Studies in Development Planning* (1971), *Redistribution with Growth: An Approach to Policy* (1974), and *Patterns of Development, 1950–1970* (1975) (with M. Syrquin). Chenery is known for his two-gap model. The two gaps refer to two key factors that affect a nation's potential for growth in gross national product (GNP): the availability of imports and the level of domestic savings to finance required investments. The trade gap is the excess of required imports over possible exports, and the savings gap is the extent to which domestic savings fall short of investment needs. Theoretically, these two gaps are equal, but in the short run they may be unequal because of disequilibria. Chenery argues that countries should adjust to the international market to achieve equality of these two gaps.

Significance   Chenery represents the scholar-doer par excellence. He has not only engaged in development activities but has reflected seriously about the development process. Particularly interested in comparative patterns of development, he has also been concerned about growth with distribution and the equity aspects of development policy. For this reason he devoted special attention to careful study of the South Korean model of development. He is also noted for his emphasis on examining the relations between efficiency and equity.

Crawford, Sir John (66)

An Australian well known for his many contributions to the development field, particularly in the area of agriculture. Crawford led the agricultural team of the World Bank's Bell Mission to India in October 1964. He spent much time in the field to become close to the realities of rural life in India. Based on his fieldwork there, Crawford stressed the importance of an integrated approach to agriculture, involving use of credit, price incentives, new seeds, and extension. Sir John felt that institutional changes alone were not sufficient to foster agricultural growth. India's Ministry of Agriculture was later to implement a number of elements of the Crawford strategy, though India's dramatic increase of its grain output was the result of many interrelated factors. Between 1973 and 1980 Crawford visited India regularly on behalf of the World Bank. In recognition of his growing reputation in the international agriculture field, in 1971 Crawford was named the first chairman of the Technical Advisory Committee (TAC) of the Consultative Group on International Agriculture Research (CGIAR). The committee established a number of new applied agricultural research centers, inspired by the earlier successes of the International Rice Research Institute (IRRI) in the Philippines and the International Maize and Wheat Improvement Center (CIMMYT) in Mexico. As chairman of TAC, Crawford clearly demonstrated his skills as an institution builder. The recent book, *Policy & Practice: Essays in Honor of Sir John Crawford* (1987), provides an excellent account of Sir John's many contributions to international development.

Significance   Sir John Crawford's successes in the international development field confirm that a single individual can make an important difference. His accomplishments also reflect Australia's growing role in the international development arena. His broad range of experiences have made him a classic inner-and-outer, a specialist who moves back and forth among government, industry, academia, and international organizations. Personal factors contributing to his success in the development field were a keen sense of politics, a rare combination of steadfastness and clarity of mind, understanding of the other side's interests, and an ability to find a reasonable consensus.

Curle, Adam   (67)
A member of the Harvard group that provided technical assistance to the Pakistan Planning Board (later, Commission) in the 1950s and 1960s. Unlike most technical assistance advisers, Curle reflected seriously and openly about his advising experiences. These critical reflections were published in his book, *Planning for Education in Pakistan: A Personal Case Study* (1966). In this volume, Curle is highly critical of the traditional role of foreign advisers who expect to share their

wisdom with developing countries and prescribe solutions to the countries' problems. Curle calls instead for advisers to be much more subservient and humble, doing all they can to help achieve the goals defined by the hosts, not the outsider.

Significance   Curle's critical openness about the pitfalls of foreign advising is unusual. He views conventional technical-assistance advising as a subtle continuation of colonial domination. Given the growing indigenous intellectual capacity of developing countries, Curle's perspective is even more relevant today than when he wrote about it in the 1960s. Curle's valuable insight that advisers need to engage in substantial "unlearning" reflects the highly differential conditions found in areas such as the Middle East and South Asia. Philip Coombs pays an elegant tribute to Curle and his success as an unusual development expert:

> One wishes that the many hundreds of technical assistance experts around the world—specialists away from home—all possessed his sensitivity, perspective, and wisdom. (Fry and Thurber 1989:107).

Currie, Lauchlin   (68)

Economist-farmer noted for his economic advising work in Colombia. As with Adam Curle's writings on his Pakistani work, Currie has reflected on his technical assistance experiences in Colombia in *The Role of Economic Advisers in Developing Countries* (1981). In this book, Currie describes openly his successes as well as his mistakes in providing economic advice to the Colombian Government Planning Agency. The report of the World Bank mission that Currie directed mirrors significantly Colombian economic policy over the years. In fact, Currie contributed to the development of close relations between Colombia and the World Bank. Unlike most technical assistance advisers, Currie developed a real commitment to Colombia by becoming a local national and a dairy farmer. Modest about his successes, Currie claims that in his nearly 40 years in Colombia he may hold the record for the number of his policy recommendations that have been rejected. Despite Currie's modest claims, his working paper, *Operation Colombia* (1961), appears to have had considerable impact on Colombian agricultural policy in the 1970s.

Significance   Despite Currie's modesty about his successes as an economic adviser, he displayed considerable talent in what Aaron Wildavsky describes as "speaking truth to power." Currie's impact on economic policy in a developing country reflects the controversial era of "the ugly American" in which thousands of Americans worked abroad in technical assistance and tried to export their solutions to the problems of developing countries. Radical development theorists argue that their advice generally caused far more harm than good since they emphasized inappropriate capital-intensive Western approaches to development. As developing countries have increased their economic expertise in the last decades of the twentieth century, their need for external experts has declined accordingly. Currie's life and experiences as an economist/farmer in Colombia provide valuable empirical data for assessing the role of the economic adviser in a developing country.

Deming, W. Edwards (69)

An intellectual consultant known as the father of quality control in Japan. In the late 1940s and early 1950s, Deming introduced the concept of statistical quality control to the Japanese, and stressed the importance of committed service to customers. In his lectures in Japan, Deming voiced optimism that the quality of Japanese goods could become the best in the world. The Japanese then took responsibility for spreading Deming's ideas more broadly throughout Japan. Ironically, Deming was not known in his own country, the United States, until around 1980, when Americans began to take special interest in Japanese approaches to management and industry. Deming's major ideas and observations on his work in Japan are contained in a volume published by MIT in 1982 titled *Quality, Productivity, and Competitive Position. See also* TECHNICAL ASSISTANCE, 305.

Significance Deming's career illustrates the potential of technical assistance and the ability of a single individual to make a real difference in the development field. The Japanese created an annual Deming Prize, which is given to the Japanese company most successful in quality control. Deming's success may be partially explained by his rich interdisciplinary background and his experience as an inner-and-outer, who moves back and forth among government, industry, and academia. The Deming case, in sum, is an extraordinary example of the right man being in the right place at the right time, and of the impressive Japanese capability to learn from foreign experience.

Deng Xiaoping (70)

Second-generation political leader of the People's Republic of China who orchestrated that nation's major economic reforms in the late 1970s and 1980s. Like Mao Zedong, Deng was a revolutionary leader who fought valiantly against both the Chinese nationalists of Chiang Kai-shek and the Japanese. During World War II Deng was politcommissar of the 129th Division (the Liu-Deng Army), and was the highest-ranking commander in the important 1949 battle of Huaihai during the civil war. Deng's political career was marked by a series of rises and falls. Three times he was toppled from positions of influence only to rise again to positions of critical importance. Beginning in the early 1950s, Deng served as both deputy premier and minister of finance. In 1966, at the time of the Great Proletarian Cultural Revolution, Deng and his family suffered seriously. Were it not for Zhou Enlai, Deng might not have survived the Cultural Revolution. In 1973, Deng was recalled by Mao, primarily because of his influence with the Second and Third Field armies of China. In a critically important address to the UN General Assembly in 1974, Deng condemned the imperialistic expansion of the two superpowers (the First World in Mao's and Deng's view), identifying China with the interests of the Third World. (In the Mao-Deng view, the Second World was comprised of countries such as Japan and Canada that were striving to remain independent of the two superpowers.) Deng promised that China would never seek to be a superpower. The years from 1978 to the present can be considered the Deng era, in which he has attempted to reform the Chinese economy by introducing elements of privatization and capitalism, welcoming international foreign investment to certain zones of China, and allowing a major opening to the outside world. The German writer Uli Franz has provided a valuable biography, *Deng Xiaoping* (1988), now available in English translation. *See also* MAO ZEDONG, 82; PARADIGMS OF DEVELOPMENT, 116; RURAL RESPONSIBILITY SYSTEM, 186; CULTURAL IMPERIALISM, 220.

Significance   As China's innovative leader of the late 1970s and 1980s, Deng, always noted for his pragmatism, attempted to implement a mixed model of Marxist socialism and capitalism. Basic modes of production such as land remain under the control of the state, but Deng abolished Mao's system of communes, which was eventually replaced by a rural responsibility system, in which peasants lease individual plots from the state and are able to retain profits beyond their basic rent. This system has led to enhanced agricultural production as well as increased economic disparities. Under the new system, various state enterprises and local governmental units also have been able to retain profits for their own use.

A number of special economic zones, primarily in coastal areas, have been established to attract international capital and foreign investment. Thus, Deng has played a major role in liberalizing and internationalizing the Chinese economy, and the Deng era has been one of impressive economic growth and increase in international trade. Deng also articulated the four modernizations: agriculture, industry, science, and defense. He has orchestrated agreements with the United Kingdom (1984) and Portugal (1987) for the return to China of Hong Kong in 1997 and Macao in 1999. To assure the citizens of Hong Kong and Macao that their basic economic systems would remain in place for at least 50 years after coming under Chinese sovereignty, Deng introduced the formula of "one country, two systems." Depending on the success of the Hong Kong and Macao transitions, this formula might make possible the reunification of Taiwan with China. Since 1983, Deng has supported a campaign against spiritual pollution and contamination, indicating that though China would like the benefits of Western technology, the country does not necessarily want commonly associated cultural changes. In June 1989, by allying with the Gang of Old, Deng clearly showed his opposition to political liberalization in his suppression of the prodemocracy movement. Continuing debate about the extent to which Deng has brilliantly combined the best features of socialism and capitalism to achieve growth with equity is likely. Some economic critics, both within and outside China, see Deng's model of development as combining capitalist demand with socialist supply, a clear formula for inflationary pressures and economic imbalances. On the other hand, if Deng's economic formula succeeds in quadrupling China's GNP during the 1980–2000 period, his major development goal, China will be poised to be a genuine economic power of the twenty-first century, and the Chinese will owe much to Deng for his courage in reforming China's brand of Marxist economy.

Dooley, Tom (1927–1961)   (71)

Young U.S. doctor whose humanitarian service in Southeast Asia was made famous by a feature film and by the title of a popular ballad of the Kingston Trio about a folk character of the same name. Dooley wrote a trilogy about his health work in Southeast Asia, the profits from which were devoted to his medical work, primarily in the extremely poor country of Laos. Dooley's commitment to this type of mission was inspired by his personal acquaintance with Albert Schweitzer. He stated his basic philosophical orientation toward the work of his team in Laos:

> I am not interested alone in the amount of antibiotics that circulate in the bodies of our patients. But I am most interested in the amount of

education that circulates in the hearts and minds of the people of our high valley. After *our departure* this will last longer than will their blood level of penicillin. (Fry and Thurber 1989:111).

Significance   Dooley worked in Laos roughly at the time Lederer and Burdick published *The Ugly American* (1958), and he provided a strong contrast to the image in that novel. Writing about Dooley in 1956, Sen. Mike Mansfield stated,

> If the United States had abroad more ambassadors like Dr. Thomas A. Dooley, I think it not only would be better off, but would be better understood in the countries which are underdeveloped and which need understanding at this time. (Fry and Thurber 1989:112).

Thus, Dooley and his colleagues in Laos represented a youthful and idealistic ethic of international personal service. Some even speculate that Dooley's example might have had an impact on senators Hubert Humphrey or John Kennedy who proposed the Peace Corps concept when Dooley's work in Laos was attracting national and international attention. Despite Dooley's heroic image (he died of cancer in 1961), a careful reading of his trilogy reveals some disturbing elements of paternalism and ethnocentrism. Nevertheless, Dooley represents an inspiring role model of personal sacrifice and commitment to help the poor in developing countries such as Laos to meet their basic medical and health needs.

Fuller, William P.   **(72)**
A development practitioner who has primarily worked in the Asian arena and is noted for his able administration of major aid programs. Fuller's first major development experience was field research in India dealing with the economics of education. Later Fuller served in the Ford Foundation's Office for Southeast Asia. While with Ford, Fuller assisted three ministries of the Thai government in developing analytical policy research capacity. He also helped the National Education Commission of Thailand, part of the Office of the Prime Minister, conduct a major Coleman type study on the equality of educational opportunity in Thailand. After completing his work in Thailand, Fuller became the Ford Foundation's representative in Bangladesh in the late 1970s. There he encouraged many innovative development projects, most of them related to improving the income-generating capacity of rural women and techniques such as oral rehydration therapy to increase satisfaction of basic needs. In the 1980s Fuller moved to the U.S. Agency for International Development (AID) to direct its program in Indonesia, one of the United

States's largest aid programs. After completing his Indonesian assignment, Fuller was reassigned to Washington, where he headed AID's Middle East and North African desk. In July 1989, Fuller became the president of the Asia Foundation in San Francisco.

Significance   Though Fuller had excellent scholarly potential with advanced degrees from Stanford and Harvard, he chose to employ his energies and creativity to direct development efforts. His support of a study of equality of educational opportunity in Thailand provided critical data relevant to a major educational reform movement that has changed the face of contemporary Thai education. He also played an important role in helping foster a proactive nonformal education movement in Thailand; that country today has achieved a 91 percent literacy rate. Fuller's development work in Bangladesh showed that important progress could be made even in extremely adverse developmental settings. In Indonesia, Fuller achieved recognition for his efforts to carefully coordinate U.S. AID with that of many other donor agencies. Fuller is an exceptionally committed and responsive aid administrator, and his appointment as the president of the Asia Foundation augurs well for that organization.

Gandhi, Mohandas K. (1869–1948)   (73)

World-renowned advocate of nonviolent action and a key figure in India's struggle for independence, whose life was a vivid demonstration of vision, courage, and compassion. Born in 1869 and married at age 12, Gandhi trained in law in London. After several years of practice in Bombay, he moved to South Africa where he founded the Natal Indian Congress in 1894. He took over a weekly publication to advance the cause of Indians in South Africa in 1904 and introduced his concept of *satyagraha*, a doctrine of nonviolence that translates as "a force born out of true love." Upon his return to India in 1915, Gandhi began to organize resistance against the British, for which he was imprisoned on numerous occasions. He soon became a central figure in the Indian independence movement and helped found the Congress party, from which he resigned in 1934 because of its unwillingness to commit totally to principles of nonviolence.

Gandhi's philosophy of peace and nonviolence carried strong implications for development, which he defined as "the realization of human potential." Gandhi's vision of India's development stood in sharp contrast to that of the other great figure in India's modern political history, Jawaharlal Nehru. Instead of following the path of modernization through the establishment of large-scale industrialization, Gandhi advocated the development and support of cottage industries as the main form of economic activity. He took up the spinning wheel to demonstrate self-sufficiency, a particularly meaningful gesture in light of the British attempt to destroy the Indian textile industry. Cottage industries, he believed, would provide meaningful employment and income for the largest number of people as well as fostering self-reliance at the village level. This self-reliance included the abolition of the caste system, and would be accompanied by a decentralized political system that stressed highly participatory decision making. Gandhi also warned against the materialist and consumptive nature of industrialized societies and concerned himself with both spiritual and environmental consequences of the conventional path to national and international development. He was assassinated on January 30, 1948. *See also* JAWAHARLAL NEHRU, 90; CHIPKO MOVEMENT, 358.

Significance   Gandhi's life and teachings stand as a challenge to materialistic and centralized development models. He was an advocate of self-sufficient, holistic, and participatory development long before these became popular notions in the development literature. His methods of nonviolence and concept of *satyagraha* have served as a model for social and political change throughout the world, including the civil rights movement in the United States. Gandhi's thoughts on development serve as a basis for later alternative development strategies, which emphasize local action and humanistic approaches to human betterment. Above all, Gandhi is considered by many to be one of the most inspirational figures of the twentieth century and a symbol of "positive peace," that is, the need for greater social justice.

Grant, John (1890–1962) (74)

China-born son of Canadian missionaries, who played a major role in the Rockefeller Foundation's health programs in China in the 1920s and 1930s. From 1921 to 1938, Grant was in China with the International Health Board of the Rockefeller Foundation and taught for 14 years at the Peking Union Medical College (PUMC). Grant's qualifications for such a role were impeccable. He was fluent in Chinese, had an M.D. degree from Michigan, had taken follow-up training in public health at Johns Hopkins, and had U.S. practical experience with innovative public health programs in North Carolina. Given his intimate knowledge of Chinese culture and language, Grant was able to develop close working relationships with key figures in the Chinese health bureaucracy, which facilitated his success in helping strengthen China's public health system and institutions. His son,

James Grant, has also had an important impact in the development field as director of the United Nations Children's Fund (UNICEF).

Significance   In many respects, Grant's work was an inspiring example of effective technical assistance. Showing remarkable ability in adapting his expertise to local Chinese conditions, he trained hundreds of Chinese in the health field. Over time, the percentage of PUMC staff members who were Chinese steadily increased. Grant had a strong commitment to institution building and enhancement of local capacity. However, one criticism is that PUMC was built as an elite institution. Mary Brown Bullock, a scholar who has carefully studied Grant's work in China, ably summarizes the essence of Grant's approach to technical assistance:

> Perhaps it is because Grant worked so diligently to overcome the institutional encumbrances of Western medicine that one reflects favorably upon his career. But perhaps more revealing is the fact that he did not make himself indispensable to the progress which he started. Therein lies the measure of his success. (Bullock 1980:161).

Hanna, Paul (1902–1988)   (75)

A noted development educator and founder of the Stanford International Development Education Center (SIDEC). Hanna, a former professor in Stanford's School of Education, became interested in education and development primarily as the result of working on various AID and UN projects in developing countries, particularly in the Philippines. As the result of such experiences, Hanna believed that it was important to create a center to train both U.S. and Third World nationals who would understand the important role of education in development and the complex relations between education and political, economic, and social development. Thus, he persuaded Stanford to establish SIDEC in 1965. Since that time, hundreds of Third World and U.S. nationals have received formal training in international development education at the master's and doctoral levels.

Significance   In his later years at Stanford, Hanna became a rather controversial figure primarily because of his allegedly uncritical view of the role of education in development. His association with the "right-wing" Hoover Institution also alienated him from a much more liberal and radical SIDEC community which diverged rather dramatically from Hanna's original ideology. While Hanna's work as a development expert overseas may have had some impact, his major legacy is SIDEC and a remarkable archive established in the name of Hanna and his wife at Stanford, called the Hanna Collection on the

Role of Education in the Twentieth Century. This archive contains the papers and documents of hundreds of prominent individuals who worked overseas in the twentieth century in the area of education and development, including such persons as Philip Coombs, Hugh Wood, Eugene Staley, John Montgomery, Frank Moore, Milton Friedman, L. S. Stavrianos, and Arthur Young. Created by the financial generosity of the Hannas, the archive provides rich primary data for the study of technical assistance in developing countries, and is a valuable source for current and future generations interested in international development issues.

Hoffman, Paul G. (76)

A key postwar development leader who directed the Marshall Plan and was the first director of the United Nations Development Programme (UNDP). Before World War II, Hoffman achieved fame as a highly successful, human relations–oriented president of Studebaker. In the early 1940s, along with other progressive businessmen, Hoffman founded the Committee for Economic Development, which he headed. President Truman selected Hoffman to direct the Marshall Plan and head the newly created Economic Cooperation Administration in 1948. Based on his successful implementation of the Marshall Plan, in 1951 he was appointed president of the Ford Foundation. While at Ford he launched new overseas development programs and became a strong political advocate for U.S. foreign aid. After a falling out with Henry Ford II, Hoffman became president of the Fund for the Republic and returned to Studebaker. Hoffman completed his illustrious development career by moving to the United Nations in 1959 where he was director of the Special Fund and the first director of the newly established UNDP (1966–1971). Hoffman was highly successful in expanding the funding available for UN development programs and efforts. *See also* UNITED NATIONS DEVELOPMENT PROGRAM, 447.

Significance With genuine humility, Paul Hoffman was the epitome of the progressive development diplomat. Walter Lippmann said of Hoffman, "The outside and the inside are all the same stuff." In an example of Hoffman's forward thinking, while directing the Marshall Plan, he strongly resisted tied aid, which would impose "buy American" restrictions. Hoffman also had an ability to attract talent to his staff. While at the UN, for example, he brought in the West Indian future Nobel laureate, W. Arthur Lewis, to be his first deputy director. A fair and careful scholarly study of Hoffman's life and activities in the development field has been written by Alan R. Raucher (1985), aptly describing him as an architect of foreign aid.

Holmberg, Alan (77)

A Cornell anthropologist who became known as the father of the Vicos community development project in Peru. With farm roots in rural Minnesota, Holmberg was a deeply committed liberal. In developing the Vicos project, Holmberg "felt that he was developing a model that would aid greatly in solving universal problems of poverty, exploitation, and racism" (Mangin 1979:67). Holmberg spend most of 1951 and 1952 working with Peruvians to establish the Vicos project and arrange for Cornell University to assume the lease of the Vicos hacienda. Over the next nine years, he spent most of his summers working on the Vicos project, which emphasized the integration of applied research and political action. Holmberg devoted enormous amounts of time and energy to implementing and administering the project. Although his own top priority was the rural development of Vicos, not scholarly research, he was highly supportive of U.S. and Peruvian researchers' use of Vicos as their laboratory for studying rural development. *See also* VICOS PROJECT, 376.

Significance   Holmberg's missionary zeal and good intentions typify a special genre of overseas development personnel that was ironically idealized in the hero in *The Ugly American.* Holmberg's willingness and desire to play a major management and leadership role in the project was also a common pattern, particularly in long-term development projects in the 1950s and 1960s. Holmberg's commitment of time and energy to the multifaceted dimensions of the project was impressive. In retrospect, however, Holmberg's role should have been much less dominant and prominent, given his goal to create a replicable model of rural development. Because Holmberg himself has not yet reflected critically in extensive writing on the Vicos experience, an opportunity for both participant-observer research and action research of considerable depth unfortunately has not been realized. Holmberg's preoccupation with practical action to make Vicos a viable community development project is understandable and reflects a major dilemma of the development field. Practitioners of development frequently have too little time to reflect on their activities critically and creatively. Similarly, development scholars often have too little opportunity to participate actively in the development process.

Hussein, Aziza (78)

A prominent advocate of family planning and women's rights in Egypt. Nationally and internationally prominent, Hussein is a past president of the International Planned Parenthood Federation (1977) and has represented Egypt frequently at major international meetings concerning family planning and women's issues. Among her initial activities in community development programs for village women, Hussein played a leading role in developing the Sandyoun project, which attracted international attention because of its success in persuading rural Muslim women to participate in community development activities. Central to the project were a child-care center and courses training village women to improve their practical and income-earning skills. Hussein played the lead role in the establishment of the Joint Committee of Family Planning in Egypt in 1963. By 1966, Egypt had announced an official population program and in 1967, the joint committee was subsumed under the Egyptian Family Planning Association under the Ministry of Social Affairs. Egypt was the first Middle Eastern country to announce a population planning program. Hussein's next challenge was to enhance women's rights, particularly in legal matters related to family. She started the Commission for Women in Egypt after serving as the first Egyptian delegate to the UN Status of Women Commission in 1965. After important successes in liberalizing family law, Hussein, in the 1980s, again turned her energies to promoting family planning and started an organization called Family of the Future (FOF), which has promoted, for example, the broader use and acceptance of condoms. *See also* POPULATION PLANNING, 254.

Significance Despite her elite background as daughter of a physician and spouse of a cabinet minister, Hussein has shown remarkable commitment to develop programs to benefit marginalized rural women in Egypt. Like Meechai Viravaidya in Thailand, she has influenced her country to promote greater access to family planning services. She has used her abilities to develop programs and advocate policies to benefit all women in Egypt. Hussein's accomplishments reflect the important social entrepreneurial roles played by Third World women.

Khan, Hasina (79)

A Bangladeshi noted for her contributions to the establishment of women's groups at the village level in Bangladesh. For her initial work with the Rural Women's Project of the Family Planning International Association, Khan received her primary training in Washington, D.C., at the Centre for Development and Population Activities. Eventually Khan left this project, which involved promoting family planning among rural women, because she felt that the manner of administration was too hierarchical. In 1979 she joined Save the Children as its first women's program officer. Her major goal was to involve village women in self-help groups to expand their income-earning opportunities. Given traditional Muslim customs confining Bangladeshi women within the household, Khan faced a major challenge in involving village women in participatory development. Under Khan's charismatic leadership, the number of women's groups in Bangladeshi villages in her region grew dramatically, from 400 women in 1979 to 410 groups with 4,200 members in 1987. Khan often had to walk from village to village, because of cultural constraints against women's using bicycles or motorbikes. Khan eventually resigned from Save the Children and took a teaching job in order to devote more time to her own family and children. Within two years, she was appointed headmistress of her school. *See also* WOMEN IN DEVELOPMENT, 256.

Significance   Through her charismatic and diplomatic leadership, Khan was at the vanguard of changes occurring for women, particularly in rural Bangladesh. Khan demonstrated the effectiveness of participatory development and was particularly skillful in encouraging village women to "speak their words" and express their needs. She opened new possibilities for village women to generate their own income through such activities as raising livestock and poultry and making fishnets and ropes. Khan has been praised for the "extraordinary diplomacy and persuasiveness she exhibited in her dealings with the rural hierarchy of men" (Levy 1988:55). Khan's success with Save the Children is an inspiring example of what a single individual can accomplish in local-level participatory development.

Ladejinski, Wolf (1899–1975)   **(80)**
Known as the controversial Mr. Land Reform for his tireless efforts to bring land to the tiller, a process he considered vital to agricultural and national development. Born in the Ukraine, he worked for the U.S. Office of Foreign Agriculture Relations (OFAR) from 1935–1945. Ladejinski spent the last 30 years of his life in Asia working for the U.S. government, the Ford Foundation, and the World Bank. Upon his arrival in Japan in 1945, he was already known for his expertise in agricultural reform as a result of his writing and research for the OFAR. In postwar Japan under Gen. Douglas MacArthur, he was renowned as a practitioner. A major architect of

the highly successful, comprehensive Land Reform Program, he helped lay the groundwork for Japan's remarkable economic recovery. Ladejinski was called to Taiwan in 1949 to work with the Joint Committee for Rural Reform, which he considered a model for other U.S. technical assistance programs. By 1955 he had helped orchestrate a full-fledged reform program that facilitated Taiwan's dramatic and balanced growth in both agriculture and industry. From 1955 to 1961, as a U.S. official, Ladejinski worked for the government of Vietnam under Diem. His efforts there were frustrated by the chaotic state of affairs and lack of support from both governments. After three years with the Ford Foundation, Ladejinski spent his last 11 years (1964–1975) with the World Bank working throughout Asia, primarily in India. *See also* LAND REFORM, 183.

Significance   Wolf Ladejinski's journals and articles, collected and published as *Agrarian Reform as Unfinished Business* by Oxford University Press for the World Bank in 1977 (edited by Louis Walinsky), reveal a profound understanding of the rural poor and the economic and political realities of rural development. Ladejinski frequently visited the countryside to listen to the views of the rural populace. He was convinced that land reform was inevitable, through either enlightened top-down initiatives or rural revolution. Ladejinski saw overemphasis on industrial development as a major error in development thinking. His opinions and insights are now considered conventional wisdom, if not practice, by many development strategists and the World Bank.

Lenin, V. I. (1870–1924)   (81)

Founder of the Russian Communist party, leader of the Bolshevik Revolution (1917), and first Soviet head of state. Born Vladimir Ilich Ulyanov, Lenin was trained in law and became an adherent of Marxism in 1889. As an exile in Western Europe prior to the October Revolution, he formulated his interpretation of the events unfolding in Russia. In *Development of Capitalism in Russia* (1899), for example, Lenin argued that while Russia had not advanced to the same stage of capitalism as the rest of Europe, it was nevertheless in a state of capitalist development. He held that Russia, of necessity, must achieve a full state of capitalism before the establishment of a socialist state. In light of the revolution of 1905, however, he modified his theory and entertained the possibility of an earlier proletariat revolution, which in fact occurred in 1917 as soldiers returned from World War I. From the time of the revolution until his death in 1924, Lenin guided the Soviet Union through its formative years. Major features of his development strategy were central planning, collectivization, Communist party rule, and rapid industrialization. *See also* IMPERIALISM, 204; REVOLUTION, 213.

Significance   Given the unique circumstances of the Russian Revolution, the Soviet Union had few models to follow in formulating its national strategy. Lenin, for better or worse, provided the direction for the precarious new nation-state. The revolution he led served as impetus for a wave of revolutions to follow. One of his great intellectual contributions, which also had much practical impact, was his assessment of the role of the peasant class in the revolutionary process. He recognized that by promising them the land of their overlords, the peasants could be mobilized to support urban workers and the aims of the proletariat revolution. His formulation of Marxism-Leninism has served as the framework for the economic and political policies of the Soviet Union and other Marxist states. Lenin helped lay the groundwork for dependency studies in his writings on the development of capitalism in backward nations. His theory of imperialism challenged the notion of empires as benign outgrowths of European civilization. Rather, he contended, they were systems of exploitation that always favored the imperial powers. While Lenin's ideas grew in influence during the post–World War II period, in the 1980s their relevance was seriously challenged, primarily as the result of frustration with highly bureaucratic states that possessed a monopoly of political and economic power.

Mao Zedong (Mao Tse-tung) (1893–1976) (82)

The father of the Chinese Communist revolution and the ruler of the People's Republic of China (1949–1976) who formulated an alternative, autarkic Marxist path to development adapted to Chinese and Asian conditions. Of peasant background himself, Mao's goal was to create a socialist society free from the inequalities and inequities of feudal China, in which all individuals would be able to meet their basic needs and all basic production would be controlled by the state. Mao founded the Red Army in 1927 and led a long revolutionary struggle against the nationalist government of Chiang Kai-shek, which resulted in the eventual victory of Mao and the Communists in 1949 and the opportunity to put his radical ideas of development into practice.

Initially, Mao's China was strongly influenced by the Soviet Union and its development consultants, who emphasized the need for a rapid transition from a rural to an industrial society. After the Sino-Soviet split in 1960, direct Soviet influence was eliminated. In

1953, Maoist China introduced its first Five Year Plan (1953–1957). In 1958 Mao announced the Great Leap Forward movement, which led to the spread of communes and the goal of doubling steel production within a year. Mao had hoped to create a society free of money and wages, but that proved impractical. Instead, his philosophy of development emphasized equality for all, particularly the majority of the nation who were living and working in communes. From 1966 to 1976, Mao supported the Cultural Revolution, which was launched to purify the revolution and to ensure the maintenance of its fundamentally Communist philosophy. Mao's death in 1976 and the subsequent arrest of the Gang of Four in October of that year led to the emergence of a new alternative development paradigm in China under the eventual leadership of Deng Xiaoping. *See also* SELF-RELIANCE/SELF-SUFFICIENCY, 120; PARADIGMS OF DEVELOPMENT, 116; GREAT LEAP FORWARD, 361; DENG XIAOPING, 70.

Significance   As the political leader of the world's most populous nation, Mao undoubtedly influenced more individuals with his development perspective than any other ideology ever. Mao's major achievement was to move China quickly from a feudalistic rural society with vast poverty and injustice into a socialist society where the basic needs of all could be met. By cutting China's economic ties to the West and outside, he demonstrated the country's potential to be self-reliant and independent. Despite such isolationist policies, Mao provided technical and development assistance to countries in Africa such as Tanzania. Mao also introduced in China important and impressive programs of afforestation. Mao's biggest mistake was to provide active support of the Red Guards and the Cultural Revolution, which had a highly adverse effect on the lives of educated individuals and intellectuals, many of whom were sent to work in remote areas or factories. Despite the excesses of the Cultural Revolution, Mao's development strategy enabled China to respond reasonably quickly to the basic needs of its people and provided a solid economic base for the later economic reforms introduced by Deng Xiaoping.

Maude, H. E.   **(83)**
A British colonial servant noted for his commitment to the peoples of the South Pacific and his scholarly work on the history of the area. Maude worked as a colonial officer primarily in the Gilbert Islands from 1929 to 1939. He served in a variety of posts such as census officer, administrative officer, native lands commissioner, and adviser to Queen Salote of the Kingdom of Tonga. Finally, in the postwar period he was executive officer for social development of the South

Pacific Commission. While working for the Western Pacific High Commission, Maude helped the Banabans, who had been badly exploited by the British Phosphate Commission. Perhaps Maude's most impressive accomplishment was his effort to establish a cooperative movement in the Gilbert Islands. Commerce had been controlled by foreigners, but when Maude left after 17 years of service, all major commerce was in the hands of native-run cooperative societies. Maude was also noted for a shy, unassuming style and his command of the Gilbertese language, which facilitated his emphasis on "listening to the people."

Significance   Maude represents an important genre of sympathetic colonial officials who worked for decades in developing areas and who often became noted scholars on the areas where they had served. Other such individuals were J. S. Furnival (with extensive Burmese and Southeast Asian experience); W. A. R. Wood (Thai experience, author of *Consul in Paradise* [1965]); Austin Coates (Hong Kong, author of *Myself a Mandarin* [1969]); Eduard Douwes Dekker (Indonesia, author of *Max Havelaar* [1974], a devastating critique of Dutch colonialism in Southeast Asia); Anthony Burgess (Malaya and Brunei, author of *Malayan Trilogy* [1972] and *Devil of a State* [1961]); and B. Willis (Argentina, *A Yanqui in Patagonia* [1948]). Both Maude's development work and his related scholarly work have contributed importantly to the preservation of the rich cultural diversity of the South Pacific.

McNamara, Robert   (84)

Former president of Ford Motor Company, secretary of defense under Presidents Kennedy and Johnson, and president of the World Bank, who had a major impact on international development in the 1970s. During McNamara's 13 years as World Bank president (1968–1980), its lending increased twelvefold. In his final year of office, the bank was supervising more than 1,600 projects in more than 100 developing countries, with a total budget of approximately $100 billion. McNamara made the bank the largest international donor agency, though as of 1989 Japan had surpassed it. McNamara saw two principal goals of development: to accelerate economic growth and to eradicate absolute poverty. The intrinsic relationship was elegantly expressed in the following statement:

> The pursuit of growth without a reasonable concern for equity is ultimately socially destabilizing, and often violently so. And the pursuit of equity without a reasonable concern for growth merely tends to redistribute economic stagnation. (McNamara 1981:629).

McNamara's extensive, pragmatic thinking on development issues is summarized in a collection of his World Bank speeches and presentations, *The McNamara Years at the World Bank* (1981). *See also* WORLD BANK, 454.

Significance   As U.S. secretary of defense, McNamara managed a war of destruction and violence in Vietnam. Becoming World Bank president gave McNamara the opportunity to "redeem himself" by working to alleviate global poverty and suffering. McNamara had two major impacts on the bank. First, he dramatically increased its financial base and volume of lending. Second, he broadened the bank's orientation to make possible much greater lending in "soft" areas such as health and education, where benefits tend to be long-term in nature. As early as 1970, the bank required environmental impact assessments for projects. During the last McNamara years, China became part of the World Bank as well. However, several criticisms of the bank under McNamara have been stated. The first relates to the dominant role of the United States in the bank's decision making. Though McNamara and the bank recruited many highly qualified international executives and analysts, the United States maintained basic control. The second criticism is that the bank emphasizes extremely large projects and is not open to smaller projects, which might be more responsive to local needs. Finally, during the McNamara years, the bank was not reluctant to pressure countries to accept loans. Such pressure was important to demonstrate quantitative success and expansion. Despite such criticisms, there is considerable praise for McNamara's commitments to development and decisive management of the bank. As of 1990, McNamara was still active in the international development field as a speaker and as a member of various governing boards. He has perhaps had more impact on development practice in the 1970s than any other single individual.

Mendes Filho, Francisco (Chico) (1944–1988)   (85)
A union organizer of Brazilian rubber tappers who was assassinated in a remote part of the Amazon on December 22, 1988. Founder of the union of rubber tappers, he fought vigorously against clearance of the tropical Amazon rain forest and the threat to his group's way of life presented by the clearance. He helped establish a dozen extractive reserves—areas to be harvested perenially without doing harm to the forest. Mendes and his followers were credited with saving thousands of acres of rain forest from destruction. For these efforts he received the Global 500 award from the United Nations Environmental Program. In his posthumously published book, *Fight for the*

Forest (1989), based on his last major interview conducted just weeks before his tragic death, Mendes described his life's work.

Significance   Chico Mendes is seen as a martyr whose death has important symbolic meaning. Each year about 11 million acres of tropical forests and woodlands are destroyed, threatening the long-term viability of our global ecosystem. Countries such as Brazil, Nigeria, the Ivory Coast, Sri Lanka, Costa Rica, El Salvador, Indonesia, and Thailand face serious problems of deforestation. Illegal deforestation in Thailand, for example, contributed adversely to the effects of a flood disaster in the fall of 1988. Ironically, Mendes's death is mirrored in Thailand's most important environmentally oriented novel, *The Teachers of Mad Dog Swamp* by Khammaan Khonkhai (1982). The hero of this novel is murdered by illegal loggers for his attempts to expose their dastardly acts. The import of Mendes's assassination by a hired gun and his martyrdom goes far beyond the boundaries of Brazil and its precious Amazon forests.

de Miralda, Reyna   **(86)**
A prominent leader of a national movement for peasant women in Honduras. As a widowed mother of seven who grew up among the rural poor, de Miralda had great empathy for the conditions of poor rural women in Honduras. She became involved with social action and community development as the result of her participation in training courses provided by Caritas, the social-action wing of the Roman Catholic Church. Eventually, she became a paid community health worker for Caritas, working with Housewives' Clubs. As a result of political repression in 1975, Caritas stopped funding the Housewives' Clubs and de Miralda lost her job. Working with other rural women, de Miralda later successfully launched FEHMUC (Federacion Hondurena de Mujeres Campesinas [Honduran Federation of Peasant Women]), and in 1976 became its secretary. The basic goal of FEHMUC was to "struggle to organize the poorest of rural women and teach them the skills they needed to improve their lives." De Miralda was particularly active in organizing groups in the impoverished Olancho region of Honduras. By 1985 FEHMUC had 350 women's groups with approximately 5,800 members, including 89 clubs in the Olancho region. *See also* WOMEN IN DEVELOPMENT, 256.

Significance   Reyna de Miralda's work in Honduras has shown that it is possible to organize one of the most marginalized groups in Honduras, peasant women. She has also shown an impressive ability to seek external funds from organizations such as Oxfam, FAO, and

PACT (Private Agencies Collaborating Together) to facilitate her work with peasant women in Honduras. De Miralda's major problem has been factionalism within FEHMUC and the attempt of formal political parties to incorporate the organization. Unable to accept this, she has withdrawn from the national organization to focus her work on the groups in the Olancho region. Despite massive obstacles such as factionalism, opposition of rural men, political interference, and repression, de Miralda has shown enormous courage and dedication in leading a national movement to give peasant women a greater economic and political voice in their daily lives.

Mother Teresa (87)
Revered servant to the poor, founder of the Missionaries of Charity, and recipient of the Nobel Peace Prize in 1979. She continues to serve as the organization's director. Mother Teresa was born Agnes Gonxha Bojaxhiu in Uskup, Turkish Empire (now Skopje, Yugoslavia), in 1910 to a family of Albanian Catholics. At 18, she began her life of service by joining the Sisters of Loretto, a teaching order with a missionary school in Calcutta. After 15 years as a teacher and principal, she became convinced that her calling was to leave the convent to live and work directly with the poor. She took Indian citizenship and in 1950 founded the Missionaries of Charity. The charity operates schools, hospitals, food kitchens, leper centers, homes for the dying, and orphanages in India and more than 60 other countries. There is also an affiliated laity organization, the International Association of Cooperators with Mother Teresa. Mother Teresa is known throughout the world for her complete dedication and service to the poorest of the poor in Calcutta, a city that has come to symbolize destitution. In addition to several honorary degrees, she has received numerous international awards, including the Kennedy International Award for Outstanding Service to Mankind (1971), Pope John XXII Peace Prize (1971), Jawaharlal Nehru Award for International Understanding (1972), Templeton Prize for Progress in Religion (1973), and the Nobel Peace Prize (1979). She is the subject of at least ten books.

Significance Mother Teresa's life embodies charity in the best sense of the word. While many recognize that development involves changes in social, political, and economic systems, Mother Teresa reminds us of the continued importance of selfless, face-to-face service to the poor. Her life has been devoted to caring for those people who are missed or overlooked by government services and international development agencies and programs. The order she founded now in-

cludes more than 1,600 sisters operating 230 houses on three conti-
nents. Seeking to reaffirm the value and dignity of all human life, she
and her coworkers offer hope to those seen as beyond hope by their
neighbors.

Mutua, Elvina   (88)
Director of Tototo Home Industries and a dynamic leader in expanding income-producing projects for poor women in Kenya. Tototo
Home Industries was established in 1972 as a successor to Home Industries, which had primarily worked with individual craftswomen. In
contrast, Tototo under Mutua's leadership has focused on the
launching of a network of women's groups engaged in small busi-
nesses such as poultry raising, ferryboat service, sale of water, food
processing, bakeries, and tea shops. Tototo, which literally means
perfect in Giriamo, the language of the Kenyan coast, reflects the philosophy of *harambee* (pulling together) introduced in Kenya in 1964
as a major self-help movement. Through Mutua's entrepreneurship,
the program has attracted the attention of international development
organizations such as World Education and the Ford Foundation.
The former organization, with its emphasis on participatory nonformal education, has helped finance training aspects of Tototo, while
Ford has provided revolving loan funds to facilitate the access of such
groups to critically needed credit. Mutua, who is from a village outside Mombasa on the Kenyan coast, also played an active role in the
UN Decade for Women Conference (1985) as a delegate of the
Kenyan government. Further details on Mutua's life and activities are
provided in Marion F. Levy's *Each in Her Own Way: Five Women Leaders of the Developing World* (1988). *See also* HARAMBEE, 363.

Significance   Mutua has demonstrated the leadership potential of
women in innovative rural development. Her program, Tototo
Home Industries, is considered the best grassroots agency in Kenya.
As of October 1985, Tototo had 45 groups with more than 14,000
participants. As a result of Mutua's efforts, many more poor rural
women in Kenya have learned how to generate cash income through
small-business activity. While Mutua has been extremely successful in
attracting funds from organizations such as World Education and the
Ford Foundation, questions remain regarding long-term financial
sustainability without external assistance and the potential dissemination of the innovation to other developmental settings.

Nasser, Gamal Abdel (1918–1970)   (89)
President of Egypt from 1956 to 1970, a key figure in the Council of

79

Revolutionary Command which overthrew the Egyptian monarchy of King Farouk in 1952, and a leading proponent of Arab socialism. Nasser's early political thinking was published as statements of the revolution. In a May 13, 1961, speech, he outlined his program of Arab socialism. Rejecting the Marxist view of the inevitability of class struggle, he called for a mixed economy and for elected councils in factories and in local and national governments (Sigmund 1972: 149). Several months later, he nationalized most business enterprises in Egypt and placed limits on landholding. A strong internationalist whose interests transcended the political and economic development problems of Egypt, Nasser emphasized three international circles: (1) the Arab circle of nations with Arabic populations, (2) the African circle of African nations, and (3) the Islamic circle of countries with Islamic populations in Africa, the Middle East, and Asia. *See also* SUKARNO, 98; MAO ZEDONG, 82; JAWAHARLAL NEHRU, 90; ASWAN HIGH DAM PROJECT, 355.

Significance   Like Mao, Sukarno, and a number of other Third World leaders, Nasser governed under a one-party dictatorship. One of the most prominent Third World leaders of the 1950s and 1960s, Nasser was also a major leader of the Pan-Arab movement. In his later years, he focused more on the internal problems of Egypt and its relations in the Middle East. While many charismatic leaders fail to provide for successorship, Nasser's vice-president, Anwar el-Sadat, supplied able leadership in the years following Nasser's death. Nasser will always be remembered as the father of modern Egypt and a key proponent of the Pan-Arab and Pan-Islamic movements.

Nehru, Jawaharlal (1889–1964)   (90)

First prime minister of independent India from 1947 until his death. Born in 1889, Nehru was trained as a lawyer, after which his interests turned to politics and Indian nationalism. Working closely with Mohandas Gandhi, he rose quickly in the ranks of the Congress party and became its president in 1929. In the same year he presided over the Lahore session that proclaimed complete independence as India's political goal. After independence and the death of Gandhi in 1948, Nehru became the central figure in Indian politics and architect of the nation's development. Internationally, he attempted to guide India along a path of political neutrality, at times playing the two superpowers against one another. Domestically, he promoted national unity and development through a system of secular democratic socialism.

Significance   Nehru's vision of Indian development had a profound impact on the world's second largest nation. In many ways, Nehru was a bridge between East and West, tradition and modernism, even Marx and Gandhi. He was convinced of the correctness of Marx's interpretation of history, yet he considered war and conflict as completely avoidable. A close follower of Gandhi, he shared his profound concern for the welfare of India's people, especially the poor. However, while Gandhi envisioned a nation of self-sufficient villages drawing on the best of India's traditions, Nehru attempted to move India into the modern age of advanced science and technology. He supported massive industrialization as a means of eliminating poverty, in sharp contrast to Gandhi. Under Nehru's direction, India developed a mixed economy guided by a series of five-year plans. The First Five Year Plan (1951) was designed to redress problems resulting from World War II and partition. The Second Plan (1956) encouraged rapid industrialization, particularly in the textile industry. The Third Plan (1961) gave greater emphasis to agriculture and marked the final period of high-volume public expenditures for development. Nehru's experiment, a process he called democratic socialism, was to combine the national planning of the communist and socialist countries with democratic participation. He also intended that India would undergo a social as well as an economic transformation, with the latter contingent upon the former. Nehru's national plans, as epitomized in the Community Development Program which was designed to revitalize the rural areas, assumed a level of cooperation, commitment, and social development that was never realized in practice.

An overall assessment of Nehru's leadership is difficult, given the circumstances in which he governed. The nation made impressive gains in education and industrial productivity, and saw economic growth averaging seven percent per year while Nehru served as prime minister. Agricultural productivity, however, barely kept pace with population growth until the arrival of Green Revolution technology in the 1960s. On the international scene, Nehru helped elevate India's status and maintained neutrality during the cold war. He was a founder of the Non-Aligned Movement, although India's support of the Soviet invasion of Hungary in 1956, its border war with China in 1962, and growing tensions with Pakistan were setbacks for India and for Nehru as a leader of the movement. Above all, Nehru provided the political and moral leadership so badly needed by India following independence. He helped hold together, in relative calm, a vast, diverse nation struggling to define itself and its place in the modern world. The paradox of India's present scientific, industrial, and technological accomplishments combined with its persisting poverty is a legacy of Nehru's mixed political-economic system.

Nyerere, Julius (91)

An influential African thinker, statesman, and politician who was leader of the republic of Tanzania (earlier known as Tanganyika) from 1962 to 1985. Nyerere is particularly known for his advocacy of African unity, African socialism (*Ujamaa*, literally meaning family-hood), and self-reliant development. Despite his extensive administrative and political responsibilities, Nyerere has been a prolific writer and speaker on African development issues. Many of his major ideas are included in an important volume titled *Ujamaa, Essays on Socialism* (1968), published by Oxford University Press. Other major works are *Freedom and Development* (1960) and *Nyerere on Socialism* (1969). *See also* UJAMAA, 375.

Significance   As a political leader, Nyerere is known for his charisma and statesmanship. He is one of few Third World leaders who voluntarily retired from leadership of his country. Tanzanians take great pride in Nyerere, who has become a highly respected leader in the African community and a prominent world figure. Intellectually, Nyerere is controversial since he challenged the conventional wisdom of both the West and the East by going back to his African roots. He rejected Western capitalism because of its overemphasis on individualistic materialism and the related exploitation of man by man. He also rejected Western Marxism because of its emphasis on class conflict and violence as essential steps in the evolution toward genuine socialism. Instead, he proposed a return to African socialism based on the values of traditional African society which emphasized the extended family, sharing, and mutual help. Nyerere's concept of the extended family was extremely broad, including ultimately the entire world. The extent to which his highly idealistic views are reflected in the economic performance of Tanzania is a debated empirical question. Tanzania's achievements in the social sector (education and health) have been quite impressive as has been its political stability. However, both Tanzania and Africa have faced difficult environmental and external forces that have adversely affected Nyerere's ability to accomplish all his ideals of African socialism, self-reliant economic development, and African unity. Nevertheless, Nyerere must be considered a major development thinker and an inspirational leader with integrity who was willing to challenge the conventional capitalistic and Marxist paradigms.

Ouedraogo, Bernard Ledea (92)

Founder and leader of Africa's largest and most successful grassroots movement for self-reliance and corecipient of the Africa Prize for Leadership for the Sustainable End of Hunger in 1989. Ouedraogo is from Burkina Faso (formerly Upper Volta) and has a 1977 doctorate in the social sciences of development from the Université René Descartes de Paris Sorbonne. In 1967, while he was a government counselor for rural youth training in agriculture, he founded the Naam movement. The Naam movement was based on a traditional group in Mossi society called Kombi-Naam, which gathered all the young men and women in a village for agricultural, cultural, and social activities. Ouedraogo used this traditional structure as a means to develop self-help groups open to all and it became a positive force for development. Ouedraogo is also general secretary and cofounder of the International Six-S Association, a nongovernmental aid and training organization that is Africa's largest peasant-farmer network, consisting of federated organizations of hundreds of thousands of members in nine West African countries—Burkina Faso, Chad, the Gambia, Guinea Bissau, Mali, Mauritania, Niger, Senegal, and Togo. Six-S stands for *Se Servir de la Saison Seche en Savane et au Sahel* (using the dry season in the savannah and the Sahel). *See also* NAAM MOVEMENT, 367.

Significance The distinctiveness and originality of Ouedraogo's Six-S organization is based on two factors: the organization is run by the farmers, and funds are provided as block loans on easy terms to peasant-farmer organizations which themselves determine how such financial resources will be used. Projects that have been supported include cereal banks, grain mills, improved livestock breeding, gardening, crafts, vegetable drying and storing, weaving, and building handcarts. Ouedraogo's approach is an excellent example of participative, endogenous development that emphasizes local participation, self-motivation, and local accountability with respect to financial autonomy and rigorous management. This type of endogenous development has apparently already helped reduce the rural exodus common in West Africa. The approach has also facilitated a powerful form of informal education in which farmers learn from the experiences of each other.

Salam, Abdus (93)

First Nobel laureate from Pakistan, and founder and director of the International Centre for Theoretical Physics (ICTP), a major think tank that addresses the important issue of science in developing countries. As a brilliant young physicist who had studied at Cambridge, Salam became extremely frustrated with conditions for doing quality science in Pakistan and moved back to England to continue his career. He deeply regretted that he was forced to choose between remaining in science or staying in his native country. As a result of his entrepreneurial efforts, the ICTP was created in Trieste in 1964. A major goal of the center is to provide a milieu for scientists from developing countries to spend time interacting with colleagues from the North and the South. Salam's intent was to stem the brain drain by providing this type of short-term opportunity for bright scientists from developing countries. Despite Salam's many administrative responsibilities, he is a brilliant scholar in his own right and shared the 1979 Nobel Prize in physics for his work on electro-weak force. Salam's scholarship extends well beyond physics, and his general thinking on development issues is included in a valuable anthology edited by Z. Hassan and C. H. Lai, *Ideals and Realities: Selected Essays of Abdus Salam* (1984). *See also* SCIENCE AND DEVELOPMENT, 304.

Significance　　Salam's life and career can serve as an inspiration to young science students in developing countries. Salam is deeply concerned about nurturing young talent in developing countries as a means to "grow science" and reduce intellectual and scientific dependency. Though Salam has lived in the West for several decades, like Sir Arthur Lewis at Princeton and others, he has contributed significantly to the cause of developing countries. Salam has not lost his ties with Pakistan and Islamic culture. He was the personal science adviser to President Ayub Khan of Pakistan and was involved directly with the formulation of science policy in Pakistan from 1960 to 1974. Salam's contributions to Pakistani science development illustrate some of the dilemmas of the brain drain. In international circles, he has been a strong advocate of the developing countries and stressed that science is the shared heritage of mankind and should serve all the world's people. Salam has also retained his bonds to Islam and emphasizes the compatibility between science and religion. Over time, Salam has encouraged the ICTP at Trieste to focus increasingly on science issues relevant to developing countries. Salam's career and his many contributions to the developing countries reflect the idealism expressed in the meaning of his name, Servant of Peace.

Schweitzer, Albert (1875–1965)　　　　　　　　　　(94)
Famous German physician, theologian, teacher, musicologist, medical missionary in Africa, and Nobel laureate. After receiving his doc-

torate in religious philosophy in 1899, he became an accomplished and well-known Biblical scholar, educator, preacher, and musician. Reading of the needs of a Congo mission in 1904, he studied to become a doctor in order to offer medical assistance. Schweitzer established a mission hospital at Lambaréné, Gabon, in French West Africa just before the outbreak of World War I. In 1917 he and his wife were held in France for a year as prisoners of war. Schweitzer returned to Lambaréné in 1924 where he lived for the next 41 years until his death. He was a prolific writer throughout his life. His impressions of life in Africa are recorded in *On the Edge of the Primeval Forest: Experiences and Observations of a Doctor in Equatorial Africa* (1948). Schweitzer was a man of inexhaustible energy whose work and writings became well known in Europe and North America, the sources of support for his growing but simple medical complex. He drew a good deal of attention to health conditions in tropical Africa. Though autocratic and paternalistic, he nevertheless sought technologically appropriate and culturally sensitive ways to meet the health needs of the Lambaréné area. Even in the 1960s his mission remained "unsanitary," with minimal amenities and electricity only in the operating rooms. Schweitzer was awarded the Nobel Peace Prize in 1953 for his work in Africa and his "reverence for all life." He used the $33,000 prize to build and supply a leper hospital, which by the time of his death housed 200 patients.

Significance   Schweitzer was a man of enormous intellect, talent, and conviction. In his Nobel lecture he spoke of the irony of technological and scientific advances being used to reach new heights of inhumanity and called for a new ethical mentality. He attempted to live out such an ethic in service, and his contributions to humanity must be judged in light of the era in which he lived. His hospital and medical work directly served thousands in Africa and inspired the establishment of many more health facilities throughout that continent and the world. Schweitzer's work and idealism, for example, inspired Tom Dooley to carry out his medical work in Laos. Schweitzer's writings, his commitment to Africa, and his central role in the international campaign to ban nuclear testing, mark him as a remarkable man of peace and service.

Senghor, Leopold Sedar   **(95)**
Prominent Senegalese intellectual and politician who called for a humanistic, democratic African socialism. Senghor opposed both capitalistic and communistic materialism. Prior to independence, Senghor was elected four times as a Senegalese representative in the

French National Assembly and held cabinet posts in French governments. He was elected president of Senegal in 1960. An active proponent of cultural revival, through his own poetry and writing Senghor helped to disseminate appreciation of the richness of indigenous African culture. Senghor published four volumes of his poetry and an anthology of African poets. He was the only African ever elected to the French Academy. Senghor's intellectual openness was illustrated by his view that African values were not in opposition to European values, but were a complement to them.

Significance   Like Nyerere in Tanzania, Senghor stands out as a thinking, reflective politician and statesman. Also like Nyerere, Senghor gave up political power voluntarily. Senghor is recognized for showing awareness of the issue of ethnic politics and supporting the notion of a federal democracy to allow for local political and cultural diversity. Through his extensive writing Senghor contributed significantly to defining and promoting the concept of negritude as a complex of rich African values. Among such values he identified the sense of communion, the gift of mythmaking, and the talent of rhythm. In his thinking about colonialism, Senghor demonstrated considerable openness in recognizing some positive cultural effects of French and British colonialism in Africa. Senghor's idealistic integration of humanism and internationalism is reflected in a quotation from his speech, "What Is 'Negritude'?," delivered at Oxford University on October 4, 1961:

> ...The neohumanism of the twentieth century stands at the point where the paths of all nations, races, and continents cross, "where the four winds of the spirit blow."

Soedjatmoko (1922–1989)   (96)

An influential Indonesian author, scholar, diplomat, statesman, and development thinker who was the first rector of the United Nations University (1980–1987). From 1971 to 1980, Soedjatmoko was adviser on social and cultural affairs to the National Development Planning Agency (BAPPENAS) of Indonesia. A recipient of the Magsaysay Prize in 1978, Soedjatmoko was active in the independence struggle against the Netherlands and later served as a member of the Indonesian parliament. Among his extensive publications are *The Primacy of Freedom in Development* (1985) and *Policymaking for Long-Term Global Issues* (1988).

Significance   Soedjatmoko was deeply concerned about the political and cultural dimensions, as well as the human rights and social justice dimensions, of development. Despite his extensive international experience, including a stint as ambassador to the United States (1967–1971), Soedjatmoko retained a deep appreciation of the importance and richness of traditional Indonesian village culture and the need to ensure the preservation of such culture as an integral part of the development process. Soedjatmoko also argued for the need to construct theories of development that relate freedom and development. Concerned about the need to actualize conflicting values simultaneously, Soedjatmoko criticized the conventional fields of development economics and political science for not providing an in-depth understanding of the dynamics of social change associated with development. Prominent Western leaders and scholars such as Elliot Richardson and Harlan Cleveland had the highest respect for Soedjatmoko. Richardson considered him an extraordinary man, with remarkable vision, depth of understanding, wisdom, and insight. Cleveland viewed Soedjatmoko as one of the great wise men of our times. Soedjatmoko was a genuine internationalist deeply committed to a humanistic and culturally sensitive approach to development problems and issues.

Strong, Maurice F. (97)

A prominent Canadian environmentalist and international official who was the first president of the Canadian International Development Agency (CIDA). Prior to becoming head of Canada's External Aid Office, the predecessor to CIDA, he was president of the Power Corporation of Canada. From 1970 to 1972, Strong was secretary-general of the UN Conference on the Human Environment, which resulted in the creation of the UN Environment Program (UNEP). In 1985–1986, Strong served as under secretary–general of the UN and executive coordinator of the UN Office for Emergency Operations in Africa. In the latter role, he coordinated and mobilized an international relief effort to assist 35 million people in 20 sub-Saharan countries.

Significance   Few development practitioners have had the impact that Maurice Strong has had. As a member of the Brundtland Commission, Strong is a strong advocate of sustainable development and is deeply concerned about the environmental degradation associated with conventional development. Strong views sustainable development as an essential element of food security. His ideas on sustainable development are clearly presented in his paper, "Ending Hunger through Sustainable Development," presented in Tokyo in 1989. Strong is one of the preeminent development practitioners of the second half of the twentieth century.

Sukarno (1901–1970) (98)
Father of the modern Indonesian republic and a major leader of the Third World in the 1950s and early 1960s. In Indonesia, Sukarno was a revolutionary hero who fought against the Dutch to attain independence in 1949. Sukarno (popularly known as Bung Karno) was president of Indonesia from 1949 to 1967, and in 1963 was declared President for Life. He ruled Indonesia under the rubric of guided democracy, a euphemism for a personalismo style of dictatorship. By hosting the famous Bandung Conference of 1955, Sukarno established himself as a leader of a politically neutral Third World, aligned with neither of the two superpowers. Sukarno was a highly charismatic leader whose rhetoric was extremely radical, despite an extravagant bourgeois life-style. Sukarno introduced the guiding ideology of Indonesia, the five pillars of which were belief in God, humanism, unity, democracy, and social justice. For example, he evicted the Peace Corps from Indonesia and opposed the formation of the Federation of Malaysia in 1963 as an imperialistic plot. Sukarno had a vision of an empire of Maphilindo, which would bring together politically all the Malay peoples of Southeast Asia, including those of Malaysia and the Philippines. Through brilliant diplomacy, Sukarno added the western part of New Guinea, Irian Jaya, to the Indonesian nation. Sukarno fell from political power in September 1965, after an abortive communist coup d'état, which resulted in a political victory for the Indonesian army and the right wing. Because of his general popularity Sukarno was not formally removed from the office of the presidency until March 1967, though after September 30, 1965, he was only a figurehead in Indonesian politics.

Significance Sukarno was a brilliant political nationalist who fought valiantly for independence and created an Indonesian nation from an area of more than 17,000 islands with hundreds of distinct languages and cultures. Sukarno showed considerable political and cultural insight in not making Javanese, the language of Indonesia's dominant ethnic group, the national language and in not making Indonesia an Islamic state. In fact, unity in diversity was one of Sukarno's many motifs. Sukarno was much less brilliant as an economist and a democrat. His economic policies resulted in hyperinflation and he failed to achieve the social justice promised in his rhetoric. His tacit approval of the attempted 1965 communist coup was his major political blunder. Despite that loss, Sukarno will always be remembered as the father of modern Indonesia and an important actor in the formation of the Third World as a major force in world politics.

Tinker, Irene   (99)
American development practitioner and educator, and founder of the International Center for Research on Women and the Equity Policy Center. Tinker received her Ph.D. in political science from the London School of Economics. Her early work focused on South Asia, and she was associated with the Modern India Project at the University of California, Berkeley from 1954 to 1957. In addition to holding a post at Harvard University, she worked for the American Association for the Advancement of Science as director of the Office of International Science, a program she helped establish. She was appointed director of the ACTION Office of Policy and Planning by President Jimmy Carter and served as a U.S. delegate to the UN Commission on the Status of Women. In addition, she represents the United States on the board of trustees of INSTRAW. Tinker specializes in comparative development, educational planning and curriculum development, population, and the impact of development on women. She is coeditor of three books, *Leadership and Political Institutions in India* (1959), *Women and World Development* (1975), and *Population: Dynamics, Ethics, and Policy* (1975). She is the author of *Energy Needs of Poor Households* (1982) as well as numerous articles and studies. *See also* WOMEN IN DEVELOPMENT, 256.

Significance   Tinker has been a key figure in the field of women in development (WID). Her contributions have been amplified by the establishment of the Equity Policy Center and the International Center for Research on Women. She has actively worked within the United Nations system to infuse more awareness of WID into its agencies and to foster the gathering of reliable information on women.

Werner, David   (100)
American founder of the Hesperian Foundation and author of *Where There Is No Doctor: A Village Health Care Handbook* (1977). Werner, a biologist and former high school teacher, began his health care work in Mexico in 1963 where he helped establish a remote regional clinic to assist villagers in meeting their own health needs. Werner soon

became convinced that with a few months' training using appropriately designed manuals, people with little formal education could learn to attend to 90 percent of their medical problems. In 1973 the Hesperian Foundation was established to support Project Piaxtla, the community-based health care program that grew out of the initial clinic and referral center activities. In that same year the foundation produced *Donde No Hay Doctor,* the original Spanish-language version of *Where There Is No Doctor,* which was soon used throughout Latin America. The focus of Project Piaxtla has evolved from curative health care to an emphasis on preventive measures, including action to change political and social factors that affect health. The program has been run and staffed completely by local villagers since 1976. In 1982 Werner coauthored *Helping Health Workers Learn* with Bill Bower. Werner's most recent work is *Disabled Village Children: A Guide for Community Health Workers, Rehabilitation Workers, and Families.* The book is an outgrowth of Project PROJIMO, a sister program to Project Piaxtla. Begun in 1981, the project has grown rapidly into a multiservice rehabilitation center run mostly by disabled villagers. *See also* PRIVATE VOLUNTARY ORGANIZATIONS, 300.

Significance   Werner's work has had a strong impact on health care in developing countries. *Where There Is No Doctor* has been translated into 30 languages and is used as a handbook and training manual in rural health programs in more than 100 countries. More than one million copies have been distributed, mostly on a nonprofit basis, and the book is standard issue for Peace Corps volunteers. Werner is rare in the development field in that he is both a doer and a writer. As a result, he has helped bring attention to the great potential of villagers to meet their own needs in health care. Many of the principles he has applied to developing low-cost and effective health care practices and systems can be applied to meeting other basic human needs at the village level.

2. Basic Development Concepts

A. Definitions of Development

Barefoot Revolution (101)

A new self-help approach to development emphasized in a special report to the Club of Rome. The report by Bertrand Schneider (1988), the club's secretary-general, "brands the past 20 years of development effort, characterized by sophisticated Western-style projects, as a costly disaster and looks at new small-scale farm, health and education programs across Latin America, Africa and Asia." The Barefoot Revolution calls for a complete overhaul of 20 years of economic strategy that has not fulfilled its promises. The report cites as examples specific projects in countries such as Egypt, Tanzania, and Brazil that have had adverse, unanticipated consequences. As an alternative development strategy, the report emphasizes the role of self-help, rice-roots projects supported by nongovernmental organizations (NGOs). *See also* NONGOVERNMENTAL ORGANIZATIONS, 295; UNINTENDED CONSEQUENCES, 237.

Significance Despite the forceful and compelling nature of the arguments for a new Barefoot Revolution, it is unlikely that conventional development strategies will be totally replaced by smaller, more decentralized NGO efforts. However, the critique provided by the Barefoot Revolution report will, it is hoped, move development agencies to reassess their efforts and to consider channeling more of their assistance through innovative and creative NGOs. Indigenous NGOs also represent an important but neglected source of creativity and innovation, worthy of much greater financial support and political encouragement.

Basic Needs (102)

The most fundamental material goods needed by human beings to

91

live healthily without pain or suffering. The five core basic needs are usually considered to be nutrition, education, health, shelter, and water/sanitation. The International Labor Organization in Geneva also considers employment a basic need. Sidney Webb would add leisure as a basic need. Others would include land ownership for peasants, public safety, and opportunities for sexual gratification as basic needs. *See also* DEVELOPMENT, 107.

Significance   Basic needs is one of the most important, but also the most complex, concepts in the development field. As Paul Streeten has pointed out, the key question relates to *who* determines basic needs. Do the people themselves decide their own basic needs, or should basic needs be determined by objective technocrats specifying levels of nutrition and minimal housing standards, for example? Individual consumers influenced by modern advertising may choose to consume television sets, alcohol, cigarettes, and soft drinks, while neglecting more basic needs. A related concern is the key political question of participation. Is political participation itself a basic need, and what mechanisms exist to enable people to participate in defining their own basic needs? Basic needs may vary with climate and environmental conditions. Housing needs, for example, in tropical countries are dramatically different from those in colder climates. How much education is basic? Does that amount vary from society to society? The amount of living space needed also clearly varies with cultural patterns. A universal specification of a priori basic needs is problematic. Finally, the basic needs approach represents a response to the unequal development patterns associated with the conventional emphasis on macroeconomic growth.

Buddhist Development/Economics   (103)

Two closely interrelated concepts that place the individual human being, rather than profit or capital accumulation, as the central focus of an economy. The concept, presenting an alternative form of development, was introduced and popularized by E. F. Schumacher in his book, *Small Is Beautiful: Economics As If People Mattered* (1973) and *Good Work* (1979). Schumacher's concept derived primarily from his experiences working as an adviser in India and Burma, where he was strongly influenced by both Gandhian and Buddhist philosophy. This approach to development emphasizes self-reliance, small-scale organizations, counterdependence, modesty in life-styles, social justice, priority of the satisfaction of basic needs, and, perhaps most important, reverence for life. The Buddhist approach is also elegantly presented in Erich Fromm's work, *To Have or To Be* (1976). *See also* E. F. SCHUMACHER, 45; DHAMMIC SOCIALISM, 109.

Significance   As global environmental pressures and stress increase as a result of excessive materialism and waste, the concept of Buddhist development becomes increasingly relevant. Both neoclassical and Marxist modes of development emphasize the maximization of economic growth and capital accumulation and are inconsistent with the long-term carrying capacity of Spaceship Earth. Despite its intellectual appeal, Buddhist development in practice is rare. Perhaps the development cases best reflecting this approach were attempted in the pre–Cultural Revolution China of Mao and in Burma under Ne Win until the political riots of 1988. These two societies emphasized self-sufficiency, modest living, and the dangers of becoming part of a capitalistic world system that promotes consumption of nonessential goods and services. Some highly ethnocentric writers, such as I. R. Sinai, author of *Challenge to Modernization* (1965), have argued that traditional Buddhism contributes to "backwardness." The economic dynamism of Buddhist-influenced countries such as Japan, South Korea, Taiwan, Singapore, Hong Kong, and Thailand illustrates the fallacious nature of Western perspectives that see traditional religions like Buddhism as obstacles to development. The real challenge is to find ways to implement Buddhist development more broadly as a means to ensure more humanistic values and to protect our fragile global environment. Globally, more and more political parties, such as the Greens in Western Europe, are beginning to incorporate elements of Buddhist development into their political philosophies. A new Buddhist-oriented political party called the Moral Force Party in Thailand is attracting considerable attention. Headed by the charismatic "half-man half-monk" Maha Chamlong Srimuang, the current governor of Bangkok Province, the party won 14 seats in Thailand's July 1988 national elections and easily won the Bangkok gubernatorial race of 1990. The implementation of Buddhist development in any society represents a complex challenge to integrate political, economic, and religious values.

Center-Periphery   (104)

A concept developed to explain the inequalities and inequities inherent in the world and national systems. Key proponents of this concept have included Immanuel Wallerstein and Andre Gunder Frank. The basic theory of center-periphery stresses the dominance of the center, that is, the advanced industrial countries, over the poor countries in the periphery which are highly dependent on the center in nearly all developmental dimensions. The poor countries provide the center with natural resources and markets for its industrial and manufactured goods. Communications are nearly always channeled through the center, with places such as Los Angeles, New York, Paris, London, and Tokyo dominating communication networks. In contrast, communications from one part of the periphery to another tend to be difficult and slow. These center-periphery patterns are viewed as central to the failure to achieve the development goals articulated by various international bodies and agencies. Individuals such as G. William Skinner have also applied the center-periphery concept to national systems, such as China, to explain patterns of inequality and areas of relative economic deprivation within nation-states. Nearly all nation-states and particularly those in developing areas contain specific geographic areas that have lagged significantly behind national levels of economic performance. Examples would include Northeast Brazil, Northeast Thailand, parts of Southwest Korea, and the Baluchistan region of Pakistan. *See also* DEPENDENCY THEORY, 106; ANDRE GUNDER FRANK, 15; IMMANUEL WALLERSTEIN, 58; SEMIPERIPHERY, 167.

Significance   The center-periphery and core-periphery concepts continue to have relevance in explaining inequality at both global and national levels. The theory is also highly relevant to discussions of subnational conditions and related disparities. However, with the development of newly industrialized countries (NICs) such as South Korea, Taiwan, Hong Kong, Singapore, and Brazil, and the emergence of industrial Asia, this theory can no longer be universally or mechanically applied. The NICs are now major sources of manufactured goods being exported to developed countries. Industrialized countries are increasingly shifting basic production facilities offshore to remain internationally competitive. Thus, among the developed nations, new centers have emerged or are emerging, such as Seoul, Taipei, Shanghai, Bangkok, Singapore, Hong Kong, and São Paulo. These areas are also becoming financial and communication centers. Thus, the basic center-periphery idea remains relevant but must be modified to take into account dramatic changes in the economic structure of the Third World.

Community Development (CD)   (105)

Village-based organization and activities established to improve welfare and self-reliance in rural areas. Community development, as a movement and development strategy, received considerable attention and support in the 1950s and 1960s, especially in Asia. India's CD program, launched in 1952, was envisioned as a self-help movement that would dramatically improve the lives of the rural poor, who make up most of the population throughout the developing world. The CD strategy was partly based on a system of extension programs to bring services to the rural areas, mainly in the form of technical assistance. Its purpose was to help villagers meet their "felt needs" as well as to increase productivity. The strategy focused on the organization of the villagers by village level workers (VLWs) who would marshall expertise in agriculture, health, education, and public works, made available (in theory if not always in practice) through district or regional development bodies. There was little provision of new technology or supplies. Interestingly, increased productivity was not initially one of the expressed goals of the CD movement. Nehru envisioned the movement as a self-propelled, bootstraps strategy. The program in India and elsewhere stressed decentralization and conveniently required little input from the government. CD efforts received strong support from the Ford Foundation and the United Nations. It was also tied to the cold war effort of the United States, which saw CD as a means of simultaneously addressing political disaffection and poverty in unstable regions.

In the United States itself, CD has became associated almost exclusively with urban programs such as the Community Action Program (CAP) begun in 1964, and the Model Cities Agency set up in 1966. Both programs have since been terminated. CD was a prominent theme in the early days of the Peace Corps, but there has been little systematic interaction between the fields of domestic and overseas community development. *See also* PARTICIPATORY DEVELOPMENT, 117; SARVODAYA SHRAMADANA, 373.

Significance   By the 1970s the CD approach to development was receiving little attention. It had clearly not lived up to its expectations, which may have been exaggerated from the start, as were the expectations of development efforts in general during the first two development decades. Several factors contributed to the relatively disappointing results. The VLWs were often stretched too thin as in India where one worker was expected to cover an average of five villages. Extension services were also inadequate and extension workers were often not keen to work with villagers or sensitive to their needs. The strategy was also naive regarding the diverse interests within village society. As a result, benefits often accrued disproportionately to the village elites. Further, the strategy did not address or challenge overriding structural and political arrangements that worked against the interests of the rural poor. Finally, the CD strategy did not adequately cope with the supervision/autonomy dilemma. The question remains, to what extent can or should community development be managed by outsiders? Community development implies a high level of local participation. In retrospect, one of the major problems with the CD movement was that participation occurred largely in the implementation stage but not in the planning or evaluation processes.

Despite the disappointing results of CD as implemented in the 1950s and 1960s, the CD concept remains central to sound, sensitive, and sustainable development at the local level. The basic values inherent in the community development approach to improving village welfare are reiterated in more recent strategies such as integrated rural development and farming systems research (FSR). These and other approaches that stress indigenous technical knowledge (ITK), a holistic view of change, and listening to the villagers, build on the lessons and experiences of the CD movement. For several decades, development assistance and related theory have stressed the creation of infrastructure, institutions, sectoral development, and efficient national and international policies, on the assumption that such efforts would eventually or directly benefit rural villagers. The recent and dramatic growth in nongovernmental organizations and indigenous development movements demonstrates a resurgence in community-based development efforts. Past efforts in community development can provide valuable lessons for village-level organization and the broader development field. In an interesting role reversal, community development organizations and movements in the Third World now serve as models for development projects in the poorer sectors of the more developed countries (MDCs). For example, the Grameen Bank strategy has been adopted by several organizations to bring development finance services to poor communities in the United States.

Dependency Theory (106)

A diverse body of theory on international development and underdevelopment that explains the relationship between less developed countries (LDCs) and more economically powerful nations. Using a structural analysis, dependency theorists seek to explain how the economies and development of peripheral states, or LDCs, are conditioned and dominated by the needs of the economic and political centers, that is, the advanced capitalist states and their accompanying institutions. This process of domination is described as the condition of dependence.

Dependency theory originated in Latin America in the 1960s and has been strongly influenced by writers from that region, among them Raúl Prebisch, Theotonio Dos Santos, Fernando Cardoso, Celso Furtado, and Osvaldo Sunkel. The dependency perspective, however, is the result of the work of many scholars in the social sciences, especially that of Paul Baran. The analysis rejects the notion of diffusion whereby LDCs imitate orthodox models and become developed. Prebisch argues that capitalism at the periphery results in deteriorating terms of trade for the LDCs. He and the Economic Commission for Latin America (ECLA) argued for import substitution industrialization (ISI) as a solution. The *dependistas* found the center-periphery analysis useful but did not agree that ISI would ever result in more equal economic relationships between North and South. Andre Gunder Frank, one of the leading dependency theorists, links the historic development of the center to the underdevelopment of the periphery and to both internal and international inequality. His initial writing focused exclusively on the Latin American experience, but more recently he has generalized beyond that region. He concludes that countries cannot hope to develop until they liberate themselves from the chains of domination through an anti-imperialist struggle. Adding to the theory, Sunkel draws links between the international capitalist system and inequality within nations. Furtado stresses the external dominance of peripheral capitalism. Cardoso, while critical of other *dependistas,* examines the dynamic structural relationship between internal and external political and economic forces. Other scholars, such as Samir Amin and Arghiri Emmanuel, explore the question of unequal exchange throughout the world. Finally, dependency theory forms the basis for Immanuel Wallerstein's world systems theory. Though there are many common elements among theories of dependency, "the theory" is pluralistic with important variations, particularly with regard to the extent of political radicalism associated with the theory. *See also* NEOCOLONIALISM, 210; ANDRE GUNDER FRANK, 15; IMPERIALISM, 204; UNDERDEVELOPMENT, 123.

Significance   Dependency theory poses a major challenge to orthodox economic development theory. Basing its conclusions primarily on historical analysis and critical theory, it rejects the notions of comparative advantage and stages-of-growth theory. Dependency theory suggests that development of peripheral nations within the international capitalist system is unlikely since rich nations actually develop at the expense of the LDCs. It places the discussion of economic development within the context of politics and power, effectively broadening the development debate and addressing the issues of national and international inequality. Given the diverse development experiences of Third World nations over the last three decades, dependency theory appears to vary in its explanatory power depending on culture and region. It is more useful as a method of critique and explanation than as a set of specific solutions. However, it has served to facilitate a deeper and more complete understanding of the international political and economic system.

Development (107)

Processes leading to a higher quality of life for a given population. Development involves both the determination of goals and the means of achieving those ends. Development, as a desired state that could be achieved quickly and on a massive or global scale, is essentially a post–World War II concept. However, the questions it raises as to what a "good life" is and how it might be achieved have roots in ancient philosophy and human inquiry. The notion of development grew out of postwar optimism, which in turn was premised on unprecedented levels of economic growth and technological advancement in the West. It gained further impetus among the newly independent nation-states that came to be known collectively as the developing nations or Third World.

At various times and within different schools of thought, *development* has been used interchangeably with such terms as *modernization, progress, industrialization,* and *economic growth.* Both major paradigms of development, capitalist and Marxist, tend to view development in these terms as well as in a linear, deterministic fashion. But these conceptualizations have been challenged as too narrow, materialistic, normative, and value-laden to describe adequately either the broader goals or the processes of development. As the 1950s and 1960s unfolded, it became increasingly clear that development, in terms of rapid economic growth and modernization, could in fact be accomplished. But this often proved to be an extremely uneven, if not costly, process. Certain sectors or populations might "develop" without benefit to, or even to the detriment of, others. This inequity is a recurring theme in the growing and important literature on women in development (WID). As a result, the concept of development has undergone considerable scrutiny and constant redefinition, often in an attempt to wrest the meaning away from those who would define it in overly narrow, culturally biased terms or those who perceive it in terms of a single discipline such as economics.

Development has also come to be prefaced by many sectoral terms. For example, the terms *economic, cultural, social, political, community, industrial, rural, national,* and *international development* are all commonly used. A recent and increasingly common prefix to development is *sustainable,* a reminder that development issues should be addressed in terms of the well-being not only of this generation, but also of those to come. Thus, the environment and the preservation of cultural diversity have become central issues in development. The notion of sustainability adds an ironic twist to that of development, suggesting that it involves not just change, but also preservation and conservation. This contrasts sharply with earlier definitions of development as the passing of traditional societies and the emergence of economies of high mass consumption.

The sectoral distinctions indicate that development is a multidimensional process involving various aspects of the human condition, including having, doing, and being. In Gandhi's and Nyerere's terms, it is the "realization of human potential." Denis Goulet defines development in three interconnected dimensions: life-sustenance, ability to meet basic human needs; self-esteem, meeting basic and other needs with a sense of dignity; and freedom from servitude, which involves emancipation from all forms of oppression and empowerment to choose. Similarly, Johan Galtung addresses development in terms of survival needs, well-being, identity, and freedom. Such value-based interpretations challenge any universal notion of development. They leave open the question of how development goals might best be determined and achieved, suggesting the possibility of many alternative forms of development. *See also* PARADIGMS OF DEVELOPMENT, 116; MODERNIZATION THEORY, 114; SUSTAINABLE DEVELOPMENT, 272.

Significance   Development might well be considered the grand experiment of the twentieth century. It addresses fundamental human aspirations and has proven to be one of the more compelling visions of our time. In terms of lowering infant mortality, improving life expectancy, raising literacy rates, and achieving worldwide economic growth, the development accomplishments of the last several decades are unprecedented in human history. But such indicators present an incomplete and misleading picture. Other dimensions related to quality of life, human happiness and welfare, and social equity are not so easily measured or assessed. What of contentedness, justice, the sense of satisfaction, and belonging? Have these, too, been enhanced in the development process or has alienation resulted? The record is no doubt mixed.

Given the breadth and depth of the concept of development as well as its many normative definitions, it is not surprising that the field of development studies has sometimes lacked clarity and definition. This multidisciplinary field was originally premised on rapid advancements in the hard sciences that have influenced the social sciences, and it ultimately addresses normative questions central to the humanities. Some suggest that the term *development* has exhausted its usefulness and should be abandoned, especially given its frequent ethnocentric manifestations and the many harmful outcomes of actions undertaken in the name of development. However, no suitable replacement or alternative concept appears forthcoming. A continued reconsideration and reassessment of the ideas associated with development seems more likely than abandonment of the term. Development, understood as improvement in the quality of life, is a reflection of a long-standing hope that the basic human condition can indeed be improved. As Peter Worsley suggests, "The whole of history is the history of development" (Worsley 1984:1).

Development Labelling (108)

The proliferation of a rather extensive jargon in the development field that reflects hegemony, power relations, and existing systems of social and political stratification. Such labelling is an integral part of social policy discourse. Examples of such labels are *backwardness, culture of poverty, slums,* and *developing countries.* Combining such terms can lead to a permutation and combination of hundreds or even thousands of such terms (e.g., *integrated rural development, political modernization, moral basis of a backward society, need for achievement,* and *modern man*). Labelling can serve to legitimate and dictate the nature of policy discourse. This focus on labelling is reflective of critical theory.

Significance   Too often language and the terms of social discourse are accepted uncritically, while their impact on policy-making and decision making is frequently ignored. To gain deeper insight into the development process and its impact on ordinary people, it is critically important to seek to understand their own concepts and terms for defining their reality. The problem of development labelling is described in detail in Geof Wood's *Labelling in Development Policy: Essays in Honor of Bernard Schaffer* (1985).

Dhammic Socialism (109)

A term that refers to the integration of Buddhist and socialist principles, coined by Buddhadasa Bhikku of Thailand. Buddhadasa and those advocating dhammic socialism are critical of both Western capitalism and Western Marxism. The former is perceived as preoccupied with excessive individualism and the latter considered to foster dehumanizing authoritarianism. Dhammic socialism offers a unity of the

100

human community as an alternative to the dualistic, binary, and con-
flictual competition between capitalism and communism.

> Dhammic socialism has three basic principles: the principle of the
> good of the whole, the principle of restraint and generosity, and the
> principle of respect and loving-kindness (Swearer 1986: 33–34).

The Thai term *dhamma* derives from the Sanskrit term *Dharma*. It
refers to the teachings of the Buddha and connotes the interrelated-
ness of life and nature. *See also* "SMALL IS BEAUTIFUL," 121; E. F.
SCHUMACHER, 45; BUDDHIST DEVELOPMENT/ECONOMICS, 103.

Significance   The dhammic socialist approach to development has
been popularized by E. F. Schumacher in his well-known volume,
Small Is Beautiful (1973), which presents a compelling argument for
Buddhist economics. Erich Fromm in his important, but neglected,
book, *To Have or To Be* (1978), also presents a dhammic socialist type
of perspective. Given increasing global pressures on limited natural
resources and the dehumanizing aspects of excessive materialism and
conspicuous luxury consumption, a Buddhist approach to development is becoming more and more salient. The growing voluntary
simplicity movement in certain parts of the Western countries also reflects the movement toward more Buddhist approaches. The current
irony of dhammic socialism is that many of the world's most dynamic
capitalistic societies noted for emphasizing the free market and materialism (e.g., Hong Kong, Taiwan, South Korea, and Singapore) are
located in the "Buddhist" part of Asia.

Fourth World   **(110)**
A commonly used term in the 1980s that has two distinct meanings,
both relating to underdeveloped nations. It was first used in reference to those nations that were the least developed and the most in
need of development assistance. The concept evolved in recognition
of the growing disparities among Third World nations themselves.
While countries such as South Korea and Taiwan have "graduated"
from the ranks of the poor to become newly industrialized countries,
other nations such as Ethiopia, the Sudan, Chad, and Bangladesh still
have severe poverty and serious difficulties in meeting basic needs.
These poorest of the poor countries are, thus, the Fourth World. A
more recent definition of the Fourth World refers to indigenous minorities in various nation-states who lack political autonomy and identity. They are "nations" that are not recognized internationally, or
peoples without a nation. Examples would be the Karens or Shans in

Burma, the Rama in Nicaragua, the Melanesians of Irian Jaya in Indonesia, the Miskitos of Honduras, the Kurds in Turkey, the Oromo in Ethiopia, and the Palestinians in Israel. If all these groups were to form their own nations, there would be as many as 3,000 to 5,000 nations in the world today. *See also* LESS DEVELOPED COUNTRIES, 112; THIRD WORLD, 122; NATIONALISM, 209.

Significance   The evolution of the term *the Fourth World* recognizes the absurdity of a monolithic concept of a Third World. Variations among Third World nations are dramatic and growing. It makes little sense to lump together countries as different economically as Taiwan and Ethiopia. In its second sense, the term also recognizes the growing importance of ethnic nationalism and the struggle for subnational political and cultural identity. While the twentieth century may well have been one of nationalism, the twenty-first century may well be one of both transnationalism and subnationalism, resulting in a gradual waning of the traditional nation-state.

Industrialization   (111)

The process whereby capital and labor shift from agriculture and household production to factories and manufacturing operations. Industrialization is an increase in the capacity of a country to process primary resources for marketing and consumption. The industrial process, as illustrated in Adam Smith's famous example of pin manufacture, seeks to exploit the advantages of scale, mechanization, and specialization to boost productivity. The industrial age, which began in the mid-eighteenth century in England and Northern Europe, witnessed not only dramatic increases in productivity, but marked sociological and political changes in the industrializing nations and worldwide. Colonial expansion was fueled by an increasing need for raw materials, and new markets were needed for the surplus products. Further, with growing resistance to the abuses of the labor force in the industrialized countries, the most undesirable tasks were, and continue to be, shifted to nonindustrialized or semi-industrialized areas of least resistance. Industrialization is closely tied with urbanization and the development of capital, though agriculture itself can be industrialized and urbanization may occur apart from industrialization. There have always been well-fed and healthy populations that are not industrialized but there are no capital-rich nations, with the exception of a few oil-exporting countries, that are not highly industrialized. The degree of industrialization of an economy may be measured by the International Standard Industrial Classification of the United Nations. The standard divides economic activities into the following sectors for comparative purposes: agriculture, comprised of agriculture, hunting, forestry, and fishing; industry, activities related to mining, quarrying, manufacturing, electricity, gas, water, and construction; and services, pertaining to wholesale and retail trade, restaurants and hotels, transport, storage and communications, finance, insurance, real estate, business services, and community and social services. *See also* PARADIGMS OF DEVELOPMENT, 116; EXPORT OF POLLUTION, 264.

Significance   Industrialization has widely been assumed to be the central element of the development process, especially where development is understood primarily in economic terms. Industrialization leads to greater efficiency and productivity, which in turn lead to surplus goods and capital accumulation. Both major development paradigms (Marxism and capitalism) accept this central assumption. Their disagreements are based on the degree of exploitation that occurs within the industrialized state and in the world system. Most argue that the revolutions that Marx predicted for industrialized societies did not come about because workers' lives improved significantly, especially in terms of real wages, as the industrial age advanced, facilitated by colonialist and imperialist expansion. Much of post–World War II development literature equates development, modernization, and industrialization. In quantitative terms, the development of the industrial sector is seen as a major indicator of advancement. In the spirit of Max Weber, writers in the social sciences, such as David McClelland, Alex Inkeles, and W. E. Moore, have shown that traditional, preindustrial values, institutions, and organizations often were not compatible with the values of modern, industrialized man. The factory in developing countries was viewed as a transitionary institution that embodied modern values, efficiency, temporal precision, productivity, monetary reward, and discipline. Of course, the social sciences have also pointed out the detrimental social aspects of industrial society, particularly alienation.

Alternative development thinkers call for a broader concept of development and question models that tend to equate material productivity and modern consumption with development. Gandhi, for example, stressed cottage industry as a path to Indian development. Schumacher popularized the notion of Buddhist economics, intermediate technology, and "small is beautiful." Numerous writers have pointed to what they consider a spiritual and moral void in industrialized societies. Recent emphasis on sustainable development calls into question the viability of the industrialization of the Third World as a means of development, at least as industrialization has been advanced in the MDCs. As the North enters the "postindustrial" age of information and increasing environmental concern, the LDCs may become the inheritors of "dirty industry," just as they are increasingly the site of a cheap industrial labor force. Since few if any LDCs eschew industrialization, it is imperative for the well-being of their citizens that the many pitfalls of industrialization be critically assessed to facilitate the development of creative adaptations and/or alternative development paths.

Less or Least Developed Countries (LDCs) (112)

A crude grouping of Third World nations as differentiated from more developed countries (MDCs). The term is used throughout development literature without specific designation as to which countries fall into which of the two categories. LDCs refers to nations of low to moderate levels of industrialization and GNP. Such countries represent roughly two-thirds to three-quarters of the world's population. If the world's 176 nations are divided into those with per capita incomes above and below $1,000 per year, 143 countries receive the LDC designation. The term *least developed country* was adopted in the 1970s by the UN, which originally designated 24 countries as LDCs and targeted them for special assistance. By 1990, 42 countries were categorized as LDCs by the UN. *See also* THIRD WORLD, 122; FOURTH WORLD, 110; UNDERDEVELOPMENT, 123.

Significance   *Less developed countries* is a term of convenience, especially in its acronym form. It is less value-laden than alternative general designations such as *poor, backward,* or *undeveloped.* LDC also is perhaps more accurate than *developing nation* since it is not clear that all nations are indeed developing. The designation also recognizes that all nations have developed to a degree. Finally, it can be useful for purposes of development assistance to identify which countries are least developed and what features they hold in common.

Liberation (113)

The act or process of being freed from a system or state of oppression. Liberation is most commonly used to mean either a change of individual consciousness and condition or, in political terms, freedom from oppression for a particular individual, community, class, or nation. These two types of liberation are often closely related, an idea central in the writings of Paulo Freire, one of many writers who draw close connections between liberation and development. Freire contends that liberation begins when consciousness is raised, or when oppressed people begin to understand the roots of their oppression.

Further, they must come to see that their condition of oppression and related poverty is not inevitable or destined. In similar fashion, Denis Goulet describes development in terms of freedom from servitude to ignorance, others, institutions, and beliefs. The poor and oppressed must begin to envision themselves as something other than naturally poor. As such, liberation is not just a goal of development but also its starting point. Such an interpretation assumes that genuine development cannot occur in a situation of oppression, even though changes often defined as development, such as economic growth, may take place. *See also* COLONIALISM, 195; NATIONALISM, 209; LIBERATION THEOLOGY, 233.

Significance   Consideration of liberation thrusts the concept of development squarely into the arena of ethics and values. What is the goal of development and who determines those goals? Can the development process be participatory without empowerment and liberation? The assumption of liberation movements, both violent and nonviolent, is that development within oppressive systems only serves the powerful and elite. Thus "liberation" may be a better expression of the aspirations and values of the poor than "development." At best each concept informs the other. Both liberation and development can be considered to be parts of the same process whereby people are empowered to achieve greater mastery of their own destiny.

Modernization Theory   **(114)**
An approach stressing the existence of a universal syndrome of sociopsychological values and attitudes associated with development. Modernization theories can be classified into two groups. The first is exemplified by Marion J. Levy, Jr., author of *Modernization and the Structure of Societies* (1966), who contrasts the characteristics of modern societies with those of traditional societies. A key element in Levy's definition of modernization is the extent to which a society uses tools and inanimate sources of power. He then identifies a number of pattern variables associated with relative levels of modernization, such as rational versus traditional, universal versus particularistic, specific versus diffuse, and avoidance versus intimacy. The second group of modernization theories is exemplified by Alex Inkeles and David Smith, coauthors of *Becoming Modern* (1974), who emphasize a micro approach that focuses on individual attitudinal modernity. Other scholars who stress the micro, attitudinal approach are Daniel Lerner, *The Passing of Traditional Society* (1958), and Joseph Kahl, *The Measurement of Modernism* (1968). The Inkeles-Smith concept of individual modernity is based on the extensive

Harvard-Stanford Project on Social and Cultural Aspects of Modernization, involving interviews with 6,000 men in six developing nations, namely Argentina, Chile, India, Israel, Nigeria, and East Pakistan (now Bangladesh). In this research Inkeles and Smith developed a scale for measuring individual attitudinal modernity. Their syndrome defines modern man as the individual ready for new experiences and open to innovation and change. The syndrome also emphasizes trust, feelings of efficacy, empathy, women's rights, concern for distributive justice, planning, and an emphasis on the present and future instead of the past. Inkeles and Smith use modern psychometric techniques to demonstrate the reliability and validity of their measurement scale. They find that the best predictors of modern attitudes are prior exposure to formal schools, factories, and the mass media. *See also* DEVELOPMENT, 107; N ACHIEVEMENT, 235.

Significance   The work of modernization theorists such as Levy and Inkeles has caused considerable controversy among social scientists interested in the process of development. Many radical development thinkers see the work of modernization theorists as both ethnocentric and culturally imperialistic. In a more recent volume, *Exploring Individual Modernity,* Inkeles has attempted to answer some of these charges. Those with a more anthropological orientation often express concern about the implication of modernization theory with respect to the preservation of certain traditional values such as respect for the elderly. Perhaps the most serious criticism of modernization theory faults its assumption that development must follow a linear path. This assumption is unacceptable to those who emphasize existential choice and the possibility of skipping, reversing, or modifying conventional stages of development. Whatever position an individual takes vis-à-vis modernization theory, such theorists have contributed to a vitally important debate about fundamental values and attitudes associated with the development process.

Modernization without Development   **(115)**
A distinction developed by the sociologist Norman Jacobs to explain and categorize differential development performance. Though this distinction is not a standard one in the development field, it does raise important theoretical and historical questions. Jacobs defines modernization as denoting "the maximization of the potential of the society within the limits set by the goals and the fundamental structure (or forms) of the society" (Jacobs 1971:9). In contrast, development denotes "the maximization of the potential of the society, regardless of any limits currently set by the goals or fundamental structure of

the society" (Jacobs 1971:9). Thus, modernization may be considered an integral part of development, but modernization per se does not mean development. Modernization is also more easily measured by gross quantitative economic indicators such as the rate of growth in gross national product. Development, in contrast, is a much more complex qualitative process involving fundamental structural transformations that cannot be measured by overly simple macroindicators. *See also* MODERNIZATION THEORY, 114; DEVELOPMENT, 107.

Significance   The distinction between modernization with development and modernization without development seems to have considerable explanatory power, at least for certain periods and contexts. For example, in the century 1870–1970, countries such as Chile, Argentina, and Thailand certainly experienced modernization, but not the type of development characteristic of Japan. Given the impressive natural resource bases of Argentina and Thailand, in 1870 it would have been conceivable to predict confidently that those two countries would now be much more developed than countries such as Japan or Singapore. The validity of Jacob's distinction remains debatable, given the difficulties inherent in empirically operationalizing it. Many development anthropologists and indigenous Third World scholars might also find this distinction ethnocentric, since it seems to imply that traditional social and political systems may be incompatible with development.

Paradigms of Development   (116)

General theories or world views of development and their underlying values and assumptions. Development paradigms include both articulation of goals and strategies for achieving those ends. The two major competing paradigms or models of development during the last four decades have been capitalism and Marxism. These are sometimes referred to as orthodox and radical paradigms since Marxism is essentially a critique of capitalism. Marxism and other theories that question the basic assumptions of capitalism—for example, dependency theory—are also referred to collectively as the political economy paradigm. There are, of course, many interpretations and variants of both major paradigms. Given the many possible combinations of political and economic systems among nations, generalizations regarding the two paradigms must be made with caution. However, capitalism has largely been associated with Western democratic, free market systems, and Marxism, until quite recently, with the centrally planned, socialist systems of the Soviet Union and Eastern Europe. Both paradigms are deterministic in their views of history and progress, and both stress economic growth and industrialization as means and outcomes of the development process. The capitalist paradigm emphasizes individual opportunity, the dynamics of the market, private goods, and individual rights. The Marxist models tend to stress state/public ownership, public goods, equality, and societal rights such as full employment and job security. Further, Marxism views class conflict as integral to capitalism. The two paradigms differ fundamentally in their assessment of the factors underlying the failure of many Third World nations to develop. In the orthodox literature, underdevelopment usually refers to societies that have not yet advanced through the stages of economic development. By implication, underdevelopment persists as a result of incorrect policies, low productivity, and a lack of human and capital resources. The Marxist paradigm, in contrast, views underdevelopment primarily as a result of the exploitive nature of capitalism, imperialistic domination, and subservient neocolonial regimes whose elites are co-opted. *See also* DEVELOPMENT, 107; UNDERDEVELOPMENT, 123.

Significance In practice, countries following capitalist policies have often achieved rapid economic growth at the cost of greater inequality. Many Latin American countries reflect this pattern of development. In contrast, a few of the socialist countries, such as China and Cuba, have made considerable advances in meeting basic human needs while falling behind their counterparts in overall economic growth. Various forms of both paradigms have guided the development thinking of many Third World countries, and both superpowers (the United States and the Soviet Union) have gone to great lengths, with military and economic assistance, to bring to power and maintain leaders and governments supportive of their respective ideologies.

Many Third World leaders and writers, such as Gandhi and Nyerere, have strongly questioned the viability or appropriateness of either paradigm for the LDCs. Pointing out that both models grow out of Western modes of thought, they stress the need for developing countries to devise models of development more appropriate to their particular settings, needs, and values. Also, in the 1990s, new paradigms of development are emerging in the industrialized nations that question the basic assumptions of both capitalism and Marxism. Such models emphasize environmental conservation, decentralization of political and economic decision making, and nonviolent change. Other sources of alternative paradigms stem from a resurgence of religious values among groups that question Western material wealth and consumerism as societal goals. In the current decade and in the century ahead, pluralistic development paradigms are likely to supplant the binary and polarized approach of the past.

Participatory Development   (117)
A development philosophy that encourages people to "own development" and have critical input into the nature of development projects. This approach contrasts dramatically with elitist top-down national or international orientations in which outsiders decide what is best for local people. Guy Gran, author of *Development by People: Citizen Construction of a Just World* (1983), is one of the most articulate advocates of participatory development. He sees eight key characteristics of participatory development projects: (1) significant involvement of those affected in project initiation, design, operation, and evaluation; (2) inclusion of those affected in project design mechanisms for regular participation to guide administrative, productive, and distributive elements of the project; (3) larger external linkages of the project that are functional for those at the bottom; (4) cultural feasibility and appropriateness; (5) ecological soundness; (6) potential for self-reliance and reduced further dependency; (7) potential for self-sustainment after cessation of project; and (8) enhancement of self-directed learning and avoidance of intellectual dependency. *See also* COMMUNITY EMPOWERMENT, 197.

Significance   A major problem in the development field has been the frequent failure to provide ordinary individuals an opportunity to participate in key decisions regarding projects that will affect their daily lives. Thus, there is often an imbalance between genuine needs and the development assistance provided. Long-term continuation of projects is significantly enhanced if those affected are involved in decision making from the start. Though it may be impossible to utilize the philosophy of participatory development in all projects and programs, greater emphasis on local involvement in project determination, design, and implementation could certainly enhance the effectiveness of many development programs. With the increasing involvement of indigenous, private, voluntary organizations and nongovernmental organizations in the development process, there may be greater potential for the actualization of participatory development.

Political Economy   (118)
A subfield of political science concerned with the political context of

economic systems and the relationship between the political and economic systems. Political economy also refers to a broad range of theories and critiques of the dominant capitalist system which draw in part from the writings of Marx. Critical theory and dependency theory, for example, address capitalism in the context of power, hegemony, and stratification. Charles Wilbur, editor of *The Political Economy of Development and Underdevelopment* (1988), offers an even broader meaning. He refers to the "political economy paradigm" of development, which

> challenges economic growth as a static end-goal, contending instead that the nature of the process of economic development is crucial. What is important is the means by which economic development is pursued and how these means affect the everyday lives of people. This approach appreciates the dialectic relationship between society, the polity, and the economy. (1–2)

See also PARADIGMS OF DEVELOPMENT, 116.

Significance   Broad-ranging, multidisciplinary approaches are needed to understand the various models of development, including the political economy models. Conventional economic approaches to development have tended to ignore or inadequately address the more political, normative, and distributional dimensions of the development process. Political and economic aspects of development are complexly interrelated. The political economy perspective emphasizes both the impact of economic systems on the polity and the role of political forces in transforming economic structures. Ironically, recent events in Eastern Europe dramatically confirm such linkages, but with outcomes quite different from those predicted by Marxist or radical theorists of development.

Predevelopment   (119)
A level of development achieved by a number of traditional societies prior to contact with colonialism and the Western World. The geographer Keith Buchanan introduces this concept in his work, *Southeast Asian World* (1967), and mentions that in the twelfth and thirteenth centuries, parts of Southeast Asia were considerably more developed than Europe at that time. He describes, for example, the advanced irrigation and hydraulic systems of the Angkor civilization in Cambodia. Similarly in Mexico, Guatemala, and Peru there were relatively advanced civilizations before contact with Europeans. In the South Pacific, the ancient Polynesians displayed remarkably advanced navi-

gational skills which enabled them to explore the broad Pacific. *See also* UNDERDEVELOPMENT, 123.

Significance   With the focus on contemporary problems of development, it is easy to ignore the historical and prehistoric contexts of development. An understanding of predevelopment can enhance appreciation of the potential for future development and foster greater respect for Third World nations and cultures. The richness of indigenous Third World culture is far greater than most realize. Examples of predevelopment can still be found at such sites as the Mayan complex in the Yucatan, Angkor in Cambodia, Borobodur in Indonesia, Pagan in Burma, and Incan remains in Peru.

Self-Reliance/Self-Sufficiency   (120)
A strategy that attempts to minimize reliance or dependency on external resources in the development process. Albania, Burma, and the People's Republic of China are among the few nations in recent history that have adopted strict autarkic or isolationist policies for extended periods. On a national scale, self-reliance is most often advocated by revolutionary states wary of outside interference or eager to break ties with former oppressors and systems of dependency. Self-reliance on a sectoral or communal basis is a much more common goal than national self-sufficiency. For example, self-sufficiency in food production or energy supply is a commonly expressed goal of developing countries. The advantages of self-sufficiency, be they political, economic, or cultural, must be weighed against the advantages and disadvantages of participation in extracommunal or international systems of communication, trade, and politics.

Significance   Self-reliance is essential for maintaining some degree of communal or national identity, dignity, and sovereignty. Many developing nations, once comprised of many highly self-reliant subnational groups, find themselves dependent and vulnerable within the modern international economic system. The current debt crisis is a vivid reminder of such vulnerabilities. At the same time, many groups within developing nations are reassessing their dependence on national systems of service delivery and seeking to create new systems of self-reliance or to reconstruct past systems of communal security. In general terms, the world is becoming increasingly interdependent, and attempts to move toward self-reliance contradict that trend. Nevertheless, self-reliance remains an important development option, especially for those cultures that have not been well served by the modern world system. Further, environmentalists remind us that systems of self-reliance are often more ecologically sound than the international systems serving the affluent nations.

"Small Is Beautiful" (121)
A concept highly critical of conventional capitalistic and socialistic economics and their emphasis on maximizing growth. The concept was popularized by the European economist, E. F. Schumacher, author of *Small Is Beautiful: Economics As If People Mattered* (1973). The idea derived from Schumacher's consulting work in Burma where he became intimately acquainted with both Theravada Buddhism and Ghandian concepts of development. Schumacher is highly critical of the big-is-better philosophy which emphasizes maximizing economic growth whatever its costs. Peter Berger in *Pyramids of Sacrifice* (1974) has carefully documented the excessive costs of big development in Brazil and China, despite the dramatic differences in the ideologies of the two countries. A basic assumption underlying the "small is beautiful" perspective is that extremely large organizations tend to lack responsiveness to human needs and their approach frequently results in alienation and anomie. Also, large-scale economies involve many complex interdependencies and dependencies, resulting in uncertain vulnerabilities. *See also* E. F. SCHUMACHER, 45; APPROPRIATE TECHNOLOGY, 276; DHAMMIC SOCIALISM, 109.

Significance   Many conventional economists question the feasibility and practicality of the "small is beautiful" philosophy of economics in a world where transnational corporations are growing in power and influence. Many small-scale economies such as those in the South Pacific often lack adequate economies of scale. Despite such skepticism, Schumacher's idea still remains popular among environmentally oriented development thinkers and practitioners. The political "greens" whose influence is growing in various polities around the world often incorporate some of Schumacher's thinking into their policy platforms. In the debate about centralization and decentralization of bureaucratic authority, both public and private, decentralization reflects the "small is beautiful" perspective and often results in a more efficient and responsive delivery of public goods and services. The Japanese have applied the Schumacher concept to the manufacturing process with their impressive mastery of miniaturization. Japan's success in this realm is elegantly described in O-Young Lee's *Smaller Is Better: Japan's Mastery of the Miniature* (1984). With increased emphasis on sustainable development, the concepts of "small is beautiful" and Buddhist economics are likely to grow in influence and relevance as we move into the twenty-first century.

Third World   (122)
A loosely defined, diverse group of nations and territories, including the developing nations of Africa, Asia, Latin America, the Middle East, and the Pacific. Many Third World countries have achieved political independence since World War II. The term excludes OECD and Eastern Bloc countries. The origin of the term is generally attributed to Alfred Sauvy, a French demographer who used it in 1952 in reference to the developing nations outside the two major power blocks. *Third World* is an allusion to the *tiers état* (third estate) of pre-revolutionary France, a diverse segment of the populace sharing the common traits of marginality and powerlessness. Irving Horowitz's book, *Three Worlds of Development* (1966), helped bring the term into prominence. Because the term includes "third," which may be interpreted as hierarchical and value-laden, scholars sometimes prefer alternative terms such as *South, nonindustrialized, nonaligned, Group of 77, LDCs,* or *two-thirds world.* As Peter Worsley points out in his classic book on development, *The Three Worlds* (1984), different conceptions of the Third World have led to different political conclusions about its meaning. *See also* FOURTH WORLD, 110; LESS OR LEAST DEVELOPED COUNTRIES, 112.

Significance   While a term that groups together such diverse nations is of dubious theoretical and analytical usefulness, its widespread and frequent use testifies to its utility. The concept has stimulated discussion and comparison of obstacles to development faced by the LDCs. Further, it highlights shared characteristics, including, with few exceptions: colonial histories, low GNP per capita, unstable or stagnant economies, intellectual and scientific dependence, high vulnerability, and peripheral status within the international economic community. The term's widespread use by Third World citizens and organizations attests to its continued usefulness and positive connotation. Attempts by intellectuals from the right and the left to reject the term have met with little success.

Underdevelopment   (123)
The state of a nation or region that lacks basic development. Most often used in the context of economic analysis, it implies that some level of economic development has already taken place. As with the concept of development, the notion of underdevelopment is

inherently value-laden and normative. In linear-stage theories of capitalist development, it refers to the stages following the "undeveloped" condition and preceding the establishment of mature industrial and capitalist systems. The assumption is that economies can and will emerge from their natural state of underdevelopment, an assumption that Paul Baran, Andre Gunder Frank, and the *dependistas* called into question. Frank argued that underdevelopment was not a natural state, but rather the end result of an exploitive and extractive colonial and neocolonial system. He observed that peripheral areas most drawn into the world capital system were least likely to develop in comparison to surrounding and similar areas that were spared early incorporation into the system. Other Marxist analyses also speak of underdevelopment as a result of economic exploitation and political impediments to self-determination. *See also* DEPENDENCY THEORY, 106; DEVELOPMENT, 107.

Significance   The idea of underdevelopment is used frequently throughout the development literature. It is important to understand the assumptions of the writers utilizing the term. Proponents of orthodox capitalist development assume that underdevelopment is a condition to be overcome through proper economic policies of industrialization, savings and investment, and concomitant establishment of modern finance and cultural value systems. Writers utilizing a Marxist analysis view underdevelopment as a result of exploitation by the dominant capitalist powers. Others, stressing cultural relativism, question the basis for ranking and comparison of political, economic, and social systems implied by the term. Additionally, they point out that economically developed societies could be considered culturally underdeveloped or maldeveloped and that the opposite may also be true. Those who challenge the conventional uses of the term *development* inevitably find the notion of underdevelopment equally inappropriate.

B. Economic Development

Austerity Program   (124)
Harsh economic policies adopted by a government to cope with an economic crisis. Historically, economic austerity has been associated with wartime economies when resources were diverted to the military effort. More recently, austerity programs have come to be associated with the debt crisis and more specifically with the policies of the International Monetary Fund (IMF). No longer able to secure credit from commercial banks and to pay off existing loans, many less devel-

oped countries (LDCs) have turned to the IMF, the lender of last resort. The extent of the crisis has led countries once severely critical of the IMF to turn to the organization for capital, sacrificing a degree of sovereignty for economic survival. Typically, the terms of an IMF loan involve "structural adjustment," more commonly refered to as an austerity program. This includes devaluation of the nation's currency, withdrawal of government subsidies of all types, promotion of export expansion, privatization of national industries, and budget cutbacks in government services. The immediate result of these measures may be lower wages, food price hikes and shortages, and the loss of vital services to many. The macroeconomic gains from such programs are mixed at best. *See also* INTERNATIONAL MONETARY FUND, 420; DEBT CRISIS, 134.

Significance   Austerity programs have come under increasing international criticism because of their often profound and immediate detrimental effects on the poor. Rapidly rising food costs and curtailment of services have resulted in "IMF riots," such as those that occurred in the Dominican Republic in April, 1984, and public outcry in many countries. Supporters argue that such adjustments are necessary for meeting the long-term needs of the nation, including the needs of the poor. Critics point out that the poor are the first to suffer from such policies and the last to benefit from any economic improvements they might engender. UNICEF's recent study, *Adjustment with a Human Face* (see Cornia 1987), is an unprecedented attack by one multilateral development agency upon the policies of another. The report questions whether it makes human or economic sense to sacrifice the minds and bodies of the next generation on the altar of adjustment policy.

Balanced Growth   **(125)**
A basic concept that refers to the need to pursue effective growth in both the agricultural and industrial sectors simultaneously. Balanced growth has been emphasized in the development literature for several decades in such important volumes as *The Theory of Economic Growth* (1955) by Sir Arthur Lewis, a Nobel laureate in development economics. The origin of this important concept was a 1943 article by Paul N. Rosenstein-Rodan which appeared in *Economic Journal.* In unbalanced growth, for example, if agricultural growth lags behind, food shortages will occur and food prices will be driven up, contributing to inflationary pressures that will make a nation's products less competitive. Also, without increases in agricultural productivity, growing supplies of labor will not be released to the industrial,

manufacturing, and service sectors. On the other hand, if industrial growth lags behind, the demand for the products of the agricultural sector will be more limited and supplies (machinery, for example) to improve agricultural productivity will be less available. Finally, and perhaps most importantly, without industrial growth attracting labor from the rural sector, there will be much less incentive to increase agricultural productivity. *See also* SIR ARTHUR LEWIS, 33; INTEGRATED RURAL DEVELOPMENT, 182; DUALISM, 139.

Significance   Though balanced growth has been promoted in the literature for several decades, too many developing nations have ignored the fundamental wisdom of this concept and have pursued developmental policies that greatly favor the industrial and urban sectors. In many countries, the agricultural sector has lagged dramatically behind the industrial sector, resulting in growing economic disparities and inequities. Nearly all developing countries have a region that lags behind others, such as the Northeast of Brazil, the Northeast of Thailand, the Northwest and Southwest of China, the Southwest of Korea, and the high plateaus of Peru and Bolivia. The implementation of genuine balanced growth implies political policies and demands the courage to make difficult choices. It should be added that no society can attain perfectly balanced growth.

Big Push Doctrine   (126)
The notion that a country needs a massive investment program to "take off" into sustained economic growth. This perspective was originally emphasized by Paul Rosenstein-Rodan and later by Walter Galenson and Harvey Leibenstein in the 1950s. The emphasis of the big push doctrine is heavy capital investment in the industrial sector and the development of an economic infrastructure. There is also stress on the introduction of modern technology on as large a scale as possible, implying the use of modern equipment and relatively high initial capital/labor ratios. Countries that have tried to follow this doctrine include Brazil, India, and China. *See also* INFRASTRUCTURE, 155; CAPITAL-INTENSIVE TECHNIQUES, 128; PAUL ROSENSTEIN-RODAN, 41.

Significance   The big push doctrine has been hotly debated. Critics of the approach argue that its emphasis on capital-intensive techniques is inappropriate in countries with surplus labor and serious problems of unemployment and underemployment. They are also concerned about the imitation of industrial models that may not be appropriate in other settings or for which the timing may be premature. Despite these criticisms, the doctrine does address the basic problem of inadequate levels of savings and investment. For sustained economic growth to occur, dramatic increases in savings and investment are essential. Basic economic infrastructure such as roads, stable electrical supplies, and communication systems are central to industrial development. The big push doctrine also transcends debates about political ideology. Regardless of the type of political system, some form of "big push" does seem important, though the push need not necessarily be industrial. A "big push" involving extension of rural roads, extensive small-scale irrigation, and agricultural diversification could be more effective than inappropriate and overly capital-intensive industrial development.

Capital Accumulation (127)

An increase in a nation's stock of real capital, that is, its net investment in fixed assets. Examples of such assets would be factories, dams, various kinds of production equipment, scientific laboratories, and hotels, which generate services to tourists. Capital goods are those produced for use in the production of other goods or services. To increase its capital accumulation, a nation must increase its savings and related investments as a percentage of its gross national product. If a nation's total GNP were devoted to consumption, there would be no funds remaining for capital accumulation and, consequently, for economic growth.

Significance Regardless of a nation's political ideology, it must find ways to enhance its capital accumulation if it seeks increased long-term economic growth and improved economic welfare for future generations. Nations and peoples differ in the ways in which they value the present versus the future. An emphasis on long-term capital accumulation reflects a strong future orientation. Countries such as Japan, South Korea, and Taiwan have been noted in recent decades for their emphasis on capital accumulation.

Capital-Intensive Techniques (128)

An economic development strategy emphasizing the use of capital relative to other factors of production. This approach is based on the assumption of the need to increase productivity as quickly as possible. It is also emphasized by transnational corporations, which are a major source of capital goods. A prestige-enhancing demonstration effect also fosters the use of capital-intensive techniques: countries are proud to show that they are using the most current production

technologies. *See also* LABOR-INTENSIVE TECHNIQUES, 157; APPRO-
PRIATE TECHNOLOGY, 276; DEMONSTRATION EFFECT, 135.

Significance   An overreliance on capital-intensive techniques can
have adverse effects on development, particularly with respect to
meeting basic needs. With an overemphasis on capital intensity,
major development projects will generate far too few jobs. An overemphasis on capital-intensive processes may also contribute to a foreign exchange drain and a growing debt crisis. Capital-intensive
techniques are appropriate in those areas where they are crucial for
international competitiveness and related technological capability.

Capital versus Consumption Goods   (129)

A distinction between types of economic production and priority with
important implications for a country's long-term development potential. Capital goods are basically those that can be used to produce
other goods. In contrast, consumption goods are those to be consumed as an end in themselves, with no implications for future productive capacity. Examples of capital goods would be factories and
other production facilities, machinery, equipment, computers, and
scientific laboratories. A capital good par excellence would be robots
that produce other robots. Consumption goods would include luxury
automobiles, housing, movie theaters, and stadia.

Significance   Generally, an emphasis on capital goods reflects a
long-term perspective and a willingness to forego consumption in the
present to enhance future economic productive capacity. Japan's neglect of public and private housing in the postwar period typifies such
an orientation. In contrast, the United States has invested much more
heavily in the consumption good of housing. Some balance in emphasis between capital and consumption goods is necessary. Without a
certain degree of access to consumption goods, individuals may lose
incentives to work productively or may seek to migrate to societies
where they may enjoy access to consumption goods. Effective fiscal
policies can have a major impact on a country's relative priority on
capital versus consumption goods. For example, U.S. tax law allowing
the deduction of mortgage expenses encourages an emphasis on the
consumption good of housing. In contrast, Japan's tax laws that encourage savings provide an incentive for greater investment in capital
goods such as robots and computers. Countries that emphasize the
short-term and give priority to consumption goods inevitably have
more limited long-term economic growth prospects.

Central Place Theory (130)

A deductive theory developed by the German geographer Walter Christaller to explain the distribution of towns in any society. His theory was described in a 1936 volume titled *Die Zentralen Orte in Süddeutschland,* translated into English in 1966 by C. W. Baskin and titled *Central Places in Southern Germany.* An integral part of the theory was that key goods and services would tend to be concentrated in central places. He proposed a hierarchy of central places with a hexagonal spatial configuration. Capitalist markets were viewed as a key element in shaping the distribution of central places. As an empirical indicator for assessing such centrality, Christaller proposed the number of inhabitants per telephone. An alternative formulation of central place theory was developed in 1940 by August Lösch, a German regional economist.

Significance   Though Christaller developed his concept based on German experience, it has much broader implications for understanding the economic interdependence of urban and rural areas. G. William Skinner, for example, has used central place theory in explaining urbanization patterns in traditional China. Many developing countries are dominated by prominent central places, such as Mexico City, Manila, Bangkok, and Cairo. Since central places clearly serve as poles of development, most regional planners and economists are concerned about the development of policies to enhance the spread of central places to remote backward areas to facilitate broader access to important and essential goods and services.

Commodity Agreements (131)

International agreements between major producers of a basic commodity designed to control fluctuations in its price. Primary commodities generally have long production cycles that make it difficult for producers to adjust to short-term fluctuations in demand. Further, many developing countries depend heavily on the export earnings of one or two basic commodities. Jamaica, for example, gains half of its export earnings from bauxite, and Bolivia 30 percent from tin. Individual producers, especially highly indebted countries, tend to increase production to increase earnings, but the cumulative effect is lowered prices. Commodity agreements are tools of producer associations to coordinate and regulate production and supply. These associations also work to improve their position vis-à-vis transnational corporations involved in production, shipping, and processing of raw commodities. The best known and most successful of the producer associations is the Organization of Petroleum Exporting Countries (OPEC). Other agreements have met with less success as indicated by the steady drop in commodity prices over the last decade. Producer associations and commodity agreements have been formed for nearly every major commodity. These include: the Intergovernmental Council of Copper Exporting Countries (CIPEC, 1967); International Bauxite Association (IBA, 1975); Association of Iron Exporting Countries (1975); International Tin Agreement (ITA, 1956); Inter-African Coffee Organization (IACO, 1960); Malagasy African Coffee Organization (OAMCAF, 1960); International Coffee Agreement (1962, revised in 1976); Cocoa Producers' Alliance (COPAL, 1962); Group of Latin American and Caribbean Sugar Exporting Countries (GEPLACEA, 1974); International Sugar Organization (1954); Union of Banana Exporting Countries (UPEB, 1974); International Tea Committee (ITC, 1933); Association of Natural Rubber Producing Countries (1976); Asian and Pacific Coconut Community (1969); African Groundnut Council (1964); African Lumber Organization (1975); Pepper Community (1972); and Jute International (1975). *See also* ORGANIZATION OF PETROLEUM EXPORTING COUNTRIES, 429; NEW INTERNATIONAL ECONOMIC ORDER, 161.

Significance   Many of the organizations and agreements listed above were formed in the mid–1970s in the wake of OPEC's success and at the height of the debate concerning the New International Economic Order (NIEO). They are part of a broader attempt on the part of many developing countries to gain greater control of their own economies, systems highly dependent upon the export earnings of commodities. Some of the agreements helped stabilize prices, and others succeeded in temporarily raising prices. Still others, such as the bauxite and copper agreements, failed within a few years. None matched the dramatic success of OPEC in forming an effective international cartel. But even with their limited success, it may be argued that without the commodity agreements, terms of trade for many LDCs would have deteriorated even further.

Comparative Advantage   (132)
An economic concept derived from classical international trade theory that assumes that each nation should concentrate on the production of *only* those goods it can produce more efficiently than its international competitors. Through a free international trade regime, a nation can trade for those commodities or goods in which it lacks a comparative advantage. By following the principle of comparative advantage, worldwide productive efficiency will be maximized. Prob-

lems of inequality could then be dealt with through explicit schemes of redistribution rather than the inefficient distortion of optimal trade flows. Despite the attractiveness of the ideal of comparative advantage, its practical realization is limited by a number of factors. First, the assumption of pure international free trade does not apply, since there are numerous distortions imposed by government trade barriers, tariffs, and subsidies. Second, there is the problem of static versus dynamic conditions. Less developed countries (LDCs) with rich tropical rain forests may not have a contemporary comparative advantage in biotechnology, but in a dynamic framework with a time horizon of several decades, they could potentially develop such a comparative advantage. Third, international exchange rates are sometimes distorted and thus true costs are not accurately reflected. A fourth and serious challenge to comparative advantage is the inherent problem of vulnerability. If an LDC has a comparative advantage in only a small number of goods or commodities it could become highly vulnerable to shifts in international markets and prices. Thus, to reduce vulnerability, such countries may choose to ignore comparative advantage in favor of increasing economic diversification. *See also* INFANT INDUSTRY, 154; ECONOMIC DIVERSIFICATION, 142; COMMODITY AGREEMENTS, 131.

Significance   Despite the contemporary limitations to the application of the principle of comparative advantage or comparative cost, its policy relevance persists. For example, gross economic inefficiencies may result in promoting prestige, showcase projects in which a nation seriously lacks any comparative advantage. Similarly, efforts to maximize economic diversification without regard to comparative advantage can result in dramatic economic inefficiencies and waste. The real challenge to both international and development economists is to achieve a proper balance between static and dynamic conditions and a similar balance between the need to achieve economic diversity to reduce vulnerability and the need to respect differential conditions affecting potential variations in the economies of production.

Countertrade (133)
An agreement that allows a mix of payment for sales in goods and foreign exchange. Currently countertrade represents 20 percent of global trade. Among many forms of countertrade are barter, counterpurchase, reverse countertrade, compensation/buyback, bilateral clearing and switch, evidence accounts, offset trade, countertrade linkage, and joint ventures. The informative volume titled *Countertrade: Practices, Strategies, and Tactics* (1987) by Costas G.

Alexandrides and Barbara Bowers contains a detailed description of each of these types of countertrade. The most rapidly growing type is buyback, which normally involves a company or corporation building a production facility in an LDC and agreeing to buy back the production.

Significance   There is a common mistaken notion that countertrade is the result of the 1982 global debt crisis. Actually, countertrade has a long tradition and has been an important mechanism for those economies with severe foreign exchange constraints. Eastern Bloc countries have had long experience with the practice. Countertrade does represent a response to issues raised by UNCTAD concerning trade opportunities for LDCs and fundamental issues related to NIEO. Countertrade facilitates export diversification and access to global markets. Unlike their Japanese counterparts, U.S. corporations have been slow to realize the need for countertrade to enable them to remain internationally competitive. Only with the Export Trade Company Act of 1982 were U.S. banks and other corporations allowed to form general trading companies, which are essential for effective countertrade. Among countries heavily involved in countertrade are the People's Republic of China and Japan. The Japanese corporations, Mitsubishi, Mitsui, Marubeni, and C. Itoh, have been actively involved in countertrade and have impressive information systems relevant to such a trading strategy. The dramatic economic changes in Eastern Europe in the late 1980s and 1990s will likely result in increased economic ties with the West, resulting in the need for even greater use of flexible economic devices such as countertrade.

Debt Crisis   (134)
The condition of chronic and massive indebtedness experienced by many developing countries. Cumulative Third World debt stood at $1.3 trillion in 1990. The beginning of the crisis is commonly identified as Friday, April 13, 1982, though the seeds had been planted much earlier. On that day Mexico declared its inability to make interest payments on its $80 billion debt, the first major debtor to do so.

The main roots of the debt crisis can be traced to the oil crisis of 1973. The rapid rise in oil prices dramatically increased the revenues of oil-exporting nations, especially those of the Arab gulf states, while raising the energy budget outlays of most LDCs. A large share of the massive revenues accruing to the OPEC nations was deposited with international banking institutions. This wealth, in turn, led to lower interest rates and greater inflation on a global scale. Consequently, while the flow of official development assistance (ODA) to developing countries remained fairly constant, private lending, private investment, and export credits involving the LDCs increased rapidly from the mid-1970s until the global recession of the early 1980s. Net lending by commercial banks to non-OPEC developing countries peaked at $35 billion in 1981. By 1984 this figure was a negative $10 billion. Within a short period the combination of rising interest rates, a world trade slump, capital flight, commodity price drops, and misplaced investments created a situation whereby debt service payments began to consume a high portion of total export earnings of developing countries. Many countries were unable to service their debts to private banks, the lenders of roughly two-thirds of the $1.3 trillion figure, and turned to the multilateral lending institutions, primarily the International Monetary Fund (IMF), taking new loans to pay off previous loans. IMF lending to the LDCs peaked in 1983. From 1980 to 1985, more than 90 countries arranged loans with the IMF. This, too, was a temporary solution. By 1986 the IMF, along with the commercial banks, was taking in more funds from the LDCs than it was lending. In fact, the total flow of capital from less to more developed countries between 1982 and 1986 was an estimated $220 billion. During that period Brazil, Latin America's "economic miracle" which had become the largest LDC debtor, paid $70 billion to service its debt while adding $20 billion to its total debt. In 1987 Brazil and 10 other nations suspended all debt payments for periods of varying duration. Peru declared that it would not pay more than 10 percent of its export earnings to service its debt. The debt crisis has since been characterized by stopped, delayed, and partial payments; considerable rescheduling arrangements; and limited forgiveness, involving the IMF and related structural adjustments. Meanwhile, no developing country has significantly reduced its overall foreign debt under any program. In addition to rescheduling (an extension in the payment time period), two of the more creative partial solutions are debt-for-equity and debt-for-nature swaps. These involve third parties that pay off part of a country's loan at greatly reduced rates in exchange for stock or industrial investments or nature reserve acreage in the debtor nation. Equity swaps have helped retire $14 billion in debt while nature swaps have been much more limited in scope. Both arrangements involve debtor nations relinquishing some control over national assets and, by implication, a degree of sovereignty.

The Latin American countries account for the greatest share of the total LDC debt figure while the African share continues to rise. Many of the Asian nations are also heavily indebted but generally have lower debt-service ratios owing to large export earnings. The annual net flow of capital from South to North is estimated at $43 billion.

International debt is an increasing concern of several Eastern European nations as well, Poland and Hungary in particular. The United States is by far the world's largest debtor nation, but with the largest economy, it maintains a relatively low debt service ratio. *See also* DEBT SERVICE RATIO, 316; INTERNATIONAL MONETARY FUND, 420; DEBT-FOR-NATURE SWAPS, 259.

Significance   The international debt crisis has emerged as the central issue in North-South relations and, with no dramatic or even adequate solutions in sight, it is likely to remain so for years to come. No country has yet chosen bankruptcy lest it become a pariah in the international financial system. The internal cost of such a decision would also be enormous, considering the dependencies on imports and foreign capital that exist in the debtor countries. Likewise, it would not be prudent for the lending institutions to allow total default as some return is better than none at all. For these reasons, the idea of a debtors' cartel, as proposed by Fidel Castro and others, has never materialized. The debts of the LDCs continue to be considered and renegotiated primarily on a bilateral basis. The prospects of any nation's meaningfully reducing, let alone retiring, its entire debt anytime in the foreseeable future appear dim. Meanwhile, lending institutions and debtor countries struggle to find arrangements that allow for repayment without diminishing the ability of the debtor to sustain economic growth.

The real crisis has not had a great effect on the private lenders. Third World loans only account for an average of 6 percent of the portfolios of the private international banks, and few lenders have taken significant losses on loans to debtor countries. The IMF, in effect, covers the loans of private banks and the World Bank. IMF loans are frequently received under terms of structural adjustment, programs designed to increase export earnings and reduce national deficits, which have found some measure of success in reducing debt-service ratios. However, because the adjustment programs involve currency devaluation and curtailment of many subsidies and services to the poor, the immediate social and political costs can be quite high. It is the poor, most of whom never realized any marked benefits from the original loans, who feel the effects of the debt crisis most directly. Thus the debt crisis has proven to be detrimental to both macro and micro systems, ultimately increasing the vulnerability of the poor in the world finance system. The debt crisis points to a need to reconsider the ability of the current international economic system and its major mechanisms to foster sustained growth and development among the majority of developing nations.

Demonstration Effect (135)

The tendency for those living in developing nations to imitate the economic, technological, and cultural patterns of the developed nations. The demonstration effect concept is closely related to cultural imperialism, but with fewer negative connotations. An example would be the building of modern automotive expressways in cities such as Jakarta, Bangkok, and Mexico City to relieve modern traffic congestion. Another common example is the increasing use in developing nations of the latest, most modern conveniences, such as color television and videocassette recorders. *See also* CULTURAL IMPERIALISM, 220; CAPITAL-INTENSIVE TECHNIQUES, 128; APPROPRIATE TECHNOLOGY, 276.

Significance The demonstration effect is clearly a two-edged sword. Some patterns of modern industrial societies are clearly worthy of emulation, while others are highly inappropriate in numerous developmental contexts. In a positive example of the demonstration effect, Singapore and Malaysia are encouraging their people to "look East" to emulate the Japanese in areas such as industrial quality control, family stability, and organizational commitment. Perhaps the most common negative example is an overemphasis on the consumption of luxury consumer goods. In *The Pacific Century* (1986), Staffan Linder discusses what may be the most important demonstration effect, one related to a growing desire to emulate the economic dynamism of key Pacific Basin nations, such as Korea and Taiwan.

Devaluation and Depreciation (136)

The lowering of the value of a national currency with respect to its exchange value with major world currencies such as the U.S. dollar, Japanese yen, or German mark. The lowering in value may come as a result of market forces affecting a floating rate (depreciation), which changes on a regular basis, or as an explicit governmental policy decision to alter the exchange rate of a country (devaluation). The major reasons for explicit devaluations are to improve export performance and/or to increase tourism by making a nation's products and services cheaper on the world market. A devaluation or depreciation will also increase the cost of imports and thereby contribute to inflationary pressures. Patterns or histories of devaluation also strongly encourage both legal and illegal capital outflows. There are basically three approaches to studying and analyzing the impact of devaluations: (1) an elasticities methodology, which focuses on the impact of the devaluation on relative export and import levels associated with changes in their prices; (2) an absorption approach, which emphasizes the effect of the devaluation; and (3) a monetary approach, which focuses on the effect of the devaluation on the real value of money holdings in the economy and its related impact on spending. *See also* AUSTERITY PROGRAM, 124.

Significance   Much thinking about devaluation tends to be overly simplistic. In some cases, devaluations represent only adjustments. For example, if the dollar has been appreciating rapidly during a period, a currency tied to the dollar may be depreciated, but in fact the devaluation may keep it stable vis-à-vis other important international currencies. Also, the success of a devaluation in increasing exports and reducing imports depends on relevant economic elasticities. For example, if there is strong world demand for rice, regardless of price, the demand for rice is inelastic with respect to price. In such a case, a devaluation may actually result in lost revenues. Similarly, if the demand for imported brandy is inelastic relative to price, devaluation may lead to an even greater import bill. Thus, devaluations need to be based on a careful analysis of relevant international market elasticities. Another issue related to devaluation is the critical need for confidentiality. Open parliamentary or perhaps even cabinet-level discussions of a possible devaluation are impossible, for they would automatically generate rational capital flight in anticipation of a possible devaluation. Thus, discussions of policies related to devaluation must take place in secrecy, with the utmost discretion. The discrepancy between official and black-market foreign exchange rates in some countries is a clear sign of an overvalued currency. Devaluations are often politically unpopular and can adversely affect the stature of local political leaders. For this reason, there is common resentment against outside pressure from international bodies such as the IMF to devalue a national currency.

Development Decades   (137)
Goals and strategies for development during the 1960s, 1970s, 1980s, and 1990s laid out by the United Nations General Assembly near the beginning of each decade. Goals for the First UN Development Decade were adopted in 1961. The plan stressed general goals of development common to nearly all nations and more specific goals such as 5 percent annual economic growth for all nations, but the plan offered little in the way of specific strategies. In an effort to rectify this shortcoming, and given the somewhat disappointing results of the first half of the decade, the General Assembly in 1968 requested the secretary-general to prepare a preliminary framework for

the international development strategy for the 1970s. The framework was used to set more specific goals and strategies for different sectors in the international development strategy for the Second Development Decade. General Assembly Resolution 2626 called for 6 percent worldwide growth in gross domestic product (GDP), 8 percent annual expansion of manufacturing output, 4 percent growth in agricultural production, and other sectoral goals. The strategy was based on the premise of continued rapid economic growth in the LDCs, coupled with increases in official development assistance. The Western industrialized nations were asked to contribute 0.7 percent of their GNP to aid. The overall GNP and industrial output goals were in fact met during the 1970s. But rapid population growth contributed to an actual decline in per capita GNP rates in many countries. Agricultural production barely kept pace with population, and the Third World's share of world trade actually decreased. Few Organization for Economic Cooperation and Development (OECD) countries met the 0.7 percent goal and the gaps between rich and poor nations continued to grow. With this in mind, the heads of government of the nonaligned countries, at their Sixth Conference in Havana (September 1979), postulated a new international development strategy, which stressed the need for implementation of the systematic reforms of the international economic system previously called for in the 1974 UN proposal for the new international economic order (NIEO). Thus the tone was set for the UN debate regarding the Third Development Decade. The trend of the 1980s, however, was not toward multilaterally led reforms but toward further concentration of economic policy decisions by the Group of 7 of the world's leading free-market industrialized countries (Canada, France, Germany, Great Britain, Italy, Japan, and the United States). As a result of the debt crisis and the further relative impoverishment of many LDCs, the 1980s are often referred to as the lost decade. *See also* DEVELOPMENT, 107; MULTILATERAL AID AGENCIES, 291.

Significance The formulation of world development goals, as set forth and evaluated in the international development strategy, helped establish important benchmarks for the members of the United Nations. The development decades provide a useful framework for assessing the trends and patterns of international development and the evolution of development thinking and policy. Ideas and issues do not, of course, fall neatly within ten-year periods, but periodic, directed reflection by the United Nations is a valuable tool for establishing specific development strategies. In establishing the First Development Decade, the General Assembly sought to dramatize the world's development efforts, to call for long-range planning, and to mobilize and sustain support by both North and South in the effort to achieve self-sustaining growth in the LDCs. Despite major failures, these remain the goals of the United Nations and its members in the decade of the 1990s.

Disarmament and Development (138)

The set of issues and the debate revolving around the relationship between world military spending and development. On the most basic level, outlays for the military and arms are juxtaposed against spending on other sectors such as health and education. Ruth Leger Sivard's *World Military and Social Expenditures: Annual Report on World Priorities* provides a well-documented statistical overview of national and international priorities on a yearly basis. Given the unmet basic human needs of many of the world's citizens, the nearly $1 trillion spent each year on military research, weapons, and armed forces is one of the great tragedies of our day. In addition to direct military costs, Sivard points out that one-quarter of the world's scientists are engaged in military research and development while 1.6 billion people do not have access to safe drinking water.

The disarmament and development debate is a central issue in North-South relations. In the 1970s, discussion of the issue increased, with the focus on the superpower arms race. A 1972 UN report, A/8469, gave a fairly straightforward estimate of the resources absorbed by military activities and the related adverse effects on development. In 1978 the UN formed the Group of Government Experts on the Relationship between Disarmament and Development. The group's three-year work culminated in UN document A/36/356, which came to be known as the Thorsson Report after the group's chairperson, Inga Thorsson. This was followed in 1982 by report A/37/386 to the secretary-general, "Economic and Social Consequences of the Arms Race and Its Extremely Harmful Effects on World Peace and Security." The discussion, in and outside the UN, evolved beyond quantitative analysis and comparison of expenditures to examination of both North and South militarism and militarization. The reports, for what they did and did not cover, raised further questions regarding the linkages between arms transfers, national security, social revolution, military assistance, military regimes, human rights, and broader development issues. For example, 80 percent of expenditures for arms are for conventional weapons manufactured almost exclusively in the North but used almost exclusively in the South where nearly all the estimated 22 million war-related deaths since World War II have occurred. Two-thirds of arms sales are conducted between the major arms dealers (France, the United

States, the Soviet Union) and developing countries, representing a shift of over $400 billion from South to North in the last three decades with no development benefits to the LDCs. This practice results partly from what many consider to be highly misplaced priorities on the part of LDC governments and partly from the common practice of tying economic and military "aid."

The disarmament and development question is also posed as a human rights issue, given the poor human rights records of most military-dominated governments and the willing support of the superpowers. Recently this has taken the form of support for low-intensity conflict (LIC) in situations where direct large-scale military support is considered politically unacceptable. This policy has proven to be particularly devastating to civilians migrating in the combat areas. Third World militias and military regimes have been touted as forces of modernization, guardians of infant democracies, and creators of stability deemed necessary for national economic development. As a whole, however, military governments have not proven to be the catalysts of development that some Western theorists once anticipated. Too often in developing countries, the military has been the first and only institution to modernize, thereby perpetuating a cycle of militarization, poverty, and oppression. The military is also frequently perceived by its critics in developing countries as being highly parasitical.

An excellent discussion and bibliography concerning disarmament, development, and related issues is provided by Nicole Ball in *The Military in the Development Process: A Guide to Issues* (1981). Sivard and the Swedish International Peace Research Institute (SIPRI) both provide annual reports on global military spending and disarmament. *See also* PEACE DIVIDEND, 165; LOW-INTENSITY CONFLICT, 206.

Significance   The disarmament and development debate not only encapsulates some of the most pressing issues in North-South relations, but it highlights misplaced priorities in both areas. The reduction of military expenditures in order to release resources to meet economic and social needs has been a matter of concern at the UN since 1950 when the General Assembly adopted Resolution 380. It called for every state to "agree to reduce to a minimum the diversion for armaments of human and economic resources, and to strive towards development of such resources for the general welfare, with due respect to the needs of the underdeveloped areas of the world." With rare exception, most notably Costa Rica which has no army, the nations of the world have generally ignored the resolution. Military spending in developing countries continues to divert precious resources from development efforts, though much of the increase in arms expenditures of nonindustrialized nations over the past two decades is accounted for by the purchases of high-tech items by a few oil-exporting nations. Further, instruments of internal repression can be relatively cheap. At the same time, the LDCs continue to point to the detrimental effects of the superpower military establishments, in terms of diverted world resources and of external interference with world politics.

Interestingly, the Soviet Union's decision in the 1980s to reverse the growth of its military outlay stems from the detrimental effect the expenditure was having on its own prospects for continued development. Recent speculation regarding a potential "peace dividend" anticipated as a result of easing tensions between East and West has revitalized the disarmament and development discussion, raising vital questions as to how such a dividend might best be used to enhance national and world development. The debt crisis and growing links being drawn between environment and development have also prompted a fundamental reconsideration of the notion of national security as narrowly defined in military terms. As the Brandt Commission concluded, "More arms do not make the world safer, just poorer."

Dualism (139)

The two-sector nature of developing economies, in which a relatively modern, prosperous sector exists simultaneously with a traditional, impoverished sector. Elaborate and competing economic models have been developed to explain dualism and the transitions and interactions between the two sectors. The Nobel laureate Sir Arthur Lewis was the earliest modern exponent of a classical dualistic model. Dale Jorgenson, John C. Fei, and Gustov Ranis also developed models of dualistic development. Dualism has many dimensions that go beyond merely economic differences. Six key dimensions of dualism highlighted by Kelly, Williamson, and Cheetham (1972) are: (1) social systems, (2) racial or ethnic differences, (3) production conditions, (4) demographic behavior, (5) consumer expenditures and savings behavior, and (6) links to domestic and foreign sectors. The phenomenon of nonproportional growth is central to the concept of dualism. Common reference is also made to technological dualism, which reflects the dramatic disparities in levels of technology between modern and traditional sectors. Ambiguities related to spatial aspects of dualism are common. Many urban centers such as Calcutta and Lima contain important elements of impoverished and traditional society. In contrast, there may be pockets of modernity in rural or more remote areas. *See also* UNEVEN DEVELOPMENT, 173; GROWTH WITH EQUITY, 151.

Significance   Dualism is a powerful concept whose meaning transcends the problems of developing countries. Michael Harrington's insightful and shocking *The Other America* (1963) illustrated that even the world's richest economy has important elements of dualism. With respect to developing countries, Peter Berger in *Pyramids of Sacrifice* (1975) has described Brazil as a blend of Sweden (the modern sector) and Indonesia (the traditional sector). Similarly, he writes of Mexico and "the other Mexico," and Pakistan and "the other Pakistan." The condition of dualism reflects the outcomes of uneven development and unfortunately appears to be a common phenomenon of the development process.

Dutch Disease (140)

An economic backlash suffered by a number of nations, both developed and developing, that export large quantities of oil and natural gas and earn enormous amounts of foreign exchange, but that eventually encounter the problems of domestic inflation, higher unemployment, and stagnation of the oil economy (Gillis et al., 1987). The name derives from the situation faced by the Netherlands, which had enjoyed considerable economic prosperity after World War II until 1975. The Dutch economic performance until that time was remarkable in almost all respects: low inflation rate, low unemployment rate, and consistently good growth in GNP. This occurred because the Dutch traditional export sector, one-third of which is agricultural products, was highly competitive in the world economy. Nevertheless, by 1975 natural gas exports had increased to account for 10 percent of Dutch exports, and the nation had a significant trade surplus. Government expenditures, especially on social welfare, were increased because of the higher taxes obtained from gas exports. An unexpected result was the dramatic increase of the inflation rate from only 2 percent in 1970 to 10 percent in 1975. Between 1973 and 1978, the inflow of foreign exchange earned from gas exports helped cause the Dutch guilder to appreciate by about 30 percent relative to its major trading partners. As a consequence, traditional exporters suffered higher domestic costs together with lower guilder earnings from a decline in exports. Therefore, agricultural and labor-intensive exports became stagnant, leading to a drastic increase in unemployment. The Dutch GNP growth rate dropped from 5 percent in the 1960s to only 1 to 2 percent by the end of the 1970s.

Significance   The implications of the Dutch disease extend far beyond the Netherlands. Other large oil- or natural gas-exporting countries such as Nigeria, Mexico, and Indonesia face similar economic traps. In fact, any country receiving windfall profits from exports of natural resources to the global market is potentially subject to the Dutch disease. Actually, the disease can be avoided by not spending the higher income from oil revenues on domestic goods or transfer payments, which will inevitably increase the domestic money supply and eventually cause inflation, but instead keeping the revenues overseas or spending them on additional imports to diversify an economy. Since most governments are forced to spend most of their revenues, a more practical solution would be a systematic policy of gradual depreciation of the currency, which will help prevent higher costs in other export sectors. Indonesia, for example, has utilized this strategy. Even though losses in other sectors in a booming oil-exporting economy cannot be totally avoided, they can be minimized by such sensible policy measures.

The Dutch disease does not apply to countries such as Japan, South Korea, Taiwan, or Singapore that have emphasized the export of manufactured goods that are tightly linked with the rest of the domestic economy and the external sector. If inflation rates in these countries grow faster than the world's rate, their currency exchange rates tend to depreciate, helping to keep them competitive in international markets. Unlike the manufacturing sector, oil and natural gas production are slightly affected by domestic costs or the external sector. Therefore, even if the rate of inflation in oil-exporting countries is extremely high, it has little impact on the profitability of oil exports.

Economic Democracy (141)

The spread of democratic principles to the economy through worker-controlled production and the extension of democratic choice to work, employment, income, and technology. The concept was popularized by Martin Carnoy and Derek Shearer in their book, *Economic Democracy: The Challenge of the 1980s* (1980). Their extremely broad concept calls for the transfer of capital from corporations to the public and a more equitable distribution of economic wealth. In the words of the British political writer, C. A. R. Crosland, economic democracy would mean "a diverse, diffused, pluralistic, and heterogeneous pattern of ownership" (Carnoy and Shearer 1980:36). Advocates of economic democracy find it unhealthy for the ownership of the productive wealth to rest in the hands of an elite minority. In Carnoy's view the ideal of economic democracy is more consistent with the laissez-faire vision of Adam Smith than are existing corporate-dominated economies. A system of economic democracy would involve a diversity of economic players such as cooperatives, worker-owned firms, community development corporations, and public enterprises. Examples of economic democracy are the Basque industrial cooperatives of Mondragon in northern Spain and the worker-owned plywood mills of the Pacific Northwest. *See also* MARTIN CARNOY, 10.

Significance   Most discussions of economic democracy have focused on countries such as the United States, Spain, France, Yugoslavia, and the Scandinavian nations. However, it is also relevant to developing countries. In fact, perhaps the most widespread use of worker self-management has been in economies such as China (particularly under Mao), Cuba, Chile (under Allende), and Nicaragua (under Ortega). It is important to note that economic democracy is not synonymous with nationalization of industry. For example although the economy of Burma is almost totally nationalized, it does not reflect economic democracy because of its totalitarian economic structure. The development successes of both China and Japan confirm the critical importance of economic democracy. In both societies, workers have had an important voice in production processes; the concept of quality control circles in Japan emphasizes the active participation of workers in decisions affecting their work lives. Singapore, which also has enjoyed impressive development success, has emphasized worker participation in quality control circles and public goods in areas such as housing, health, and on-the-job training.

In Mancur Olson's study of the growth and decline of nations, he found a key explanation of decline to be the existence of powerful, vested economic interests that resist change and innovation. Monopoly capital, the major obstacle to economic democracy, seems highly related to the vested economic interests identified by Olson. A system of economic democracy should facilitate innovations such as solar energy, high-speed public transporation (bullet trains), more energy-efficient and environmentally sound agriculture, and more cost-effective health care. The key issue in the debate about economic democracy is whether such a system would enhance productivity, investment, and technological innovation, while simultaneously increasing social justice and reducing worker alienation. Another major question is the relationship between political and economic democracy. It seems clear that the former is a necessary but not sufficient condition for the latter.

Economic Diversification   (142)
Changes in the economic structure of an economy or society resulting in a broader array of economic activities and sectors. A major

rationale for diversification is to reduce vulnerability that results from dependence on a single or few commodities and industries. Closely related to general economic diversification is export diversification, for which the basic rationale is essentially the same. Traditionally, many developing countries have relied on only one or two export products to generate needed foreign exchange. Examples include the dependence of Guatemala on the export of bananas, Cuba on sugar, Papua New Guinea on copper, and Costa Rica on beef. In such undiversified economies a dramatic drop in the price of a key agricultural commodity such as coffee or sugar would have a devastating effect. Countries of the South that have recently been successful in pursuing economic diversification include Chile, Brazil, Mexico, Thailand, the Philippines, Indonesia, and Malaysia. As a dramatic illustration of diversification, only 12 percent of Thailand's foreign exchange earnings currently derive from the export of rice, rubber, and tin. *See also* COMPARATIVE ADVANTAGE, 132.

Significance   Despite the apparent appeal of the diversification concept, it raises complex international economic-policy issues. For example, a potential inconsistency exists between the strategy of diversification and comparative economic advantage, which often suggests the need to specialize in those products in which a nation has special advantages. To diversify into areas in which a country lacks a comparative advantage may result in waste and inefficiency. Another problem is the lack of agreement as to how to measure the extent of diversification. For example, one measure might be the percentage of the economy accounted for by the leading industry. A more comprehensive measure would be to compute a coefficient of variation, based on variations in the percentages of the total economy of a specified number of leading sectors. The larger such a coefficient, the less diversified would be the economy. A perfectly diversified economy would have a coefficient of zero, indicating the equal importance of each of the numerous sectors. Obviously, perfect diversity is an ideal condition to which no actual economy even comes close. An appropriate balance between diversity to reduce vulnerability and comparative advantage to enhance efficiency represents a major challenge to economic planners and policymakers.

Economic Surplus   **(143)**
A key development concept defined as production minus consumption. In his influential volume, *The Political Economy of Growth* (1957), Paul Baran makes a distinction between actual and potential economic surplus. The higher the rate of economic surplus, the greater

the rate of economic growth. This element in Baran's thinking is consistent with conventional development theory which employs the capital-output ratio as a central determinant of economic growth. But Baran diverges dramatically from conventional development theory in his stress on a normative potential economic surplus, which is defined as potential production minus essential consumption. Potential production could be obtained if individuals were fully employed or diverted away from nonproductive employment (e.g., arms making, prostitution, advertising) to productive employment. Essential consumption excludes wasteful or superfluous luxury consumption unrelated to basic human needs. Baran argues that the actual economic surplus in capitalistic developing countries diverges significantly from the potential economic surplus, citing statistics showing that the actual economic surplus ranges from approximately one-fifth to one-third of the potential economic surplus. *See also* PAUL BARAN, 5.

Significance   Though Baran introduced the concept of economic surplus more than 30 years ago, it continues to have salience as we approach development problems of the twenty-first century. The country that perhaps best reflected the implementation of Baran's concept was China under Mao in the years after the revolution and prior to the Cultural Revolution. Excessive luxury consumption continues to be a barrier to increasing local savings and investments in many developing countries. Another barrier is that many countries are unable to utilize labor effectively and experience much underemployment and unproductive employment. Given Baran's arguments, the potential economic surplus would be unattainable under conventional capitalism and thus socialist revolutions are necessary. What Baran fails to address is the inefficiency of overly centralized, excessive bureaucracies associated with state socialism.

EMF Index   **(144)**
The Emerging Markets Free index, developed by Morgan Stanley and Company. The EMF index is an aggregate figure that reflects the stock-market performance of seven select nations from the developing world, namely, Argentina, Chile, Jordan, Malaysia, Mexico, the Philippines, and Thailand (Yemma 1988:11). For example, from January 1, 1988, to July 29, 1988, this index increased 38 percent. During the same period, the U.S. stock market, in contrast, increased only 9.1 percent and the world market increased 11.4 percent. Though the index includes only seven nations, they represent three major regions of the developing world: Latin America, the Middle East, and Southeast Asia.

Significance   In recent years investors have expressed growing interest in diversifying their investments more globally. The economic dynamism of certain parts of the developing world such as Southeast Asia have stimulated investor interest. Thus, Morgan Stanley and Company developed the EMF index to enable investors to track the stock-market performance of key developing economies. The Templeton mutual fund group, a major pioneer in international investing, in early 1987 created a new Templeton Emerging Markets Fund, which is traded as a closed-end mutual fund on the American Stock Exchange. This fund provides investors an opportunity to invest in the stock markets of select developing nations. Investments in such funds obviously involve special risks since certain developing nations such as Mexico have unstable foreign exchange rates. Given the dramatic economic success of some developing countries, the Morgan Stanley EMF index provides a convenient indicator for assessing the potential of investment in developing countries.

Equality versus Equity Distinction   **(145)**
A differentiation between two related and often confused concepts central to discussions of the distributional dimensions of development. The MIT economist Lester Thurow, in his important work, *Generating Inequality* (1975), emphasized this distinction. Equity is the more philosophically and economically complex concept because it is highly normative and focuses on the just distribution of economic resources. Fairness is also an integral part of the equity concept. In contrast, equality is a more straightforward mathematical concept that reflects the extent of differences with respect to the possession of any desired goods, resources, or services. Equality does not necessarily imply equity. For example, since costs of living normally vary from region to region within a country, a per capita income equality across states or provinces might not be equitable. Similarly, for everyone in an organization to receive an equal salary would be grossly unfair, given differences in responsibility, experience, education, and competence. Another related concept is equality of opportunity. This concept normally denotes that the life chances of an individual, particularly in the educational realm, should not be adversely affected by ascriptive characteristics such as gender, race, socioeconomic status, or geographic origins. *See also* SOCIAL JUSTICE, 214; GINI COEFFICIENT, 325.

Significance   C. G. Weeramantry, in *Equality and Freedom* (1976), argues that equality is the burning global issue. Thus, it is important to avoid confusion among equality, equity, and equality of opportunity. The British geographer David M. Smith, author of *Where the Grass Is Greener: Living in an Unequal World* (1982), provides creative and insightful tools for understanding equality and equity issues. The highly normative nature of the equity concept also reflects the inherently subjective nature of the social sciences. Another influential work relevant to the equity versus equality distinction is *The Theory of Justice* (1971) by Harvard philosopher John Rawls.

Export Expansion Strategy (146)

An outward-oriented strategy that emphasizes the development of industries capable of exporting to world markets. The postwar successes of Asia-Pacific economies, such as those of Japan, South Korea, Taiwan, Hong Kong, and Singapore, have inspired other nations to attempt to utilize this strategy of economic development. Integral to export expansion strategy is an emphasis on export diversification, in terms of both products and geographic markets. The success of this development strategy is contingent upon the willingness of industrial countries to open their markets to imports of manufactured goods from the Third World. Increased South-South trade also facilitates this strategy. *See also* NEWLY INDUSTRIALIZED COUNTRIES, 163.

Significance Though all countries seek to achieve trade surplusses, it is economically impossible for all to reach that goal. There must be net importers to balance out net exporters. Thus, the export expansion strategy may not be appropriate for all developing countries. A key advantage of this strategy is that it makes possible important economies of scale. Also, this approach combined with global free trade should enhance overall global welfare by making available to all the lowest priced goods. An adverse effect of this strategy observed in certain rural areas is a negative impact on nutritional status in villages orienting their agricultural production excessively to foreign exports such as cassava. An export expansion strategy of development also makes an economy highly vulnerable to external shocks from shifts in foreign economies.

Export Processing Zone (147)

A special geographic region usually found in developing countries where foreign investment is encouraged to stimulate export expansion and diversification. In such a zone, also known as a special economic or free trade zone, special laws may apply to provide incentives for foreign investments in export processing. For example, tax holidays may be offered on land sold at less than market price or rental.

The People's Republic of China has actively developed such a strategy with its many special economic zones (SEZs) located primarily in the coastal areas of China near such port cities as Canton and Shanghai. In the SEZs of China, hundreds of joint ventures have been established involving close cooperation between foreign and Chinese economic entities. Such zones have even been created in the North, particularly in economically depressed areas seeking the employment associated with new industrial development.

Significance   The creation of export processing zones reflects an outward-oriented and export-driven strategy of economic development. Such zones have one major economic disadvantage and one possibly beneficial cultural dimension. They may lead to a growth in regional economic disparities. This appears to be the case in China, for example, where outward-oriented coastal economies have tended to advance much more rapidly than remote inland areas. From a cultural perspective, such economic enclaves may minimize broader cultural disruptions associated with a significant influx of expatriate personnel, who naturally bring with them considerable cultural baggage. Competition among countries for new industry has resulted in the popular emergence of export processing zones. Those countries and political units without such economic incentives and special geographic zones can be at a serious disadvantage in attracting foreign investment.

Foreign Exchange Constraint   (148)

The lack of access to an adequate supply of international currencies to utilize for developmental needs. Those nations engaged in national planning must carefully estimate the foreign exchange costs of their targeted levels of growth and investment. Countries particularly vulnerable to this problem are those with limited sources of foreign exchange or those dependent on only a small number of commodities whose international value fluctuates widely. Many key capital goods essential to the development process are only available in countries such as Japan, Germany, or the United States and must be obtained with foreign currency. A number of small microstates in the South Pacific have this constraint, but are fortunately able to receive considerable assistance from countries such as Australia and New Zealand to provide them with critically needed foreign exchange. *See also* HARD VERSUS SOFT CURRENCY, 152; COUNTERTRADE, 133.

Significance   The problem of foreign exchange constraints reflects the mutual interest inherent in basic development problems. The industrialized countries look toward developing countries as potential markets for both their capital and consumption goods. But developing countries need foreign exchange to be able to buy critically needed capital goods from industrialized countries. Thus, they need access to the markets of developed countries to sell their own products to earn foreign exchange. Without adequate foreign exchange resources, such countries will be continually dependent and subject to the vagaries of the politics of foreign aid and the related humiliation and vulnerability. Three new trends in the world economy may help to lessen the burden of foreign exchange constraints. First, there has been significant growth in countertrade, which enables trade without foreign exchange resources. Second, tourism is now the world's second largest industry and many developing countries have excellent tourist potential, which can be a major source of new foreign exchange. Third, and perhaps most important, the Mikhail Gorbachev initiative may lead to the 1990s becoming a decade of peace. With fewer resources devoted to arms and defense, more countries may be able to reach the goal of 0.70 of official development assistance (ODA), thus enhancing the availability of funding in the 1990s and the next century.

Four Little Tigers (149)

The four newly industrialized countries of Asia (South Korea, Taiwan, Hong Kong, and Singapore), which are recognized for their success in achieving export-led rapid economic growth. These countries are also noted for their relative success in areas such as land reform, family planning, and growth with equity. Though the four areas share many common economic successes and related public policies, each has its own political/cultural distinctiveness, a factor often ignored in media accounts that overstress their similarities. *See also* NEWLY INDUSTRIALIZED COUNTRIES, 163.

Significance There is a common tendency to cite the success of the "four little tigers" to justify various theoretical and ideological approaches to development. Free market advocates see their success as vindicating the virtues of an economy free from excessive governmental control, regulation, and planning. Educators emphasize the commitment of these countries to human resource development. The rate of educational expansion at all levels in South Korea and Taiwan has been remarkable. Others see these countries as demonstrating that non-Western cultural values such as the Confucian or Buddhist ethic are compatible with rapid economic growth and modernization. The success of these countries is inspiring in that none is blessed with abundant natural resources, and they represent compelling support for Fred Harbison's (1973) notion of human resources as the wealth of nations.

General Agreement on Tariffs and Trade (GATT)   **(150)**
Initiated in 1947, a series of agreements related to tariffs and potential trade disputes, with a major goal to facilitate free and fair trade and thereby to contribute to a healthy global economy. GATT is not a formal institution or organization, though it does have staff support (approximately 350 individuals working in Geneva). GATT initially had 23 members and grew to 99 members as of 1990. Two-thirds of its members are developing countries. The Long GATT Agreement has 4 Parts and 38 Articles. Article 2 is particularly important because it "makes national obligations with regard to tariff schedules an integral part of the GATT" (Graham 1982:443). Another major goal of GATT is to minimize and detect the presence of nontariff barriers to trade. A special concern of GATT is secret export subsidies which provide unfair trade advantages. Since its inception in 1947, there have been eight rounds of trade negotiations, with the most recent and far-ranging called the Uruguay round, 1986-1990.

Significance   GATT is the principal forum for global negotiations of trade questions and issues. GATT has, however, no formal power or authority to enforce agreements. The developing countries complain that they do not have an equal voice in discussions and negotiations and that GATT is dominated by the richer, economically more powerful nations. The voting structure of GATT is dominated by major economic nations such as the United States, Japan, United Kingdom, and Germany. Among current key issues being discussed at GATT meetings are 1) the question of farm subsidies and differing U.S. and European Community views on this issue, 2) intellectual property rights, 3) textile trade, 4) safeguards against "import surges" (*Christian Science Monitor*, December 16, 1988). Though GATT is by no means a perfect mechanism for promoting and ensuring free trade, it does provide a forum for North-North, North-South, and South-South trade negotiations in a multilateral, international atmosphere. Given the diversity of its membership and imbalances in its power structure, GATT's achievements in promoting free trade should not be dismissed. A world with GATT contrasts rather dramatically with the tragic pre-World War II period, when the United States escalated tariff barriers with its passage of the Smoot-Hawley Act of 1930, helping to trigger the great world depression. Ish Singhal (1990) of Agriculture Canada has provided an excellent overview of GATT, particularly its links with developing countries and related agricultural trade policies and issues.

Growth with Equity (151)

The ideal of high economic growth with reasonable levels of equity. Rapid economic growth has often been associated with dramatic inequalities as seen in Brazil or, at times, Mexico. Reflecting on this policy dilemma, Johan Galtung has referred to the "with" versus the "with-not" nations. The "with" nations are those that have attained both growth and equity, while the "with-nots" have failed to attain equity with their growth. Frequently cited examples of "with" nations are South Korea, Taiwan, Singapore, People's Republic of China, and Sri Lanka. Brazil, Mexico, Kenya, Venezuela, the Philippines, and Colombia would be considered examples of "with-not" nations. *See also* PARADIGMS OF DEVELOPMENT, 116; EQUALITY VERSUS EQUITY DISTINCTION, 145; UNEVEN DEVELOPMENT, 173.

Significance The growth with equity dilemma represents one of the major policy debates in the development field. More conservative development economists argue that in the short run, growing inequality is an inevitable element of the development process and the associated profits and rents may be channeled into productive investment. In the longer run, with the greater wealth resulting from prolonged economic growth, redistribution can occur and greater equity be attained. More radical development economists, seeing no incompatibility between growth and equity, argue that greater equity can foster faster growth by providing for broader participation in the development process and enhancing a nation's overall pool of human resources and talent. The debate over growth and equity is so significant that numerous revolutions have resulted to resolve it. For example, the revolutions of Cuba, Nicaragua, the Philippines (against Marcos), and Iran (against the shah) all had roots in systems of growth without equity. Along with the question of the environment, equity may well be the most burning development issue of the next century.

Hard versus Soft Currency (152)

An important financial distinction related to the international convertibility of a nation's currency. A hard currency can be converted freely to other currencies in international financial markets, while soft currencies have limited, if any, value in international markets. Countries with soft currencies normally have strict controls with respect to the import or export of their currencies. Hard currencies, in contrast, move freely with few, if any, restrictions across national boundaries. Examples of countries with soft currencies are the People's Republic of China, Indonesia, India, Cambodia, Myanmar (formerly Burma), Laos, and Vietnam. Many Eastern Bloc countries such as the Soviet Union, Hungary, and Poland also have soft currencies. In many countries with soft currencies, there is a black market for the exchange of the local currency for various hard currencies, normally at rates substantially below official bank rates. Developing countries frequently overvalue their currencies for political or non-economic reasons. Several developing countries such as Singapore, Malaysia, Hong Kong, and Brunei now have hard currencies. *See also* FOREIGN EXCHANGE CONSTRAINT, 148; DEBT CRISIS, 134.

Significance   Having a hard currency suggests economic maturity and the attainment of a substantial degree of development success. In some respects it is a sign of "graduation" to developed status. A nation's ability to produce sufficient goods and services desired by those beyond its national boundaries is essential for attaining hard currency status. The Japanese yen, for example, provides access to a massive market of diverse products and services. For countries in a transitional stage, there are both advantages and disadvantages of having a hard currency. The presence of a hard currency greatly facilitates foreign investments, since international investors have confidence that their returns can be repatriated and exchanged into their own national currency. A hard currency also facilitates the development of international banking and financial services, as illustrated by the cases of Hong Kong and Singapore. On the other hand, once a nation's currency is hard, the nation loses some control over its own money supply and its economy can become more vulnerable to international financial movements. For example, foreigners now hold large quantities of U.S. dollars and thus can influence the American economy by their economic actions.

Import Substitution   **(153)**
A strategy that stresses the development of local industries to manufacture products that previously were purchased from abroad. Initially such industries normally need protection with tariffs and government subsidies, given their infant industry status. This strategy of development was particularly popular in the 1950s and 1960s. Eventually such industries should become able to compete without subsidies and tariff protection, even in world markets. India is an example of a South nation that has consistently emphasized this strategy. *See also* INFANT INDUSTRY, 154; INDUSTRIALIZATION, 111.

Significance   Considerable controversy exists as to the effectiveness of import substitution as a development strategy. Its advocates stress the need to develop industrial self-reliance and to reduce vulnerability associated with linkages with the world economic system. They also stress the valuable technological learning that occurs when countries develop their own industries. Critics, however, see import substitution as frequently contributing to the development of overly capital-intensive industries with an emphasis on nonessential consumption by local elites. In countries with overvalued foreign exchange rates, new industries have an incentive to import foreign capital goods and foreign exports originating from rural areas. Finally, import substitution is inconsistent with the philosophy of free trade, since protectionism is essential in the initial stages of this strategy of development.

Infant Industry   **(154)**
A relatively new industry that is not yet internationally competitive, and is provided protection through tariffs while it develops competitiveness. As developing countries seek to diversify their economies and to compete in manufacturing industries, there are inevitably targeted industries that cannot take off without initial protection against foreign products and in many instances considerable governmental support and subsidies. Korea's steel industry, for example, was once an infant industry. Many of India's current industries were initially of the infant industry genre. *See also* INDUSTRIALIZATION, 111; COMPARATIVE ADVANTAGE, 132; ECONOMIC DIVERSIFICATION, 142.

Significance   The infant industry concept is at the heart of debates about pure and modified free trade. The pure free trade argument sees infant industries as contributing to global inefficiencies. From this perspective, a country like Indonesia should not be inefficiently trying to manufacture helicopters but instead should buy them with funds from industries or economic sectors in which it has a comparative advantage. However, without an infant industry policy, it is extremely difficult for developing countries to diversify their economies and to move to a different stage of development where comparative advantages may shift dramatically. The infant industry concept recognizes the long-term dynamic nature of international economic forces. The basic persisting problem is to determine the time when an industry advances from infant status to compete on regular terms as an "adult" in international markets without tariff protection. This is sometimes referred to as achieving competitiveness.

Infrastructure (155)
The structural elements and activities of an economy that enhance productivity and facilitate the flow of goods and services. These include systems of transportation, communication, housing, education, finance, health, and public order. The term was introduced in NATO studies in the 1950s and has since been adapted to development theory and literature. Development economists also use the term *social overhead capital,* which is comprised of economic overhead capital, necessary for infrastructure development, and social capital, investment in public services. *See also* WORLD BANK, 454.

Significance Infrastructure is a necessary but not sufficient element for economic development. Much of the debate about infrastructure centers on the types of systems to be developed, the extent of centralization, and the timing of its establishment. An infrastructure can serve as a catalyst for development and change or, if too expensive and inefficient, can create a burden on national economies. Infrastructure is generally conceived as massive in scale, capital-intensive, and highly centralized. The vast majority of international loans have been given for the construction of roads, dams, buildings, irrigation systems, and other systems components of electrification, communication, industry, and agriculture. Such projects have become symbols of both national pride and massive development aid boondoggles. The type of infrastructure most suitable for developing countries is hotly debated in the context of appropriate technology. Critics of large-scale projects such as massive electrical generating plants argue that intermediate technology and a more decentralized system of power generation should be considered. Similar choices must be made in human services such as health care and education, on questions such as whether to invest limited resources in centralized systems such as hospitals and universities or in decentralized services such as basic health care and elementary education. Recognizing that this type of aid will encourage investments by capital-rich nations and multinational corporations, thus bolstering world capitalism, the World Bank Group has been particularly active in providing loans for infrastructure development.

Intellectual Property Rights (156)
The legal protection of the economic benefits associated with a broad range of knowledge-oriented products and other outputs of human creativity. Among such products are books and literary works, computer software, new patented pharmaceuticals, audiocassettes, videocassettes, and films. The concept originated in the 1883 Paris

Convention and is mentioned in the U.S. Constitution. The protection of such rights has led to considerable controversy and disputes, particularly between North and South nations. At the 1986 meeting of GATT, ministers agreed that intellectual property rights should be central to future discussions of world trade. Representatives of developing countries often view intellectual property rights as contributing to the persistence of global inequalities. In reply, those from developed countries argue that creative intellectuals have the rights to benefit economically from their work and that financial incentives are important to encourage innovation and creativity. The World Intellectual Property Organization (WIPO), a specialized agency of the UN, has been generally sympathetic to the perspective of the South nations and it sanctions violation of intellectual property rights by countries where certain products, such as critical pharmaceuticals, are considered vital to national well-being and security, or where the North country is not actively marketing a product in a particular South nation. *See also* INTERNATIONAL UNDERTAKING ON PLANT GENETIC RESOURCES, 288.

Significance   The issue of intellectual property rights is currently one of the most hotly debated policy issues affecting North-South relations. In the spring of 1988, the Parliament of Thailand was ostensibly dissolved as the result of a debate concerning intellectual property rights. In a number of South countries, intellectual property rights have been blatantly ignored. For many years, for example, Taiwan openly copied books and literary works without payment of royalties to their authors. Throughout the Third World systematic pirating of audiocassettes and videocassettes commonly takes place. It is naive to simply call this cheating when numerous North nations (for example, Japan and the United States) systematically subsidize their agricultural sectors and through such violations of free trade adversely affect farmers in South nations. In essence the protection of intellectual property rights is integral to a free trade regime. From the perspective of incentives for intellectuals to be creative and maximally productive, the systematic violation of intellectual property rights represents global inefficiency and may even adversely affect South intellectuals themselves. Questions of inequality, inequity, and income distribution could be more appropriately addressed directly rather than through open violations of intellectual property rights.

Labor-Intensive Techniques   (157)
An economic development strategy that emphasizes the use of labor relative to other factors of production such as capital in various

industrial and other development projects. The assumption underlying this strategy is that labor is relatively cheap compared to capital in developing countries. In many developing countries that have serious problems of unemployment and underemployment, labor supply is not a serious constraint and provision of more employment is a critical basic need. In contrast to local labor, capital often must be imported and represents a foreign exchange drain. *See also* CAPITAL-INTENSIVE TECHNIQUES, 128; APPROPRIATE TECHNOLOGY, 276; UNDEREMPLOYMENT, 171.

Significance   While the emphasis on labor-intensive techniques may be appropriate in many contexts, the mindless application of this strategy can have adverse effects on development. To remain internationally competitive, countries must improve their productivity levels. Capital and related technology are often relevant to such productivity improvements. An example would be computer-assisted design (CAD) and computer-assisted manufacturing (CAM) in the textile industry, an important sector in many developing countries. It is reductionist to think that only labor-intensive techniques can be employed. Central to sound development is an appropriate mix of labor and capital-intensive techniques.

Lomé Conventions (158)

A series of trade and economic agreements involving the European Economic Community (EEC) and countries of the African, Caribbean, and Pacific states (ACP). The first agreement, signed in 1975 in Lomé, Togo, by 46 African, Asian, and Pacific states, replaced and expanded the number of participants of the Yaounde Conventions of 1969 and the Arusha Agreement of 1968. The second convention was concluded in 1979 and the third in 1985. The ACP participants now number 64. *See also* TERMS OF TRADE, 349; COMMODITY AGREEMENTS, 131.

Significance   The signing of the first Lomé Convention gave all ACP manufactured goods and 96 percent of agricultural products duty-free access to the EEC. The agreement also encouraged technology transfer, new industrial partnerships, and increased private investment in ACP countries. The convention provided for financial and technical aid to be financed by special drawing rights (SDRs) issued to the European Development Fund and the European Investment Bank. Finally, the convention established an export-revenue stabilization scheme (STABEX) to guarantee set levels of commodity export earnings for ACP countries. The second convention addressed issues of migrant labor, energy policy, agricultural development, and stabilization of export earnings on minerals. The third convention, signed in 1985, extended the provisions of the previous conventions and emphasized increased commercial and development cooperation between the EEC and the ACP countries. Overall, the Lomé Conventions have helped counteract the decline of the trading position of the ACP nations in relation to the industrialized nations.

Multinational/Transnational Corporations (159)
(MNCs/TNCs)

These terms, referring to corporations that operate internationally, have several definitions. The United Nations defines MNCs simply as companies or corporations operating in more than one country. More specific definitions are also common. For example, an MNC may be defined as an international company with sales of more than $100 million, with its foreign branches accounting for more than 20 percent of its assets or one-quarter of its output. The gross annual sales of many MNCs exceed the GNPs of the Third World countries in which they operate. The term *MNC* was introduced after World War II by large international concerns based in North America and Western Europe that had expanded their networks of foreign investment and operations using local labor in other countries. Those who use the term *transnational* often do so in a critical sense to emphasize that the interests and concerns of the corporations transcend those of either their nation of origin or of the countries in which they operate. For example, at the Third UNCTAD Session in 1972, the Vatican representative referred to "large private empires, escaping the control of state authorities and international organizations, with the result that in practice they are outside of any control subordinated to the common good of humanity" (Osmańczyk 1985:529). TNCs operate overseas for several reasons, including tax breaks and lax regulations as in environmental laws, for example, in countries seeking investment; lower labor costs than in the country of origin; expansion of markets and production to take advantage of economies of scale; and, in some cases, virtual monopoly status within a country. *See also* NEW INTERNATIONAL ECONOMIC ORDER, 161.

Significance   There is considerable controversy regarding the role of MNCs/TNCs in international development. For example, Henry Kissinger views the MNCs as "one of the most effective engines of development growth" (LaPalombara 1979:1). In sharp contrast, Richard Barnett and Ronald E. Müller, coauthors of *Global Reach: The Power of Multinational Corporations* (1974), conclude that MNCs are powerful impediments to Third World development. Both the OECD and the Group of 77 have attempted to devise codes of conduct to regulate MNCs, which potentially hold powerful sway over the internal affairs and conditions within developing countries. Transnational policies and activities were central issues in the call for a new international economic order (NIEO) in the mid–1970s. In 1976 the United Nations formed the UN Committee for Multinational Corporations and has since pushed for international codes of conduct for transnational corporations. The MNCs argue that they provide much-needed investment, employment, and technology transfers to developing nations. Critics respond that nearly all the profits revert back to the more developed countries (MDCs) and that MNC operations distort local and national economies, bringing benefit to only a few. They also note that technology transfers seldom translate into technological advances outside of the MNC production plant. MNCs have also been widely criticized for double standards regarding safety regulations, wages, and benefits for workers, depending on the standards and enforcements of the country of operation. Another concern is the aggressive marketing of products considered inappropriate and detrimental to the welfare of Third World citizens. Nestlé Foods Corporation, for example, has been subject to considerable criticism and an international boycott of its products for its promotion of its infant formula to replace breast-feeding in developing countries. Other MNCs market products, such as pharmaceuticals and pesticides, deemed illegal and unsafe in the MDCs. These can be particularly hazardous in societies with high rates of illiteracy. Finally, MNCs argue that, given their transnational status, they have a strong vested interest in international development and peace. Without development they cannot expand their markets. Without political stability and international cooperation their operations are further limited. However, their concern for political stability has often meant the support of highly repressive governments favorable to their interests. This has been the source of much cynicism regarding the role of MNCs/TNCs in Third World development. MNCs have the potential to play a vital role in alleviating poverty in developing countries. Thus, nearly all governments continue to seek their investments. Unfortunately for the people of the less developed countries, they have often failed to live up to this potential.

Nationalization (160)

The transfer of control of a private economic enterprise to the government. All economies have a certain degree of nationalization; for example, the control of postal services by governments throughout the world. Public utilities such as electricity and telephones are often controlled by the government, as may be banking, medical care, transportation, and communications media. Government-owned and government-controlled enterprises are often called state enterprises. Such enterprises may operate at profitable levels, break even, or be highly subsidized through taxes and other revenues. As countries develop, certain infant industries may be initially controlled by the government and sold to private enterprise once they become profitable. In many developing countries there is pressure to nationalize foreign companies involved in the extraction of natural resources. Such companies frequently have anxieties about potential nationalization and seek insurance from their own governments against such risks. When foreign companies are nationalized, considerable variation exists with respect to how much, if any, economic compensation they may receive from the nationalizing government. Nationalization can be contrasted with expropriation, which involves the government's seizure of classes of property owned by both citizens and aliens. *See also* INFANT INDUSTRY, 154.

Significance   Nationalization is one of the most hotly debated policy issues in developing countries. Proponents of privatization, deregulation, and the minimization of nationalization associate it with economic stagnation, inefficiency, personalism, and cronyism. Controversies surrounding nationalization were a major factor leading to the 1973 coup against Allende in Chile. Opponents of nationalization view many state enterprises as "public parasites" highly dependent on public revenues and thus lacking in incentives to perform efficiently. Excessive nationalization is also often associated with bureaucratic pathology and lack of responsiveness to popular needs and demands. Those concerned with the protection of political democracy see excessive nationalization, particularly of areas such as the media and communications, as a serious threat to individual liberties. In contrast, proponents of nationalization emphasize the need for government control and planning in key areas such as banking, land-use planning, environmental protection, transportation, medical care, and public welfare. Powerful labor unions associated with state enterprises strongly oppose privatization and the financial uncertainties associated with the free play of market forces. Given the relative failure of many economies with high levels of nationalization, privatization seems to be the popular pattern in the 1990s. Despite the popularity of privatization, increased public regulation and involvement are essential in numerous critical areas, including environmental protection, land use, medical care, transportation, alternative energy development, and conservation of limited natural resources.

New International Economic Order (NIEO) (161)

A set of proposals and demands of the developing nations calling for a comprehensive reform of the world economic system. Supporters contend that the international system is based on structures of inequality and does not serve the interests of poor nations. The concept, rooted in the analysis of dependency theory, was brought to the forefront at the Sixth Special Session of the United Nations in 1974. Inspired by the success of OPEC, the Group of 77 proposed multilateral and systematic reforms in North-South economic relations designed to enhance the development and economic self-determination of the LDCs. The proposals were adopted by the UN General Assembly in May 1974, with little support from the OECD members, as set forth in the Declaration and Programme of Action on the Establishment of a New International Economic Order. The program calls for increased foreign aid, renegotiation of Third World debt, more favorable terms of trade including support for international commodity agreements, greater control by LDCs over MNCs and natural resources, easier access to technology, and a greater decision-making role for developing nations in international bodies, including the IMF and the World Bank. In a follow-up action in December 1974, the General Assembly adopted the Charter of Economic Rights and Duties of States, which reemphasized the need for international economic relations based on equity, equal sovereignty, and interdependence of developed and developing countries. *See also* NEW WORLD INFORMATION AND COMMUNICATION ORDER, 252; MULTINATIONAL/TRANSNATIONAL CORPORATIONS, 159; DEPENDENCY THEORY, 106.

Significance   The NIEO never became a catalyst for the reforms envisioned by its proponents. Without the support of the major economies it has led to few tangible results. Detractors regarded it as unnecessary, irrelevant, or inefficient, no more than a Third World wish list. Nevertheless, the NIEO has served as an effective tool for articulating the goals and frustrations of the LDCs and the underlying nature of North-South conflict. It helped create an agenda for North-South dialogue, even on a bilateral basis, and it became a rallying point and symbol of unity for the Group of 77.

Newly Industrialized Agro-Based Countries (NIACs) (162)

Countries experiencing rapid economic growth associated with a strong agricultural base. Characteristic of this status are increasing diversification of the agricultural sector, expansion of agricultural exports, improvement of agricultural productivity, and development of agriculture-related industry. Examples of modern countries that have followed this path of development are Denmark and New Zealand. *See also* NEWLY INDUSTRIALIZED COUNTRIES, 163.

Significance   With so much focus on the challenge of becoming a newly industrialized country (NIC), it is easy to forget that many developing countries have factor endowments that will be strongly agricultural for a long period into the future. Therefore, their development paths will differ considerably from current NICs with few agricultural resources such as Hong Kong and Singapore. Countries with NIAC potential include Thailand, Indonesia, Costa Rica, and Pakistan.

Newly Industrialized Countries (NICs)   **(163)**
A term that became popular in the 1980s to refer to those developing countries that have succeeded in establishing a major industrial and manufacturing sector. Among those countries clearly considered NICs are the Republic of Korea (South Korea), Taiwan, Hong Kong, and Singapore (the "four little tigers"). Countries such as Brazil, Argentina, Mexico, and Israel are also usually included among the NICs. Such countries have normally been quite successful in expanding their export of manufactured goods, which has contributed to the development of economies of scale and the building of their industrial base. Though criteria have been identified for defining NIC status, there is still debate as to whether a given country is a NIC or not. For example, there is considerable current debate as to whether Thailand has achieved NIC status. Economists have established four criteria for determining NIC status: (1) manufacturing products as 30 percent of GDP; (2) manufactured exports as 50 percent of total exports; (3) a shift in employment from agriculture to industry; (4) per capita income of at least $2,000 U.S. *See also* NEWLY INDUSTRIALIZED AGRO-BASED COUNTRIES, 162; FOUR LITTLE TIGERS, 149.

Significance   The NIC terminology reflects the emergence of highly differential development conditions. The NICs are for the most part development successes, and the gap between them and the richer countries is decreasing. At the same time, the gap between the NICs and more stagnant developing economies is growing dramatically. In fact, NICs such as South Korea and Taiwan are in the process of becoming donor nations that are beginning to share their development experience through technical assistance and other developmental aid. Contributing to attainment of NIC status, particularly in the Asia-Pacific region, have been (1) effective land policies, (2) family planning and population control, (3) commitment to investments in education at all levels, and (4) export-driven growth. Because of the export-driven growth of the NICs, they are vulnerable to possible external shocks associated with potential protectionism, particularly in developed countries such as the United States. Though the number of NICs is small, their example may be an inspiration to other developing countries, which may learn from their experiences, both positive and negative. For example, in several instances, the environmental costs of rapid economic growth have been high.

Opportunity Costs (164)

An economic concept highly relevant to international development referring to the economic activities that are foregone because of a decision to allocate funds for a specific purpose. It is also commonly used in the economics of education and human resources to refer to the earnings that individuals give up while they take on training or schooling activities. An easy way to conceptualize the inherent nature of opportunity costs is to assume that funds not devoted to a development project were instead invested in a banking system to provide a given economic return. The alternative maximum financial returns that could be received in lieu of that development investment reflect its opportunity cost.

Significance Opportunity cost is a powerful economic concept reflecting the limited and constrained nature of all economic resources. There are important economic trade-offs inherent in all decision making related to development. For example, women who decide to work at home without pay incur the opportunity cost of the earnings they forego by not entering the labor market. Perhaps the most pertinent opportunity costs in many developing countries are the financial resources foregone because of relatively high levels of military spending. Though it may not have been computed explicitly, it is likely that the opportunity cost of the Vietnam War exceeded $1,000 billion. By 1990, the $200 billion that the United States "invested" in Vietnam could have brought alternative economic returns of a rather staggering amount.

Peace Dividend (165)

A rather massive sum of funds potentially available for nonmilitary purposes, primarily as the result of the end of the cold war in the late 1980s and early 1990s. These released funds may be a prime factor in the economies of the Soviet Union and the United States, both of which experienced spiraling defense spending during the 1980s. A multitude of articles have been published about the prospective peace dividend and competing needs for the released funds. Prior to the current popularity of the term, most discussions focused on economic conversion and the relationship between disarmament and development. Ironically, as pointed out by many in the Third World, the West's eagerness to aid the reformed economies of the Eastern European countries may distract from development assistance marked for the LDCs. *See also* DISARMAMENT AND DEVELOPMENT, 138.

Significance   While a major use of the peace dividend will be to help restore the soundness of the Soviet and U.S. economies, far greater funds than in the past may be available for international development and related environmental efforts. As the end of the cold war increasingly becomes a new international reality, for the first time there may be a genuine opportunity to turn "swords into plowshares." Many questions of economic conversion have yet to be answered. Clearly one of the major policy debates of the 1990s in the United States, the Soviet Union, and Europe will be on how to spend the windfall peace dividend and how much of it should be devoted to international development efforts and needs.

Segmented Labor Market Theory   **(166)**
An alternative perspective for viewing the relationship between education and the labor market, particularly in developing countries. This theory postulates that there are three distinct labor markets, each with its own characteristics—primary, primary subordinate, and secondary. The impact of educational background varies dramatically from sector to sector. In the primary labor market, individuals have secure, stable employment, and considerable opportunity for self-initiative and independent judgment. Those in the primary subordinate market have secure and stable employment, but have little opportunity for self-initiative and control over their work lives. Those in the secondary labor market lack job security and are placed in highly routinized job situations requiring minimal decision making and self-initiative and providing little opportunity for growth and skill enhancement. High job turnover is typical of this sector.

Significance   This theory is highly relevant to those concerned with educational planning and policy-making. According to the segmented labor market theory, the impact of education and schooling are directly conditioned by the labor market context. For example, additional years of schooling may have little impact for the individual in the secondary labor market, but may bring significant benefits to the employee in the primary labor market. The validity of this theory can be empirically tested by disaggregating data according to the postulated labor markets. Major proponents of the theory include Michael Piore, Martin Carnoy, and Henry Levin. This structural, macro-oriented theory represents an alternative to human capital theory, which assumes that all individuals benefit similarly from investments in their education or training with variations primarily dependent on human abilities.

Semiperiphery (167)

An adaptation of core-periphery and world systems theory to allow for a third tier of countries between the core rich and powerful nations and the impoverished, dependent countries of the periphery. Immanuel Wallerstein introduced this concept as part of a trimodal system in his volume, *The Capitalist World Economy* (1979). Ruy Mauro refers to these nations as subimperial states and Johan Galtung calls them go-betweens. The concept of semiperiphery derives from social class theory. According to this perspective, the wealthy in any society favor the creation of a middle social group or class that will feel superior to the lower class but not inferior to the wealthy, and thus will support the status quo. Those in the middle class also represent a model of success that proves the reality of possibilities for upward social mobility. Thus, the presence and strength of such a middle group defuses potential for radical uprisings of the poorer segments of society. Similarly, the presence of a middle group of countries serves the same function in a bipolar world system, contributing to stability and helping to defuse polarization. Examples of countries in the semiperiphery would be South Korea, Taiwan, Singapore, and Hong Kong. *See also* IMMANUEL WALLERSTEIN, 58; CENTER-PERIPHERY, 104.

Significance The concept of semiperiphery extends the explanatory power of world systems theory by accounting for anomalous cases that do not fit an overly simplistic concept of a bipolar world. Many of the best-performing developing economies of the Asia-Pacific region have steadily reduced the economic gap between themselves and core countries through rapid economic growth and the dramatic expansion of manufactured exports. The basic problem with the semiperiphery is definitional. There appear to be no clear criteria for determining membership in the semiperiphery. Are rapidly industrializing countries such as Brazil, Mexico, and Thailand part of the periphery or the semiperiphery? Wallerstein also implies that the development conditions of those in the semiperiphery are created by the core. Such a view fails to recognize important indigenous economic and cultural factors contributing to economic performance and semiperiphery status in countries such as South Korea. At the international level, the semiperiphery concept clearly suggests a type of Horatio Alger myth. Such a myth tends to help legitimize the existing world structure, as highly successful models of capitalist economic growth such as South Korea, Hong Kong, Taiwan, and Singapore are used to "prove" that countries can succeed within the current world capitalist system.

Spatial Aspects of Development (168)

A subfield of development studies that focuses on the organization of geographical space in developing countries. Theorists, planners, and policymakers have tended to neglect the spatial dimensions of development. The result has been persisting problems of uneven development with large, parasitic cities surrounded by a multitude of small villages. For proponents of an emphasis on the spatial aspects, the key to development is urbanization of the core region with better distribution of central places and intermediate cities and towns. This perspective draws heavily upon the theoretical work of the German geographers Walter Christaller (the father of central place theory) and August Lösch. G. William Skinner has also utilized such perspectives in his studies of historical regional development in China. The major volume articulating the spatial perspective on development was written by E. A. J. Johnson, *The Organization of Space in Developing Countries* (1970).

Significance The issue of uneven development and the related concentration of economic wealth and public services in one or few large cities is one of the most critical development problems. John P. Lewis argues that genuine planning is "inherently spatial in character." Rigorous and committed regional planning is needed to create policies to foster a better spread of central places and intermediate cities and towns, and requires major investments and the identification of promising growth points. Perhaps a major reason for the difficulties of achieving genuine regional planning and the related spread of development benefits is that this perspective implies greater decentralization and deconcentration of both economic and political power.

Subsistence (169)

A concept generally referring to the economic situation of poor farmers or urban workers in developing countries in which

155

individuals are able to obtain only the basic economic necessities of life. The subsistence farmer has no funds with which to obtain amenities or luxury goods of any type, and all efforts go into maintaining basic subsistence. Such farmers are often much more rational than commonly believed, doing everything possible to minimize the possibility of falling below the basic subsistence line. There are, of course, problems in defining precisely what constitutes a subsistence line. Generally, adequate food supplies to avoid hunger and famine, and basic shelter from the elements are the core elements of subsistence. Major threats to subsistence are the natural vagaries of weather, which can bring devastating droughts or storms, and political or economic actions that adversely affect farmers' access to agricultural land and basic inputs. *See also* BASIC NEEDS, 102; SELF-RELIANCE/SELF-SUFFICIENCY, 120.

Significance A life of subsistence in a village setting may offer numerous advantages. Unlike nonsubsistence farmers, these farmers are much less vulnerable to global or national shifts in commodity prices or price-support systems. Careful observers of rural settings have noted that children in villages of subsistence farmers are frequently far healthier than children of wealthier farmers who are primarily engaged in producing for national and world markets. Emphasis on the production in Thailand of tapioca pellets for European pigs, for example, may reduce the availability of local protein for children. Funds from cash crops such as tapioca pellets may be used for various luxury items such as liquor, tobacco, television sets, and motorcycles. Though subsistence farmers are materially poor and subject to threats from natural disasters and the vagaries of weather, under normal times they show remarkable resiliency in their ability to survive, and their basic life-styles in terms of personal warmth and hospitality, love and care for children and elders, conviviality, security from crime, and access to a pollution-free environment, are commonly superior to those in modern concrete urban "jungles."

Trickle-Down Effect (170)

The notion that the benefits of development will eventually reach the poorer segments of society through a natural process, a type of modern-day "invisible hand." Policymakers and development specialists who believe in the trickle-down effect tend to emphasize gross macrostatistics such as the economic growth rate or rate of industrialization as measures of development. Because of the assumed trickle-down effect, such thinkers tend to be less concerned with distributional or equity issues. The trickle-down concept has been borrowed from American domestic politics where it is used to describe a governmental policy that is aimed at helping the rich get richer, with the expectation that much of this wealth will filter down to the poorer classes. *See also* DUALISM, 139; EQUALITY VERSUS EQUITY DISTINCTION, 145.

Significance   The trickle-down effect assumption has critically important development implications. It is difficult to test empirically because of ambiguities related to length of time and scope of geographic area covered. For example, development in a country might "trickle down" to key regional towns, but not to genuinely remote rural areas. Or development benefits might trickle down only after lags of years or even decades. Overly smug belief in the trickle-down effect has resulted in the persistence of backward areas and internal colonialism within developing countries. Countries where trickle-down has occurred would seem to be the "little tigers" of Asia, namely, South Korea, Taiwan, Hong Kong, and Singapore.

Underemployment   (171)
A pattern of economic activity in which individuals are unable to utilize their full capabilities in their particular employment situations. There are basically two types of underemployment. In the first type, the individual has a full-time position, but is only partially engaged and may have excessive time in which no productive activity occurs. In the second type, common in the informal sector, individuals create their own jobs by engaging in activities such as street vending since regular full-time jobs are not available to them. In the second form of underemployment, it is assumed that such individuals could undertake full-time formal employment. Both types of underemployment tend to be common in developing countries, particularly in urban areas in which there has been tremendous migration from rural areas, and in countries with high population growth rates and relatively young age structures.

Significance   The widespread existence of underemployment reflects a vast reservoir of unutilized economic potential. Individuals could shift from underemployment to full-time employment with minimal foregone economic output or services. Countries with large pools of underemployed labor thus have considerable potential for new manufacturing involving low-skill intensity. From the perspective of the underemployed, the situation is sometimes more favorable than it would appear. Full-time employees who are underemployed frequently moonlight to increase their salaries to levels more commensurate with rising urban costs and prices. Those in the informal sector frequently have far more economic freedom than their counterparts in the formal sector of factories. Studies in Peru, for example, have indicated that numerous individuals prefer work in the informal sector to highly regimented and regulated low-paying factory work. The precise measurement of underemployment is difficult, and thus while underemployment is significant in many developing countries, it cannot be accurately estimated.

Unequal Exchange (172)

A concept referring to economic transactions that transfer value and wealth from rich nations to poor ones in ways that contribute to growing global inequalities and disparities. The origins of the term are found in Arghiri Emmanuel's volume, *Unequal Exchange* (1972). Samir Amin later popularized the term in *Unequal Development: An Essay on the Social Formations of Peripheral Capitalism* (1976). Emmanuel and Amin criticize traditional international trade theory, which they view as based on false, misleading assumptions. The countries and corporations at the center have economic power that allows them to pay much less than true value for products and services from developing countries. The economic value lost from such underpayment is far greater than funds received in various forms of international development assistance. Lower levels of productivity in developing countries also contribute to unequal exchange. *See also* DEPENDENCY THEORY, 106; COMPARATIVE ADVANTAGE, 132; NEW INTERNATIONAL ECONOMIC ORDER, 161.

Significance   The concept of unequal exchange is inherently normative. In the world capitalist system, prices and values are generally not determined by concerns for social justice and equality, but by a combination of market forces and dominant economic power. The restructuring of such a system would represent a major global revolution. Given the unlikelihood of such global changes, a country confronting unequal exchange has three major alternatives: (1) to isolate its national economic system from the global one (e.g., Albania, Burma, [1962–1980], China under Mao [1949–1976], and North Korea); (2) to diversify its economy so as to benefit from exporting the types of commodities and services more valued in global markets (e.g., manufactured goods); and (3) to enhance economic productivity as a means to improve wages and profits. Countries such as South Korea, Taiwan, Singapore, and Hong Kong have followed the second and third strategies. As a result, Taiwan now has the second largest foreign exchange reserves in the world. But the success of such countries ironically has led to even greater disparities between themselves and other developing countries that confront persisting unequal exchange and are unable to diversify their economies adequately or improve their productivity substantially.

Uneven Development (173)

The differential economic performance of the regions of a nation. While the pattern tends to be more pronounced in LDCs, it is also found in developed countries. For example, Appalachia usually lags behind the rest of the United States economically, as does the Okinawa region of Japan. Nearly all developing countries have areas that lag behind. Though both Brazil and Thailand have achieved impressive macroeconomic growth rates during the past several decades, their Northeastern regions suffer from drought and neglect, with per capita income levels much lower than in other parts of the country. There are multiple reasons for uneven development. Areas of a country differ in basic factor endowments. For example, the Northeast of Brazil and the Northeast of Thailand suffer from drought and poor soil conditions. Elements of internal colonialism lead to funds being siphoned to the center as modern financial institutions spread to more remote areas. Such remote regions often lack a strong political voice to enable them to attract their fair share of public investments and services in areas such as education and health. *See also* DUALISM, 139; CENTER-PERIPHERY, 104; GROWTH WITH EQUITY, 151.

Significance Uneven development has many adverse implications. If the problems of uneven development are ignored, revolutionary forces may emerge and threaten national political stability. The Shining Path guerrillas in Peru are an example. To survive in backward regions, it may be necessary for individuals to engage in environmentally destructive activities that result in excessive deforestation, for example. The harsh human conditions associated with uneven development lead to strong push factors forcing migration into already overly congested urban areas. Migrants from such poorer regions often end up in slums or favelas and become part of serious problems of child labor and/or prostitution. Forceful government policies are essential to improve the economic and social infrastructure of neglected regions and to offer incentives to encourage private entrepreneurs and public servants to work and locate facilities in such areas. The achievement of more even development often requires major reallocation of public and private resources.

Urban Involution (174)

A concept introduced by W. R. Armstrong and T. G. McGee to explain responses by the poor to rapid urbanization in developing countries. Urban involution is an application of Clifford Geertz's concept of agricultural involution, which is based on conditions prevalent on the island of Java in Indonesia. The urban involution concept also relates to an urban type of dualism emphasized by Geertz in his book, *Peddlers and Princes: Social Change and Economic Modernization in Two Indonesian Towns* (1963), which contrasts the formal firm sector and the informal bazaar sector. Just as a given area of land in Java is able to absorb greater numbers of people through increasing agricultural intensity and shared poverty, Third World cities are able to absorb increasing numbers of migrants from rural areas into a highly elastic informal service sector. Jobs in this sector are generally characterized by low incomes with low skill intensity, and often involve serious underemployment. Common examples of such employment are hawkers, street vendors, domestic servants, and prostitutes. *See also* CIRCULAR MIGRATION, 178; UNDEREMPLOYMENT, 171; TRICKLE UP PROGRAM, 444.

Significance The number of new jobs generated by large-scale formal organizations and corporations in the cities of developing countries is often exaggerated and can in no way provide adequate employment for rapidly increasing urban populations. Thus, the informal service sector becomes an extremely important source of employment, particularly for the poor and less educated. The informal sector also provides a potentially huge pool of cheap and available urban labor that can be utilized by the manufacturing sector as a country industrializes. For example, in Thailand, many young women who previously worked as domestic servants are now employed in computer or textile factories and have left the informal sector. However, research studies in Peru suggest that workers sometimes move from private factories back into the informal sector, which allows more freedom and less regimentation. Numerous developing countries also experience circular migration in which individuals leave the urban informal sector and its disappointments to return to their rural origins. The power of the informal sector to absorb labor and accommodate shared poverty reflects the many coping strategies of the urban poor. As Dominique Lapierre points out in his work on Calcutta, *The City of Joy*, despite their dire physical conditions, the urban poor have remarkable resiliency and ability to maintain their basic human dignity. Recent research by the Peruvian economist Hernando de Soto indicates that the informal sector making urban involution possible is of far greater economic meaning than many have realized.

C. Agricultural and Rural Development

Affluent Subsistence (175)

A pattern of living characterized by a bare minimum of material goods, but a healthy and plentiful natural diet combined with a pleasant life-style. This pattern is usually found in areas with adequate rainfall and natural abundance of land and diverse agricultural resources. Affluent subsistence can be found in areas such as the Kingdom of Tonga, rural areas of Thailand such as Chantaburi, areas of China such as Hainan and Kunming, parts of Sri Lanka, parts of Costa Rica, and parts of Malaysia. *See also* SUBSISTENCE, 169; SELF-RELIANCE/SELF-SUFFICIENCY, 120.

Significance Conditions of absolute poverty and bare subsistence differ markedly from affluent subsistence. There is a tendency to overgeneralize concerning the nature of poverty in developing countries. Availability of water, type of climate, and soil conditions are key factors explaining the extent of affluent subsistence. Conditions of affluent subsistence are easily misperceived as ordinary poverty because of the lack of standard material wealth associated with development. In broader terms, the concept serves as a reminder that individuals may lead lives of high quality in the absence of modern technology and financial systems.

Agrarian Reform and Transformation (176)

Changes in agricultural economies and societies designed to enhance rural development in the areas of land distribution, tenure systems, pricing policies, taxation, agriculture management and organization, and types of production. Agrarian reform may take place in some or all of these areas and may be initiated from above or below. The term *reform* implies changes stemming from regional and national policy decisions while *transformation* suggests broad-based changes with roots in local decision making. Given the marked, rising inequality of land distribution throughout most of the world's rural developing societies, land tenure and ownership issues are central to agrarian reform. The Green Revolution brought about not only dramatic increases in overall productivity, but other economic, social, and political transformations as well. Increased productivity is only one of many goals of agrarian reform. Productivity in a given area may rise while the rural population becomes further impoverished. The neopopulists, for example, argue that the Green Revolution has resulted in growing inequality, offering advantages only to the well-endowed farmers. In fact, the record is mixed, alerting us to the need to understand more deeply the diverse sociopolitical contexts in which agrarian reform and transformation take place or are attempted. *See also* LAND REFORM, 183; GREEN REVOLUTION, 180.

Significance   Though the world is rapidly becoming urbanized, agrarian reform is critical in many countries where most of the population still gains its livelihood directly from agriculture. Yet agrarian reform is seldom given high priority by governments, which tend to show a strong urban bias in national development planning. When reform is attempted it often meets resistance from entrenched power structures or from the farmers themselves, who are suspicious and in no position to take further risks. Few attempts at reform that have not been premised on the needs and perceptions of the affected farmers have had a lasting positive impact. Zimbabwe is one of the few food-exporting and food-sufficient countries of Africa. Key to its success have been reforms leading to better prices and incentives for agricultural products, better access to credit (especially for women), and increased technical support from the government. In many cases the most effective reform is simply to find new means of support for existing farming practices embodying indigenous technical knowledge (ITK). Such policies, together with equitable land tenure systems, appear central to successful agrarian reform throughout the developing world. In turn, such reform is key to rural development.

Agroforestry (177)
The integration of growing trees and shrubs with food or other crops—with or without animals—in self-sustaining, highly productive farming systems. Actually, agroforestry has been practiced for thousands of years. The trees not only improve and protect soil productivity but represent savings and a potential cash crop. They also increase fodder supplies for animals. Interest in this age-old practice was renewed in 1977 with studies supported by the International Development Research Centre (IRDC) of Canada that resulted in the establishment of the International Council for Research in Agroforestry (ICRAF) in Nairobi, Kenya. Three of the 13 international agricultural centers (in India, Nigeria, and Ethiopia), under the umbrella of the Consultative Group for International Agricultural Research (CGIAR), have agroforestry programs. All of the major international

development banks have shown a special interest in agroforestry. During the past decade they have invested $2 billion in this area, 13 times what was invested in the previous decade. *See also* USUFRUCT LAND POLICY AND SOCIAL FORESTRY, 190; CHIPKO MOVEMENT, 358.

Significance   The growing interest in agroforestry reflects the enhanced awareness of the critical need to reverse the pattern of global deforestation. Mobilizing villagers to grow more trees will have positive economic and environmental effects, a critical benefit given growing fuelwood shortages in many areas, "the other energy crisis." Robert Chambers of the Institute of Development Studies (IDS) in Sussex, Great Britain, has carefully documented the ways that trees represent both savings and security for the rural poor. Contrary to common myths, he finds that small, poor farmers plant more trees, and sell and cut fewer than expected. Empirical studies also indicate that the funds earned from selling trees are used primarily for productive purposes. David Spurgeon, former IDRC official, elegantly summarized the benefits of agroforestry:

> Fortunately, agroforestry systems are characterized by this happy blend . . . and thereby give farmers the maximum return from the available soil, water, nutrient[s] and sunlight.

Delay in instituting agroforestry or other tree-preservation/planting programs can be devastating. In Haiti, for example, few trees remain and new trees are often cut prematurely by those desperate for fuelwood.

Circular Migration   (178)
A relatively new demographic concept that refers to the return of individuals to rural areas after experiencing the frustrations of coping with urban living. Such individuals become disillusioned after finding that urban living conditions do not conform to the common stereotypes about "bright lights," jobs, and unlimited economic opportunities. Circular migration has been common in many developing countries in the postwar period in the form of seasonal migration between rural and urban areas. The new pattern is the permanent return to villages of those who have experienced urban life.

Significance   Richard Critchfield in his important volume, *Villages* (1981), and Soedjatmoko of Indonesia in his thoughtful and insightful writings on development describe in positive terms many of the traditional values and conditions of rural life. Critchfield argues that once such villages become equipped with modern amenities, they may seem attractive when compared to overly complex industrial society. If Critchfield's and Soedjatmoko's perceptions are valid, the century ahead may see an increase in circular migration.

Farming Systems Research (FSR)   (179)

An interdisciplinary and highly participatory method of agricultural research and development. The approach emerged in the mid–1970s as a means of bridging the gap between farmers and agricultural research. Much research was being conducted on experimental plots that often did not approximate the physical, biological, and socioeconomic conditions faced by the farmer. FSR is an integrative, bottom-up strategy that starts with the concerns of the farmers and includes them directly in technology development. There are four stages of FSR:

1. Description and diagnosis. This stage involves formal and informal surveys to identify potentials and constraints within the farming system. Researchers may conduct *sondeos*—quick, informal, exploratory, and largely qualitative surveys—carried out by multidisciplinary teams.
2. Design. This should take place with input from farmers.
3. Testing. This is the on-site implementation of the design.
4. Extension. Successful projects are incorporated into regional practice.

Key developers of FSR include David Norman, who has done extensive work in West Africa, and Peter Hildebrand in Guatemala. *See also* INTEGRATED RURAL DEVELOPMENT, 182; INDIGENOUS TECHNICAL KNOWLEDGE, 248; RAPID RURAL APPRAISAL, 185.

Significance   Farming systems research represents a refinement of integrated rural development and an alternative to earlier approaches to agricultural research that tended to be top-down in practice. The strategy attempts to involve the farmer at all stages of research and development, thereby increasing the chances for successful and appropriate project and technology design. Potential conflicts of interest may still exist among the farmers, researchers, and elites, but FSR should aid in a realistic assessment of constraints and possibilities of all types. FSR also requires the coordination of multidisciplinary research teams whose members may have differing agendas and time frames. Despite such demands, FSR has proven highly effective in the field. It incorporates many lessons from past rural research and development efforts and continues to undergo its own refinement. The key to its success and value is its emphasis on genuine participation at all levels of development.

Green Revolution **(180)**

Dramatic increases in grain production, primarily of wheat, rice, and corn, resulting from the utilization of high-yielding varieties (HYVs) of seeds and related new technologies applied in the Third World. Norman Borlaug's development of a short-stemmed strain of wheat, highly responsive to fertilizers and water, gave impetus to the "revolution" in Mexico and soon after in the Punjab in India where the seeds were introduced in the early 1960s. HYVs of rice, the most broadly consumed grain in Asia, were then developed at the International Rice Research Institute (IRRI) in the Philippines. HYVs of both grains were highly dependent on an abundant water supply, mechanization, fertilizers, and pesticides since the seeds were not necessarily well adapted to local conditions. The term itself is credited to William S. Gaud who served as director of the U.S. Agency for International Development (AID) in 1968. A "green" revolution was perceived by many as the best alternative to the "red" (Communist) revolution. The Green Revolution has affected Asia most profoundly, with less dramatic results in Latin America and only nominal impact in Africa since wheat and rice are less widely grown or consumed there. A potential second Green Revolution may occur with new advances in biotechnology and/or the growing acceptance and implementation of the many alternative food-production systems whose benefits are being demonstrated on a small scale throughout the world. *See also* HIGH YIELD VARIETIES, 181; NORMAN BORLAUG, 62; SUSTAINABLE AGRICULTURE, 188.

Significance While adoption of Green Revolution technology was by no means universal, it led to unparalleled increases in world food production precisely at a time when most developing nations began experiencing unprecedented growth in population. Between 1950 and 1980, Third World food production averaged 3 percent annual growth, slightly higher than the population rate. As such, Green Revolution technology undoubtedly helped avert Malthusian type famines throughout the Third World. India and Mexico became self-sufficient in grain production in a relatively short period of time and soon became exporters. However, critics point out that the adoption of the capital- and energy-intensive technology contributed to greater concentration of wealth and subsequent impoverishment of poorer farmers. Large inputs of capital were needed to supply the technology, water, seeds, and fertilizers necessary for increased

165

production. Such inputs were most often unavailable to the poorer farmers. Supporters respond that while the income gap may have widened in many areas, the rural poor have benefited from greater productivity and lower food prices. In fact, the social and economic results of the Green Revolution have varied broadly according to the conditions into which the technology was introduced. Critics also raise concerns about the environmental effects of widespread and sustained use of pesticides, monocropping, and increased dependency on foreign products and technology for food production. As production growth rates begin to level off throughout the Third World, questions of sustainability are raised. Borlaug responds that the HYVs were never viewed as a panacea, but were necessary to buy time for the development of further solutions to world food problems. He accepts that the seed alone cannot revolutionize things, without technological and cultural change.

High Yield Varieties (HYVs) (181)
New strains of grains that became the technical foundation for the Green Revolution. Both wheat and rice plants, the two major grains involved, shared common characteristics: they were short-stemmed (dwarfs) to prevent lodging, highly responsive to and dependent on fertilizer and water, high in protein content, and resistant to major diseases. The HYVs not only resulted in high yields per hectare but matured more quickly than traditional strains, allowing double and even triple cropping in some areas. The first HYVs of wheat were developed by Norman Borlaug in Mexico in the late 1950s while the rice varieties were developed under the direction of Robert Chandler at the IRRI in the Philippines. The first HYV of rice, IR-8, was released in 1966, declared International Rice Year by the United Nations Food and Agriculture Organization (FAO). The original strains have since been replaced many times over by new varieties. Since the same varieties are planted in a wide range of settings, they may not be well adapted to each particular setting. As such, they are highly dependent on controlled inputs such as fertilizers and pesticides, and each strain has a life span of three to four years before it succumbs to natural enemies. Some refer to the seeds as high-input varieties. The short duration of each generation has resulted in what has been described as a varietal relay race where the plant breeders attempt to develop replacement strains before the previous variety becomes unviable. Through biotechnology new varieties can be developed more quickly by using genetic engineering instead of cross-pollination, the method used to develop the first HYVs. *See also* GREEN REVOLUTION,

180; BIOTECHNOLOGY, 279; INTERNATIONAL UNDERTAKING ON PLANT GENETIC RESOURCES, 288.

Significance   The cultivation of HYVs spread quickly upon availability with dramatic results in Third World grain production, especially in Asia, where population growth threatened to outpace food production. For example, with the introduction of HYVs, India tripled its wheat production from 1967 to 1982 and the Philippines doubled rice production from 1960 to 1980. Even though the HYV seeds and the inputs necessary for their nurture remain beyond the means of many poor farmers, HYVs have been planted on half the world's wheat lands and now account for more than 90 percent of the rice production. HYVs have directly improved the food supply of one-quarter of the world's population, mostly in the developing nations. Systems of production based on HYVs raise serious questions of sustainability, but they undoubtedly have prevented disastrous grain shortages typical of the past.

Integrated Rural Development (IRD)   **(182)**
A comprehensive approach to rural development with emphasis on interrelationships among various sectors. IRD stresses the indivisibility of the rural community and the need to coordinate both agricultural and nonagricultural activities designed to raise the living standard of rural populations. A multidisciplinary and multidimensional approach is utilized to understand causal relationships and anticipate how changes in one sector of the community will affect others. Supporters of IRD also emphasize the need to involve rural people in the planning and implementation of policies and programs, implying decentralization and localized management in the planning process. Through this approach it is anticipated that rural development planning will become more effective in redressing rural-rural and rural-urban inequality. Finally, IRD emphasizes sustainability in the development of human and natural resources.

Significance   Integrated rural development represents an important corrective and critique of earlier notions of rural development. Proponents of this perspective recognize the urban bias in much centralized development planning, noting that in many cases increases in rural productivity have not been accompanied by improvements in rural living standards. IRD embodies a number of key development concepts, placing greater emphasis on human resource development (popular participation), more equitable access to resources for and benefits from the development process, the need for an interdisciplinary and holistic approach to rural development, and questions of sustainability in project design. Though this concept has helped shape recent rural development policies of many governments as well as the World Bank, some remain skeptical about its practical feasibility. Such critics view rural development as occurring with various natural imbalances resulting in subsequent pressures to reduce gaps and lags.

Land Reform (183)

Changes in land tenure systems resulting in more equitable individual ownership, communal tenure, or state ownership. Nearly three-quarters of the world's population gains its livelihood directly from the land, as landlords, small farmers, tenants, or sharecroppers. Land ownership is highly concentrated in nearly every region of the Third World, and associated problems are especially acute in parts of Asia and most areas of Latin America. (Communal ownership is more common in Africa.) Landlessness is increasing nearly everywhere, as a result of both population growth and the accumulation of land into fewer hands. This trend in turn has a direct bearing on rural-urban migration and increasing rural poverty. For these reasons, land reform is one of the most discussed issues of rural and national development. Nearly every developing country has attempted some measure of reform, most unsuccessfully. Because land tenure systems embody entrenched power structures, attempts at reform inevitably meet a great deal of political resistance. Despite the overwhelming evidence that land reform is central to national development and the provision of basic human needs, few nations have achieved successful programs outside of revolutionary change. Not surprisingly, Oxfam has concluded that "unjust land tenure systems and concomittant sytems are the chief causes of hunger and poverty in the Third World." *See also* AGRARIAN REFORM AND TRANSFORMATION, 176; WOLF LADEJINSKI, 80.

Significance   Land reform can be costly and in the short run can disrupt food production and disaffect powerful elements of a society. Military coups have often followed attempts at reform. Failure to achieve reform can be even more costly. Highly unjust tenure systems have been at the heart of revolutions as in Cuba, China, Russia, and Nicaragua. Conversely, effective tenure reform has been the key to the dramatic development success of several nations that have radically different economic systems. Before the 1949 revolution China was a land of frequent famine. The People's Republic of China now manages to feed more than 20 percent of the world's population on only 8 percent of the world's arable land. South Korea and Taiwan have taken much different paths to development but both owe a great deal to successful land reforms. The United States, recognizing the appeal of the Communist "land to the tiller" promise, helped implement highly successful land reform programs in these countries following World War II under the brilliant direction of Wolf Ladejinski. The United States also encouraged land reform in Latin America as part of the Alliance for Progress and other assistance programs. These efforts, however, met with little success, because they confronted a diverse set of vested interests and objectives on the part of the U.S. economic interests and Latin rulers. Because land tenure is a volatile subject, information is often difficult to obtain. Research and related development experience suggests that land tenure systems are closely related to both productivity and sound agroecological practices. Generally, people are more apt to practice conservation if they feel some sense of ownership of a particular plot. This sense of ownership may derive from a secure tenure arrangement, communal ownership, or the actual holding of a deed. As Eric Eckholm of the Worldwatch Institute points out, land reform is central to sustainable development. The relationship of productivity to tenure varies widely. Larger systems benefit from economies of scale and are capital-intensive. On the other hand, smaller plots of comparable quality are usually more productive because they are farmed more intensely and receive better care. In most cases, land reform could lead to significant gains in long-term productivity as well as reduction in malnutrition and poverty.

Latifundios (184)

The large landholdings that account for the vast majority of agricultural land in Latin America. The term is derived from the Latin *latifundia*, which refers to the slave plantations and ranches of wealthy Romans in the second century. By definition a *latifundio* is a farm large enough to employ 12 or more people. Its counterpart is the *minifundio*, a unit too small to support a single family. Together they form the grossly unequal land-ownership distribution pattern that dominates most of Latin America. *See also* LAND REFORM, 183.

Significance   Great inequality in access to land is the prime factor in the impoverished status of most of Latin America's population. Figures from the FAO indicate that 1.3 percent of the landowners hold more than 70 percent of land under cultivation. The situation is exacerbated by the inefficient use of *latifundio* holdings, which often comprise the richest land yet do not begin to approach the per-unit productivity levels of the smaller holdings. Not surprisingly, land issues remain at the heart of continuing conflict and revolutionary impetus in Central and South America.

Rapid Rural Appraisal (RRA) (185)

A group of rural development research methods devised and promoted by Robert Chambers and the Institute for Development Studies (IDS) in Sussex, England. The RRA method was created in response to a need for more timely, relevant, accurate, cost-effective, and useful information than that provided by more conventional methods. Chambers characterizes the two most common methods as "quick and dirty," quick and superficial visits to the countryside by urban-based professionals; and "long and dirty," conventional social science research that is often overly complex or esoteric, and outdated upon completion. A successful rapid rural appraisal is an informed compromise that does not attempt to avoid all superficiality and errors, but rather controls them to achieve cost-effectiveness of time and money. Chambers stresses "optimal ignorance," that is, determining what is not worth knowing, and "proportionate accuracy," or establishing the optimal degree of accuracy needed for the purposes of a project. RRA is a set of methods designed to offset the biases so often a part of what Chambers refers to as rural development tourism. The RRA method recommends that rural appraisers (1) take more time in the field; (2) take measures to offset common biases including roadside bias, male elite bias, dry season bias, and the tendency to communicate only with the educated and with villagers already involved in a project; (3) assume less self-importance and listen to and learn from rural people; and (4) use a number of different data-gathering approaches to cross-check and verify information. In the fourth matter, Chambers suggests using existing information (which is sometimes ignored), learning local technical knowledge, determining key indicators of local welfare, and employing local researchers, direct observation, key informants, and group interviews. *See also* RURAL DEVELOPMENT TOURISM, 303; INDIGENOUS TECHNICAL KNOWLEDGE, 248; ROBERT CHAMBERS, 11.

Significance Rapid rural appraisal has received widespread attention in the applied development field. It alerts professionals to the many pitfalls and biases common to the information aspect of rural development projects. At the same time, it offers practical suggestions for overcoming these obstacles to effective and sensitive project design. RRA is a common-sense approach to fundamental needs in the development field. The criticism of RRA as a mere pointing out of the obvious does not detract from its usefulness, for whether obvious or not, the problems it addresses persist in practice and need to be rectified if more effective and responsive projects are to be designed.

Rural Responsibility System (186)

An innovative approach used in the People's Republic of China that blends socialistic and capitalistic principles to stimulate productivity improvements in the agricultural sector. This system was part of the major economic reforms introduced by Deng Xiaoping and his colleagues after the end of the Cultural Revolution and the arrest of the Gang of Four in 1976. In this system, land remains under the control of the state, and farmers pay a fixed rent based on the size of their holding, but unrelated to their total level of production. Thus, for the first part of each year farmers are working to produce enough to pay off their fixed rent. Once they have paid their rent to the state, the remaining income from their agricultural production is free for their own discretionary use. Such a system creates a tremendous incentive to maximize agricultural production. *See also* AGRARIAN REFORM AND TRANSFORMATION, 176.

Significance   The rural responsibility system represents a rather remarkable integration of the ideas of socialism (government ownership of land), Henry George (land tax), and free-enterprise market capitalism (maximum profits to the most enterprising). Despite its integration of ideas from diverse ideologies, it is a controversial system. Some argue that it has contributed to growing individual and regional income disparities in China. The increased incomes and demands resulting from the rural responsibility system could contribute to China's current problems with inflation, though the increased productivity resulting from the system should actually be deflationary. Given China's huge population and small percentage of available arable land (only 11 percent of its land area), its success in achieving self-sufficiency in agriculture is noteworthy and exemplary. Other developing countries could benefit from closely examining China's agricultural sector, including the imaginative rural responsibility system.

Small-Scale Producers (SSPs) (187)

Farmers with limited resources and small landholdings. In the concept developed by D. M. Warren, SSPs include subsistence farmers outside of the formal market system as well as emergent farmers who market some of their farm outputs. In the early days of development these groups were largely ignored primarily because of the biased attitude of Europeans and Americans toward non-Western peoples. Instead primary attention focused on large-scale commercial farmers. Beginning in the 1970s, however, more attention was given to SSPs. Facilitating this shift were several developments, namely, (1) the emergence of ethnoscience as an integral part of anthropology, (2) the establishment in the 1960s of a new network of international agricultural centers, (3) the return of Western volunteers from service among the poor in LDCs, (4) AID's 1973 mandate to give highest priority to projects to improve the lives of the poorest segments of society, (5) the emergence of farming systems research and development efforts pioneered by individuals such as David Norman, and (6) the emphasis on indigenous technical knowledge by prominent scholars such as Robert Chambers. *See also* FARMING SYSTEMS RESEARCH, 179; INDIGENOUS TECHNICAL KNOWLEDGE, 248; LAND REFORM, 183.

Significance   Small-scale producers constitute the largest segment of poor people in many developing countries. Despite their material poverty, such farmers often have valuable and insightful knowledge of indigenous agricultural systems. Much can be learned from such individuals, who appear to be more rational than traditional about agricultural decision making. During the past two decades increased interaction has taken place between technical agricultural scientists and SSPs. Individuals such as D. M. Warren argue that more cost-effective development programs can be realized by working with and through indigenous, local decision-making groups. Special concern for the needs and problems of SSPs is essential to enhance the impact of development on equity.

Sustainable Agriculture (188)

Agricultural practices and systems that seek to maintain or improve productivity without degrading the environment or jeopardizing the ability of future generations to meet their agricultural needs. Sustainability pertains to the biological, physical, socioeconomic, and legal components of agriculture systems. In practice, sustainability generally implies minimized use of artificial herbicides, pesticides, and fertilizers and other petroleum-based inputs. Proponents emphasize alternative methods of pest control such as integrated pest management (IPM) or the development of more pest- and disease-resistant varieties of plants and livestock. Regeneration of the soil is accomplished through crop rotation and the use of natural fertilizers. The term also implies control of soil erosion and questions the long-term viability of monocropping. Sustainable agriculture may be distinguished from industrialized agriculture and agribusiness by its stress on *optimizing* production as opposed to *maximizing* production. Thus the objectives are more complex. Sustainable agriculture also implies the need for more site-specific research practices since sustainability is determined by local conditions. The concept is articulated in the field of agroecology, for example, in the work of Gordan Conway, and in the permaculture and organic farming movements. *See also* SUSTAINABLE DEVELOPMENT, 272; GREEN REVOLUTION, 180; INDIGENOUS TECHNICAL KNOWLEDGE, 248.

Significance   As agricultural productivity based on Green Revolution technology levels off and the long-term environmental and economic consequences are better understood, questions of sustainability become more pressing. There is a growing recognition of the need for sustainable systems to replace petroleum-based systems. This is being accomplished through a combination of biotechnology, new innovations, and the recovery and enhancement of traditional farming practices. Since most of the world's poor dwell in rural areas, sustainable agriculture must remain central to broader discussions of sustainable development.

Tropical Seasonality   **(189)**
The importance of seasons in tropical areas and the dramatic impact that seasonal variations may have on developmental conditions. Most of the world's poor live in tropical areas that have markedly contrasting dry and wet seasons. These issues were the focus of a major conference on the Seasonal Dimensions to Rural Poverty sponsored by the IDS in England, July 4–7, 1978. Major findings of the conference are highlighted in a volume edited by Robert Chambers, Richard Longhurst, and Arnold Pacey, *Seasonal Dimensions to Rural Poverty* (1981). The conference emphasized the seasonal linkages between food, energy, morbidity, malnutrition, indebtedness, dependence, exploitation, and poverty. *See also* RURAL DEVELOPMENT TOURISM, 303.

Significance   In his insightful writing on development conditions Robert Chambers frequently mentions tropical seasonality, noting that Western and urban-based professionals prefer to travel to tropical areas during the more favorable and pleasant seasons. As a result, their perceptions of genuine rural conditions and poverty are often seriously distorted and they fail to recognize the critical importance of seasonality and how it affects developmental conditions in highly interdependent ways. A greater awareness of tropical seasonality has many practical policy and administrative implications. Perhaps the most critical relates to the timing of actions, policies, and development programs. Given concerns about regional inequalities, locational rather than timing considerations tend to dominate development planning and thinking. Thailand's dry-season public works program is an example of a response to the problem of tropical seasonality. During the dry season, Thai farmers are underemployed and face serious income shortfalls, which contribute to their indebtedness and poverty. A major dry-season rural public works program provides income to farmers who work on development projects such as fish ponds and small-scale irrigation projects. The People's Republic of China has also developed effective seasonal public works programs. Unfortunately, these examples are uncommon and too little awareness of tropical seasonality is fostered by planners and policymakers who remain so-called knights in air-conditioned offices and travel to remote rural areas only during the best of seasons.

Usufruct Land Policy and Social Forestry (190)
An innovative approach to land utilization to prevent deforestation and enhance the forestry commons and the quality of life there. Under this approach being tested by the United Nations Development Program (UNDP) and the UN Food and Agriculture Organization (FAO), farmers are not allowed to own, buy, or sell the land involved. Instead they receive certificates of usufruct, which give them the right to use the land for five years. If the land is used properly, their rights can be extended and even passed on to children. This innovation is being implemented in Thailand's Northeast, which has been adversely affected by serious deforestation. Vast quantities of tree seedlings and other important government services have been distributed to the farmers involved. *See also* AGROFORESTRY, 177.

Significance The usufruct land policy and social forestry approach represents a creative combination of capitalism, socialism, and rational choice theory. Explicit incentives encourage conservation and proper treatment of the land and soil. The wastes and injustices associated with private land ownership, profit making from land speculation, and absentee landlords are eliminated. Essential to the success of such an approach is a government bureaucracy sufficiently strong and dedicated to enforcing the sanctions and incentives associated with environmentally sound land use.

Villages **(191)**

Along with the family, the small communities that serve as the basic unit of social and political organization throughout the nonindustrialized world. Though the world's population is increasingly concentrated in urban areas, roughly one-half to three-quarters continue to live in more than 2 million villages, most of them in LDCs. No precise definition exists of what constitutes a village in terms of size. Rather, villages are most often discussed in terms of functional units that may vary greatly in size, composition, and physical characteristics. Anthropologist Robert Redfield, a pioneer in village studies, was one of the first to suggest the existence of a common or generic world village culture, in *Peasant Society and Culture* (1956). In addition to an immediate village-centered worldview, Redfield emphasizes several shared characteristics, including close ties to and reverence for the land, mixed appreciation and suspicion of city life and people, a view of hard physical labor as intrinsically good and necessary, and restraint on individualism in favor of the family and the village.

Significance   Given the great diversity of cultures throughout the world, one should approach the concept of a village culture with caution. However, villages and villagers in diverse settings do appear to share many characteristics, as pointed out by Redfield and others. To the extent that village culture may be universal in rural areas, and considering that the majority of the world's population lives in village settings, an understanding of this culture and type of community is central to development studies. Village-focused development planning and research could help offset the urban bias so common in the development field. Finally, as village journalist Richard Critchfield concludes in his book, *Villages* (1981:346):

> History suggests that there may be no adequate substitute for this universal village culture, which, for all its restraints, religious conventions and patterns of obedience, seems necessary in small communities of people living off the land. It just could be the most harmonious way of life for human beings who choose to live in groups.

D. Political Development/Development Administration

Aprismo   **(192)**

A Latin American development philosophy emphasizing anti-capitalism and anti-imperialism, the concept of Indo-America, and Latin American unity. This philosophy was adopted by the

APRA (Alianza Popular Revolucionaria Americana) or Aprista party of Peru, which was formed in 1924 in Mexico by the exiled Victor Raúl Haya de la Torre, the father of *aprismo*. Haya de la Torre, author of *A Donde Va Indo-America?* (1936) and *Treinta Años de Aprismo* (1956), apparently won the Peruvian presidential elections of 1931 and 1962 but was never allowed to take office. In fact, he was forced to spend much of his life in prison, in hiding, or in exile. The *aprismo* philosophy is considered distinct from communism, which is seen as European. It calls for an alliance between the producers and the middle class with an emphasis on the political participation of the indigenous Indians, who have historically been exploited by outside invaders and conquerors. With its emphasis on Latin American unity, this philosophy is clearly Bolívarian. Like dependency theory, *aprismo* calls for the economic independence of Latin America and views the Pan-America concept as an expression of North American imperialism. The APRA party held power in Peru from 1985 to 1990 under Alan García Pérez. *See also* DEPENDENCY THEORY, 106.

Significance   In several key respects, with its emphasis on economic independence, anti-imperialism, and anti-capitalism, *aprismo* represents a precursor to dependency theory. Particularly central to this philosophy are the notion of Indo-America and the concept that the native Indians represent the core population of Latin America who have traditionally been neglected and exploited economically, politically, and culturally. The extremely radical nature of the *aprismo* philosophy has restricted its appeal to the elite and bourgeoisie classes, who see it as a threat to their privileged position in Latin American societies. Perhaps the socialist regime in Nicaragua came closest to reflecting some of the ideals of *aprismo*. Cuba does not particularly fit the model because of the strong influence there of Hispanic and Black cultures, the dominance of European-influenced communism, and its persisting economic dependence on the Soviet Union.

Bureaucratic Pathology   **(193)**
An organizational climate or structure in which the interests of citizens, employees, and society at large are subordinated to the self-centered and self-aggrandizing goals of authoritarian leaders and officials. This milieu of bureaucratic pathology is characterized by the principle that administration is power, not service. Delays and inefficiency are common and often are used to facilitate corruption or questionable payments. Rewards in such systems are often unrelated to genuine service to the larger public or to professional commitment, but depend upon personal connections, loyalties, and favors.

Such bureaucracies grow, unrelated to actual needs for services provided. High degrees of centralization are common to such systems, with little genuine opportunity for employee or client participation. *See also* PARTICIPATORY DEVELOPMENT, 117.

Significance While bureaucratic pathology is common in all societies, it is a special problem in a number of developing countries. Many key reforms introduced in China during the 1980s were designed to reduce the level of pathology in the massive bureaucracy established during the Maoist period. Serious levels of bureaucratic pathology adversely affect the public-service infrastructure essential for effective and responsive development. Though there are many competing explanations for bureaucratic pathology, a common one relates to quality of leadership. Bureaucracies in which officials are well educated and/or well paid tend to be less subject to bureaucratic pathology. Many political scientists also argue that the existence of democratic mechanisms, such as open elections and parliamentary bodies, contributes to bureaucratic accountability and responsiveness. Others argue that democratic systems encourage political interference that may adversely affect professionalism and commitment to longer-term perspectives. Finally, and of special importance, excessive bureaucratic pathology may lead to political revolution. Empirical research indicates that an important factor contributing to the decision to rebel is maltreatment by arrogant and/or corrupt officials.

Circulation of Elites (194)

A sociological concept derived from Vilfredo Pareto denoting the openness of a political system to allow for regular changes in leadership. In a genuine circulation of elites, opportunities are open to individuals of diverse geographic and socioeconomic backgrounds. If new leaders are always recruited from a narrow class, the elite structure is still relatively closed. Political scientist William Riker argues that fair and open elections serve a vital role in facilitating elite circulation.

Significance The blocking of elite circulation frequently leads to political tension and growing popular discontent. The overthrow of leaders such as the Shah of Iran, Somoza in Nicaragua, Marcos in the Philippines, Thanom in Thailand, and Stroessner in Paraguay shows the dramatic political consequences that can result from a lack of elite circulation. Elite circulation enables a society to renew and revitalize itself. In an open elite structure, potential rebels may decide to work through normal political channels to obtain power. Without elite circulation, governments may remain unresponsive and provide minimal opportunities for popular feedback.

Colonialism (195)

A worldwide system of economic and political expansion and dominance by a small number of predominantly Western European nations. The term *colonialism* is often used interchangeably with *imperialism* and may also refer to the Japanese empire expansion that led up to World War II. Nearly all areas of Africa, Asia, the Pacific, and the Caribbean have experienced some sort of European colonial rule. The Middle East was controlled by Europe for only a short period following the fall of the Ottoman Empire at the beginning of this century. Even countries that never came under direct colonial rule, such as Thailand, Liberia, and Afghanistan, were deeply affected by the colonial system.

The colonial age began in the sixteenth century with Spanish and Portuguese invasions of what became Latin America and the Caribbean region. The Spanish were primarily concerned with a search for gold and silver which they exchanged for products imported from European neighbors. Spain also became involved in slave trade and sugar production, but was unable to maintain much political and economic control in its territories after 1821. Meanwhile, the Portuguese were joined by the British and Dutch as the premier sea powers and international merchants focusing on Asia. Trading companies were "granted territory" by their respective home governments along with military support to quell resistance, of which there were considerable episodes. The discovery of quinine as a medicine for malaria helped open the African continent to the colonial powers in the late 1800s. By the turn of the century, the majority of the world's land had been divided into colonial territories controlled by France, Great Britain, Portugal, Belgium, Germany, and the Netherlands. At the same time the United States, once a colony itself, gained control of Puerto Rico and the Philippines as an outcome of the Spanish-American War. The height of the American colonial period was 1920–1945. The colonial era began to disintegrate with the American Revolution and ended swiftly and dramatically following World War II. Since 1949, nearly 100 new nation-states have gained political independence. Only a few colonies and territories remain. The colonial legacy, however, continues to have a profound effect on many of the world's citizens. *See also* DECOLONIZATION, 200; IMPERIALISM, 204; NEOCOLONIALISM, 210; NATIONALISM, 209.

Significance   Though the colonial experience varied according to the location and the colonial power, in all locations colonial involvement was primarily extractive in nature. The colonies became sources of raw materials and agricultural products such as tea, sugar, cotton, coffee, and spices. Further, colonialism created a new international division of labor with subordinate positions allocated to the colonies. Colonialism became an extension of the Industrial Revolution, though its aim was not to bring competitive industry to the colonies. While the raw materials of the colonies fueled the industries of Europe, the colonial powers destroyed local industry to eliminate competition for European goods. A dramatic example was the demise of the textile industry in India under the British. The colonies became vast markets for European goods. The system was also detrimental to local cultures and security systems, especially where large tracts of land were seized from subsistence farmers in order to grow export crops. Importation of foreign labor in certain cases led to increased ethnic tensions and conflict.

Ethnocentrism abounding, the colonialists rationalized empire building as an extension of civilization. They brought Christianity, education, health care, and economic integration to the "uncivilized," failing to recognize the legitimacy of local cultures and systems, even ancient and highly developed political and social orders. Resistance took on many forms ranging from prolonged military resistance, as was the case with the Ashanti in Ghana and the Zulus in Natal, for example, to more subtle forms of noncooperation. Not all Europeans, and certainly not the majority of the colonized, viewed imperialism as a benign expansion of Western civilization. Lenin, for example, was harshly critical of the exploitive nature of colonialism, and set forth his views in *Imperialism: The Highest Stage of Capitalism* (1917). The imperial powers used a combination of military force and indirect rule to maintain control over vast populations and territories.

As former colonies gained independence in the post–World War II era, either through armed resistance or the voluntary withdrawal of the colonists, the indelible mark of colonialism became even more apparent. The unequal relationships established over the decades of European rule persisted despite political independence. The new nations found it difficult to develop genuine economic and cultural sovereignty and began to speak of neocolonialism, more subtle forms of dominance, and ongoing dependent relations in political arrangements, economic relations, and cultural interchange. Even foreign aid and development assistance are widely viewed as forms of continued control on the part of Western nations. In addition to economic and political independence, the former colonies continue to struggle to create and regain a sense of dignity and identity, a process that African historian Chinweizu calls the "decolonization of the mind."

Communalism (196)

The existence of competing ethnic groups within a given nation-state, primarily in the political and economic realms. In communal systems these groups have clear ethnic identities that they wish to maintain, and they reject the notion of assimilation into the dominant culture. The existence of communalism raises a range of complex issues, such as the ethnic mix of political parties, language policies, educational streaming, and affirmative-action policies to aid economically deprived ethnic groups or "penalties" for overly successful groups. Intense communalism can lead to civil strife and/or forced emigration of certain communities. The presence of "guest workers" from other countries can also lead to growing communalism. *See also* ETHNIC NATIONALISM, 229; CULTURAL DEMOCRACY, 218.

Significance   Given that many developing countries have high levels of cultural heterogeneity, communalism is both a common and a complex issue. A nation that has dealt successfully with the issue is Singapore, which has four national languages and multiethnic political parties. Indonesia, by choosing the neutral Bahasa Indonesia as its national language, defused many potential problems of communalism. In contrast, since achieving independence from England in 1948, Burma has not yet solved its communal problem and in 1989 changed its name to Myanmar to try to be more responsive to communal pressures. The reality of communalism is almost a universal constant. What varies enormously is the manner in which governments and nations allow communal groups to participate economically and politically, and the extent to which ethnic groups are allowed to preserve their cultural identities.

Community Empowerment (197)

The delegation of power and authority to local citizens to allow their voices in decisions affecting their lives. This philosophy stresses bottom-up, rather than top-down, development. In genuine community empowerment, local individuals are given control over financial resources and decision making. In pseudo community empowerment, locals are consulted, but actual decisions are made at higher levels.

An example of a community empowerment development project was Ngun Pann (pass the money down) in Thailand. Councils elected in tambols (subdistricts) were given block (lump-sum) grants to use for whatever purposes they deemed appropriate for local community development. Funds were used for projects such as new roads, fish ponds, small-scale irrigation projects, and new preschools. The Saemaul Undong program in Korea operated in a similar fashion. *See also* DECENTRALIZATION, 199; NGUN PAN PROJECT, 369; SAEMAUL UNDONG, 372.

Significance   Too often villagers at the local level are ignored in the development process and inappropriate top-down projects may be imposed on villages. Governments are often reluctant to allow community empowerment because of fear that funds will not be used effectively or efficiently or fear of slippage through local corruption. Even when nonoptimal decisions are made at the local level, important learning and thus capacity building occur. Community empowerment may also strengthen the power of local politicians, which may threaten centralized authorities. A negative but often overlooked aspect of community empowerment is that it can disrupt local social harmony, since conflicts will inevitably arise over the use of funds and resources made possible by a genuine decentralization of power. Though community empowerment has both benefits and costs, it is integral to the realization of genuine rice-roots democracy and participative development.

Corporatism   **(198)**
A concept used to describe states that incorporate key interest groups into a system of governance so as to minimize overt conflict and political competition and to facilitate the development of policies in the "national" interest. The concept, from the field of political science, became popular in the mid–1970s as an alternative to the concept of pluralism. In the past 15 years, the idea has sometimes been referred to as neocorporatism to distinguish it from earlier, inaccurate usage describing Fascist Italy and Nazi Germany. Currently corporatism is most commonly used to describe consensus-oriented democracies such as Austria, Switzerland, and Japan; authoritarian Latin American regimes (O'Donnell 1979); and Asian governments influenced by Confucian theories of harmony (Zeigler 1988:15). Many distinguish between a democratic variant called societal corporatism and an authoritarian form called state corporatism. The former characterizes countries such as Japan and Switzerland, and the latter nations such as South Korea and Taiwan. Manfred Schmidt (1982) has used

two empirical indicators to measure the extent to which a nation is corporatist: extent of absence of strikes and proportion of GNP invested in capital formation. Two valuable studies of corporatism are Peter J. Williamson's *Varieties of Corporatism* (1985) and Harmon J. Zeigler's *Pluralism, Corporatism, and Confucianism* (1988), which compares political association and conflict resolution in the United States, Europe, and Taiwan.

Significance   The concept of corporatism is one of the most debated in contemporary political science. A major problem relates to the existence of numerous alternative variants of corporatism with rather substantially different meanings and implications. Despite Schmidt's valuable work, there are no agreed-upon empirical measures of corporatism. Despite these definitional problems, the concept of corporatism has moved political science away from a narrow reliance on the dichotomy of pluralism and authoritarianism as the dominant paradigm to describe state–interest group relations in contemporary polities. Corporatism also provides an important theoretical perspective for analyzing economically dynamic non-Western political systems in Asia and nonpluralistic regimes in Latin America. Corporatism is also highly relevant to current debates about the need for explicit industrial policy and the type of government–interest group relations most compatible with such macro goals as economic dynamism (high economic growth with minimal inflation), more just income distribution, and the attainment of sustainable development (development consistent with the long-term preservation of sound ecosystems).

Decentralization   (199)

A development strategy emphasizing the dispersement of decision-making and administrative authority to regional and local governments or to nongovernmental organizations and agencies. The role of the central government has always been a key issue in the development debate. Most conventional development theory, both socialist and capitalist, in the 1950s and 1960s assumed that strong central planning was necessary to coordinate and rationalize the process of industrialization and modernization in developing nations, as typified by numerous five-year plans. The emphasis on central planning was also a reflection of the shortage of trained administrators. Growing disillusionment with centralized planning became evident in the 1970s, especially as a result of the failure of most countries to achieve growth with equity: socialist countries tended to achieve equity with little growth and capitalist nations more often achieved growth with more inequality. The development literature began to stress basic human needs, popular participation, and, in the 1980s, the potential of nongovernmental and private agencies and enterprises. Further, serious questions were raised regarding the ability of a small group of urban elites to understand and respond to the needs of the rural poor. All of these themes implied the need for decentralization of decision making. From a variety of motivations, numerous governments embarked upon programs of decentralization which took on many forms. India and Tanzania, for example, allocated more authority to local governments. A number of Latin American nations shifted planning to semiautonomous organizations. In Africa and Asia, more emphasis was placed on district and provincial administration. Another strategy was debureaucratization, the transfer of responsibilities to voluntary organizations and the private sector. The emphasis on decentralization in most cases resulted from public pressure. Central governments adopted the new policies to retain legitimacy, to redress glaring inefficiencies, and in some cases to delegate responsibilities. *See also* COMMUNITY EMPOWERMENT, 197; NONGOVERNMENTAL ORGANIZATIONS, 295; PARTICIPATORY DEVELOPMENT, 117.

Significance   Decentralization is a response to the disappointments and the entrenchment associated with central development planning and administration. Decentralization attempts to tap local knowledge and experience to understand and overcome local problems that are unlikely to be fully appreciated by urban elites. It is also a strategy for achieving greater political and economic equity and participation. In practice and policy decentralization has garnered mixed results. Local authorities and organizations are not always given adequate resources or freedom by the central government to carry out their new responsibilities. Power is not readily given up. And depending on local politics, decentralization may not always result in greater participation in decision making. In many instances, the most effective programs involving popular participation in politics and development are initiated from below rather than from central authorities. In instances such as the formation of cooperatives, governments can engage in decentralization simply by recognizing the authority of the new organization or even offering assistance. The dramatic recent growth of indigenous nongovernmental organizations and autonomy and independence movements points to the growing appeal of decentralization as a development and human rights strategy.

Decolonization   (200)
The process of terminating external control of a polity to achieve

political independence. The term *decolonization* was coined by the German scholar M. J. Bonn in 1932 and first appeared in 1952 in the title of a French book by Henri Labouret. Since the end of World War II, nearly 100 former colonies have become politically independent through the process of decolonization. The geographic areas with the greatest extent of decolonization have probably been Africa and the South Pacific. There is little similarity between the names on the maps or stamps of these two regions in the years right after World War II and those used now. In his valuable political history of African decolonization, John D. Hargreaves shares Leopold Senghor's insightful definition of decolonization:

> the abolition of all prejudice, of all superiority complex, in the mind of the colonizer, and also of all inferiority complex in the mind of the colonized. (Hargreaves 1988:2)

The attainment of Senghor's mental state of decolonization is obviously a more stringent requirement than simply the relaxation of formal external control. Radical thinkers such as Frantz Fanon, noting the conditions under which political power was being transferred in Africa, considered the transfer to be "false decolonization." Such critics see a neocolonial system, with many dependent and exploitive relations continuing after political independence under new formal arrangements that often guarantee access of former colonial powers to economic and other resources. Responses to decolonization have varied rather dramatically. Many nations, such as Singapore, Malaysia, Ivory Coast, the Philippines, and Sri Lanka, have received their political independence smoothly and peacefully. Other nations have experienced violent wars of liberation, such as in Vietnam, Algeria, Mozambique, and Indonesia. *See also* COLONIALISM, 195; NEOCOLONIALISM, 210.

Significance   As the decade of the 1990s begins, decolonization is still an important issue of political development. Areas such as French Guiana, Palestine, and Palau have not yet attained political independence. After six votes, Palau has still not reached agreement on a compact of free association with the United States. The obstacle thus far has been the insistence of the United States that it be able to use its nuclear military base in the area. Other countries with formal political independence still face important issues related to decolonization such as the two U.S. Pacific military bases in the Philippines. One group of Filipinos sees such bases as a violation of Philippine political sovereignty. In colonial island areas such as New Caledonia, Tahiti, and even Puerto Rico, debate continues concerning possible political independence. Despite the remarkable number of new states established in the postwar period as part of the decolonization process, deeper forms of colonization, suggested by the thinking of individuals like Fanon and Senghor, continue to persist in many parts of the developing world.

Development Administration (201)
A term denoting the complex of agencies, management systems, and processes a government establishes to achieve its development goals. The term was coined in the mid–1950s by George Gant, then of the Ford Foundation, and the prominent Dutch economist, Egbert de Vries. A key distinction was that between administration focusing on the management of development versus ordinary administration, which focuses on the maintenance of law and order. Bureaucratic entrepreneurship and institution building, in the view of Harlan Cleveland, were also key elements of development administration. In the 1960s, the concept of development administration was translated into reality through various institution-building development assistance projects. In 1966, with Ford Foundation support, Thailand established the National Institute of Development Administration. Also in the mid–1960s, a development administration unit was established in the prime minister's office in Malaysia. The U.S. Agency for International Development (AID) changed the name of its public administration unit to development administration in the 1960s, and the UN regional center for training and research in administration in Asia became the Asian and Pacific Development Administration Center (in Kuala Lumpur, Malaysia). In 1979, Gant published the basic textbook on development administration, *Development Administration: Concepts, Goals, and Methods.* Clarence Thurber and Lawrence Graham edited a volume, *Development Administration in Latin America*, in 1973, which provided a systematic discussion of the topic. That research was an outgrowth of Fred Riggs's seminal work on public administration in developing countries, *Administration in Developing Countries: The Theory of Prismatic Society* (1964), which was in many respects a pioneer work in the field of development administration.

Significance   The evolution of the concept of development administration reflected growing awareness that development was far more than hardware such as dams, roads, fertilizers, factories, and equipment. The concept also was consistent with Joseph Schumpeter's classical thinking related to innovation and entrepreneurship. Integral to the concept of development administration are the "innovations which strengthen the capacity of the bureaucracy to stimulate and facilitate development" (Gant 1979:25). Another key element in the concept is an emphasis on decentralization as a means to enhance both the efficiency and the responsiveness of bureaucratic systems in developing countries. As part of the development concept came the notion of rational national planning, a somewhat ironic emphasis, given that the United States itself did not engage in such planning. Another key dimension of development administration is its interdisciplinary and future orientation. Though successful development is too complex to measure empirically, it seems apparent that well-managed countries are generally those with more impressive development success stories. Examples of countries with solid management systems are Singapore, Malaysia, South Korea, contemporary Chile, and the Ivory Coast. Their current success is dramatic when contrasted with poorly managed societies such as Burma, Bolivia, and Zaire. A final and important implication of development administration is that it concerns not only the difficult task of management for development but also the development of administration itself.

Felt Needs (202)

The genuine wants and desires of individuals affected by various development programs and projects. The early literature on community development placed a strong emphasis on the importance of identifying felt needs and then facilitating the development of action programs to respond to such wants. Despite the apparent simplicity and attractiveness of this ideal, its implementation has often been problematic. Powerless individuals with limited consciousness of the total realm of alternative possibilities may find it difficult to articulate precise needs. Or certain needs may be considered politically sensitive or disruptive of important vested interests. A common example could be land reform. *See also* BASIC NEEDS, 102; PARTICIPATORY DEVELOPMENT, 117.

Significance Despite the difficulties, the ability to identify the felt needs of those populations to be affected by programs and projects is central to a responsive and participatory approach to development. The failure to listen to or consult the people has resulted in well-documented examples of waste and inefficiency in various development projects around the world (e.g., the groundnuts scheme in Ghana, the Aswan Dam in Egypt, and early steel mills in India). Experts, whether local or external, tend to think that with all their learned "wisdom" they know what is best for rural or other poor populations. Even while paying lip service to the goal of ascertaining felt needs, in direct encounters with rural people, such experts tend to be dominating, resulting in the imposition of their values on their clients. The major challenge for development workers and planners is to develop sufficient cultural empathy to ascertain the genuine needs of rural peoples and then to utilize their expertise to facilitate eventual satisfaction of such needs with the active involvement of the people themselves.

Guided Democracy (203)

A term referring to political systems dominated by one party and usually one individual, but having democratic mechanisms such as elections and parliaments. Guided democracies, a concept popularized by Third World leaders such as Sukarno in Indonesia, have usually been one-party states. Advocates of guided democracy emphasize that political development is not unilinear, so it is not necessary or even appropriate for all Third World countries to imitate a pluralistic, multiparty type of political development. Those favoring this concept also argue that in the milieu of Third World politics, a pluralistic, multiparty system may be too chaotic and indecisive, and thus fail to facilitate economic development. *See also* POLITICAL DEVELOPMENT, 211.

Significance Guided democracy is certainly a controversial and hotly debated issue. Liberal scholars of political development often view guided democracy as a means to legitimate authoritarian and paternalistic rule. Others associate it with leaders obsessed with developing a personality cult. As "people power" spreads around the Third World, there is increasingly less tolerance for guided democracy. Citizens want genuine democracy and opportunities to express themselves politically. Mechanisms for such opportunities need not necessarily follow or imitate Western patterns of political structure.

Imperialism (204)

The extension and maintenance of political and economic power or empire by dominant nation-states, resulting in the subordination or de facto loss of sovereignty of other nations. Imperialism in the modern world dates from the global exploration, conquest, and establishment of colonies in the sixteenth century by the major European sea powers, namely Spain, Portugal, Britain, and the Netherlands. At the height of the colonial period between the two world wars, much of the world had fallen under the political and economic domain of a few European powers. Motives for colonial expansion were varied, but generally involved the need to expand markets under terms favorable to the imperial power, access to natural resources and cheap labor, and the desire to spread elements of Western civilization. Imperialism was also a result of each European nation's desire to enhance its national security and international position vis-à-vis the other imperial powers. In the 1880s, for example, Joseph Chamberlain argued that the expanding influence of France and Germany necessitated further extension of the British Empire. However, such rationales were challenged by isolationists and those who criticized imperialism as a form of exploitation. In *Imperialism as the Highest State of Capitalism* (1917), Lenin provided the groundwork for many subsequent interpretations of imperialism as economic exploitation. Lenin argued that imperialism is an economic necessity for the exploitive capitalist economy, a buffer against the otherwise inevitable falling rates of profit and collapse of the system. According to many scholars, imperialism did not end with the demise of the colonial system following World War II, but rather continues in less direct, but no less effective, systems of dominance created and maintained by former colonial powers. Dependency theorists, for example, stress the notion that most Third World countries are conditioned in their development by dependence upon the economically powerful Western industrialized states. Further, they contend that neocolonialism is perpetuated by many forms of imperialism and sometimes subtle forms of dominance. The theoretical breadth of imperialism now extends to other dimensions such as cultural, intellectual, and social imperialism. *See also* COLONIALISM, 195; NEOCOLONIALISM, 210; CULTURAL IMPERIALISM, 220; DEPENDENCY THEORY, 106.

Significance   The many theories of imperialism seek to explain the nature of, and reasons for, the dominance of one country or people over another. The term *imperialism* is emotion laden; it involves interpretation of motivation and is difficult to operationalize empirically. Imperialist policies have no doubt been devastating to the development of many countries and cultures. The issue of exploitation has not been adequately dealt with in orthodox development literature. But the nature of imperialism has varied from place to place and the pattern has not been monolithic. Even the policies of a given imperial power have varied. British imperialism in Singapore, Malaya, and Hong Kong, for example, was certainly more benign than in Burma. There is also the complex issue of socialist imperialism with respect to Soviet influence on the economies of countries such as Cuba and Afghanistan. Despite the many variants of imperialism and related theories, it remains a major political issue of the twentieth century.

Kemalism (205)

The political, economic, and development philosophy/ideology of Mustafa Kemal Atatürk, the founder of the modern Turkish state. As articulated in 1931 at the congress of the Republican People's party (RPP), the ideology of Kemalism was defined as six basic principles: nationalism, republicanism, populism, secularism, statism, and revolutionism (Ahmad 1981: 145). Writing in the 1960s, Harold Lasswell and Daniel Lerner argued that Atatürk "was the nearest approximation to a genius of modernisation that any 'emerging nation' had seen in this quarter-century" (Özbundun and Kazancigil 1981:1). Another element in Kemalism was the notion of friendly relations with all nations and a rejection of Ottoman imperialistic goals. Rationalism and positivism were integral parts of Kemalism. Atatürk argued that "the true enlightenment in life is science." Atatürk also recognized the need to blend Western and Turkish civilization. *See also* KEMAL ATATÜRK, 61.

Significance Atatürk's greatest accomplishments were as an institution builder. Examples of his success in this regard are the convening of the Grand National Assembly in 1920, the founding of the People's party in 1923, the proclamation of the Republic of Turkey in 1923 after a successful war of national liberation against both external (Greece) and internal (the sultanate) forces, the passing of the Law on the Unification of Instruction in 1924, and the adoption of European law codes in 1926. All of these institutions have survived to the current day in Turkey. Though Atatürk remains a national hero in his homeland, controversy persists about his philosophy, particularly in the Muslim world. Some argue that Kemalism died with the fall of the shah in Iran and that Western civilization and Islam do not mix. Despite such criticisms, Turkey, reflecting the legacy of Kemalism, remains the most peaceful polity in the Middle East, and has a relatively impressive record with respect to most development indicators related to basic needs and equality. Kemalism in Turkey and the Meiji reformation in Japan continue to stand out as examples of effective development and institution building in non-Western settings. Kemalism deserves careful study by other nations undergoing the development process. In this regard the key question is whether Kemalism was primarily the result of a highly charismatic and dynamic personality or an eclectic ideology that has relevance and applicability beyond the borders of Turkey.

Low-Intensity Conflict (LIC) (206)

A concept developed by the U.S. military to refer to small-scale political violence, usually occurring in Third World settings. Michael Klare of Amherst has written extensively about such conflicts in volumes such as *Low Intensity Warfare* (1988). LIC normally involves violent confrontations between the military and police forces of an existing state against rebels, insurgents, or "freedom fighters." Examples of LIC are the current insurgency of the New People's Army (NPA) in the Philippines, the actions of the *contras* in Central America, the insurgency against the Vietnam-backed government of Kampuchea, the actions of the Shining Path guerrillas in Peru, and the confrontations between the Palestinians and the Israelis in the West Bank. *See also* DISARMAMENT AND DEVELOPMENT, 138; REVOLUTION, 213.

Significance   Since World War II, low-intensity conflict has been the major type of political violence. It represents a major obstacle to world peace. As the cold war has thawed with Gorbachev's peace initiatives, the United States military has increasingly emphasized LIC. Underlying the mentality of LIC and this military doctrine are distorted images and perceptions of the Third World. This part of the world is viewed as dangerous, chaotic, fanatic, unruly, less civilized, and thus a threat to U.S. vital economic and strategic interests. Since World War II the United States has seen as its mandate the responsibility to maintain world order and deal militarily with such threats, as it did in Vietnam and Central America and as the Soviet Union did in Afghanistan. Such roles represent a serious economic burden for both the United States and the Soviet Union, ironically giving the Japanese and Pacific Basin newly industrialized countries (NICs) special economic advantages since they avoid entanglements in LIC situations. The seriousness of economic problems in both the United States and the USSR could lead the superpowers to disengage gradually from external interference and promotion of LIC.

Microstates   (207)
Polities typically having extremely small geographic areas, populations, and economies. Microstates are generally defined as countries with populations of 2 million or less. Given their small size, such nations may have difficulty in achieving economies of scale in various industries. They also may have a narrow resource base, thus making them extremely dependent on international trade. Examples of microstates are the Republic of Nauru, the Kingdom of Tonga, Seychelles, the Republic of Maldives, Mauritius, Bhutan, the Sultanate of Brunei, and the Cook Islands. There are currently 43 microstates among the 160 nations comprising the membership of the United

Nations. In the 1980s, Colin Brock (1985) has written about the special educational problems of microstates.

Significance   Most conventional development theories assume a nation-state of substantial size and thus may not fit well the context of microstates. Microstates are politically and economically weak in terms of international bargaining power. As a result some microstates are beginning to form alliances, as in the South Pacific Forum, which includes many of the microstates of the South Pacific. Many microstates suffer from serious hyperdependency and large trade deficits in ratio of exports to imports. However, since many microstates are islands, they receive economic windfalls from the 200-mile exclusive economic zone postulated by the Law of the Sea.

National Planning   (208)
A systematic, rational approach to developing an economy over the long term, featuring the specification of detailed national plans, usually for periods of five years. Ironically, the United States, which has never practiced national planning, encourages national planning in developing countries through its various aid programs. The many variants of national planning range from highly controlled central planning (formerly typical of most Communist societies) to national planning in largely laissez-faire economies (for example, Thailand). In highly controlled central planning, all production levels and prices are set by the national government and all major economic activities controlled by the state. During Allende's Marxist rule in Chile, for example, technocrats attempted to computerize the workings of the entire Chilean economy to facilitate central planning. Complete central planning with rigid government controls and ownership has generally been a total failure, as reflected in the backward economies of Eastern Europe in the 1980s. In less rigid, less controlled national planning, the major focus is to develop key priorities and economic targets and to recognize potential bottlenecks associated with inconsistencies in various economic sectors. *See also* DEVELOPMENT ADMINISTRATION, 201; DECENTRALIZATION, 199.

Significance   Nearly all developing countries engage in some type of national planning. Given the failure of central planning with tight controls, the more flexible planning associated with capitalism or democratic socialism is now more common. In such contexts, national planning is extremely helpful in establishing goals and targets. Planning agencies play an important role in monitoring the extent to which such targets and goals are achieved. A major criticism is that planning agencies are often merely staff bodies with no "teeth." In other words, politicians and policymakers can ignore the planners and their priorities. Countries such as Indonesia have dealt with this problem by having both a routine and a development budget. The latter budget is controlled by Indonesia's national planning body, and thus it has far more authority than a planning body with no budgetary powers. Without some important links between budgeting and planning, national planning can be nothing more than impressive intellectual gymnastics and/or related public relations.

Nationalism (209)

An ideology that imbues people with the spirit of belonging together by stressing primary allegiance to the nation-state as opposed to smaller or larger political and social units. It is generally thought that nationalism grew out of response to the Napoleonic conquest, though the ideas of national sovereignty and self-determination certainly preceded that era. Nationalism was central to the Third World independence movements leading up to the postcolonial period. The United Nations was founded on the premise of sovereignty of each modern nation-state. Interestingly, the administrative and territorial units carved out by the colonial powers were broadly accepted as the borders of the new nations though they were often arbitrarily drawn and often cut across important cultural and linguistic groupings. *See also* DECOLONIZATION, 200; ETHNIC NATIONALISM, 229.

Significance One of the major tasks of the leaders of the newly independent nation-states of the post–World War II period has been to forge a national identity among diverse groups within internationally accepted borders. Anticolonialism served as the driving force in nationalistic campaigns, but this alone could not unite diverse ethnic groups, especially with the coming of independence. In many cases national unity and identity depended upon strong, charismatic, or authoritarian leaders to hold the nation-state together. Where this did not occur, civil war resulted as was the case in Nigeria, India, Pakistan, and Burma, for example. Many of these wars were fueled by the conflict between the superpowers. Nationalism, meaning allegiance to a particular modern nation-state, continues to be challenged on many fronts. The primary unit of identity for many of the world's citizens continues to be particular ethnic, minority, and indigenous cultures, or "nations" in another sense of the word. For many such groups the ideology of nationalism has meant forced assimilation, discrimination, and even genocide. Few modern nation-states can speak proudly of their treatment of the "nations within nations." The other major challenge to nationalism is the notion of globalism. Globalism points to the history of international conflict fueled by nationalistic interests and suggests the need for a broader commitment to meeting the needs of an interdependent world and identifying with universal values that transcend the nation-state. Individuals such as Jean Monnet, the father of the European Economic Community, see the "curse of nationalism" as a major impediment to world peace. While nationalism has been a major motif of the twentieth century, subnationalism and internationalism may well be the prominent themes of the next century.

Neocolonialism   (210)
The continued economic and cultural dominance of nominally independent Third World nations by former colonial powers. Third World scholars introduced the term in the early 1960s in their attempt to explain the quasicolonial and highly extractive nature of North-South economic interaction. Under the new colonialism the former powers maintain a system whereby strategic resources flow cheaply and consistently from South to North. This, in turn, requires the maintenence of a cheap and unempowered labor force as well as the preservation of markets for finished goods. The benefits of foreign investment accrue primarily to the investors and not to the underdeveloped country. Moreover, the system is maintained through an alliance with a compliant local elite or regime, and through strong Western influence in the education and mass communication systems. Neocolonialism may refer to any form of modern domination of poor nations, subtle or overt, by former colonial powers. *See also* COLONIALISM, 195; NATIONALISM, 209.

Significance   The concept of neocolonialism is central to the dependency theory of development and underdevelopment. It grew out of a realization on the part of newly independent nations that political sovereignty may be overshadowed by persisting economic dependencies perpetuated and maintained by economically powerful nations. This understanding formed the basis for the call for the new international economic order (NIEO) and the new world information and communication order (NWICO) in the 1970s. The notion also may help explain U.S. support of repressive governments, especially in Latin America, and the nature of European relationships with Africa and Asia, if not the current debt crisis. Neocolonialism refers to many forms of dominance and serves to question the existence of genuine independence and sovereignty for Third World nations.

Political Development **(211)**
A concept that refers to "improved" political conditions in a society, often comparable to the improved economic conditions associated with economic development. While there is extensive debate concerning the meaning of economic development, the controversy concerning the nature of political development is even greater. Among the many scholars who have tried to explicate the concept of political development are Gabriel Almond, G. Bingham Powell, David Apter, Glenn Paige, Lucian Pye, Harry Eckstein, S. N. Eisenstadt, Seymour Lipset, Guillermo O'Donnell, Samuel Huntington, and A. F. K. Organski. Many scholars of political development have been influenced by both Weberian and modernization thinking, particularly the work of Parsons, Lerner, Levy, and Inkeles. A common perspective is to view political development as evolution toward Western liberal democracy as a correlate and concomitant of economic development. Lipset presents considerable correlational data to support such a view. This optimistic perspective is consistent with the basic construct of political modernization that implies an imitation of Western institutions of participation, interest formation and articulation, and other dimensions of political institutionalization. Less Western views of political development emphasize the attainment of the political and administrative capacity to achieve a society's goals and objectives, however they may be defined. Scholars such as Huntington question the optimism and explanatory power of political modernization theorists, given the extent of political disorder in developing countries and the obvious lagging of Western-style political development behind economic development in many contexts. Huntington presents an alternative, multidimensional conceptual framework for understanding politics in developing countries. His key variables are social mobilization, economic development, social frustration, mobility opportunities, political participation, political institutionalization, and political instability. More recently Eckstein has presented a valuable and critical overview of the concept of political development. His perspective represents an integration of both historical and futuristic dimensions with an emphasis on developmental thinking.

Significance   Despite the extensive literature written on political development, the construct remains flawed and undeveloped. If defined as Western liberal democracy (an appealing approach from a human rights perspective), political development can be considered ethnocentric. If defined neutrally as enhanced capacity to achieve goals, there is the problematic category of fascist or authoritarian regimes that can get things done, but that have inadequate respect for individual human liberties. Critical dependency and political economy perspectives see economic structures leading invariably to authoritarian political conditions in many developmental contexts (O'Donnell 1979). The history of political economy in many Latin American contexts is consistent with such a perspective. As frequently defined, political development also illustrates binary Western thinking with its overly simplistic political poles of modernity and tradition. The unilinear, imitative-stage aspects of political development are also offensive to many South intellectuals. Rather than continue debating alternative definitions of political development, it is probably now best to focus on the empirical operationalization of specific political conditions reflecting more concrete political concepts such as extent of local empowerment, nature of income and wealth distribution, nature of opportunities for political participation, extent of political organizations and related interest groups, extent of systems for expressing political thoughts and ideas, types of systems of political representation, alternative mechanisms for participatory development, and the way in which political dissent is handled. It may indeed be impossible to integrate these diverse political phenomena into a single valid construct of political development.

Questionable Payments (212)
A term that encompasses various types of fees, commissions, bribes, or other forms of irregular payments often associated with doing business in many less developed countries (LDCs). Local languages contain many terms for such payments, including *backsheesh*, grease, and *baejia*, a word in Teochiew, a Chinese language commonly spoken in Thailand, that literally means tea money and refers to special extra fees associated with admission to highly prestigious primary and secondary schools. Proceeds from the tea money may actually be used for computer laboratories, sport facilities, and other educational purposes. Such fees are often expected by school administrators. Questionable payments are often associated with bureaucracies involved in various types of licensing. Customs offices are a common place for such fees to be collected to facilitate either exporting or importing. These fees often increase the speed with which papers can be processed in bureaucracies. *See also* SOFT STATE, 215.

Significance Since questionable payments obviously relate to the larger, complex issue of corruption, they represent an important dimension in the fields of comparative bureaucracy and development administration. One perspective on questionable payments is to consider them simply as user fees. In many LDCs civil servants, many with large families, are grossly underpaid, and user fees are essential to supplement their meager formal salaries. LDCs commonly have difficulty in raising sufficient revenue through direct taxation of income and property. In this sympathetic interpretation, questionable payments could be viewed as direct taxes for government services received. The problem with this interpretation is the equity implication that the rich may receive better and quicker public services. On the other hand, it may actually be more efficient to collect such taxes directly through user fees and thus avoid an excessively large bureaucracy to collect taxes and distribute revenues. Westerners also have a tendency to assume that questionable payments are always a loss to a society. Actually, from an economic perspective they represent a type of transfer payment. For example, if the recipients of questionable payments saved and invested more than those paying them saved, they could actually contribute to faster economic development. Conversely, if recipients of user fees were more likely to export funds abroad, the economic effect would be adverse. Overall, the issue of user fees, from both moral and economic perspectives, is much more complex than commonly recognized. It is important to note that such payments exist in nearly all societies, not just LDCs.

Revolution (213)

The fundamental transformation of a society's economic and political structure primarily through some type of popular and/or radical uprising, often associated with violence or massive nonviolent demonstrations. During the post–World War II period, many revolutions have been directed against colonial powers attempting to retain control over colonies and territories. Among the most successful post–World War II revolutions were the Indonesian revolution against the Dutch, the Algerian revolution against the French, the Chinese revolution of Mao, the Vietnamese revolution against the French and the United States, the Cuban revolution, the Nicaraguan revolution, and the Iranian anti-shah, anti-Western revolution. Popular uprisings such as those in the Philippines in February 1986, or in Thailand in October 1973, are sometimes referred to as revolutions. However, they are not genuine revolutions since they did not result in fundamental transformation of an existing economic and political order. Inherent to the concept of revolution is the basic question of why individuals rebel, a topic of extensive social science debate. There appears to be general consensus that absolute economic deprivation per se does not lead to revolution. Among concepts to explain revolution are relative deprivation (falling behind other visible groups); decremental deprivation (falling below future expectations);

and the J-curve of James Davies (rapidly growing discrepancy between expectations and realities). Drawing on his fieldwork in Mexico
and India and extensive ethnographic materials, Joel Migdal in
Peasants, Politics, and Revolution (1974) demonstrates how and why villagers become more political, and analyzes the revolutionary potential of peasant groups and communities. In certain contexts a
combination of excessive political repression and related bureaucratic
pathology can lead to revolutionary explosions. Political time bombs
can also be caused by dramatic and growing discrepancies between
the social demand for higher education and high-status jobs, and the
realities denying access to such possibilities. *See also* DECOLONIZATION,
200; KARL MARX, 35.

Significance   The concept of revolution is central to the fundamental debates about the nature of the just society and the most desirable
economic and political structure for a society. Radical critics of the
"development establishment" see many development programs and
projects as designed to defuse revolutionary potential and struggle
and thereby to postpone needed structural changes. In contrast,
many humanistically oriented development thinkers note that dramatic human costs often occur during revolution and during
postrevolutionary restructuring. While successful revolutions receive
the most media attention, many revolutions in developing countries
have failed, such as those in Thailand, Malaysia, Singapore, Burma,
El Salvador, Peru, New Caledonia, Jordan, and Brunei.

Social Justice   **(214)**
A highly normative concept that refers to the degree of fairness of a
country's basic institutions such as governance, the legal system, and
education. John Rawls of Harvard articulated the best known theory
of justice in his volume, *A Theory of Justice* (1971). Rawls argues that
two fundamental principles are central to justice, namely:

> 1. Each person is to have an equal right to the most extensive basic
> liberty compatible with similar liberty for others.
> 2. Social and economic inequalities are to be arranged so that they
> are both a) reasonably expected to be to everyone's advantage, and
> b) attached to positions and offices open to all. (Rawls 1971: 60).

Rawls's seminal volume has stimulated an extensive intellectual
debate and virtually thousands of subsequent articles and books dealing with his concept of justice (see Hellbank et al. 1982). *See also*
LIBERATION, 113; EQUALITY VERSUS EQUITY DISTINCTION, 145;
ATKINSON INDEX, 310; COEFFICIENT OF VARIATION, 314; GINI

COEFFICIENT, 325; KUZNETS INDEX, 331; LOG VARIANCE, 334; THEIL'S INDEX, 350.

Significance   Though Rawls did not apply his concept of social justice directly to development issues and problems, it is fundamental to discussions of the equity and ethical aspects of development emphasized by scholars such as Denis Goulet and Amartya Sen. It is also highly relevant to ongoing efficiency-versus-equity debates in the development field. In fact, some argue that the pervasiveness of inequality and the related lack of social justice is the global burning issue (Weeramantry 1976:10). Others maintain that social justice is the most important normative outcome of development and that conventional development strategies fail to address adequately issues of distributional justice.

Soft State   (215)
A concept that refers to the inability of numerous Third World polities to make tough policy decisions. Examples of soft state weaknesses are inabilities to tax, control corruption, reduce population growth, enforce laws or regulations related to the environment, eliminate waste and inefficiency, redistribute income, and ensure broad and fair access to government goods and services. Swedish Nobel laureate Gunnar Myrdal, who introduced the concept in *Asian Drama* (1971), derived it primarily from his ten years of research on the development process in South Asia. *See also* QUESTIONABLE PAYMENTS, 212.

Significance   The soft state concept is particularly controversial in that it reflects a harsh Western criticism of political conditions common in many Third World settings. The concept also makes clear that the genuine key to development is not external assistance from abroad, but internal political changes and actions. International agencies such as the IMF and World Bank have at times attempted to force Third World polities to be "harder" in their policy choices. This is generally resented as interference with economic sovereignty. Political leaders who try to become harder often encounter strong opposition from vested political interests and may even fall through votes of no confidence in parliamentary settings or in irregular military coups. Some of the more impressive examples of overcoming the soft state syndrome are Lee Kwan Yew's policies to deal with traffic congestion in Singapore, the currently aggressive population-control policies of the People's Republic of China, the harsh sanctions against crime in Saudi Arabia, the development of Costa Rica's national park system to protect its precious tropical rain forests, Thailand's restriction of civil service growth under Prem, and Indonesia's imposition of new taxes to offset lost oil revenues in the mid–1980s. A fundamental question is the nature of the relationship between democracy and the soft state syndrome. Ironically, in a democracy, it may be harder to implement unpopular policies such as critically needed tax increases or tuition hikes. Authoritarian regimes, however, may lack mechanisms for ensuring the responsiveness and integrity of government. Perhaps the key factor for confronting the soft state syndrome in any context is charismatic leadership that can persuade a populace to accept tough policies.

Weapons of the Weak (216)

A concept that refers to various forms of quiet resistance by peasants short of open revolution, riots, and demonstrations. James Scott's concept, derived from extensive fieldwork in the Muda region of Malaysia, is described in detail in his book, *Weapons of the Weak: Everyday Forms of Peasant Resistance* (1985). The major context for Scott's Malaysian research was peasant reaction to double cropping and mechanization associated with the Green Revolution. Examples of the weapons of the weak include attempts by peasants to defend their interests through boycotts, quiet strikes, theft, killing of livestock, and malicious gossip. Such weapons include anonymous acts of resistance and more ideologically oriented acts such as formal opposition to the introduction of combines.

Significance   In societies that emphasize harmonious and deferential social relations in public settings, it is easy to assume false consciousness (that is, a lack of political awareness on the part of peasants) and lack of class struggle and conflict. Scott's insightful, phenomenologically oriented research in rural Malaysia indicates the complex nature of rich-poor relations in rural settings characterized by rapid agricultural changes such as those introduced by the Green Revolution and the growth of agribusiness. The concept of weapons of the weak also provides balance in the literature on peasant resistance, which normally tends to emphasize the dramatic, but actually much rarer, forms of resistance such as riots, demonstrations, open violence, and peasant wars of liberation. The forms of resistance reflected in the term *weapons of the weak* certainly transcend conditions in Malaysia and Southeast Asia and may have almost universal applicability, even in industrialized societies.

E. Sociocultural Development

Cultural Collisions (217)

Interaction between Western and non-Western cultures that is a natural concomitant of the development process. The term *cultural collisions* was coined by a Thai educator, Khunying Amporn Meesuk, and a UN official, Nicholas Bennett. The term implies that the cultural contact between the Western and non-Western worlds may involve complex and difficult adjustments by people everywhere. As a result of these collisions, new cultural amalgams are evolving that integrate aspects of traditional and modern cultures. *See also* MODERNIZATION THEORY, 114; CULTURAL DEVELOPMENT, 219; CULTURAL IMPERIALISM, 220.

Significance   A common view exists that the cultures of developing countries are like clay pots, easily broken upon contact with a "dominant, superior" Western culture. Typical of this ethnocentric perspective are books such as I. R. Sinai's *The Challenge of Modernization* (1964), concerning Burma, and Alan Morehead's *The Fatal Impact* (1985), concerning Tahiti. An alternative view is that the cultures of developing areas are surprisingly resilient and are more like iron bowls than clay pots. In fact, Third World cultures even have an impact in the West. Examples would be reggae music from Jamaica; the popularity of Thai cuisine in large U.S. cities; the growing interest in Theravada Buddhism in Western Australia; the interest in Chinese herbal and traditional medicine; the rich and increasingly recognized creative arts from Africa, Latin America, and Asia; and growing recognition of the benefits of traditional organic farming systems. Despite the shocks associated with cultural collisions, the resilience of Third World cultures augurs well for the possibility of an enriching global cultural diversity.

Cultural Democracy (218)

"The right of all children to retain loyalties to what they have learned to value from their home and community socialization experiences and to base their identity in large part on personally meaningful aspects of those experiences" (Castaneda, et al. 1973:1). This important concept was so defined and introduced to the literature in 1973 by Alfredo Castaneda, Manuel Ramirez III, and P. Leslie Harold. Two related and possibly competing concepts are assimilation and acculturation. The former refers to the degree of participation of minority individuals or groups in the various economic, political, legal, and other important institutions (particularly those controlling major

resources). Acculturation refers to the degree to which minority individuals or groups appear to acquire the cultural and social personality
characteristics of the dominant group in a society. The extent of commitment to the dominant culture reflects the acculturation ideal. *See
also* CULTURAL DEVELOPMENT, 219; CULTURAL IMPERIALISM, 220;
ETHNIC NATIONALISM, 229.

Significance   Though the cultural democracy concept was developed in the U.S. context, it has critical relevance to all societies with
significant cultural heterogeneity. Those developing countries particularly concerned with national integration emphasize acculturation
and may fear that cultural democracy will lead to political instability
and destabilizing seccesionist movements. Wide variations exist
among societies in the extent of ethnic discrimination, a major violation of cultural democracy. Singapore's adoption of four national languages and use of these languages in its national media illustrate a
policy that fosters cultural democracy. Cultural democracy also contains economic implications. In many developing countries, ethnic
minorities represent a dynamic entrepreneurial and intellectual class
who, if not discriminated against, can make major contributions to
development, as shown in the contributions of the Chinese to Southeast Asia's economic dynamism. Cultural democracy is fundamentally
a human rights issue premised on the view that all cultures have equal
rights to preservation.

Cultural Development   (219)

A dimension of development involving the preservation, enhancement, and support of the cultural heritage resources of a society.
Such resources can be identified as the assets, both tangible and in-
tangible, that reflect or express a people's particular way of life and
serve in some way to give people a sense of cultural identity and belonging. Examples include archaeological monuments and sites;
sacred sites (natural formations or specially designated areas of the
physical or spatial environment); oral traditions, rituals, and ceremo-
nies; dance and musical traditions; the plastic arts; and institutions
such as museums and cultural centers. The concept of cultural development entails recognition of the value and role of a people's traditional culture and life-styles as positive and essential elements of the
development process rather than as impediments. A precise description of cultural development is somewhat problematic owing to
widely varying perceptions of both culture and development. Interestingly, the notion of cultural development implies that development may involve preservation while cultures are dynamic. UNESCO

has emerged as the primary international organization promoting cultural development. *See also* CULTURAL DEMOCRACY, 218; MODERNIZATION THEORY, 114.

Significance   The concept of cultural development is based on the assumption that cultural heritage resources have historical and contemporary value, give meaning to people's lives, and contribute to the spiritual and intellectual development and well-being of individuals and societies. It emphasizes the importance of preserving diversity in world culture for both ethical and more pragmatic reasons. It has become widely recognized, for example, that the success or failure of many development projects hinges on the acknowledgement of or negation of their cultural dimensions. Development involves not only material concerns but must also embody and foster the spiritual, intellectual, and cultural aspects of well-being. Further, the indigenous technical knowledge (ITK) embodied in local, long-standing cultures may serve as a key resource for the creation or preservation of sustainable development systems. Preservation of diversity appears to be central both to a vigorous world environment and to healthy and humane world cultures.

Cultural Imperialism   (220)
A highly controversial concept denoting the imposition of the cultural values of the Western industrial countries on the peoples of the developing countries. This domination occurs through such mechanisms as the media; advertising; study abroad; proselytization; adoption of new technologies; introduction of new industries and products; and use of foreign teachers, personnel, and advisers. Also reflective of this phenomenon are academic works which stress that traditional cultural values are the major impediment to modernization and development. Two examples of such works are I. R. Sinai's *Challenge to Modernization* (1964) and Edward Banfield's *The Moral Basis of a Backward Society* (1958).

Significance   A major debate in the development field is whether it is possible to modernize and develop technologically without "the cultural baggage of the West." For those denying the inevitability of cultural imperialism, Japan is often cited as an example. They point to Japan's retention of many of its traditional cultural forms despite its high level of technological and material development. The most controversial aspect of the concept of cultural imperialism relates to the dichotomy of imposition and free choice. Are individuals forced to view television, wear Western clothes, and become more materialistic? Fearing cultural imperialism, countries such as Burma, and China during Mao's rule, pursued isolationist policies. Also more recently in China, Deng emphasized spiritual pollution, a concept with overtones similar to that of cultural imperialism. *See also* DEMONSTRATION EFFECT, 135; MODERNIZATION THEORY, 114; CULTURAL COLLISIONS, 217; DENG XIAOPING, 70.

Culture of Poverty (221)

A set of common outlooks, behavior attributes, characteristics, and values of individuals living in poor communities. The famous anthropologist Oscar Lewis listed 70 traits of the culture of poverty based on his ethnographic fieldwork, beginning in 1943, which focused on several families in Mexico, Puerto Rico, and New York City. Lewis carried out his first study in Tepoztlan, Mexico, the same village studied by Robert Redfield in the 1920s. Whereas Redfield portrayed the village as almost idyllic, Lewis painted a tragic picture of social disorder and deprivation. In his culture of poverty hypothesis, published in 1961, Lewis argued that poverty created its own distinct culture, one full of fear, envy, and mistrust, and lacking organization and order. He was sympathetic to the plight of the poor but saw within their culture numerous characteristics that kept them from improving their conditions and participating in the broader culture. Edward C. Banfield's *The Moral Basis of a Backward Society* (1958) took a similar approach in attempting to explain poverty in southern Italy. *See also* VILLAGES, 191.

Significance   The notion of a culture of poverty was an attempt at developing general conclusions regarding the poor and their social interaction. Lewis's work was intriguing and received broad attention. His conclusions even influenced the policies implemented in President Lyndon Johnson's War on Poverty in the United States. Welfare would not be enough since, as Lewis suggested, it is easier to eliminate poverty itself than the culture of poverty. The poor would also have to be organized for "maximum feasible participation." In retrospect, and in light of many more poverty- and village-focused studies, many of Lewis's conclusions regarding the nature of the poor and their poverty must be, and have been, called into question. For example, subsequent studies have shown many poor communities to be highly organized though this order may not be immediately apparent to an outsider. Further, Lewis's traits are based on his fieldwork with a small number of Latin American families that cannot be characterized as typical in their own cultures, let alone within the diverse cultures of the world. Finally, the idea of a culture of poverty implies that resistance to solutions to poverty derive from the poor themselves. This belief does not take into account the external structures that help create and perpetuate the condition of poverty. As another anthropologist, Charles Valentine, argues, the culture of poverty idea wrongly implies that the poor are to blame for their own poverty.

Decade for Women (222)
The ten years following the United Nations's proclaimed International Women's Year (IWY) of 1975. The World Conference for the IWY drew more than 1,000 delegates from 133 countries to its meeting in Mexico City. Its three overriding themes were equality, development, and peace. The conference proclaimed 1976–1985 the UN Decade for Women and adopted a World Plan of Action that provided an agenda for the decade. The plan outlined steps to achieve improvements in the status of women in the areas of education, labor, and politics. A second UN conference was held in Copenhagen in 1980 to mark the midpoint of the decade and assess the progress made toward the goals of the plan of action. The conference produced a Programme of Action to update and supplement the Mexico plan, stressing problems in the areas of food and nutrition, migrant and refugee women, and women with sole responsibility for families.

The decade ended in 1985 with the Nairobi conference, officially entitled the Women's Conference to Review and Appraise the Achievements of the United Nations Decade for Women: Equality, Development, and Peace. This conference drew more than 2,000 delegates from 157 countries and representatives from nearly all of the UN specialized agencies. A 371-page document, informally known as the Forward-Looking Strategies (for the Advancement of Women), was adopted by the consensus of all delegates. The resolution called for governments to allocate more resources to women's education and training, gather better data on women, and attempt to measure unpaid women's work and include such data in a nation's GNP. Special attention was paid to the problems of specific groups of women (single mothers, victims of violence, refugees) as well as the problems specific to Third World women. Also included were issues high on the agenda of Western women, such as equal pay and day care. Another dynamic conference, Forum '85, held in Nairobi in conjunction with the UN conference, drew 13,500 women to more than 1,000 workshops on a wide variety of concerns. *See also* WOMEN IN DEVELOPMENT, 256.

Significance   The achievements of the Decade for Women are broad and difficult to quantify. The decade's success in raising the consciousness of the world regarding women's status and role in development is reflected in numerous ways: in the fast-growing number and dramatic achievements of women's organizations throughout the world; in the new and more informed considerations of the impact of programs on women, on the part of international development agencies; in the number of new programs established to improve the status of women. In addition, the decade saw the creation of seven new UN bodies dedicated to the advancement of women, including the UN Development Fund for Women (UNIFEM) and the UN International Research and Training Institute for the Advancement of Women (INSTRAW). The decade was a vital tool for bringing much needed and long overdue attention to the special issues of half the world's population.

Development Anthropology   (223)
A type of applied anthropology that involves anthropologists directly in the development process. This field is marked by controversy regarding the appropriate role for the anthropologist in development, if indeed there is such a role. Traditionally, anthropology has focused on natural cultures undisturbed by modern forces such as technology transfer and nation-state planning. The anthropologist sought to observe and understand a culture, but not to act as an agent of change. This approach was guided by the implicit notion of cultural relativism, and the implied response to development planning was a doctrine of local self-determination. Given the rapid changes throughout the world, especially following World War II, anthropologists were often faced with a dilemma: they could remain uninvolved with the inevitable disturbances and changes, or become involved to ease the burden of change, the latter choice implying intervention and loss of cultural integrity. Their initial involvement in the late 1950s and early 1960s was in defense of local autonomy. In the 1970s, as a result of broadening perspectives on development, a number of development organizations began including social scientists in the planning process for ethical and pragmatic reasons. Social assessments of development projects became common, as anthropologists offered considerable insight into what had often been written off by economic and technical planners as extraneous, i.e., cultural, factors. The first books on development anthropology appeared in the early 1970s as did new academic programs in the field. Since that time,

anthropology has become increasingly involved in the development field, both in scholarship and application, though ambivalence regarding this involvement persists.

Significance   Anthropology has both changed the field of development and been changed by its participation in the development process. Whether directly or indirectly as a result of its involvement with development, the discipline of anthropology now concerns itself with a broader scope of human behavior in varied circumstances. For example, considerable attention has been given to various forms of adaptation and rapid cultural change, and urban anthropology has emerged as a subfield. At the same time, anthropologists have had considerable impact on development practice and theory by bringing needed attention to the issues of culture, cultural preservation, and unanticipated cultural or social outcomes of development. As a direct outgrowth of these priorities came the emphasis on participatory development, bottom-up planning, and a reassessment of the "irrational peasant." Stressing the normative nature of development, anthropologists challenged the basic assumptions of modernization theory, and they continue to be at the forefront of major challenges to development theory. Development anthropologists have contributed to more culturally sensitive, and subsequently more effective, development practices at the local level.

Development Education   **(224)**
An increasingly important dimension of education related to fostering deeper understanding of the developing countries and their status. There are numerous levels of development education and frequently it occurs in the form of informal or nonformal education. Formal training in development education is available at various universities such as the Stanford International Development Education Center (SIDEC) at Stanford University; the Institute of Development Studies (IDS) at the University of Sussex in England; the Development Studies Centre at the Australian National University in Canberra; and the Comparative and International Education Program at the University of Pittsburgh. Such programs are oriented to training scholars and practitioners who will work in developing countries and/or educate others about conditions in those countries. The academic field of international development education emphasizes the interdisciplinary study of the relations between education and economic, political, and sociocultural development. Much scholarly work in this field can be found in the journal *Comparative Education Review*, published by the University of Chicago Press. Many practi-

tioners and scholars in this field are members of the Comparative and International Education Society (CIES), a worldwide organization that meets annually.

Significance The citizens of the industrial countries generally show gross ignorance of conditions in developing countries. Educational systems in Western countries tend to neglect curricular content on developing countries. Without a citizenry better informed about development issues, it is difficult to have political policies that deal adequately with these issues. The assumption that improved development education will foster greater political support for international development assistance and more effective programs of development is yet untested. Many development agencies are giving increasing attention to their role as development educators at home in addition to their activities abroad. Development education has been an important element of Canada's and Sweden's bilateral aid programs. The development education efforts of nongovernmental and private voluntary organizations in the United States are encouraged and coordinated by InterAction's Development Education Committee and the International Development Conference (IDC). They jointly publish a quarterly entitled *Ideas and Information about Development Education.*

Development Journalist (225)

A new breed of journalists who are willing to spend weeks, months, or even years in developing countries to gain a genuine understanding of conditions there. These journalists contrast markedly with conventional journalists who fly in from London or New York for a day or two to report on a natural disaster or violent coup in a developing country. Development journalists are expected to have a sense of internal interdependence and commitment to the longer range of development. Such journalists are willing to spend time away from capitals digging at the core problems facing people and governments. Reflecting the emergence of the development journalist, the United Nations published in 1987 an *International Directory of Development Journalists*, which lists approximately 1,100 development journalists from both the South and the North. For each journalist, the directory lists areas of specialization, length of time working on development issues, geographic specialization, the journals with which he or she is associated, and the individual's working languages. This project to identify the world's leading development journalists was encouraged by the Division of Economic and Social Information (DESI), part of the UN's Department of Public Information, which publishes

Development Forum. Among development journalists listed are Irving Horowitz, Tim Sharp (Thailand), Abby Tan (Philippines), Yoko Kitazawa (Japan), and Maureen Mopio (Papau New Guinea). The American Richard Critchfield and Paul Harrison of Great Britain should also be noted for their extensive time spent covering the developing world. *See also* NEW WORLD INFORMATION AND COMMUNICATION ORDER, 252; THIRD WORLD NETWORK, 443.

Significance The emergence of the field of development journalism in recent years reflects the call for a new international information order (NIIO). Developing countries themselves have become more assertive in making their voices heard on the world stage. Nongovernmental organizations in the North and the UN's DESI have encouraged more rigorous and less ethnocentric reporting on developing countries. Continued growth in the number of active, competent development journalists will help reduce the disequilibrium in information flowing between North and South and in the long term will enhance South-South communication.

Development Journals (226)
The major journals dealing with development issues. Among them are *World Development* (Oxford); *Development: Seeds of Change* (Rome); *Development and Change* (The Hague); *Development Policy Review* (London); *Development Dialogue* (Uppsala, Sweden); *The Journal of Peasant Studies* (London); *South* (London); *Third World Quarterly* (London); *The World Bank Economic Review* (Washington, D.C.); *Economic Development and Cultural Change* (Chicago); *IFDA Dossier* (Nyon, Switzerland); *Journal of Developing Areas* (Macomb, Illinois); *The Developing Economies* (Tokyo); *The Journal of Development Studies* (London); *Development Forum* (Kuala Lumpur, Malaysia); *Journal of Rural Development* (Hyderabad, India); *Journal of Philippine Development* (Manila); *National Development* (Westport, Connecticut); *Asian Development Review* (Asian Development Bank, Manila); and *Thai Journal of Development Administration* (Bangkok).

Significance The accelerated pace of change in the development field makes it critically important to be able to keep up with current developments. Given the time required for the production of books, journals are the best source of current information on development issues. The list above is by no means comprehensive, but it includes some of the major journals and examples of indigenous Third World journals now available.

Emic versus Etic Distinction (227)

Two differing intellectual orientations with important implications for methods of studying developmental issues and problems. This distinction derives from the field of linguistics and the terms *phonemics* and *phonetics*. Anthropologists have applied the distinction to the study of other cultures and values. An etic orientation focuses on the development of generalizations that are true, independent of time and space. In contrast, an emic orientation focuses on ascertaining the concepts and categories of groups being studied on their own terms. The emic-oriented social scientist emphasizes cultural differences and the uniqueness of each culture, while the etic-oriented social scientist is looking for commonalities and universal patterns. *See also* DEVELOPMENT METHODOLOGY, 319.

Significance Both the etic and the emic orientations are legitimate scientific approaches. An example of the etic approach would be the efforts of Alex Inkeles and David Smith to validate a universal construct of individual attitudinal modernity. An example of the emic approach would be the excellent anthropological history by Anthony Reid, *Southeast Asia in the Age of Commerce, 1450–1680: The Lands below the Winds* (1988). The social sciences vary in the extent to which they are emically or etically oriented. On a continuum, economics and political science tend to be the most etic, while anthropology would be the most emic. Essential to emic-oriented research is an intimate knowledge of other cultures and languages. A major challenge to social scientists is to integrate these two approaches by operationalizing etic concepts in ways that are meaningful and valid cross-culturally.

Environmental Refugees (228)

A concept describing people who flee from conditions of environmental degradation. The concept was developed by Jodi L. Jacobson of the Washington-based Worldwatch Institute, which argues that environmental refugees constitute the largest category of refugees. Officially refugees are those fleeing from political, racial, or religious persecution. Economic refugees flee their homelands to seek improved economic opportunities. Jacobson describes four major factors accounting for environmental refugees: land degradation; unnatural disasters such as floods, defined as normal events whose effects are exacerbated by human activities; toxic and nuclear contamination; and expected rising of an ocean because of global warming.

Significance   The United Nations Environmental Program estimates that 4.5 billion hectares of land, 35 percent of the earth's land surface, are in various stages of desertification. Some 850 million people live in thesé areas and thus are potential environmental refugees. As land becomes more and more marginal in terms of quality and productivity, individuals are forced to move to more productive land. Eventually, millions of such individuals will move to cities or regional towns, contributing to hyperurbanization in cities such as Mexico City, Jakarta, Bangkok, Calcutta, and Lagos, and to rapidly increasing regional urbanization in developing countries.

Ethnic Nationalism   (229)
A concept reflecting the growing consciousness of various ethnic groups whose places of residence do not coincide with national political boundaries. Many current political boundaries in the Third World are the result of arbitrary colonial decisions that were based on factors such as relative military strength, strategic power negotiations, and competition among colonial powers for valuable natural resources. Such boundaries rarely, if ever, reflected ethnic boundaries. Also, colonial powers frequently moved ethnic groups from one area to another to provide manpower for mines, factories, or plantations. The legacy of such colonial influences survives in ethnic anomalies around the world. For example, in Fiji there are more Indians than indigenous Fijians. There are far more individuals of Lao ethnicity in Thailand than in Laos. In other areas such as South Africa or New Caledonia, indigenous majorities are ruled by minorities originally from Europe. With the demise of colonialism instances of minority white rule are less common, but persisting problems include minority groups divided by political boundaries (for example, the Hausa in West Africa), and cultural groups ruled by indigenous minorities, as is common in Africa. This imbalance is one source of ethnic tensions common in Third World societies such as Nigeria, the Sudan, Iraq, Malaysia, Burma, and Sri Lanka. Much research on ethnic nationalism is conducted at the International Centre for Ethnic Studies in Colombo, Sri Lanka. *See also* NATIONALISM, 209; CULTURAL DEMOCRACY, 218; COMMUNALISM, 196.

Significance   While the twentieth century was one of nationalism, the next century may be one of transnationalism and subnationalism. Ethnic nationalism is central to subnationalism. If states were defined by ethnicity there could well be more than 1,000 nations. Given the rise of ethnic nationalism, conventional nation-states must find ways to allow ethnic minorities or majorities to express their cultural identities and to share political power. Genuine federalism is one approach that delegates considerable power to regional ethnic groups and areas. The use of a neutral national language or multiple languages can help to preserve subnational ethnic identities. As an example, Singapore has four official languages, Mandarin Chinese, English, Malay, and Tamil. A neutral national language is Bahasa Indonesia, which is not the language of Indonesia's largest and most powerful ethnic group, the Javanese, or of any single ethnic group in the country. Ethnic nationalism is expressed in two major patterns. When it is suppressed or ignored, considerable political tension and violence can occur. When it is allowed to flourish peacefully and cooperatively with tolerance and respect, it can greatly enrich the diversity of world and national cultures. A useful reference work related to ethnic nationalism is *Minorities in Conflict: A World Directory* (1989) by Patrick Thornberry and Martin Wright.

Ethnocentrism   **(230)**
A term referring to the "disease" of judging other cultures by the standards and norms of one's own. Much criticism of Third World behavioral patterns has elements of ethnocentrism, a term used perhaps most commonly by anthropologists. Since few individuals can claim to have no ethnocentrism, it may be useful to think of this concept as a continuum. Both Westerners and Third World individuals can display ethnocentrism. Those from the Third World may find fault with aspects of life in the West, based on comparing conditions with those in their own country. *See also* DEVELOPMENT METHODOLOGY, 319; MULTICULTURAL LITERACY, 234.

Significance   The genuine understanding of development studies and issues has been adversely affected by ethnocentrism. Adequate sanctions and incentives may facilitate the minimization of ethnocentrism. The careful training of those to be engaged in development work with an emphasis on the adverse effects of ethnocentrism is critically important. Given the rich ethnic diversity within and among the nations of the Third World, greater interethnic understanding is essential for national and international peace.

Informatique   **(231)**
A French term that refers to the information revolution now occurring around the world. This revolution has growing and dramatic implications for developing countries and has led to a new distinction between the "information haves" and the "information have-nots."

Reflecting this revolution, a new discipline is emerging called informetrics, which is the scientific study of the production, distribution, and flow of information and scientific knowledge. A good introduction to this emerging field is the volume *Informetrics 87/88*, which presents the select proceedings of the First International Conference on Bibliometrics and Theoretical Aspects of Information Retrieval held in Diepenbeck, Belgium, August 25–28, 1987. *See also* NEW WORLD INFORMATION AND COMMUNICATION ORDER, 252.

Significance   As we enter the twenty-first century, an increasingly popular perspective emphasizes information as the new source of power and wealth. The success of Japan's technological and economic transformation reflects this perspective. Future-oriented writers like Jean-Jacques Servan-Schreiber in volumes such as *The World Challenge* (1981) emphasize that developing countries must rapidly build up their capacity in *informatique* or be left behind in economic and political power. In response to Servan-Schreiber's challenge, countries such as Ivory Coast and Kuwait are introducing computer education into the classroom. The emerging discipline of informetrics provides a systematic methodology for measuring scientific productivity in developing countries. A related issue is that of information about the developing countries themselves. It is not uncommon to find that a North nation has more information about a South nation than the South nation itself has. Such anomalies reflect an imbalance in access to and control over information. If information in the long term proves to be the world's most precious resource, it is imperative that developing countries devote special attention to developing their capacities in *informatique*.

Language Policy   (232)

National-level decisions concerning the choice of a language or languages to be used in government, education, and society. A common language policy is to choose the language of the dominant ethnic or cultural group as the national language. Some countries opt for multiple national languages, such as the Republic of Singapore's four languages. Others choose a neutral language, that is, not the language of a particular ethnic group, as did Indonesia in adopting Bahasa Indonesia as its national language. The prominence of Swahili in East Africa reflects a similar approach. Colonial languages such as English and French function as national languages in a number of multilingual states, serving as the common language of business, government, and education. *See also* CULTURAL DEVELOPMENT, 219; CULTURAL DEMOCRACY, 218.

Significance   Language policy is one of the most delicate policy areas, particularly in countries with significant cultural heterogeneity. Language policy decisions can lead to considerable communal strife and ethnic tensions. In Malaysia after the 1969 racial riots, a new national language policy evolved, emphasizing Malay and replacing a previously multilingual approach in which both English and Mandarin Chinese were prominent. Empirically it appears that policies stressing multiple or neutral national languages tend to minimize ethnic strife and to promote cultural democracy. Language is intimately linked to cultural preservation and both are directly affected by basic educational policies.

Liberation Theology   (233)

A form of Christian theology stressing liberation from all forms of oppression as the primary message of the Gospel. Liberation theology is generally associated with Catholicism and Latin America, the region of its origin, but it now takes on many forms throughout the world. The term *theology of liberation* is attributed to Gustavo Gutierrez, the Peruvian priest whose book by the same name, *Teologia de la Liberacion* (1971), is considered the Magna Carta of the movement. The term and associated ideas played a central role in the proceedings of the Medellin (Colombia) General Conference of Latin American Episcopacy (CELAM) in 1968 which, in a sense, was made possible by the liberalizing changes evolving from Vatican II in 1962. The proceedings of the Medellin conference focused on the situation of the poor in Latin America and the church's response to conditions of poverty and oppression. The participants acknowledged poverty as "a situation of sin," implying acceptance of the idea of structural violence. Statements from the conference stressed the theme of liberation and declared the church's "preferential option for the poor." By definition, however, liberation theology emerges not by edict or statements by church leaders, but rather from laypersons reading the Bible and critically reflecting on their own conditions. This analysis of reality, akin to Paulo Freire's notion of conscientization, leads to praxis, or action taken after thorough reflection. According to Gutierrez, the purpose of theology is not just to understand the world, but to change it. The message of the Exodus and the Christ story is that God is a God of liberation. Recognizing the many forms of oppression, Gutierrez defines liberation in broad terms, including the spiritual dimension traditionally defined as salvation. In practice, liberation theology has taken shape among a fast-growing number of Christian base communities (*communidades eclesiales de base*) throughout Latin America and has gained and retained considerable support among some high-ranking church officials, most notably Dom Hélder Câmara, former archbishop of Recife in Brazil. An intense social activist and eloquent spokesman for the oppressed, he was instrumental in the development of a theology for the poor.

By the time Latin American bishops met again at the Puebla Conference in 1979, liberation theology had become central to discussions among Catholic Church leaders, though it certainly continued to have many critics. Among its detractors was Archbishop Alfonso Lopez Trujillo, who became secretary general of CELAM in 1972. Lopez Trujillo condemned liberation theology for what he considered its support of Marxism and radical politics. He was able to suppress the voices of the liberation theologians in the official proceedings of Puebla. The Puebla documents steer a middle course, condemning social injustice while discouraging priests from involvement in political activism, as did Pope John Paul II in his opening address. Lopez Trujillo was made a cardinal in 1983, a signal of the Vatican's ongoing reluctance to embrace liberation theology. While liberation theology takes on many forms, the Vatican and many opponents of liberation theology raise concerns about its association with Marxism and violence as an instrument of change. As a whole, liberation theology is somewhat ambiguous on both issues, not a surprising position given its diversity. Others in the theological community charge that it deemphasizes the transcendent and question whether it is a theology at all.

Whatever the position of Rome and the concerns of North American and European theologians, liberation theology continues to take on new dimensions and gain advocates in the North and throughout Latin America and other areas of the Third World, most notably in the Philippines. All of the major works of liberation theologians have been published in English by Orbis Books, the press of the Maryknoll Fathers. *See also* LIBERATION, 113; SOCIAL JUSTICE, 214.

Significance   In the late 1960s, liberation theology emerged as a powerful internal critique of both the Catholic Church, the largest single organization in the world, and development as advocated by the United States and its allies in leadership in Latin America. The church carried a long history of compliance with and support of oppressive social and economic systems. On the development front, many Latin Americans were completely disillusioned by the inadequacies of the Alliance for Progress, blatant and growing inequality, the bleeding of their economies by outside interests, and the growing entrenchment of heavy-handed regimes supported by the United States in the name of anticommunism and economic stability. Vatican II enhanced the position of the layperson in the church and helped open a broad discussion regarding the role of the church in situations of oppression and specific discussion regarding paths towards liberation. Both capitalism and traditional Catholic theology were rejected forthwith by many working with the poor of Latin America and often by the poor themselves, who saw no benefits from the development models in place and found no ally in the church establishment.

Liberation theology, especially as practiced in the Christian base communities (CBCs), is characterized by a number of development themes that have gained prominence in development literature since the evolution of the new theology: it stresses popular participation; community self-reliance; building on indigenous tradition, knowledge, and experience; and advocates a holistic approach to development that addresses both physical and spiritual needs. Liberation theology has also prompted further discussion regarding the meaning of liberation and the implications for development found in other religious traditions.

Multicultural Literacy (234)

Awareness and understanding of the rich global cultural diversity represented not only by Western but also by African, Asian, and Latin American civilization. Many educational systems in the Western world ignore or misrepresent the cultures of the non-Western world. Students are not exposed to the intellectual contributions of Third World thinkers and writers such as Nobel laureates Miguel Asturias (Guatemala), Wole Soyinka (Nigeria), Octavio Paz (Mexico), Naguib Mahfouz (Egypt), Gabriella Mistral (Chile), and Pablo Neruda (Chile). A recent volume edited by Rick Simmonson and Scott Walker, *Multicultural Literacy: Opening the American Mind* (1988), provides a preliminary list of concepts and ideas comprising the core of multicultural literacy. See also ETHNOCENTRISM, 230; DEVELOPMENT EDUCATION, 224.

Significance The best-selling books, *The Closing of the American Mind* (1987) by Alan Bloom of the University of Chicago and *Cultural Literacy* (1987) by E. D. Hirsch, have stimulated a heated debate about the fundamental nature of multicultural liberal education. Bloom and Hirsch have narrowly defined liberal education as basically European and Western, neglecting and ignoring the creativity and contributions of the non-Western world. As we move into a dramatically more multicultural century, literacy about the Third World becomes increasingly essential. Inherent to genuine liberal education is an understanding and respect for great ideas and thoughts, whatever their racial, religious, cultural, or geographic origins.

N Achievement (235)

A psychological concept reflecting the extent to which individuals are highly motivated to achieve. *N* Achievement was popularized by the Harvard psychologist David C. McClelland who aspired to ascertain the psychological correlates of economic development. McClelland argued that variables such as propensity to save and to invest were ultimately psychological and individual. In his book, *The Achieving Society* (1961), McClelland provides a detailed account of his methodology for measuring *n* Achievement and his empirical results in correlating it with macro development performance of diverse nations. The measurement of *n* Achievement is based on techniques from experimental psychology and the psychometric insights of Freud. A system of coding and interpretation of children's stories provides the basic data for assessing the level of achievement motivation of various cultures and nations. McClelland's empirical correlations supported his theory, showing a definite relationship between individual *n* Achievement and macro differential economic performance. For example, McClelland found significant correlations between *n* Achievement and Incremental Capital-Output Ratios (ICOR). Societies with higher *n* Achievement levels tended to have the lower ICOR values directly associated with higher potential for economic growth. McClelland examined many possible explanations for differential *n* Achievement such as religious values, child-rearing styles, climatic variations, and racial differences. Drawing upon the work of Weber, McClelland concludes that religious values, particularly Protestantism, are an important factor explaining differential *n* Achievement. *See also* CAPITAL-OUTPUT RATIO, 312; MODERNIZATION THEORY, 114.

Significance   McClelland's research on *n* Achievement reflects the genres of modernization theory, which emphasizes the importance of individual values, and national character studies that were popular in the 1950s. In recent decades such approaches have come under severe intellectual attack from methodological, theoretical, and normative perspectives. Though McClelland never claims that *n* Achievement is the only factor explaining development, he is still rather reductionist in placing so much stress on the individual psychological factor. McClelland, like other modernization theorists such as Inkeles, tends to ignore external structural factors that are often major obstacles to development. Though McClelland presents information on the validity of his tools for measuring *n* Achievement, they seem highly subjective and their validity questionable. For example, McClelland finds the *n* Achievement scores of children in Japan, German Switzerland, and the Netherlands to be signficantly lower than those of children in Pakistan, Iraq, Syria, and Uruguay. Despite these problems so apparent 30 years later, McClelland deserves credit for his creative attempts to ascertain the psychological, noneconomic factors associated with development. The contemporary economic success of countries such as Japan, South Korea, Taiwan, and Singapore, and the success of Chinese minorities in Southeast Asia and elsewhere suggest the continuing importance of individual cultural factors and values in development.

Tourism (236)

The second largest industry after oil, both wordwide and in the Third World, and the world's single largest employer. While tourism is centered in the developed countries, it represents the major source of foreign exchange earnings for many developing countries. According to the United Nations, tourism brought $55 billion to developing countries in 1988 and provided 50 million jobs. The industry is expanding rapidly throughout the Third World, primarily in response to the pressing need to deal with debt. Tourism's contribution to development, however, varies greatly and has certainly proved to be no panacea. Governments may go to great expense to attract the industry by constructing airports and roads and offering tax breaks to investors. Typically tourism becomes an enclave industry centered around major hotels built and owned by Northern financiers. This can also cause extreme distortions in the local economy, as when visitors arrive on Northern-based airlines and dine on imported food. In Fiji, for example, it is estimated that 70 percent of tourist expenditures are not retained in the country. Given the low skill intensity required for workers in this sector, most of the associated employment involves menial labor and little transfer of technology occurs. Also, tourism has often fostered a growth in prostitution and related health problems. Ironically, tourism may actually detract from economic independence.

Numerous recent studies have also emphasized the detrimental environmental, social, and cultural costs of tourism. Tourist centers are often built in beautiful but vulnerable natural settings or in prime agricultural areas. The industry may also create a social setting that promotes contact among people of different cultures, but this may only serve to reinforce stereotypes and misunderstanding since the relatively affluent tourists and the relatively impoverished locals rarely meet as equals: the locals are almost always in subservient roles. With these drawbacks in mind, a number of developing countries such as Zambia, Senegal, and parts of Indonesia are promoting a more indigenous-based form of tourism emphasizing the use of local products, local architecture, and minimal environmental alteration. Ecuador recently launched an innovative program to attend to ecological and industry needs in the creation of the Galapagos Marine Resource Reserve. At the same time, an alternative tourist industry is emerging in the North, including educational tourism, ecotourism, Third World work camps, home stays, and cultural tours designed by host countries.

Significance   Tourism has had and will continue to have a profound impact on the development of many Third World nations. The industry as a whole is growing at a rate of 4 percent a year and more rapidly in developing areas. Tourism can represent a substantial source of much needed hard currency, and it can be used as a tool to preserve traditional culture. It also has the potential to devastate local cultures and economies, depending on the manner in which it is promoted. In response to such hazards, many countries are devising creative ways to promote tourism that is environmentally sound, respectful of local culture and tradition, and beneficial to the nation as a whole.

Unintended Consequences   (237)
The unanticipated impact of development projects on the people affected by the development activities. Such consequences may be positive or adverse, but are more commonly the latter. The huge Aswan Dam project in Egypt, for example, had many unanticipated adverse effects, primarily in the areas of health, environment, and agriculture. The Green Revolution has had many unintended effects, including growing rural income disparities. The "innovative" planting of eucalyptus trees in reforestation programs in Africa and Asia has had significant adverse agricultural and environmental effects. Similarly, in Northeast Thailand, increased dependence on cassava as a cash crop has made farmers in that region more vulnerable to the vagaries of the politics of the European Common Market. The introduction of mechanized rice hullers in Indonesia eliminated an important source of income-producing employment for hundreds of thousands of Indonesian women. The development literature is rife with such examples. *See also* APPROPRIATE TECHNOLOGY, 276.

Significance   There are many factors explaining unintended consequences. By definition this term rejects the notion of explicit conspiracies. The extent of unintended consequences could be limited by allowing people affected by projects to participate actively in preproject appraisals. This simple caution and participatory approach could eliminate many unintended consequences. Small-scale experimentation before the broader dissemination of innovations and new projects could also help to minimize unintended consequences. The use of interdisciplinary teams could facilitate recognition of potential unanticipated consequences. For example, anthropologists with solid understanding of cultural nuances could anticipate negative reactions to new approaches that might be inconsistent with fundamental traditional norms and cultural values. The intention of social and environmental impact assessments prior to project approval and implementation is to minimize unintended consequences.

F. Human Resource Development

Brain Drain (238)
The international migration of highly trained and talented individuals from poorer to richer countries. Both push and pull factors contribute to the brain drain. Primary pull factors are higher salaries, better living conditions, and more facilities in support of intellectual activity in richer countries, such as scientific laboratories and computer technologies. Primary push factors are political repression and other constraints on intellectual life in many developing countries. There are important variations among countries with respect to the extent of the brain drain problem. Countries such as India, Pakistan, Iran, the Philippines, South Korea, and Taiwan have traditionally had high levels of brain drain. In contrast, countries such as Thailand and Japan have had limited brain drain. Education and World Affairs sponsored a major study of the brain drain problem titled *The International Migration of High-Level Manpower: Its Impact on the Development Process* (1970), which included case studies of the brain drain in Taiwan, the Philippines, Japan, Thailand, Korea, Malaysia, Singapore, India, Lebanon, Turkey, Iran, Tanzania, and Kenya. The study also contained case studies of the Netherlands, France, the United Kingdom, and Australia as recipients of brain drain talent. *See also* BRAIN OVERFLOW, 239; SCIENCE AND DEVELOPMENT, 304.

Significance There is much debate concerning the impact of the brain drain on development. The major adverse financial dimension is that the developing countries usually have invested in the initial primary, secondary, and tertiary education of those who eventually migrate. Thus, this initial investment in such human resources is lost. Some compensation to the country of origin may result when intellectuals send back foreign exchange remittances to family or relatives or return occasionally to share their expertise with their original home country. When talented individuals from wealthier countries migrate to poorer countries and become permanent expatriates, a kind of reverse brain drain may partially compensate for the traditional form of brain drain. To minimize the possibility of brain drain, countries such as Thailand require students on foreign scholarships to sign legal guarantees that they will return. Should they fail to return, heavy financial penalties are imposed on local guarantors who offer such financial resources as real estate as collateral. The People's Republic of China is facing increasingly serious brain drain problems as many Chinese students, particularly those in fields such as science and computer science, are finding far more lucrative economic opportunities in the United States. If human resources are indeed the wealth of nations, then the persistence of the brain drain contributes to global disparities and inequalities. In contrast, if individual freedom to pursue economic gain is commensurate with talent, and ability is highly valued, then the brain drain could be viewed positively. The international migration of talented individuals is one of the most complex and perplexing policy issues in the development field.

Brain Overflow (239)

An alternative perspective for considering the problems associated with the brain drain. While the term *brain drain* implies that the movement of highly educated individuals from the developing to the developed countries is entirely negative, the brain overflow notion reflects a more open and international view of the question of the movement of human resources across national boundaries. The term *brain overflow* suggests that various countries have different absorptive capacities for making use of higher levels of manpower. It also emphasizes the value of the maximum utilization of talent for the benefit of global welfare, regardless of the physical locus of such work. In the brain overflow perspective, talent should be free to migrate where it can be most effective, creative, and productive. *See also* BRAIN DRAIN, 238.

Significance   In some respects the brain overflow concept mirrors the concept of free trade in commodities. Minimal barriers to the flow of high-level talent from nation to nation should exist. Critics of this perspective fear that it will lead to even greater disparities in science, technology, and knowledge. Supporters of the brain overflow perspective counter that individuals with Third World origins may contribute meaningfully by returning to such countries on development projects and contributing to a deeper understanding of development by their work in developed countries. Two clear examples would be Hla Myint, originally from Burma, and Sir Arthur Lewis, a Nobel laureate in development economics originally from the Caribbean and now a distinguished professor at Princeton. Though many may reject the brain overflow perspective, it deserves careful consideration, given its relevance to training strategies as well as immigration and emigration policies.

Correspondence Principle (240)

A concept from the field of economics of education related to the way in which employment and educational conditions mirror each other. For example, children in an elite missionary school in a developing country will be socialized for roles associated with elite status in organizational or employment settings. Their learning environment will thus provide far greater opportunities for individual autonomy and decision making, which are relevant to their future occupational opportunities. In contrast, students from lower socioeconomic backgrounds in a vocational school will be socialized to move into more subordinate roles. The correspondence principle appears to have broad applicability in both developing and developed countries. *See also* SOCIAL CHARTER, 255.

Significance Competing with the common view that education is a powerful vehicle for social and occupational mobility is the belief that education and formal schooling tend to reinforce and legitimize existing systems of social stratification and status. To the extent that the correspondence principle accurately reflects reality, it lends support to the latter, more radical view. The principle does not necessarily imply any notion of conspiracy, but attempts to explicate the remarkable correspondence between schooling and work experience. The extensive study of individual modernity by Smith and Inkeles also lends support to the validity of the correspondence principle. They find that the experience of formal schooling with a structured time frame prepares individuals, often of peasant background, for the roles expected in modern factories.

Diploma Disease (Degreeism) (241)

A pattern of overeducation in which prestige rather than actual need fuels a growing social demand for higher and higher degrees. An important connotation of the concept, popularized by Ronald Dore of the University of Sussex, is that individuals seek degrees rather than the learning or abilities associated therewith. An example of the diploma disease at work is the tendency in numerous Third World contexts to require high-ranking administrators to hold doctorates, even though their jobs may have no research dimension. Another

221

reflection of this pattern is political action seeking to upgrade teachers' or technical colleges to comprehensive universities. As a result of the diploma disease, considerable educational inflation has occurred and the educational requirements for any given job have spiraled upwards. *See also* EDUCATIONAL INFLATION, 243.

Significance   Though human resource development is clearly central to the development process, overeducation and unnecessary educational qualifications can lead to considerable waste and inequality. Unnecessary overseas education can represent a substantial loss of limited foreign exchange resources. Upgrading of colleges into comprehensive universities also requires significant public investment. One policy alternative to discourage excessive degreeism would be to impose a degree tax to be paid after a graduate begins regular employment and to be recycled into the financing of the educational system. Such funds could also be used to expand access to education. Dore has made a major contribution to the development field by questioning the sacred cow of educational inflation.

Easterlin Supply-Demand Theory of Fertility (242)
Determination
An economic-oriented theory developed by the economist Richard Easterlin to explain motivation for individual fertility control. Easterlin's theory represents an attempt to understand the factors underlying the demographic transition to lower fertility. A major element of the Easterlin hypothesis is that a threshold exists between two modes of fertility regulation. Prior to the threshold, fertility is determined by natural social, cultural, and environmental forces, with no explicit attempt to regulate fertility. After the threshold, families make explicit decisions about the desired number of children. To explain motivation for fertility control in the period after the transition, Easterlin posits three key factors: the demand for children, the supply of children, and costs of fertility regulation. Tests using empirical data from such countries as India, Sri Lanka, Kenya, and Colombia in a system of econometric equations implied by his model support Easterlin's theory. Full details on Easterlin's theory and methodology are presented in his book coauthored with Eileen Crimmins and titled *The Fertility Revolution: A Supply-Demand Analysis* (1985). *See also* DEMOGRAPHIC TRANSITION, 317; FERTILITY REDUCTION, 246; POPULATION PLANNING, 254.

Significance   The transition to lower fertility is an integral part of the development process. Understanding the factors underlying this process of transition has been a major challenge to modern demographers. Drawing on economic, rational choice and modernization theories, Easterlin has developed a systematic model of fertility determination consistent with empirical data from developing countries. In his integration of economic and social-psychological approaches, applied to a fundamental demographic problem, Easterlin demonstrates an impressive interdisciplinary orientation that guides his rigorous econometric analyses. Since Easterlin finds that modernization favorably affects all three factors in his model explaining reduced fertility, his theory is basically optimistic, suggesting that the population explosion will end naturally as the modernization process spreads around the globe.

Educational Inflation   **(243)**
The notion of an ever-spiraling demand for greater educational qualifications to carry out specific jobs or pursue given occupations. For example, some less developed countries (LDCs) now have the notion that all top administrators should hold doctorates even though many such jobs involve no explicit research dimension. As the pool of educated individuals enlarges, employers can escalate educational requirements for given jobs. Educational inflation appears to be a global phenomenon that feeds increasing social demand for higher and higher levels of formal schooling. *See also* DIPLOMA DISEASE, 241.

Significance   Given the labor-intensive and service nature of education, its costs tend to increase faster than GNP. Thus, unnecessary educational inflation represents an important economic burden to countries with limited resources for public and government expenditures. Given the flexible mixes of schooling associated with many jobs, educational inflation is extremely hard to operationalize. Nevertheless, to the extent to which this trend represents only status enhancement, it is a wasteful drain of limited public resources.

Educational Planning   **(244)**
An organizational process for determining the rational production of trained citizens in accord with demographic trends, occupational needs, and developmental goals. Even though the United States does not engage in educational planning, ironically, through its aid programs it has encouraged developing nations to plan for education. Without educational planning, a nation may overproduce or underproduce schools and teachers. For example, in the 1970s both the United Kingdom and the United States had surplusses of teachers

because of declining school enrollments associated with reduced fertility in the 1960s. Another critical dimension in educational planning is the need for coordination among the different levels of education. The teacher-training system, for example, needs to provide enough teachers for the primary and secondary school systems.

There are three basic alternative approaches to educational planning: manpower planning, cost-benefit analysis, and social demand. The manpower-planning approach popularized by Fred Harbison and others emphasizes producing educated graduates in accord with changing labor-market demands associated with developmental needs. The cost-benefit approach analyzes the economic returns from investing in various forms of schooling and bases educational plans upon the findings of such research. The social-demand approach, the most political and the most populist, bases educational plans on the common educational aspirations of the population at large, unrelated to specific national needs or economic returns. All three approaches have inherent weaknesses. An alternative approach, called the tracer study, has been applied by Singapore and calls for the follow-up evaluation of the market success of graduates from various streams of education. The results from such studies are fed back into the educational planning process and may result in budgetary reallocations and shifts in priorities. The major international agency promoting educational planning is the International Institute for Educational Planning (IIEP) located in Paris and an autonomous unit of UNESCO. The IIEP has trained many educational planners in various developing nations and has provided extensive technical assistance to improve educational planning. *See also* TRACER STUDY, 353; MANPOWER PLANNING, 251.

Significance   Given the rapid demographic and economic changes in developing countries, educational planning takes on special salience. Countries with limited economic and personnel resources can rarely afford the luxury of overproducing schools and teachers or tolerate critical manpower shortages resulting from underproduction. Despite its importance, educational planning has been difficult to implement effectively, and the various methodological approaches have had serious flaws. Educational planning agencies are often only staff bodies with little administrative power to enforce their plans. Popular political pressures often result in a victory of the social-demand approach over more rational technocratic plans that may, for example, try to limit the proliferation of lower-quality institutions of higher education. The major challenge of educational planning is to integrate creatively technical, rational approaches and the inevitable populist political pressures for unplanned educational expansion.

Educational Reform (245)

A major shift in educational policies toward greater efficiency and equity, normally introduced as a result of substantial political changes. In some cases, as in Cuba or Nicaragua after major political revolts, the educational reforms represent genuine social and economic transformations. In other cases, the changes are more much marginal and may have limited impact on basic structures of stratification and opportunity. Some reforms place greater stress on efficiency issues, while others may be largely concerned with equity dimensions. In the 1970s Peru and Thailand experienced important educational reforms, and China carried out significant reforms in the early 1980s.

Significance Educational reforms can have dramatic political consequences. For example, attempts in Ghana to have college students pay a higher percentage of the costs of their instruction led to the downfall of a government. The opening of two major open universities in Thailand greatly facilitated the defusion of a political time bomb associated with a rapidly rising social demand for higher education. Reforms in Malaysian education have resulted in considerable ethnic tension and feelings of discrimination among minorities. But these same reforms have significantly improved the educational opportunities of rural Malays. Marginal or cosmetic educational reform, such as changes in names or numbering systems, have limited impact. Unfortunately, few systematic, rigorous before-and-after studies have been carried out to assess the impact of various educational reforms in developing countries.

Fertility Reduction (246)

A drop in the average number of children borne by women. Fertility reduction is normally considered an integral part of the development process. The total fertility rate is the average number of children that women will bear during their lifetimes. Among developing countries in 1986, Rwanda in Africa had the highest total fertility rate of 8.0, while the People's Republic of China had the lowest rate of 2.3. Three key variables at the individual level affect potential fertility reduction: age at marriage, duration of breast-feeding, and use of contraception. Broader macro factors affecting potential fertility reduction are increased urbanization; improved education, particularly for women; enhanced health care, particularly the reduction of infant mortality; rising levels of income associated with economic development; employment, particularly of women; and the status of women. Developing countries that showed the greatest reduction in total fertility rate between 1965 and 1986 include the People's Republic of China, a drop of 4.1; Thailand, 3.3; Colombia, 3.3; Singapore, 3.0; Costa Rica, 3.0; and Mexico, 3.0. *See also* POPULATION PLANNING, 254.

Significance   A complex interdependence exists between fertility reduction and the development process. From one perspective, it is argued that the development process itself will automatically lead to fertility reduction. Others maintain that a lack of fertility reduction represents an obstacle to the very development that could lead to fertility decline. The latter view implies an interventionist strategy to affect individual fertility by encouraging contraception, breast-feeding, delayed marriage, and improved health care. Data indicate vast differences in the capabilities of developing countries to reduce their fertility rates. Africa has shown the least success in reducing fertility rates. In fact, in some African countries (for example, Niger, Burkina Faso, Zaire, and Ethiopia), total fertility rates actually increased between 1965 and 1986. In 1986, Kenya still had a remarkably high total fertility rate of 7.7. Countries with the greatest success in reducing fertility have been Pacific Basin states such as China, Thailand, Hong Kong, South Korea, and Singapore. The close correspondence between fertility reduction and economic dynamism in the Pacific Basin suggests the synergistic relationship between fertility and development.

Human Capital (247)

The concept of the human being as an asset in which investments are made to improve productivity and development. Common forms of human capital include on-the-job training (OJT), schooling, nonformal and informal education, information and knowledge related to employment opportunities, health, and migration to improve economic opportunity. Gary Becker, the University of Chicago economist of education, popularized this concept in his book, *Human Capital* (1964, 1975). Becker and other advocates of human capital theory have been heavily influenced by economist Theodore Schultz. Since the appearance of the first edition of *Human Capital*, there has been a dramatic growth in research on education and investment in human beings, such as Fred Harbison's *Human Resources As the Wealth of Nations* (1973). The rising interest in human capital was stimulated by empirical studies of the determinants of economic growth that indicated that physical capital explained only a relatively small part of the growth in per capita income of nations.

Significance   Though the term *human capital* has only been popular for several decades, the concept is not new. Classical economists such as Adam Smith and Alfred Marshall were certainly aware of human capital. In *Principles of Economics,* Marshall states that "the most valuable of all capital is that invested in human beings" (cited in Becker 1975). The relative success in meeting basic needs and achieving development by countries such as South Korea, Taiwan, Hong Kong, Singapore, Thailand, Sri Lanka, Tonga, and Costa Rica, all of which are known for their commitments to human resource development, lends support to the thinking of Marshall, Schultz, Becker, Harbison, and other advocates of the human capital theory. However, this theory is controversial. First, seeing this theory as too materialistic and economic, opponents argue that it is dehumanizing to consider human beings as capital. They argue that much education, for example, is an end in itself and should not be evaluated in terms of its impact on individuals' productivity. Second, some radically oriented economists argue that investments in human beings only have high payoffs when those individuals are from higher socioeconomic backgrounds or favored ethnic groups. They contend that the poor and disadvantaged do not necessarily benefit from investments in their training and education, because of discrimination and unemployment in relevant labor markets. Despite the criticisms of human capital theory, many in the development field still argue that the human being is the most important resource in the development process.

Indigenous Technical Knowledge (ITK)   (248)
The body of technical knowledge held by a local people, also commonly referred to as local knowledge. Once referred to as folk wisdom, the concept is not new, but its value in the development process has not always been appreciated. Such indigenous knowledge has often been dismissed as anachronistic and unscientific, even though it may have emerged over centuries in response to needs specific to a particular environment and social setting. Whether for reasons of racism, gender bias, or a strong sense of superiority, outsiders have failed to appreciate this valuable resource. Too often the holders of ITK came to dismiss the value of their own experience and knowledge as well. ITK may be held in many areas, including all aspects of agriculture and health care. Examples are knowledge of systems of intercropping and cultivation, and herbal medicines.

Significance   Appreciation of ITK is a key to sound development planning, and a vital aspect of appropriate technology, popular participation, and basic needs. Research in the field of human ecology and the experience of practitioners converge in recognizing that ITK can be an invaluable resource for development. Failure to recognize its value has no doubt been at the heart of many project failures. ITK is gaining further recognition with the recent emphasis on sustainable development. Researchers are finding many indigenous agricultural practices and systems, such as biological pest control, that are productive and environmentally sound. While much ITK has already been lost, special efforts are now being undertaken to preserve the "wisdom of the ages." Finally, ITK is important because it may represent the only resource over which the poor have much control. ITK is no panacea, of course. Indigenous knowledge may be faulty just as outside information and notions may be. But recognition of ITK enhances the dignity of the poor and puts them on a more equal footing with outsiders, making a partnership more likely.

Literacy (249)
The ability to read and write one's own language. Literacy is considered to be one of the basic needs of all people and a particularly helpful skill in the Third World development process. It is important to distinguish between functional literacy and literacy as measured in a national census. The latter may only mean that an individual is able to write and read his or her own name. In contrast, functional literacy refers to the ability to read and write adequately to cope with the basic requirements of society. Adult literacy is also a special concern, since many adults in LDCs may not have adequate primary schooling to ensure sustained literacy into adult life. Literacy rates vary dramatically from nation to nation and between the sexes. Among developing countries, for example, literacy in Costa Rica is 94 percent for both men and women; in Burkina Faso it is only 21 and 6 percent respectively. Adult literacy is one of three key empirical indicators constituting Morris Morris's Physical Quality of Life Index (PQLI). *See also* LANGUAGE POLICY, 232; PAULO FREIRE, 16.

Significance   Most people agree that literacy is inherently a valuable and important basic need. Though many jobs can be performed by illiterates, nevertheless, literacy is important for empowering individuals and in helping them cope with increasingly complex societies. Without basic literacy, a farmer, for example, may have difficulty in seeking a small loan. Literacy may be essential for farmers to protect their land rights, which may be stated in written documents. In terms of political development, literacy affords individuals a much better understanding of the various political parties and their orientations. Various demographic studies have shown consistent relations between female literacy and reduced fertility. Impressive gains have been made in countries such as Cuba and Nicaragua, which both launched campaigns that proved highly effective in dramatically raising national literacy rates. Countries such as Sri Lanka, Tonga, Thailand, and Costa Rica have also placed high priority on human resource development and adult literacy. The Brazilian Paulo Freire has introduced powerful techniques for teaching literacy to adults by linking such basic cognitive skills to raising political consciousness.

Malthusian Theory (250)

The belief that the human population tends to increase more rapidly than food production, also known as Malthus's principle of population. Thomas Malthus, an English demographer, clergyman, economist, and professor of history, published his ideas on population trends in 1798. He observed that population tends to increase geometrically while food production only grows arithmetically. Similar observations had been noted in the writings of William Petty 150 years earlier but little attention was given to them. Malthus pessimistically predicted that population growth would soon be limited by starvation and disease with only a slight chance that people would take preventive measures, especially sexual continence, to avert or postpone such disaster. *See also* POPULATION PLANNING, 254.

Significance   Malthus is one of the more controversial figures in social thought. In his day, his theory was widely accepted and seemed to be supported by the available evidence. Further, his notions were embraced by English politicians who used the theory as part of a rationalization for neglect of the growing numbers of poor: better conditions for the masses would only lead to more children and further impoverishment, they believed. During the next century, however, Malthus's theory fell out of favor in light of the rapid economic growth, technological change, and dramatic increases in food production.

With the rapid population growth rates in the twentieth century, especially in the poorest countries, Malthusian theory has been revived and revised by neo-Malthusians. They warn of the impending danger of population once again outstripping resources, and argue that the earth is quickly reaching its maximum carrying capacity. If dramatic measures are not taken to achieve zero population growth soon, the environment will suffer irreparable damage, thereby further lowering its carrying capacity. Economists such as Julian Simon and Herman Kahn, editors of *The Resourceful Earth* (1984), downplay such doomsday predictions and place their trust in market forces and technological innovation to solve the problems of population, environment, and resources. Others emphasize the need for better resource distribution and changes in the consumptive choices and behavior of the rich nations to extend effectively the earth's resources.

Manpower Planning (251)

A key concept in educational planning, stressing that plans and priorities should be consistent with any society's economic structure. Popularized by Fred Harbison and Charles Myers in their volume, *Education, Manpower, and Economic Growth* (1964), the concept was extremely popular in the late 1960s and 1970s because of its logical elegance. The fundamental assumption was that educational requirements could be inferred from varying levels of economic development. By examining the educational patterns associated with countries at higher levels of economic development, educational planners in developing countries could ascertain the necessary educational paths. Considerable technical assistance in the 1960s and 1970s was provided to help developing countries implement manpower planning. *See also* HUMAN CAPITAL, 247; EDUCATIONAL PLANNING, 244.

Significance   Despite its intellectual elegance and previous broad popularity, considerable skepticism now exists concerning the use of manpower planning. There are several difficulties. First, predicting future economic and technological changes in any society is difficult. Second, substitutions among various types of educational manpower are far more feasible than previously realized. Thus, there are many possible educational mixes associated with a particular level of economic development. Even in socialist economies, where the government has much more control over economic and educational policy choices, manpower planning has failed to achieve its potential. Despite these fundamental problems and the sexist nature of the term, manpower planning did serve to highlight the critical importance of human resource development, emphasized in Harbison's later book, *Human Resources As the Wealth of Nations* (1973). Analyses derived from manpower planning also helped to document serious imbalances in educational systems; for example, the neglect of technical or science education.

New World Information and Communication Order (252) (NWICO)

A call for major reforms in the international communication and information system that would redress current imbalances in the political, legal, technical, and financial spheres of communication between developed and developing nations. The calls for reform are also known collectively as the new international information order (NIIO). The concerns of Third World nations in this area were first jointly articulated at the 1973 Algiers conference of developing countries, which demanded the reorganization of existing communication channels considered the legacy of the colonial past. The call for a new communication order was informed by dependency theory and grounded in critical theory as applied to the field of information. What came to be known as the NWICO expressed deep concern on the part of developing nations about the quantity and content of information flowing between the North and South, and the imbalance of such flows. The concern is the extent to which information, most of which originates in rich nations, undermines national and cultural development in the Third World. In 1976, the ministers of information of the nonaligned nations met at the Delhi conference to solidify and articulate the call for reforms. This was followed by the "Declaration on the Mass Media," adopted by the 1978 UNESCO General Conference. The declaration and subsequent formation of the McBride Commission placed UNESCO at the center of the NWICO debate. The key issues that comprise the call for a new communication order generally involve: the quantitative imbalance of information flow, absence of information about the South and Third World perspectives, the willful domination of the South by the North (neocolonialism), the rights of recipients of information, and access to the electromagnetic spectrum for broadcasting. Proponents also stressed the right of correction, whereby information deemed incorrect or misleading could be redressed by the offended state. Critics of the proposal see such activity as censorship. Because supporters of a NWICO tend to view information as a social good, not as merchandise, they find themselves in ideological opposition to the modus operandi of the Western developed nations that generate and control most communication technology, information, and copywritten entertainment. The reforms sought in the NWICO express the South's distrust of the current order to meet its development needs and suggest possible correctives. *See also* CULTURAL DEVELOPMENT, 219; NEW

INTERNATIONAL ECONOMIC ORDER, 161; NEOCOLONIALISM, 210; EQUAL
MEDIA, 399; CULTURAL IMPERIALISM, 220.

Significance   International debate and negotiation related to the
concerns of a NWICO peaked with the publication of the McBride
Commission report in 1980. However, the report serves more as a
summary than a guide to solutions of issues. Actual changes in policy
resulting from the debate have been minimal. As with the Third
World's efforts to create a new international economic order (NIEO),
the reforms proposed for the creation of a new communication order
find little support among those nations most vital to reform since the
old order has served them well. Many of the calls for reform have
been opposed on ideological grounds, others simply ignored. Ironically, the call for a new information order has sometimes led to polarization of viewpoints and a breakdown in communication between
North and South. UNESCO's support for the NWICO was a major
factor in the United States's and Great Britain's withdrawal from the
organization. Nevertheless, the NWICO served to provide a forum
for articulating the views and frustrations of developing nations. The
call for an NIEO stemmed from a growing realization by developing
nations that national sovereignty is severely threatened in the absence
of genuine economic independence. Similarly, the call for a NWICO
reflects the contention that true national sovereignty and cultural
identity cannot be maintained under the current international information and communication system. Many nations experience the current world communication system as an extension and promoter of a
world economic and political system that fosters a growing gap between rich and poor nations. Unprecedented development of communication technology in the North has resulted in an exponential
growth in information flow that may have dramatic implications for
the development of the LDCs. The call for a new communication
order is an attempt by the developing nations to ensure that these
changes will enhance the development of the South and not simply
enrich the nations of the North.

Nonformal Education   **(253)**
A type of education that differs from formal schooling. The key
points of difference are: (1) the timing of the training or education is
flexible, not restricted to fixed days during the week; (2) access tends
to be open to all regardless of age, gender, ethnicity, or extent of
prior formal education; (3) teachers are not necessarily hired based
on educational credentials but may be community members with special skills or expertise developed through experience; and (4) there is

not an emphasis on degrees or diplomas. Nonformal education differs from informal education in that it is explicitly organized and funded to meet specific educational needs of the community. In contrast, informal education is more spontaneous and unplanned and is often related to media and direct experience.

Significance   Since formal schooling in many developing countries fails to meet the needs of significant segments of a population, particularly in rural areas and urban slums, interest in nonformal education has grown during the past two decades, and programs have sprouted in a number of developing countries. The influential writings of intellectuals such as Paulo Freire and Ivan Illich have undoubtedly helped stimulate interest in nonformal education. The expansion of nonformal education programs has contributed importantly to rising literacy in countries such as Cuba, Nicaragua, and Thailand. Critics of nonformal education argue that it provides a second-class type of education for those of lower socioeconomic background and may help to "cool them off" politically.

Population Planning   (254)
Measures taken by governments and international agencies to raise or lower birth rates of a given population. Where population is to be reduced, programs usually involve some combination of methods including economic incentives, public education, distribution of contraceptives, and sterilization. Many highly industrialized nations face declining birth rates and even declining populations. In 1987, the growth rate of all more developed countries (MDCs) was 0.5 percent. In the Third World the growth rate stands at 2 percent due primarily to declining death rates. While the world population growth rate has declined from 2 percent (1965) to 1.7 percent (1987), the total absolute population continues to grow due to the broadening age/structure base. Countries such as Kenya, Honduras, Iraq, and Ghana, with growth rates exceeding 3 percent, face the prospect of their populations doubling in size in just two decades. Countries comprising more than 90 percent of the world's population, nearly all of them developing countries, have adopted some sort of population policy based on the premise that continued population growth will adversely affect development efforts. Actual investment in population planning, however, has been quite limited. India was the first country to implement a population program in 1952 when its population was around 400 million. Today that figure has more than doubled. According to the Population Institute, 90 percent of Indian couples know of at least one method of birth control but only 39 percent

actually use one. In contrast, the People's Republic of China has dramatically reduced its growth rate to 1 percent, compared to 2.4 percent for the rest of the LDCs. Its crude birth rate dropped from 32 in 1972 to 18 in 1985. (It has since risen.) Of the two countries, India's experience is more typical of LDCs' efforts. Few countries have markedly lowered their growth rates or population sizes. Countries that have achieved a notable degree of success in family planning, in addition to China, are Cuba, Colombia, Costa Rica, Fiji, Indonesia, Jamaica, Mexico, Thailand, South Korea, Sri Lanka, Taiwan, and Venezuela. Numerous international organizations are engaged in family-planning research and projects. Best known are the UN Fund for Population Activities (UNFPA), the International Planned Parenthood Federation, and the Population Council. *See also* FERTILITY REDUCTION, 246; DEMOGRAPHIC TRANSITION, 317.

Significance   Population policies and the relationship of population to development have been subjects of much heated international debate. With regard to development, two opposing viewpoints can be called neo-Malthusian and cornucopian. The former emphasizes limited resources and the strain of growing populations upon those resources, especially natural resources. This interpretation was popularized by Paul Ehrlich's influential book, *The Population Bomb* (1968). The cornucopians downplay the limited availability of natural resources and stress human resources. Greater numbers are capable of more production and productivity (because of economies of scale), which in turn lead to economic growth. They further question the viability and effectiveness of population planning. They view reduction of population growth as a natural response to economic growth and security. The neo-Malthusians counter that high population growth rates make economic growth less likely to occur. Among intellectual skeptics, many Marxists reject population growth as a key variable affecting development, since they view macro and international structural factors as the major causes of underdevelopment. Environmentally oriented skeptics emphasize consumption patterns rather than numbers of people per se as the major factor putting pressure on global resources and environment.

Most Third World countries have adopted policies promoting both economic growth and population growth reduction, viewing the two goals as mutually reinforcing. However, attitudes toward birth control and family planning vary widely throughout the world and within countries. Both multilateral and national programs have been received with a good deal of suspicion and skepticism on the part of local populations. Reproduction issues are not only political and economic in scope; they are grounded in personal and cultural preference. Programs initiated at the national and international level are often considered impositions with little meaning at the village level. In other cases, the women in particular may desire contraceptives and family planning information but have access to neither. As such, population planning is often filled with contradictions and conflicting goals and values. The efficacy of cutting population growth is widely acknowledged and evident in the number of nations and international agencies engaged in population planning. The urgency of the world population problem is borne out dramatically in the population growth in Third World urban centers. The effects of overpopulation on rural areas may be more subtle but nonetheless important. Urban growth is no doubt precipitated by rural population growth. But while the need for population planning is widely acknowledged at the national and international levels, means to achieve effective and humane population planning are still being debated.

Social Charter (255)
A concept introduced by the sociologist John Meyer that refers to perceived individual attributes associated with certain types of education. Schools may have specific goals to socialize students into certain behavioral modes and styles. For example, graduates of Oxford or Harvard are perceived as being bright and successful. Given the social charter, these graduates are defined as having the attributes necessary for success in modern society. In contrast, graduates of community colleges are perceived as individuals having limited futures. *See also* CORRESPONDENCE PRINCIPLE, 240.

Significance   The social charter phenomenon tends to appear in any society with modern schools or colleges, and leads to intense competition for places in highly chartered schools. Some countries have coaching schools for preschoolers to prepare them for entrance examinations to highly chartered schools. Graduates of chartered institutions often carry into the labor markets bonds of loyalty and commitment to each other. The social charter phenomenon reflects the persistence of education and schooling as central to the process of social stratification and inequality.

Women in Development (WID) (256)
An increasingly important dimension of the development field focusing on the impact of development upon the lives of Third World women and their contributions to the development process. A seminal work in the field was Ester Boserup's *Women's Roles in Economic*

Development (1970). By identifying female and male farming systems, this study drew attention to differential effects of colonialism and industrialization on women in various parts of the Third World. The WID field now consists of four related dimensions of research: female empowerment and women in the political process; the effects of the development process upon women's lives; the marginalization of women in modern economic systems; and women in the new international division of labor. A major volume highlighting the past and ongoing process of gender discrimination, including male bias in development planning, is *The Domestication of Women: Discrimination in Developing Societies* (1980) by Barbara Rogers. Women's economic roles and contributions to productivity are the subjects of an influential collection of studies, *Women and Development: The Sexual Division of Labor in Rural Societies* (1982), edited by Lourdes Benería. WID research demonstrates that women frequently lack opportunities to participate in decisions that vitally affect their lives, especially in the political and economic realms. The growing number of documented accounts of women's lives illustrates both the detrimental effects that development has often had on their well-being and the need for various forms of empowerment of Third World women. Appropriately, scholars from developing countries such as Kumari Jayawardena, Noeleen Heyzer, and Fatima Mernissi are major contributors to WID. The working paper series of Michigan State University's Office of Women in International Development has helped coalesce the field. The major professional organization for WID is the Association of Women in Development (AWID). The United Nations Research and Training Institute for the Advancement of Women (INSTRAW) serves as the primary WID organization within the UN system. *See also* DECADE FOR WOMEN, 222.

Significance   The field of women in development represents one of the most important critiques of the development process to have emerged in the last two decades. Outside of the WID field, inadequate attention has been given to the impact of development on the lives of women and to the vital role of women in maintaining the well-being of Third World societies. For example, women are the major actors in most phases of local food production, and therefore their role is critical to eliminating hunger and malnutrition. Women are also becoming increasingly involved in the global assembly line and in the urban informal sector. What are the effects of these and other changes on women and their families? Development research, theory, and planning have often ignored the specific circumstances faced by the female half of any society's population. The rapidly growing field of WID has served as a major catalyst for new consideration of the plight and potential of women in the Third World, thereby greatly enhancing the development field.

G. Development and Environment

Brundtland Report (257)
A study conducted by the World Commission on Environment and Development (WCED) to provide proposals for "long-term environmental strategies for achieving sustainable development to the year 2000 and beyond." The report, officially titled *Our Common Future* and published in 1987, is known by the name of the prime minister of Norway, Dr. Gro Harlem Brundtland, who is also chairperson of the WCED. Development practitioners and scholars from 21 countries representing all regions of the world comprised the group of eminent commissioners who prepared this important study. A major emphasis of the report is "sustainable development, a term which implies meeting the needs of the present without compromising the ability of future generations to meet their own needs." The report also emphasizes the need for a more equitable distribution of goods, social justice for all, and broader participation of all citizens in decisions affecting their own development and welfare. *See also* SUSTAINABLE DEVELOPMENT, 272.

Significance   This important report, prepared in response to a 1983 UN resolution, provides global consensus in support of the concept of sustainable development. In previous decades many Third World intellectuals viewed environmental problems as primarily a luxury concern of the wealthier countries and believed that developing nations had other, far more important priorities. The consensus developed in the Brundtland Report transcends such a we/they false dichotomy with a visionary concept of *Our Common Future,* the title given the published report. The challenge is to turn the idealistic statements of the report into developmental realities. A key question is whether the major aid donors such as Japan and the World Bank will give priority to facilitating cooperation between developed and developing countries to achieve the goals and recommendations of the Brundtland Report.

Common Heritage of Mankind Principle (258)
A concept articulated as part of the Law of the Sea that reserves the resources of the high seas for the benefit of all people. The term was coined by Prince Wan of Thailand during the early stages of the

negotiation of the Law of the Sea covenant, and is a remarkable example of peaceful and cooperative international relations. Under the Law of the Sea, all resources beyond the exclusive 200-mile economic zone will be shared by all nations and their use will be regulated by an international body, the International Seabed Authority. Thus, poor landlocked countries such as Laos, Nepal, and Bolivia would be guaranteed a share of the enormous wealth of the oceans. *See also* LAW OF THE SEA CONVENTION, 269.

Significance   Given the potential wealth of the ocean commons, including manganese nodules and other minerals, energy supplies, and various aquatic resources, the common-heritage element of the Law of the Sea is both its most important and most controversial feature. The United States, for example, objected to this aspect of the Law of the Sea and refused to sign the covenant. Without this principle, the resources of the high seas will go exclusively to those nations with the greatest technological capacities to utilize them. Another danger of not having this principle, from an ecological perspective, is the so-called tragedy of the commons. Individual nations acting in their own self-interests may excessively utilize and consume the resources of the oceans. If regulations for use of ocean resources are ambiguous, private firms may be reluctant to invest in such operations. Full implementation of the common heritage principle provides an alternative to potentially violent confrontations over the use of ocean resources such as oil in the South China Sea. The principle is also relevant to other resource domains such as the high frontier, that is, outer space. The implementation of the common heritage of mankind principle would result in an impressive new level of cooperative rather than competitive and confrontational global relations. It would also augur well for the future of more environmentally conscious international regimes.

Debt-for-Nature Swaps   **(259)**
The exchange of a reduction in a developing country's debt for funds to implement environmental preservation and conservation projects. The idea was first proposed by Thomas Lovejoy of the World Wildlife Federation in 1984. The practice involves international conservation groups who pay off part of a nation's debt at a discounted rate acceptable to the lender. In exchange, the debtor country either transfers local currency to in-country conservation groups or agrees to set aside land for conservation reserves. Among countries that have experimented with this innovation are Bolivia, Ecuador, and Costa Rica. For example, in 1987 Conservation International (CI)

"purchased" $650,000 of Bolivia's $4.5 billion foreign debt from a Swiss bank for $100,000. Bolivia then created a four million acre conservation area, the Beni Biosphere Reserve, and set aside $250,000 in local currency to administer the area. *See also* DEBT CRISIS, 134.

Significance   Debt-for-nature swaps provide an innovative way to increase funding for environmentally oriented development while addressing the need for debt relief in developing countries. In practice, however, the swaps have been plagued with logistical, economic, and political problems not unlike many conventional development projects. The Beni Biosphere Reserve, for example, is highly controversial. The Bolivian government has been slow to allocate funds for the project. Further, the indigenous tribal groups that populate the area see the project as legitimating extensive logging operations that threaten rather than protect the Chimanes Forest. Debt-for-nature swaps also need to be limited in scope lest they contribute to runaway inflation or simply replace external with internal debt. Finally, the goals mandated by international organizations may not necessarily fit the needs of local environmental organizations or the national government and thus may be perceived as a threat to national sovereignty. Debt-for-nature swaps have a relatively short history. It remains to be seen if such problems can be overcome. If so, they hold promise as partial and complementary solutions to two pressing international problems, environmental destruction and the debt crisis. Debt-for-nature swaps have also inspired emerging debt-for-education swaps, based on similar principles and strategies.

Dumping   (260)
Any of a number of activities involving the transfer of goods from a country where they are illegal, unsaleable, or obsolete to another country that will accept them. The term is also used to describe the marketing of highly subsidized exports. The most common dumping involves transfer of goods from industrialized nations with stronger legal restrictions on products to less regulated, less developed countries (LDCs). Industries most frequently involved in dumping disputes are the pharmaceutical and petrochemical industries. For example, drugs that await approval or are rejected by the U.S. Food and Drug Administration are made readily available or even donated to many LDCs. Banned petrochemical products, such as certain pesticides, may be legally exported provided the buyer is informed that the product is illegal in the United States.

Recently, much attention has focused on the attempts and practice of industrialized nations to dispose of toxic waste in developing countries desperate for hard currency. Because of stricter regulations in the North, many companies find it more economically viable to ship toxic waste and even common garbage to willing LDCs than to engage in proper and legal disposal in the country of origin. This practice has been dubbed "garbage imperialism." Although more than 40 developing countries now officially ban the import of hazardous waste, illegal trade continues. In response to growing concern over such practices, the UN Environmental Program (UNEP) in 1989 convened a meeting, attended by 114 nations, to create international guidelines for the export and import of hazardous waste. The resulting convention requires waste exporters to obtain written permission from importing countries before shipments commence. It also obliges exporters to take back illegally shipped waste. A group of 40 African nations refused to sign the agreement, stating the need for stricter regulations. *See also* GARBAGE IMPERIALISM, 265; EXPORT OF POLLUTION, 264.

Significance   The practice of dumping raises numerous legal, economic, and moral issues. If a product is deemed illegal in one country, should it be permitted to be exported? What obligation do industrialized countries have to dispose of their waste within their own borders? As regulations on products and waste disposal grow stricter in the North, the incentives to dump products in the South become greater while indebted developing countries have greater economic incentives to purchase or accept them. In one extreme case, Guinea-Bissau was offered nearly $500 million, about three times the nation's GNP, to take hazardous waste from the United States and Europe. It refused. Sadly, these products, such as pharmaceuticals, petrochemicals, and hazardous materials, are more likely to be detrimental in LDCs than in the more literate societies that have banned them. Protection from dumping can be considered a human right, as well as an economic and environmental issue, requiring greater international regulation and cooperation.

Ecocultural Revolutions   (261)

Major shifts in the relations between people and their environment. The first ecocultural revolution was the use of fire by hunters, which had a major impact on the distribution of forests and grasslands. The second revolution, normally referred to as the agricultural revolution, involved the domestication of plants and animals. The third revolution was the adoption of techniques of irrigation. The fourth was the spread of global markets and the resultant impact of cash economies on traditional societies. The fifth and future revolution postulates a new affinity for nature. Key elements in the fifth ecocultural revolution are self-sufficiency, local responsibility, symbolism, and spiritualism. These five ecocultural revolutions have been defined and described by two Swiss-based conservationists, Jeffrey A. McNeely and Paul S. Wachtel, authors of *Soul of the Tiger* (1988). *See also* SUSTAINABLE DEVELOPMENT, 272.

Significance   McNeely's and Wachtel's fifth ecocultural revolution is directly related to the call for sustainable development and the need for deeper concern for the impact of development on environmental conditions and critical global interdependencies. McNeely and Wachtel speculate that individuals from Third World areas with rich rain forests, such as Southeast Asia, will be the leaders and the beneficiaries of the fifth ecocultural revolution. The concept is consistent with Fritjof Capra's notion of the turning point and the Salks' concept of a transition from an Epoch A emphasizing competition and destruction of nature to an Epoch B bringing about greater cooperation and respect for nature.

Ecofeminism   (262)
A radical form of feminism that has gained increasing prominence in environmental and feminist movements over the last two decades. Many view Rachel Carson's *Silent Spring* (1962) as an important catalyst for the movement. Ecofeminism developed from a recognition of similarities between violence toward and domination of women, and violence toward and domination of the environment. Much of the discourse within ecofeminism has centered not only on these parallels, but also on women's relationships with the natural environment. A particular focus has been on cultures that imagine the divine as female and nurturing. *See also* SUSTAINABLE DEVELOPMENT, 272; WOMEN IN DEVELOPMENT, 256.

Significance   Development efforts have often been criticized for their negative effects on both women and the environment. As a result, special sectors have been created in many development organizations to address these issues. Nevertheless, many ecofeminists claim that the notion of development is inherently flawed because it has been based on Western, patriarchal, and hierarchical paradigms that stress control over nature, if not women. They see overwhelming evidence that such models undermine the security of women and the quality of the environment. For example, development tends to promote the establishment of cash-based economies either directly through for-cash projects or indirectly by introducing technology that requires cash to be purchased and maintained. Women in many parts of the world are strongly tied to natural resource–based economies. Their security is frequently undermined by development projects that degrade the environment. In addressing these issues feminists have focused on questions of equity in the development process. Ecofeminists have gone a step further to question the very concept of development since it so often has undermined the welfare of women and their security base—the immediate and broader environment. They suggest that ultimately this is everyone's security base. As such, ecofeminists call for new models of change based on nonhierarchical, sustainable, and feminist principles.

Entropy (263)

A measure of disorder as embodied in the second law of thermodynamics stating that matter and energy can only be changed in one direction, from usable to unusable, from ordered to chaos. Only through the consumption of energy on one level can order be maintained on another. The net result is always increased chaos. Jeremy Rifkin, in *Entropy: A New World View* (1980), argues that, if properly understood, the notion of entropy has profound implications for world development, which he claims has always been based on the assumption of unlimited exploitation of resources and the ability to control nature. He quotes the Nobel Prize–winning chemist, Frederick Soddy, who states that the laws of thermodynamics "control, in the last resort, the rise and fall of political systems, the freedom or bondage of nations, the movements of commerce and industry, the origins of wealth and poverty, and the general welfare of the race" (Rifkin 1980:8). Rifkin suggests that a new development paradigm that recognizes the implications of entropy needs to replace the Newtonian world machine concept. Further, moving toward a low-entropy society would entail a radical transition in societal and economic systems. The new paradigm would call for an economic system based on renewable energy. *See also* SUSTAINABLE DEVELOPMENT, 272; SOFT ENERGY PATHS, 271.

Significance Rifkin's interpretation of entropy has proven to be a useful point of departure for environmentally oriented discussions of sustainable development. The implication is that further "progress" based on consumption of nonrenewable resources, specifically fossil-based fuels, is not viable for either the industrialized nations or the Third World. The current system of industrialization is approaching its natural limits and polluting the globe. Pollution is just one manifestation of entropy. Rifkin disputes the notion that science will find a quick-fix solution to the depletion of energy resources other than greater efficiency. The solar age, he contends, is inevitable and not far off. This suggests that the Third World should give up dreams of maximal Western-style industrialization and focus on intermediate technology, its agricultural base, and conservation of nonrenewable natural resources. The developed world should prepare now for the inevitable transition to the solar age by reducing wasteful, nonessential consumption and subsequent pollution levels. Much of the entropy paradigm serves as the basis for more recent writings on sustainable development.

Export of Pollution (264)

The establishment by industrialized countries of the dirtiest and most polluting industries in developing countries. In such countries, where industry is often sought to provide employment for young and rapidly growing labor forces, environmental controls and regulations are commonly lax in comparison with the standards in industrial countries. *See also* DUMPING, 260; GARBAGE IMPERIALISM, 265.

Significance The exportation of pollution represents a gross injustice in that consumers of the products of such industries in rich countries do not have to pay for the environmental costs involved in the production of such commodities. Many developing countries competing for foreign factories as a source of new employment are frequently unwilling to impose strict environmental controls for fear that industries may move to other nations. How to deal fairly and creatively with this problem represents a major challenge to the United Nations Environmental Program in the decades ahead.

Garbage Imperialism (265)

The export of toxic wastes from rich, industrialized countries to developing nations. It is estimated that in the years 1987–1988, 3.5 million metric tons of toxic waste were shipped to developing countries and Eastern Europe. The financial cost of dumping in developing countries in Africa, for example, may be as little as $3 a ton in contrast to industrial countries where cost may be as high as $1,250 a ton. *See also* DUMPING, 260.

Significance Many developing countries already face serious environmental problems, which are exacerbated by the dumping of toxic wastes. The United Nations, seeking alternative international policies to deal with this growing problem, is working on a "Global

Convention on the Control of Transboundary Movements of Hazardous Wastes." The two major policies could be an outright ban on such shipments or tight controls that would allow developing nations to store safely or recycle certain toxic wastes from industrial countries. Environmental organizations such as the Natural Resources Defense Council (NRDC) are pushing hard for a total ban in the trade of wastes. Several LDCs such as Ivory Coast and Nigeria have enacted new laws with severe sanctions for those found importing or dumping hazardous wastes from abroad. The Organization of African Unity and the 101-nation Non-Aligned Movement (NAM) are on record in support of a complete ban on hazardous waste trade.

Hyperurbanization (266)

The excessive growth of many of the world's major cities, which exceeds the carrying capacity of their environments. Common in hyperurbanized cities of developing countries are inordinate traffic congestion; inadequate housing reflected in sprawling barrios or *favelas;* polluted rivers, canals, and air; excessive underemployment and unemployment; and growing rates of modern diseases such as cancer. Major cities that exemplify hyperurbanization are Mexico City, São Paulo, Lagos, Bangkok, Manila, and Calcutta. *See also* PRIMATE CITY, 343.

Significance Hyperurbanization represents a major global developmental problem. Its causes, involving both push and pull factors, are relatively easy to identify. Pulling people into such cities are the many associated amenities and economic prospects that are perceived to be more favorable. Pushing individuals into the cities are rural poverty, deteriorating agricultural conditions such as soil erosion, and demographic factors including large rural families. The problem of hyperurbanization is virtually insoluble in that an improvement in urban conditions attracts even more rural influx and the building of barriers between urban and rural areas would represent a denial of economic and educational opportunities to the less advantaged.

Integrated Industrial Development (267)

Refers to increased levels of industrial activity and related technological changes in harmony with culture and the environment. It is implied in the thinking of the Thai intellectual-entrepreneur, Sippanondha Ketudat (1990), and his collaborator, Robert Textor, in their work on the future of Thailand as part of an East-West Center project on sociocultural change in Southeast Asia. The concept is obviously an ideal type. No society or organization has yet attained the ideal of integrated industrial development. There are, however, examples of movement toward this ideal in various settings. The Japanese concept of "garden and machine" society reflects this genre of thinking. The bird and water parks of the Jurong Industrial Estate in Singapore reflect an attempt to achieve a more aesthetic form of industrial development. The Eastern Seaboard Project in Thailand is being developed with considerable concern for cultural and environmental impacts. The new Nike World "Campus" in Oregon with its lake, jogging trails, park and picnic areas, and art work also reflect this ideal. The concept of integrated industrial development as being defined here has several dimensions. Primary is the concern for industrial development to be environmentally and culturally sensitive. Other dimensions connoted by the concept are 1) the growing merger of city and village in the mega-metropolitan areas of developing countries and the integrating of urban and village values, without the destruction of or disrespect for the latter; 2) the importance of including an aesthetic dimension in industrial development; 3) the need to treat multicultural work forces without discrimination or ethnic bias; and 4) finally, and perhaps most importantly, that human welfare maximization should take priority over profit maximization. *See also* SIPPANONDHA KETUDAT, 51; EASTERN SEABOARD PROJECT, 359; SUSTAINABLE DEVELOPMENT, 272.

Significance   Though there is an extensive literature on integrated rural development, the concept of integrated industrial development is conspicuously absent from the development and social science literature. Thus, this is a new emerging concept with increasing salience in the 21st century as environmental concerns become critical. To move toward the ideal of integrated industrial development will require visionary and farsighted political leadership and private entrepreneurship. This concept also is related to the ideas of corporate culture, socially responsible investment, and sustainable development.

Interdependence   (268)
A concept stressing the mutual dependence and intertwined fates of the earth's political, economic, and environmental systems and their various components. The concept of interdependence is central to understanding global environmental issues as well as the international economic system. For example, transborder pollution, global warming, and desertification all illustrate how the actions and policy decisions of individual nations may have profound impacts on other

countries and, in some instances, the entire planet. In the area of economics, interdependence can be illustrated by the current debt crisis. Debtor nations cannot afford to default on loans, being dependent on national and international institutions for continuing financial support. Those institutions and supporting countries cannot afford to let them default, lest they recover nothing from their prior investments. The economic development of any country depends on healthy markets for its products, that is, viable trading partners.

Significance   Interdependence is a notion of increasing importance in international development. It stands as a reminder, at the sectoral level, that development cannot be approached in a piecemeal fashion. Political, economic, and environmental decisions are interconnected. At the international level, the concept stresses the shared economic and environmental fate of the world's nations. This, in turn, points to the need for new methods, agreements, and forms of international cooperation that transcend immediate, narrow national interests since we ultimately share the same interests. As rather dramatically put by Barbara Ward, "We are going to become a community or we are going to die."

Law of the Sea Convention   (269)

An international agreement, or a "constitution for the oceans," that addresses cooperation in maritime law and the management of the open sea resources. The first United Nations Conference on the Law of the Sea (UNCLOS I) was assembled in Geneva in 1958; UNCLOS II met in Geneva in 1960 but failed to resolve major issues. The central issues were navigational rights through straits, and the extension, by most nations, of the territorial seas limit from 3 to 12 miles. During the 1960s interest grew in declaring the oceans the common heritage of mankind to be managed by an international body such as the United Nations. As a result, the UNCLOS III Conference began work on a global LOS Convention, which was completed in 1982. The convention updates and codifies previous maritime agreements and provides a comprehensive framework for the management of marine resources and protection of the ocean environment. Most notably, the convention establishes and defines exclusive economic zones (EEZs), the 200-mile territory over which coastal nations are granted exclusive economic control. EEZs account for 40 percent of the world's ocean surface and seabed area. The remaining 60 percent remains open for traditional freedom of the seas while the wealth to be drawn from the seabed is to be considered the common heritage of mankind. In a unique arrangement, the convention establishes the

International Seabed Authority (ISA) and grants it domain over the seabeds outside of the EEZs. The ISA may tax the proceeds of exploitive operations and distribute earnings among all nations according to a predetermined formula. Fifteen industrialized nations most capable of exploiting the deep seas withheld their signatures from the convention in opposition. However, 119 nations signed the convention in 1982, and all participants except Turkey signed the final act, entitling them to attend the meetings of the agencies created by the convention. Since 1982, 40 more nations have signed the convention, which gives it the force of law upon ratification by 60 nations. As of 1989, 39 nations had formally ratified the agreement. *See also* COMMON HERITAGE OF MANKIND PRINCIPLE, 258.

Significance   The Law of the Sea serves as an invaluable and timely tool for global cooperation in the management of the oceans. It replaces the outdated maritime treaties and arrangements and recognizes the need for cooperation, not only in navigation and fishing rights, but also in the ecological management of the seas. The LOS reflects the growing awareness of the interdependence of all nations and addresses a number of emerging global development issues such as food security, resource management, trade, regional cooperation, the rights of landlocked states, and the control and benefits of information and technology. The Law of the Sea is the outcome of the largest and longest ongoing international conference in history. It reflects a new genre of cooperative rather than confrontational international relations in which competition for valuable resources can be essentially resolved through peaceful international negotiations. The treaty, for the first time in the history of the states system, creates a limited world government with powers and authority to govern the world's oceans and their seabeds. Failure of the United States to sign or ratify the treaty has encouraged other states to refuse implementing actions, jeopardizing the entire project.

Overdevelopment   (270)
Refers to the state of economies based on comparatively high levels of consumption. The concept of overdevelopment emphasizes the great disparity in resource consumption between rich and poor nations, particularly of nonrenewables such as oil. Japan, Western Europe, the United States, and the Soviet Union, together comprising roughly one-quarter of the world's population, account for 80 percent of the world's annual consumption of resources. The United States alone, with less than five percent of the population, accounts for one-third of resource utilization. At the same time, the share of

pollution output is roughly equated with the level of consumption. An individual in the overdeveloped countries has 30 to 50 times the environmental impact of a person in an LDC economy. Thus some would contend that the highly industrialized nations are, in terms of per capita resource consumption and pollution production, the most overpopulated countries in the world.

Significance   The concept of overdevelopment helps frame the broader debate regarding global environmental and economic justice. Developing nations are concerned that much of the world's resource base is being depleted and will not be available for their development purposes. They also point to the global environmental impacts of the Northern industrialized nations to which they are vulnerable. The principle of the common heritage of mankind, as embodied in the Law of the Sea legislation, reflects this concern. The concept of overdevelopment further points out the sad irony of vast poverty persisting in a world of plenty.

Soft Energy Paths   (271)
The alternative energy policies first proposed by Amory Lovins and others in the mid–1970s to reduce dependence on oil. The oil shortages of the early 1970s raised the awareness that the world economy had become highly dependent upon a nonrenewable resource and many industrialized nations depended upon imported oil. Lovins proposed that the world, particularly its high-energy users, begin planning for alternative sources and conserving oil supplies for the inevitable conversion to a new energy system. He described two paths—hard and soft. The hard path would involve high-output, highly centralized, capital-intensive production, such as nuclear energy, coal gasification, and prolonged dependence on ever scarcer and costly oil. The soft path would use renewable sources such as solar and wind energy. It would be diverse and decentralized, low-tech but not necessarily unsophisticated. Moreover, the soft path is coupled with greater efficiency. Lovins speculated that the economic vitality and quality of life in the high-consumption countries could be maintained while they dramatically reduced their energy consumption. He suggested that energy policies should stress efficiency, not greater production. Lovins also noted that the hard and soft paths are culturally and politically incompatible with antithetical social implications. *See also* ENTROPY, 263; ENERGY/EFFICIENCY RATIO, 321.

Significance   The general sense of urgency regarding energy supplies and conservation that developed in the 1970s and led to support for soft energy paths faded in the 1980s as oil prices and supplies stabilized. Much of the momentum toward alternative energy sources and systems created in the wake of the energy crisis of 1973 was lost. Most of the highly industrialized countries continue to rely heavily on imported oil as their chief energy source. In the Third World, non–oil-producing countries often spend the greater share of their budget on oil, contributing greatly to their national debt. The discovery of new oil fields has postponed by several decades the practical depletion of the world's oil reserves. But soft path alternatives are gaining support for both economic and environmental reasons. No country has yet devised a satisfactory method of disposing of waste from nuclear power plants. Few Third World countries can afford to own and operate nuclear generators. Oil explorers face growing opposition in environmentally conscious regions. In 1989, the United States imported a higher percentage of its oil than it did prior to the energy crisis, renewing concerns of economic dependency. The viability of the hard path for both the advanced industrialized and the developing countries begs reconsideration. Interestingly, Lovins's prediction of sustained economic growth with comparatively less energy consumption has been borne out in nearly every industrialized country over the last two decades, reflecting conservation measures introduced in response to the oil crisis. Many sectors of the Third World already follow, by tradition, what could be considered the soft path. The soft energy philosophy suggests building upon and improving such systems rather than viewing them as backward and antithetical to development.

Sustainable Development   (272)
The enhancement of productivity and living standards in ways that are consistent with the preservation and maintenance of global and local ecosystems. This concept has been emphasized in the late 1980s and 1990s as intellectuals, policymakers, and citizens are becoming increasingly conscious of the severe environmental consequences of limitless, mindless economic growth. The roots of the sustainable development notion derive from concepts such as stewardship, conservation, and respect for nature as well as new scientific insights into the undesirable consequences of the major development programs and paradigms. Specific pioneering works from the 1960s and 1970s include Rachel Carson's *Silent Spring* (1962), Paul Ehrlich's *The*

Population Bomb (1968), the Club of Rome's *The Limits to Growth* (1972), and E. F. Schumacher's *Small Is Beautiful* (1975). More recent work in the field of agroecology, such as that of Gordan Conway and Miguel Altieri, has been particularly important in advancing and clarifying the concept of sustainable development. *Our Common Future* (1987), the report of the World Commission on Environment and Development, or the Brundtland Commission, has also prompted broad discussion and recognition of the importance of sustainable approaches to international development. Michael Redclift, in *Sustainable Development: Exploring the Contradictions* (1987), provides an excellent discussion of the emergence and complexities of the concept. With the widespread adoption of sustainable development rhetoric and practice throughout the development field, various interpretations and definitions have emerged.

Significance   Though many intellectuals in developing countries initially saw environmental problems as primarily a luxury of the rich nations, as environmental conditions have deteriorated in many areas of developing countries in the 1980s and 1990s, recognition has increased that environmental concerns are of the highest priority in the development agenda. The relationship between development and the environment has been ignored by many in the development field for too long. The concept of sustainable development calls into question the long-term viability of current industrial-development models based on the consumption of a large share of the earth's natural resources and resulting pollution. The viability is questioned for both the North and the South, site of some of the world's most diverse, valuable, and vulnerable ecosystems such as the tropical rain forests of the Amazon Basin, Costa Rica, Indonesia, and Thailand. Preservation of such biological diversity is also related to the cultural identity of many minority groups living within these areas. In Africa, increasing desertification poses a serious threat to a continent already struggling to feed a rapidly growing population. Empirical research suggests that it is the poorest of the poor who often suffer the most from environmental degradation in urban and rural areas. In fact, throughout the Third World, the leading proponents of more environmentally sound development are the poor themselves, who clearly understand the relationship between poverty and environment. For these reasons, sustainable development must be a key priority in the decades and century ahead. However, it remains to be seen whether the concept of sustainable development represents a major development paradigm shift in practice or merely another passing fad in the development field. Governments and development groups must continue to search for creative ways to balance economic, cultural, and environmental considerations with immediate and long-term development goals.

Voluntary Simplicity (273)

A decision on the part of affluent individuals and societies to live more simply, particularly in terms of consumption of limited resources. The notion was popularized in the early 1980s in a book called *Voluntary Simplicity* written by Duane Elgin. The notion of simplicity as a virtuous life-style can be found in most of the world's cultures and religions. While drawing connections between Western materialism and Third World suffering, Elgin points to the spiritual void of the affluent consumer society. Choosing to live more simply, he contends, addresses both worldwide environmental and poverty-related concerns and individual spiritual needs. "The widespread simplification of life," he writes, "is vital to the well-being of the entire human family" (Elgin 1982:4). *See also* OVERDEVELOPMENT, 270.

Significance   The notion and practice of voluntary simplicity emphasize the interconnectedness and interdependence of all societies and individuals, ecological concepts cast in social and political terms. Elgin's book is part of a broad range of recent writings calling into question the long-term viability of Western consumer society in both environmental and moral terms. The concept reflects both Schumacher's principle of "small is beautiful" and the classic question raised by Erich Fromm, "To have or to be?" Voluntary simplicity is presented as one response to a growing awareness of how the choices of people in affluent societies affect not only their own well-being, but the health and choices of those in less affluent nations. This effect is particularly true with regard to the amount and types of goods produced and consumed in countries such as the United States. While some dismiss the notion as idealistic, in many types of practices, voluntary simplicity appears to be a growing reality and should not be so easily dismissed as a passing fad. The idea has sparked considerable reassessment of values and priorities, and discussion on the part of the world's more privileged societies as to what constitutes responsible individual choices.

H. Development Assistance and Technology Transfer

Absorptive Capacity (274)

A country's ability to utilize foreign aid effectively for developmental purposes. Related to absorptive capacity are the physical and human infrastructures of a nation, which vary widely among developing countries. Also relevant to absorptive capacity are the system of governance and its efficiency in utilizing external funds. One way of assessing a country's absorptive capacity is to evaluate rigorously its use of past aid funds. However, there is no agreed upon empirical measure of absorptive capacity. One possible measure would be to compute a country's success in meeting basic needs relative to its increases in gross national product (GNP). Another relevant measure might be the degree of equity achieved relative to increases in GNP. *See also* INFRASTRUCTURE, 155.

Significance   There is often an inverse relationship between a country's economic needs and its absorptive capacity. Commonly, the neediest countries have the most limited absorptive capacity. In contrast, countries such as Singapore may have high absorptive capacity but minimal needs. In an important way, the absorptive capacity issue relates to the fundamental question of equity versus efficiency. Allocating limited development funds to the developing countries with the greatest absorptive capacity may maximize efficiency but contribute to growing global disparities. In contrast, giving priority to needier countries with less absorptive capacity may contribute to greater equity but result in reduced efficiency in the use of limited aid funds. Quality technical assistance may contribute to strengthening the absorptive capacity of developing nations.

Alliance for Progress   **(275)**
The comprehensive, multinational program for the social, political, and economic development of Latin America begun during the 1960s. The Alliance for Progress was initiated by President John Kennedy in 1961 as a means of promoting regional development and the hemispheric security interests of the United States. The Cuban Revolution and Vice-President Richard Nixon's disastrous trip to Latin America in 1958 had helped alert the United States to growing discontent in the region. The alliance was envisioned as a means of achieving political stability through social, agrarian, and financial reforms; technical assistance; and improved trade relations. The plan, which was adopted by agreement of all 20 member states of the Organization of American States (OAS) at Punta del Este, Uruguay, called for a $100 billion investment in various plans and projects over the period of a decade. The United States was to provide $20 billion in development assistance, primarily through the Inter-American Development Bank, International Bank for Reconstruction and Devel-

opment (IBRD), and the U.S. Agency for International Development (AID), which was the major coordinating agency for U.S. efforts. However, no long-term funding mechanism or commitment was ever established. Following an initial $1 billion commitment, congressional support faded during the Johnson administration, especially with increased U.S. involvement in Vietnam. Total official development aid (ODA) from the United States to Latin America during the 1960s amounted to only $3.3 billion, and assistance of all types did not exceed $5 billion. With the advent of the Nixon administration in 1969, the alliance as originally envisioned was discontinued. While total regional investment associated with the plan did exceed the $100 billion envisioned by its originators, the results were clearly disappointing. Average economic growth in the region during the decade was only 1.3 percent and growth in industrial output was negligible. Land reform programs, essential to agricultural and equitable economic development, met staunch resistance from the landed elite. Agricultural output barely kept pace with population growth and the region witnessed the entrenchment of authoritarian regimes. *See also* FOREIGN AID, 285.

Significance   The Alliance for Progress was initiated during a period of considerable optimism regarding development and development assistance and cooperation. In retrospect, it was naively ambitious and laden with contradictions and fickle support. The alliance faced opposition from members of Congress who questioned the expediency and effectiveness of foreign assistance. Many Latin Americans also grew skeptical of the program. They suggested that the alliance was another form of U.S. intervention that benefited the United States more than its neighbors to the south. The program called for fundamental economic, social, and political changes that threatened the privileged positions of those most capable of initiating reform within Latin America. For the United States, this dilemma often meant a choice between supporting stable authoritarian governments or reform-minded leaders who drew internal opposition leading to political and economic instability. Such choices were further complicated by disagreement over the primary purpose of assistance to Latin America, whether it was to stave off revolution and communist expansion, to establish markets for U.S. goods, or to foster humanitarian purposes. Further, while the initial plan emphasized support for the poorest countries of the region, development assistance, increasingly in the form of loans as opposed to grants, was most often directed to the richer OAS members, most notably Brazil and Chile. Finally, many of the projects essential to the success of the Alliance for Progress were poorly planned, administered, and coordinated. Increasingly, foreign aid to Latin American states shifted from economic and technical to military.

Appropriate Technology (AT)   **(276)**
A concept that evolved in the late 1960s in response to the observation that modern technology may be highly disruptive and detrimental to social, economic, and environmental systems within developing societies. AT refers to a wide range of technologies generally characterized by the following: simplicity in production, operation, and maintenance; labor-intensive as opposed to capital-intensive in production and operation; highly adapted to particular social and cultural environments; sparing in their use of natural resources, especially nonrenewables; and having minimal adverse environmental impact. The term may also refer to innovations in organization and management. What is appropriate in any particular setting is highly normative. In the development literature the term often refers to technology that is understood by, accessible to, and controlled and maintained by villagers. The AT concept encompasses intermediate technology, i.e., that which is an improvement upon traditional technology but not a direct and unquestioned import of modern technology, as articulated by E. F. Schumacher in his influential work, *Small Is Beautiful* (1973). AT may also refer to soft technology, a concept that stresses the importance of creating and adapting technology for development with nominal detrimental impact on the physical environment, and minimal disruption of cultural and social environments. Some writers and practitioners prefer the term *local resource technology* as a more specific and less normative concept. *See also* E. F. SCHUMACHER, 45; SOFT ENERGY PATHS, 271; TECHNICAL COOPERATION AMONG DEVELOPING COUNTRIES, 306.

Significance   The concept of appropriate technology is central to a broader ideological and cultural critique of industrialization, particularly large-scale and energy-intensive industry, as the principal means of development. It stresses that development itself is a normative concept. Its importance is difficult to assess in quantitative terms, but the rapidly growing number of organizations in the North and the South committed to the promotion of AT reflects its importance. What was considered a marginal movement in the late 1960s now boasts support from more than 1,000 organizations and nearly every less developed country (LDC) government. Third World critics of the AT movement consider it a detraction from the more pressing issues of the relatively high cost of acquiring advanced technologies and the restrictions imposed by intellectual property rights. Others view it as another, even if an alternative, imposition of Western ideas and concepts. Nevertheless, most developing nations have supported the movement and together fund research and development of AT in amounts equal to the developed countries. This in turn has laid the groundwork for increased technical cooperation among developing countries (TCDC). While generally used in context of the Third World, the concept also stimulates discussion as to what is appropriate technology in the First World.

Bilateral Aid (277)

Development assistance provided from one country to a second country. About 60 percent of development assistance is in the form of bilateral aid. Donor governments often require that such aid be "tied" for political reasons. In tied bilateral aid, goods and services associated with development assistance must be purchased from the country giving the aid or from companies within that country. Thus, the actual new flow of funds from the developed to the developing country is only a fraction of the total amount of development assistance. Such strings make aid more politically acceptable and create vested business interests to support development assistance. *See also* BILATERAL AID AGENCIES, 278; FOREIGN AID, 285; MULTILATERAL AID AGENCIES, 291.

Significance In the development field there is considerable controversy concerning the desirability of bilateral aid versus multilateral aid provided by international organizations and usually not tied to purchases in any particular country. Opponents of the bilateral approach stress that such aid is often primarily motivated by strategic political reasons. Empirical studies have shown, for example, relatively low statistical correlations between the amount of U.S. development assistance and genuine development needs. Countries receiving the most U.S. bilateral aid are those in strategic political locations such as Israel, Honduras, Egypt, and Pakistan. Opponents of the multilateral approach stress the inefficiency of large international bureaucracies such as UNESCO and the lack of strict accountability. With multilateral aid, however, countries are free to select goods and services from the source offering the lowest price and best quality, regardless of nationality. Such openness can certainly enhance the efficacy of development assistance expenditures. The Scandinavian and Benelux countries have been those most supportive of multilateral aid.

Bilateral Aid Agencies (278)

Government agencies whose purpose is to administer the disbursement of official development assistance (ODA) to other countries. Generally the aid involves the transfer of public funds from one of the Organization for Economic Cooperation and Development (OECD) or Organization of Petroleum Exporting Countries (OPEC) governments directly to the government of an LDC with some understanding as to how the funds will be utilized. The agencies also administer the concomitant provision of technical assistance. Bilateral agencies may support development efforts overseas through provision of funding to private or multilateral agencies. The OECD bilateral agencies include the U.S. Agency for International Development (AID), Canadian International Development Agency (CIDA), Swedish International Development Authority (SIDA), British Overseas Development Agency (ODA), Australian International Development Assistance Bureau (AIDAB), Danish International Development Agency (DANIDA), Japan International Cooperation Agency (JICA), Belgian Administration for Development Cooperation, France's Ministry of Development Cooperation, Norway's Agency for International Development, Finnish International Development Agency (FINNIDA), German Development Corporation, and the Swiss Development Corporation. *See also* BILATERAL AID, 277; FOREIGN AID, 285; MULTILATERAL AID AGENCIES, 291.

Significance   The bilateral development agencies are highly visible representatives and managers of foreign aid. It is their responsibility to carry out the development assistance mandates of their home countries. Given the diversity of opinion regarding the purpose of foreign aid, the agencies often must respond to various, even contradictory, directions emanating from their government. As is appropriate, their performance comes under the scrutiny of the general public, governmental bodies, the recipient country, and the broader development field. Overall, it is difficult to reach any general conclusions regarding the performance of such a diverse group of agencies. Much of the criticism leveled at the agencies themselves stems from criticism of bilateral aid in general, particularly with respect to tied spending requirements often dictated by the national politics of aid. Bilateral agencies are increasingly working in cooperation with private development agencies in an attempt to improve efficiency and effectiveness of aid delivery. There is also increased coooperation with multilateral agencies. But the agencies themselves continue to administer the greatest share of international development assistance.

Biotechnology (279)

Techniques using living organisms to create or alter a product, usually plant and animal products of economic importance or microorganisms that act on the environment. Biotechnology is not new but is of growing importance in its implications for development. The majority of biotechnological research concerns plant agriculture. New developments in this area could have profound impacts on Third World food production depending on how the findings are utilized. The impact will be governed by affordability and access, the ability and willingness of developing countries to engage in their own research, and research directions. For example, biotechnology might be used to develop more disease-resistant strains of grains, thereby reducing dependency on herbicides and pesticides. Petrochemical firms, however, are more likely to develop herbicide-resistant strains allowing heavier applications of their product. *See also* INTERNATIONAL UNDERTAKING ON PLANT GENETIC RESOURCES, 288; INTELLECTUAL PROPERTY RIGHTS, 156.

Significance Biotechnology has become a central issue in the broader debate regarding intellectual property rights, in this case international patent agreements. Potentially, biotechnology could help lower the cost of food production by elimination of petrochemical inputs required by Green Revolution plants. It could also shift the emphasis from a few common cereals back to more traditional crops such as yams, cassava, amaranth, and quinoa that have not been a part of the Green Revolution. Biotech could also lead to the development of drought-resistant plants, thereby avoiding the need for capital- or labor-intensive irrigation projects. Some new strains of vegetables can now be grown in salt water, an especially important development considering the tremendous population growth occurring in the arid and semiarid tropics. All of these developments imply more environmentally sound and sustainable agricultural practices. Most biotechnology research and development, however, is conducted by for-profit corporations seeking to maximize profits, not necessarily to benefit developing nations. Of course, these two interests are not necessarily mutually exclusive. Biotechnology can also mean the development of cheaper substitutes for Third World commodities or products. For example, the production of high-fructose corn syrup has meant a decrease in U.S. sugar imports from 4.6 million to 2.5 million tons between 1978 and 1985. Biotechnology represents tremendous potential for meeting human needs, especially in food production. However, it is no panacea. As with any technology, who benefits will largely depend on who produces and controls the products.

Brandt Commission (280)
A committee of distinguished international statesmen and leaders who carefully examined the world's major development issues in the late 1970s. Chaired by Willy Brandt, former chancellor of the Federal Republic of Germany and former mayor of West Berlin, the commission also included as members Adam Malik of Indonesia, Eduardo Frei Montalva of Chile, and Olaf Palme of Sweden. Acting independently of governments and various international agencies, the committee was formally known as the Independent Commission on International Development Issues. The commission worked during 1978 and 1979 and published its final report, *North-South: A Program for Survival*, in 1980. Funding for the work of the commission came from a variety of sources such as governments (both North and South), the Ford Foundation, the International Development Research Centre (IDRC), and the German Marshall Fund. The Dutch government generously covered nearly half of the commission's expenditures. The following were among the major needed reforms recommended by the commission: (1) reform of the international monetary order; (2) a new approach to development finance with a substantial increase in World Bank lending and the channeling of more funds through regional institutions; (3) greater transfers of appropriate technology from North to South; (4) a rollback of protectionism of industrialized countries against the exports of LDCs; (5) increase of ODA to 0.70 percent of GNP by 1985 and to 1.0 percent before 2000; and (6) a new world development fund. Prior to arriving at consensus on such recommendations the commission consulted broadly in meetings around the world and sought out the views of eminent development thinkers such as the Nobel laureates Sir Arthur Lewis and Jan Tinbergen, Raúl Prebisch, and Barbara Ward.

Significance   Of special importance was the Brandt Commission's emphasis on the *mutual* interests of North and South nations and its conviction that development issues are not zero-sum games in which one side wins and the other must inevitably lose. Unfortunately many of the commission's specific recommendations have not been implemented. Ironically, the recommendations may be more relevant to the 1990s than to the 1980s, given the thawing of the cold war as the 1980s ended and Gorbachev's remarkable initiatives which may make possible the turning of "swords into plowshares." Though the commission's recommendations have not necessarily been adopted, the Brandt Report did have a major impact on development thinking. The cover of the report, for example, shows a Peters global projection and a North-South geographic division. This projection presents a more realistic and less Eurocentric view of the world than the conventional Mercator projection. In fact, the Brandt Report popularized the North-South terminology as a substitute for more ethnocentric terms such as underdeveloped or Third World nations. The 1990s may well represent a far more meaningful opportunity to respond to the challenges articulated by the Brandt Commission than the decade of the 1980s.

Development Foundations (281)
Nonprofit philanthropic organizations that provide important assistance to international development by making financial grants. Generally such foundations specialize to some extent according to function or region of the world. Among the best known development foundations are the Ford Foundation, the Rockefeller Foundation, the Asia Foundation, the Aga Khan Foundation, the Japan Foundation, the Toyota Foundation, Winrock International, and the Volkswagen Foundation. With respect to functional specialization, for example, Rockefeller has emphasized health, agriculture, and economics, while Winrock International emphasizes agriculture. With respect to geographic focus, the Aga Khan Foundation focuses on Islamic developing countries. Some smaller foundations such as the International Foundation for Development Alternatives in Nyon, Switzerland, concentrate almost exclusively on information dissemination and the exchange of innovative ideas.

Significance Though the funds of development foundations are limited, particularly when compared to the United Nations, the World Bank, and bilateral aid agencies, they have considerable flexibility in supporting innovative approaches to development. Foundations make grants, not loans, and thus they do not contribute to the international debt problem. Also, foundations such as Ford and Rockefeller are genuinely international in focus with none of the requirements associated with tied bilateral aid. Some critics, however, argue that foundations promote cultural imperialism and by their actions tend to legitimize the existing political and economic order both in and among nations (*see* Arnove 1980). Despite such criticism, it is clear that foundations have played an important role in encouraging innovative projects and ideas in developing countries and in providing funds to enable the sharing of innovative information among developing countries.

Development Trust Fund (282)

An experimental approach to development assistance that provides an endowed trust fund to a developing country as an alternative to conventional annual grants and loans. This innovation was developed by Tuvalu's Minister of Finance, Henry Naisali, with the support of the United Nations Development Program. On June 16, 1987, the government of Tuvalu established such a trust fund totaling $19.2 million U.S., with contributions from the United Kingdom, New Zealand, Australia, Tuvalu, Japan, and the Republic of Korea. The money is managed by Westpac of Australia, and the Tuvalu government then utilizes interest earnings from the fund to finance its recurrent and capital expenditures.

Significance   Despite its limited applicability (primarily to microstates with limited resources), the development trust fund approach to development assistance has many appealing aspects. Most importantly, it gives a developing country the opportunity to control its own economic destiny without having to ask for outside assistance on a continual basis, which has humiliating dimensions. Funds from a development trust fund are totally untied and its use is completely up to the discretion of the individual developing country. Though the needs of most developing countries would be too large to be met in such a way, this approach could be used for specific domains or sectors, to reduce long-term dependency and enhance local choice and decision making. An irrigation or public health department, for example, might be given an endowed development fund.

Disaster Relief (283)

Material and technical assistance provided to areas in response to natural disasters, such as floods, earthquakes, and drought, by governments and local and international organizations. Over 1,000 voluntary agencies (volags) are geared to respond to disasters. International efforts are coordinated in Geneva by the League of Red Cross Societies (LORCS) Volag Steering Committee composed of the Red Cross, Catholic Relief Service (CRS), Lutheran World Federation, Oxfam, and the World Council of Churches. Other major relief organizations include CARE, Caritas Internationalis, Church World Service, and World Vision. Disasters may be short-term and cataclysmic, such as earthquakes, or longer in duration as with droughts. Disaster relief attempts to provide timely assistance to alleviate the suffering of victims. In this regard it is distinguished from development assistance, though the two are closely linked and often carried out by the same organizations.

Significance　　The obstacles to effective, efficient, and sensitive international disaster-relief efforts are related to effective development assistance. Unfortunately, little has been written regarding the relationship. Of notable exception is *Disasters and Development* (1983), a book written by Frederick Cuny and sponsored by Oxfam America. Cuny notes that because disaster relief is a clearly humanitarian effort it is too often considered above question. But, as with development assistance, even the sincerest of efforts may result in "the second disasters." Alongside effective, well-conceived, and much appreciated relief efforts, we find shipments of inappropriate materials, inappropriate technology, and paternalistic planning. As with international development aid, disaster relief may undercut local efforts, create new dependencies or reinforce old ones, foster unrealistic expectations through spot provision, and fail to consult the victims about their own perceived needs and desires. Conversely, effective programs are participatory and take into consideration the cultural, climatic, and political settings in which efforts are to be implemented. Cuny suggests that disaster relief should not be considered as an operation distinct from development and that the two activities should be conducted with similar criteria.

The dramatic international news coverage given to disasters often provides a windfall of support for private development agencies involved in relief work. However, the support is usually as short-lived as the sense of urgency created by the disaster. Thus, agencies face the challenge of carrying through with their work and moving from disaster to long-term development assistance. Some even consider disasters as opportunities to bring about needed structural changes. Disaster relief is not an apolitical activity. It sometimes can lead to the creation of new community-based organizations as was the case in Guatemala following the 1976 earthquake. In other cases it may reinforce existing power structures, depending upon the channels of assistance. In Nicaragua, the earthquake and the subsequent pocketing of relief funds by Somoza no doubt served as catalysts for the eventual revolution against him.

Finally, disasters themselves are linked with development and maldevelopment. Most disasters, though they may be thought of as natural, are in some way related to human activities. The recent increase in flooding in Bangladesh, for example, is directly related to deforestation in the Himalayas. The droughts in the Sahel are exacerbated by the loss of vegetation due to overgrazing and cultivation. Also, the poorest sectors of society are often forced to live in the areas most susceptible to natural events. Thus, natural events such as floods and landslides take on tragic dimensions when the poor must find shelter in ravines and on the sides of steep inclines, often the only space available to them. In the same manner, farmers forced onto marginal lands become more vulnerable to drought, erosion, and flooding. As such, disasters and disaster relief are closely tied to the need for long-term, sustainable development practices.

Food-for-Work Programs (284)

An innovative development strategy that provides food to poorer, unemployed or underemployed families in exchange for work on important development projects. The beauty of this concept is that it mutually benefits the donors and the recipients. Farmers in donor nations with surplus food (e.g., the United States, Thailand, Canada, and New Zealand) are pleased with enhanced markets for their agricultural commodities. In countries with serious food deficits, as in Bangladesh where such an experiment has been implemented, the program can help to strengthen fulfillment of the most basic need of all, food essential for health, well-being, and economic productivity. The employment generated can then be utilized for important development projects (e.g., digging of fish ponds to increase the indigenous supply of protein).

Significance Food-for-work programs have many appealing features. First, and perhaps most important, they are noninflationary. In contrast paid-in-cash development work can contribute to inflationary pressures, since gross demand may be increased more rapidly than GNP. Second, benefits provided to the unemployed or underemployed go directly toward basic needs, with little opportunity for diversion to nonessential expenditures such as alcohol, gambling, or other luxury consumption. Third, this approach can result in a greater increase in jobs for the unemployed and underemployed, since it is much less expensive (in monetary terms) than conventionally supported development work. The greatest criticisms of food-for-work programs are: (1) they foster cheap labor and raise the question of why the poor receive only payment in kind for their hard work, and (2) they foster continued dependence on other nations for basic food supplies. There is also concern about the quality and productivity of resulting development projects. For countries with significant food deficits and large sectors of unemployed/underemployed, the food-for-work strategy is highly relevant. Such programs also facilitate the important redistribution of global food resources. As is universally recognized, global hunger and starvation do not result from shortage of food, but from the lack of adequate systems for food distribution and redistribution. Food-for-work programs offer an important policy option for dealing with both problems of unemployment/underemployment and basic needs.

Foreign Aid (285)

Economic assistance from one country's government to the people or government of another provided outside of regular international market forces. It includes all forms of official development assistance and military assistance, though the latter should be distinguished from development assistance. Foreign aid may take the form of bilateral aid or be channeled through multilateral agencies. Since World War II, foreign aid or assistance has become a central aspect of international relations. Discussion of foreign aid revolves around three key issues. The first is the moral and humanitarian aspect of development assistance. Nearly all countries with bilateral programs have, from the beginning, couched the rationale for assistance in terms of moral obligation, as reflected in Sweden's policy statements, Kennedy's speeches, the French Jeannery Commission Report of 1964, and the British White Papers on foreign aid. The Pearson Commission also reiterated the moral premise of aid. All indicate that the richer nations have a moral obligation to assist in the development of their poorer neighbor states. Such a premise remains unquestioned, for the most part. At the suggestion of Lester Pearson, the United Nations has adopted 0.70 percent of GNP as the ODA outlay target for the Organization for Economic Cooperation and Development (OECD) countries. Only five non-OPEC nations exceed this amount: Norway, the Netherlands, Denmark, Sweden, and France.

The second element of aid, the question of how best to provide assistance, remains much more controversial. Central to foreign aid theory has been conventional economic development theory as reflected in or based upon the writings of John Maynard Keynes, W. W. Rostow, Harrod and Domar, and Hollis Chenery, among others. The dramatic success of the Marshall Plan in the reconstruction of Europe spurred the concept of foreign assistance to developing countries. Economic growth was assumed to be the central factor in development, and was virtually equated with development. It was assumed that all countries could and would develop in a linear fashion over time, moving through certain stages of development. Foreign aid could be used to speed up that process by providing the catalyst of increased capital accumulation, a key to growth. Foreign capital was, and continues to be, made available to developing countries in several forms: long-term loans, soft loans at very low interest rates or to be paid back in local or soft currencies, outright grants, and sale of surplus or subsidized products at lower than market price and purchased in local currency. The P.L. 480 or Food for Peace program of the United States is an example of the latter. Technical assistance is often offered as part of financial assistance to improve the absorptive capacity and efficiency of countries in their use of economic assistance. In light of the disappointing economic performance of many recipient countries, orthodox economic development theory and subsequently foreign aid theory have been challenged. The 1970s witnessed considerable upheavals in the international economic system and a widening gap between rich and poor nations despite record levels of foreign aid. The Third World called for not only more assistance, but radical changes in the world economic system so that its nations might better meet their needs, under the sentiment of "trade, not aid." The 1980s is referred to by some as the lost decade despite continued record levels of foreign aid. In response to the growing indebtedness of many developing countries, foreign aid became increasingly tied to structural adjustment programs.

Finally, foreign aid has always been closely tied to the strategic foreign policies of the donor country. If moral obligation serves as the basic rationale for aid and economics the theory, political interests have most often dictated who receives aid and in what amounts. Anti-communism, for example, has played a major role in U.S. foreign aid beginning with the Truman Doctrine. European donors have worked primarily with former colonies for strategic and practical reasons. Even with considerable discussion over the importance of assisting the poorest countries and meeting basic human needs, the records clearly show that development assistance has largely been determined by political interests. The United States, for example, has in recent years sent the greatest share of its assistance to two countries, Egypt and Israel, following the signing of the Camp David Accords. Japan's largest contributions go to Asian countries, the site of increasing Japanese trade and investment.

A common practice of donor countries is to give tied aid. For example, loans are made with the provision that the money will be used to purchase equipment or goods in the donor country. For this reason, most of the development assistance funds never leave the country of origin. Development assistance is also closely tied to military assistance and in some cases the two are presented in one aggregated figure. Much controversy has also resulted from the provision of aid to repressive regimes and the withholding of aid as a form of leverage in trying to influence the domestic policies of recipient nations. The political aspect of foreign aid has been the source of the most criticism and cynicism regarding the purpose and appropriateness of development assistance. *See also* OFFICIAL DEVELOPMENT ASSISTANCE, 296; BILATERAL AID, 277; U.S. AGENCY FOR INTERNATIONAL DEVELOPMENT, 451.

Significance   Foreign aid is a relatively new but vital aspect of international relations, as well as the dominant form of development assistance. It has been widely accepted in the North and the South as a moral obligation in a world of great disparities. At the same time foreign aid has been subject to a diverse set of criticisms. Given the mixed results of aid, many claim that it simply does not work. Others of a more cynical bent might claim that foreign aid is not necessarily intended to work as a development strategy, only as a strategic political and economic tool for the richer nations. Another criticism is that development assistance often creates a new set of unhealthy dependencies rather than stimulating growth and enhancing economic sovereignty. Nevertheless, few countries have adopted a policy that precludes the receiving of foreign aid, and within donor countries few would suggest the abolition of foreign aid.

Global Poverty Reduction Act   **(286)**
A new foreign aid bill developed by the U.S. Congress. In 1988, the United States spent $14.4 billion on foreign aid, and continual debates have been conducted about the effectiveness of such expenditures. In 1988, a bipartisan coalition of 153 representatives and 18 senators in the U.S. Congress drafted a new Global Poverty Reduction Act as a means to increase the responsiveness and relevance of the U.S. foreign assistance program, which is currently implemented primarily on the basis of the 1961 Foreign Assistance Act. The new act, if adopted, would "instruct the president to develop a plan to ensure that United States development assistance contributes measurably to eradicating the worst aspects of absolute poverty by the year 2000" (Kidder 1988:17). It postulates three basic goals to be achieved by the year 2000: (1) an infant mortality rate (for children under five) of no more than 70 deaths per 1,000 live births, (2) a female literacy rate of 80 percent, and (3) not more than 20 percent of a nation's population living in absolute poverty (an income level so low that minimum nutrition and nonfood requirements are not affordable). The act allows for the U.S. president to supplement these three basic goals with additional operational measures. *See also* FOREIGN AID, 285; OFFICIAL DEVELOPMENT ASSISTANCE, 296.

Significance   This proposed act makes explicit in operational terms the goals of U.S. development assistance and reflects an international application of the concept of accountability to our foreign assistance programs. A key question relates to the type of sanctions that might be applied by the Congress should such goals not be attained. There is also the complex question of assessing the causes of developmental outcomes, of which development assistance is only one of many factors. What is perhaps most notable about this act is the central importance it attaches to the education of women in developing countries. The education of women has been a neglected dimension in the development strategies of many countries, particularly in Africa, Latin America, and parts of the Middle East.

Institution Building   (287)
An approach to development and technical assistance that gave priority to enhancing the quality and efficiency of key public organizations in developing countries. Institution building was emphasized particularly in the 1950s and 1960s. For example, the Rockefeller Foundation provided extensive funds to help develop medical schools, agricultural research centers, demographic institutes, and faculties of economics in various parts of the Third World. Such assistance consisted primarily of fellowships abroad in the West and outside expert services to promote local training and research. The Ford Foundation similarly offered substantial funding to help build educational-planning institutions and applied social science faculties and institutes. *See also* TECHNICAL ASSISTANCE, 305; DEVELOPMENT ADMINISTRATION, 201.

Significance   Given both the high costs of study abroad and the provision of large teams of advisers, this approach to development and technical assistance is now less feasible. Many developing countries also now have strong and viable indigenous institutions, many of which received technical assistance in previous decades. The major criterion for measuring the success of institution building is to examine the long-term effectiveness of such institutions and their ability to sustain themselves without additional external assistance. In reality, there are many examples of both notable successes and failures in institution building. Even in cases where institutions may have folded or dramatically shifted their mandates, individuals who have received quality training through institution-building projects will continue to contribute to the development process in new settings and roles.

International Undertaking on Plant Genetic Resources (288)
A principle established by Resolution 8/83 of the Food and Agricultural Organization (FAO) as an expression of concern for preserving genetic diversity of seed varieties and the control of old and new varieties. The resolution, passed at the FAO's twenty-second biennial conference, encourages worldwide preservation, evolution, and exchange of plant germ plasm under the authority of the FAO, based on the premise that "plant genetic resources are a common heritage of mankind and consequently should be available without restrictions." Proponents of the resolution, primarily Third World nations, insist that intellectual property rights should not apply to seed varieties since the raw material for new varieties and related plant germ plasm most often originate in the South. Moreover, they point out that the rights of Third World cultivators should be recognized since farmers have contributed to the conservation, improvement, and availability of plant genetic resources. Also at issue is the cost of the developed products, which can prohibit their use by poor nations. Nations undertaking most of the research in new seeds refuse to endorse the resolution on grounds that they must be compensated appropriately for their investments. However, they are cooperating in germ plasm conservation through the creation and support of the International Board for Plant Genetic Resources, an autonomous body created in 1974, over which Third World governments have no control. An excellent overview of plant genetic-resource issues is provided in *Seeds and Sovereignty* (1988), edited by Jack Kloppenburg, Jr. *See also* BIOTECHNOLOGY, 279; HIGH YIELD VARIETIES, 181; INTELLECTUAL PROPERTY RIGHTS, 156.

Significance Cooperation in plant germ plasm preservation is essential to the security of future world food supplies. It is especially vital in the Third World where food shortages are most likely to occur and where many national economies are based on agricultural production. The undertaking points to the growing concern about genetic diversity, ecological stability, and sustainability within rapidly changing agricultural systems. Further, the issues of concern in the resolution are similar to those raised in the call for a new international economic order (NIEO) and the new international information order (NIIO), i.e., what obligations do the technologically advanced nations have to the Third World, particularly when the raw material for a product originates in the South? Parties in the North tend to see the resolution as an assault on free enterprise, and a contributing factor in the politicization of science. Proponents counter that if intellectual property rights are to apply, they should be extended to the recognition of the rights of farmers who have developed and preserved local seed strains for centuries. Both North and South nations recognize the importance of cooperation in this area, but have failed to agree on the nature of that interaction.

Marshall Plan (289)

Common name for the European Recovery Program, the massive aid plan of the United States for Western Europe following World War II. In the spring of 1947 Western Europe appeared to be on the verge of economic collapse after a hard winter and the removal of wartime economic controls in the United States. The extent of Europe's needs had been underestimated and the United States feared that further economic difficulties would strengthen the appeal of the Communist parties. These circumstances prompted U.S. Secretary of State George C. Marshall to propose, in a June 5 commencement address at Harvard University, that the United States adopt a cooperative plan for the systematic reconstruction of Europe. The program consisted of an effort by 17 countries to harmonize their recovery efforts and determine what U.S. assistance would be necessary. To this end, the Organization for European Economic Cooperation was created with its seat in Paris. In April 1948, the Economic Cooperation Act was enacted by the United States, providing nearly $13 billion in assistance over the next five years. During this period the GNP of the countries involved rose 25 percent annually. The objectives of the Marshall Plan were to foster European economic recovery in a short period of time, thus creating viable economic partners for the United States, and to contain communism. To these ends it was quite successful. *See also* FOREIGN AID, 285.

Significance The Marshall Plan was a dramatic example of what could be accomplished with a massive influx of financial and technical assistance. Western Europe recovered economically from the destruction of World War II in a few years. The success of the program lent impetus to the stages-of-economic-growth theories of the 1950s and 1960s, which suggested that with massive injections of capital and the creation of an industrialized infrastructure, developing countries, most of which would gain political independence in the two decades following World War II, would be able to pursue successfully a path of economic development and modernization. Such assumptions, however, failed to take into account the vast differences in the conditions faced by postwar Europe and those faced by the new nations of the Third World. The newly independent nations did not possess the same traditions, institutions, human capital, and infrastructure as those of Europe. As such, the Marshall Plan, while achieving dramatic results for Europe, did not represent a viable development model for the Third World. Even within countries that managed to create pockets of modernization and industrialization, the benefits usually accrued to an extremely small sector. In response, many countries and development organizations began a shift toward a more direct basic-human-needs approach to development.

Miyazawa Plan (290)
An innovative plan developed by Japanese Finance Minister Kiichi Miyazawa in 1988 to deal with the global debt crisis. The plan combines debt relief and new funds to promote economic growth in exchange for serious economic reforms. Under the plan, a country's debt is divided into two parts. One part would be converted into long-term, deferred-interest bonds, guaranteed by the deposit of a portion of a country's foreign exchange reserves into a special trust account to be administered by the International Monetary Fund (IMF). The remaining part of the debt would be rescheduled to be paid back in 10 to 20 years. The plan does not involve writing off any debt but would involve below-market interest rates. New development funds would also be made available to those debtor nations that adopt tough economic reforms. *See also* DEBT CRISIS, 134.

Significance   The Miyazawa Plan reflects Japan's attempt as the world's largest creditor nation to show more global economic responsibility. Thus far the United States has opposed the plan and prefers its own Baker Initiative which requires that all debtors pay full interest at market rates on all that they owe. Though the Miyazawa Plan is inherently generous and sympathetic to the economic needs of the debtor nations, it nevertheless has elements that impinge on the economic sovereignty of the debtor nations.

Multilateral Aid Agencies (291)
A diverse set of development banks and regional and UN organizations that offer or coordinate international development assistance rendered to member nations. Roughly 40 percent of all international development assistance is channeled through such organizations as the International Bank for Reconstruction and Development (IBRD), the Food and Agriculture Organization (FAO), the World Health Organization (WHO), the International Monetary Fund (IMF), and the United Nations Development Program (UNDP). Most multilateral

organizations are functionally focused and serve to coordinate regional and global efforts in such areas as health care, education, environment, industrial development, agriculture, and investment capital. *See also* organizations listed in this section.

Significance   Multilateral agencies allow nations to pool resources to address specific global development needs. They are the agents of multilateral aid, a vital part of the aid triad, along with bilateral and private or nongovernmental aid. While these various forms of development assistance address similar problems, each has specific strengths and weaknesses. Multilateral agencies, for example, usually are not limited by the economic and political interests of specific countries as is the case with bilateral agencies; thus there is no tied aid. Further, they can often generate more widespread support than can private agencies. They are particularly important given the global or international scope of many development problems that cannot be adequately addressed in bilateral or private forums, such as those linked to international monetary, environmental, and labor issues. Multilateral aid is especially important for small developing countries, which often cannot deal on equal terms with the More Developed Countries (MDCs). Yet multilateral agencies do not have authority over individual nations, and their effectiveness is dependent upon widespread cooperation. Thus they both promote and depend upon international cooperation. The multilateral agencies have been effective in promoting both North-South and, increasingly, South-South development cooperation. However, the agencies are not without their critics. Many are viewed as highly top-heavy, inefficient, and not adequately monitored. There are also problems regarding interagency cooperation, overlap, and competition. Some agencies have also become highly politicized. Many countries, for example, view the World Bank and the IMF as promoters of U.S. policy and interests because of the weighted voting system that gives the United States 20 percent of the vote in their management. On the other hand, the United States has expressed discontent and has often refused to participate in policies and programs because of anti-Western rhetoric of agencies where member countries have equal say in policy regardless of the size of their budget contributions. This was a major contributing factor in the American and British withdrawal from UNESCO. Interestingly, some agencies have been criticized for being apolitical, that is, not willing to address the political obstacles to development within specific countries lest those governments take offense. Despite these criticisms, however, the UN and subsequently its specialized agencies have recently witnessed a resurgence of respect resulting from a growing recognition of the global scope of development problems and the interdependence of nations.

Mutual Benefit Thesis (292)

The critically important assumption that development of the poor countries will simultaneously benefit the rich nations of the world, and that development is thus not a zero-sum game. In zero-sum games, one party must always win and the other necessarily lose; it is impossible for both sides to win. Mutual benefit would occur if, for example, African countries were to take off into sustained development in the 1990s and the twenty-first century, constituting a growing and important market for Europe, Japan, and the United States. Already certain West African countries have become new markets for the exports from Thailand. Classic international trade theory reflects the mutual benefit thesis with its emphasis on how all nations benefit from the principle of comparative advantage. In contrast, dependency theory, with its emphasis on conflicts of interest and exploitation, rejects the optimistic mutual benefit thesis. *See also* INTERDEPENDENCE, 268; COMPARATIVE ADVANTAGE, 132; DEPENDENCY THEORY, 106.

Significance　Few of the industrial countries have met the UN target of 0.70 percent of GNP for development assistance. Zero-sum–game thinking governs much discussion of foreign aid, which is often viewed by the public as a drain on the national budget and as having much waste. Serious efforts are necessary to educate both the public and politicians in the developed countries to increase acceptance of the mutual benefit or non–zero-sum thesis. Without such greater public consciousness of the interconnectedness of the developed and developing nations, commitments to international development will continue to lag.

Needs Assessment (293)

Efforts to ascertain what the population of a developing country genuinely wants from the development process or from specific projects. Too often highly educated elite development administrators, both local and foreign, have assumed that they knew what "the people" needed most. Underlying this assumption was the implicit notion that ordinary people were too ignorant to articulate their own needs. In the last two decades increasing emphasis has been placed on allowing the people "to speak their words" to use Paulo Freire's apt term. Unfortunately there is no commonly accepted methodology for needs assessment. Among many alternative possibilities are the following:

1. Direct quantitative surveys of needs using standard research instruments.
2. More qualitative and ethnographically oriented approaches that stress developing rapport with ordinary citizens and then probing informally to ascertain needs.
3. Special search conferences to bring together the clients of development programs and development administrators to discuss needs.
4. Reliance on normal democratic political processes to provide for interest articulation through both local and national political bodies such as parliaments and provincial assemblies.
5. Literacy campaigns such as those of Paulo Freire that encourage ordinary citizens to become more assertive in articulating their problems and related needs.

Significance   Needs assessment is one of the most critically important concepts in the development field. Despite its importance, it remains a somewhat nebulous concept, and its implementation is still commonly influenced by hypocrisy and adversely affected by hierarchical communication patterns. Too often those claiming to be open to genuine needs assessment have preconceived ideas of what should be done and ultimately impose their views on the powerless and the less articulate. Also, without having experience with programs of the type advocated by Freire, ordinary villagers may not be comfortable expressing political assertiveness. In societies with long traditions of political oppression, ordinary citizens may be extremely reluctant to state publicly their genuine needs and views. Needs assessment can only become viable when governments have a real commitment to local community empowerment and to discourse free from hierarchical constraints.

New Directions   (294)

Name given to the policy changes mandated by Congress for official U.S. development assistance programs as clarified in the 1973 amendment to the Foreign Assistance Act of 1961. The amendment was intended to address the growing perception that U.S. development assistance was not dealing with the immediate needs of the poor in developing countries, that it had instead benefited only the well off. The new policy amendment stated:

United States bilateral development assistance should give the highest priority to undertakings submitted by host governments which directly improve the lives of the poorest of their people and their capacity to participate in the development of their countries. (1973 Amendments to Chapter 1, section 102 of the Foreign Assistance Act of 1961)

The policy changes were, of course, directed at AID. At the same time, Robert McNamara was advocating similar changes at the World Bank. In both cases, New Directions represented a radical departure from past policy and practice, which had stressed efforts to bring about macroeconomic development and to attend to the strategic and political goals of the United States The new policies emphasized humanitarian concerns and the distribution of development benefits. *See also* U.S. AGENCY FOR INTERNATIONAL DEVELOPMENT, 451; BASIC NEEDS, 102; PRIVATE VOLUNTARY ORGANIZATIONS, 300.

Significance   Upon passage of the New Directions legislation, an immediate question arose as to how it was to be implemented? The New Directions policy called for a complete reorientation of the world's largest bilateral development agency, which had little experience in working directly with the poor, let alone in a highly participatory manner. The World Bank was even less well equipped to support development efforts of this type. New Directions prompted a good deal of new research focusing on the rural poor of developing countries and how they might be involved in the development process. The results were mixed. The reorientation proved difficult for AID, which was simply not oriented toward smaller, grassroots projects. One approach that AID took was to subcontract projects to U.S. private voluntary organizations (PVOs), many of which already had extensive experience in working more directly with the poor. The PVOs were brought into a broader system of accountability while benefiting from the new source of funding and broader recognition for their work. AID benefited from their experience. The results for the poor are difficult to assess. The new mandate would be difficult for any large development agency to implement. The rhetoric was more prominent than the practice. Almost any project could be shown to involve the poor in some manner. In addition, AID remained under pressure to conform to the political and strategic needs of the United States as interpreted by the State Department. Thus, AID continued to receive mixed messages about its mandate. As a result, Egypt and Israel continued to receive the major share of U.S. official development assistance quite apart from the mandate of New

Directions. Nevertheless, New Directions helped to focus more development efforts on attempting to meet the direct needs of the poor and served as a reminder that economic development cannot be assumed to automatically benefit the poorest sectors of societies. It was, and remains, an important corrective to previously stated policies.

Nongovernmental Organizations (NGOs) (295)

An amalgam of nonprofit citizens' organizations and agencies not affiliated with official governments. These include special interest groups, development and relief agencies, environmental organizations, self-help associations, human rights organizations, public watchdog groups, labor organizations, and research and policy institutes. NGOs may be domestic or international in scope. Once primarily associated with the MDCs, such groups have dramatically grown worldwide during the past two decades, especially in the Third World. The majority of the new NGOs in developing countries are women's associations. There are now more than 12,000 internationally oriented NGOs based in a single country, including local groups, and 5,000 international groups (INGOs) defined as those having activities in more than three countries. The term *nongovernmental organization* originated in the UN system. The United Nations defines an NGO as "any international organization not established by intergovernmental agreement." NGOs can gain consultive status if they act within the field of interest of the UN Economic and Social Council (ECOSOC) and abide by the spirit of the United Nations. Category I NGOs must be concerned with most of ECOSOC's activities. They are entitled to submit written statements to the council, to be granted hearings, and to propose agenda items. Category II organizations have specific competence in some area of interest to ECOSOC. They cannot submit agenda items. Category III NGOs are those able to make occasional contributions to the work of ECOSOC. They can only submit written statements. Listed among Category I organizations are the International Cooperative Alliance, World Federation of Association of Friends, World Veterans Federation, Women's Council, and the League of Red Cross Societies. The NGO presence at the UN is coordinated by the NGO Liaison Office. Volume 15 of *World Development* (1987) is a valuable compilation of articles on international NGOs. An excellent overview of the growing role of NGOs in local and international development is provided by Elise Boulding in her recent book, *Building a Global Civic Order* (1988) and David Korten in *Getting to the 21st Century: Voluntary Action and the*

Global Agenda (1990). *See also* PRIVATE VOLUNTARY ORGANIZATIONS, 300.

Significance   The NGO community has a brief but impressive history of work on the leading edge of development, environmental, and justice issues. NGOs have acted as catalysts for change in direction and policy of many governments and multilateral organizations. For example, the first international conference on the environment, the 1972 Stockholm Conference, which established the UN Environment Program (UNEP), was primarily a result of the work of NGOs. NGOs have played an important role in every UN special-topic conference since Stockholm. Since NGOs stem from direct and specific citizen concerns, they tend to be highly participatory in nature. They have proven to be particularly innovative and effective in relief and development work, serving as a direct link among citizens of different nations. NGOs are truly international or transnational organizations. Groups such as Greenpeace, Amnesty International, and Oxfam can often more effectively call governments to accountability for their environmental, human rights, and development policies than can other governments. Collectively, this diverse group of organizations is making dramatic gains in numbers of organizations, competence, and impact on global development.

Official Development Assistance (ODA)   (296)

The total of net disbursements of loans or grants made at concessional terms by nations to enhance the economic development and welfare of less well-off countries. The sum of official development assistance includes disbursements to both developing countries and multilateral development institutions. Loans made at normal commercial market rates would not be considered development assistance. This definition also is intended to exclude military assistance, though some governments may intentionally or inadvertently include some military assistance as part of their total disbursements. The definition does include technical assistance and cooperation. Net disbursements equal gross disbursements less payments received related to the paying off of past loans. The normal measure for judging a country's commitment to international development is to calculate its ratio of official development assistance to gross national product. The UN target is 0.70 percent. Among OECD countries with the highest ratios are the Netherlands (0.98); Denmark (0.87 in 1987); Sweden (0.84 in 1987); and France (0.82 in 1986). OPEC countries such as Saudi Arabia (4.29 in 1986) and Kuwait (2.90 in 1986) provide impressively high levels of official development assistance, which is directed primarily to poorer Muslim countries in Africa and Asia. Though ODA is normally associated with OECD or OPEC countries, other nations such as the People's Republic of China, Eastern European countries, Cuba, the Republic of Korea, and Taiwan are now providing official development assistance to other countries. Countries also vary widely with respect to their levels of receipt of ODA as a percent of GNP. Among low-income countries with the highest levels of receipt of net disbursements in 1986 were Zambia (31.2); Somalia (27.8); and Mauritania (23.8). Among middle-income or lower middle–income countries, those receiving the greatest ratio of disbursements were Jordan (12.0); Papua New Guinea (10.9); and Botswana (10.4).

Significance   Though the aggregate of official development assistance is an imperfect measure of a nation's commitment to share its wealth and expertise with poorer nations, it provides an overall estimate of the extent of a nation's commitment to contribute to international development and to reduce the gap between rich and poor nations. The measure's imperfection derives primarily from: (1) its lumping together of loans and grants; (2) its lumping together of bilateral and multilateral assistance; and (3) occasional inclusion of non-development-oriented assistance. The measure also excludes the extent of profits deriving from development assistance that accrue to firms and corporations in the country of origin of aid.

Oral Rehydration Therapy (ORT)   (297)
A medical treatment in which an oral solution is given to replace the water and salts lost from diarrhea. The solution is called oral rehydration salts (ORS). This simple technology was developed in 1971 by Dr. Dilip Mahalanabis, an Indian scientist at the Johns Hopkins Centre for Medical Research and Training in Calcutta, who used it with patients suffering from cholera. The global effort to promote ORT is being coordinated by the World Health Organization's (WHO) Diarrhoeal Control Program.

Significance   The United Nations Children's Fund (UNICEF), a major promoter of ORT along with WHO, estimates that this simple technology now prevents more than 1 million deaths a year associated with diarrhea among children under five years of age. Nearly 60 developing countries now produce ORS. Of UN-distributed ORS, approximately 65 percent is manufactured locally and is now being used by one of three families in the Third World. Countries with impressive ORT promotion programs include Egypt, Honduras, Algeria, China, Ecuador, and Bangladesh. The rapid spread of ORT is an example of how social mobilization and simple, affordable technology can bring dramatic improvements in Third World health. The development and dissemination of ORS reflect the potential of positive development efforts simultaneously involving indigenous research and development, South-South cooperation, and North-South cooperation.

Pearson Report (298)

The report of the Commission on International Development published in 1969 as *Partners in Development.* The commission, chaired by former Canadian Prime Minister Lester Pearson, was founded at the behest of the World Bank. In 1967, the president of the bank, George Woods, suggested the need for an overview assessment of the state of international development cooperation. He envisioned a prominent group to "meet together, study the consequences of twenty years of development assistance, assess the results, clarify the errors and propose the policies which will work better in the future" (Pearson 1969:vii). In August 1968, Pearson accepted the invitation of the new World Bank president, Robert McNamara, to form such a commission. Pearson invited colleagues from seven countries: Sir Edward Boyle (United Kingdom); Roberto de Oliveira Campos (Brazil); C. Douglas Dillon (United States); Wilfried Guth (Federal Republic of Germany); W. Arthur Lewis (Jamaica); Robert E. Marjolin (France); and Saburo Okito (Japan). The commission was assisted by a staff of 14 experts in various fields of development, who began by conducting a review of the history of development cooperation with a view toward long-term recommendations. Through four meetings, correspondence, and consultation with numerous international and national development agencies, the commission completed its work in less than a year.

Significance   The Pearson Report serves as an important benchmark in tracing development thought and practice. It reflects the primary concerns of the late 1960s, the widening gap between rich and poor, and the growing disillusionment with development assistance. In contrast to the overly optimistic plans and projections for the UN's First Development Decade, the report presented a more realistic assessment of the potential and limitations of development cooperation. As such, it helped shape the agenda and direction of the UN Second Development Decade as well as the policies of the World Bank. The report particularly criticized AID, the World Bank, and the UN, pointing to the complexity and rigidity of their programs and the need to adopt to the unique situation in each developing country. The report does not, however, question the fundamental assumptions of development assistance, as would the supporters of the call for a new international economic order within a few years of the release of the report. Another noticeable absence, in retrospect, is any mention of the special role and needs of women in development and concerns for the environment. Although it is critical of many development practices the report generally reflects conventional wisdom regarding development and development assistance of the late 1960s, a perspective that would face considerable challenge in the years to come.

Point Four Program (299)

A technical and financial foreign-assistance program proposed by President Harry Truman in his 1949 State of the Nation address. Congress authorized the novel, long-term program, the first major foreign aid program after the Marshall Plan, with the passage of the Act for International Development in 1950. The program came under the direction of the Technical Cooperation Administration established within the State Department with $45 million allocated the first year. With this program, the United States was breaking new ground. There was no clear consensus regarding its scope, purpose, and method of implementation. The State Department saw development assistance as a means of winning the "hearts and minds" of the people of poor nations, especially those considering the Communist path. In many cases, development aid was coupled with military assistance, an extension of national security interests. Aid also appealed to the humanitarian sentiments of the American public living in a land of plenty. Technical and financial assistance were the twin pillars of the program, but how they were to be effectively administered remained open to conjecture. *See also* FOREIGN AID, 285.

Significance The Point Four Program quickly mushroomed in size and scope to become a multibillion-dollar amalgamation of programs, the beginning of what remains the world's largest set of bilateral assistance programs. It was born simultaneously out of the post–Marshall Plan optimism and the cold war mentality. The program was launched in an era of confidence regarding the potential of development assistance and the ability of the United States to lead the world down the path of development and democracy. While it soon became apparent that such a task faced innumerable obstacles, the Point Four Program thrust development assistance into the center of U.S. foreign policy, where it has remained.

Private Voluntary Organizations (PVOs) (300)

A diverse group of nonprofit, nongovernmental, international agencies and foundations working primarily in development assistance and emergency relief. Sometimes referred to simply as voluntary agencies or volags, they are included in the broader category of nongovernmental organizations (NGOs). The organizations provide technical, organizational, and material assistance, usually in localized, people-to-people operations. The Organization for Economic Cooperation and Development (OECD) lists over 1,600 such organizations worldwide with emphases including education, health services, refugee assistance, entrepreneurship, financial services, and increasingly environmental issues, political lobbying, and advocacy. While most PVOs operate out of, and originated in, North America and Western Europe, many being church-related, the number of indigenous private voluntary organizations (IPVOs) is growing rapidly throughout the developing world. Better known PVOs include CARE, American Friends Service Committee (AFSC), Catholic Relief Service (CRS), Church World Service, Mennonite Central Committee, Save the Children, World Neighbors, World Vision, and Oxfam. The agencies are supported by private contributions and government grants. Several organizations seek to enhance cooperation and coordination among North American PVOs. These include the American Council of Voluntary Agencies for Foreign Service (ACVAFS), Inc.; Coordination in Development (CODEL), Inc.; Private Agencies Collaborating Together (PACT); and the American Council for Voluntary International Action (InterAction). A valuable discussion of the role of PVOs is provided in *Private Voluntary Organizations as Agents of Development* (1984), edited by Robert Gorman. *See also* NONGOVERNMENTAL ORGANIZATIONS, 295.

Significance   While it is difficult to measure the collective impact of this diverse group of private voluntary organizations, there is widespread consensus that their overall contributions to development are substantial. PVOs are broadly recognized for their history of effective, if often small-scale, development assistance at the grassroots level. Their size and use of highly dedicated volunteers and low-paid staff, combined with the experience of working directly with assistance recipients, often result in resourceful, innovative, and culturally sensitive projects. While this may not always be the case, PVOs are generally better suited to assisting the poorest segments of society in a participatory manner than are their bilateral and multilateral counterparts. PVOs are increasingly working in cooperation with bilateral agencies, particularly in Canada and the United States. Accepting government contracts and goods helps solve the perpetual funding problems of many PVOs and no doubt enhances the quality of the work supported by the bilateral agencies. But it also raises questions as to the private nature of PVOs that receive a large percentage of their support from public funds. Catholic Relief Service, for example, receives more than 70 percent of its support through government funding and the World Vision Relief Organization 87 percent (1986). In total, U.S.-based PVOs now receive over $1.5 billion from government sources. However, this figure still does not exceed private support. Several organizations, such as Oxfam and AFSC, seek no government funding. They wish to maintain their strong ties with their constituency at home and their nonnationalistic image abroad. The PVOs' value also lies in their role in development education in the developed countries. This function, once considered of peripheral importance by many PVOs except as a byproduct of promotional material, has increasingly been granted higher priority by many groups. Returned field workers often serve as educational resources and act as advocates for Third World peoples.

Privatization of AID (301)
A strategy stressed during the Ronald Reagan administration to emphasize contracting development projects to private and consulting companies. The rationale was to increase flexibility and reduce costs. The policy has resulted in the growth of large numbers of development-oriented consulting firms in the Washington, D.C., area bidding for various development projects. These firms have been sarcastically referred to as belt-line bandits, implying a narrowness of vision and an excessively profit-oriented self-interest. Actually a number of private firms doing development work have excellent professional reputations. Particularly well known for excellent development work are the Transcentury Corporation, Robert Nathan Associates, the Institute of International Research, and Winrock International. *The Development Directory* is an excellent guide to such organizations.

Significance   The privatization of development assistance in the United States raises important questions related to accountability. To whom are such private firms accountable? To what extent is their objectivity compromised by their desire to continue winning contracts?

280

To what extent does privatization discourage bright young individuals from entering the development field because of the uncertainties associated with short-term contract employment? How effectively can private development firms, compared to the U.S. Agency for International Development itself, represent the interests of U.S. taxpayers and the interests of the poor and needy abroad? There are no easy answers to these questions and few if any rigorous or systematic studies exist comparing the effectiveness of private versus public development assistance.

Program-Related Investments (302)
A special type of development assistance used by some foundations to supplement normal grant-making activity. With this type of assistance, funds are provided to a group or organization to undertake an innovative development project that is expected to have positive financial returns. For example, a group of women might start a rural rabbit cooperative. If the project proved successful, the granting foundation would receive a return of its principal, plus modest concessionary interest. These funds could then be recycled by the foundation to support other innovative development projects. *See also* TRICKLE UP PROGRAM, 444; GRAMEEN BANK OF BANGLADESH, 405.

Significance   Small groups of poor people with innovative ideas may find it extremely difficult to obtain credit through normal private banking channels in developing countries. Such microenterprises are often too small to receive project funds from many donor agencies, such as the World Bank or Japan. Program-related investments can be of direct benefit to such groups. The investments are normally made in priority areas of the foundation or donor agency. For example, if a foundation had an active women-in-development program, then innovative projects related to enhancing the earnings of rural women would be a natural area for program-related investments. The Ford Foundation has occasionally employed this approach to development assistance.

Rural Development Tourism (303)
Superficial short-term visits to rural areas by development experts, most often during the most pleasant seasonal conditions. Such visits often result in highly misleading and uninformed perspectives on rural development conditions. The term was popularized by Robert Chambers of Sussex University. As in conventional tourism, there is an emphasis on visiting the most successful and exemplary projects,

which may not be at all representative of overall rural conditions. Those individuals in rural areas with the most serious health, agricultural, or environmental problems often remain hidden from the view of the rural development tourist. Given the concern for image building, such tourists may be "wined and dined" to make their short stay in the rural areas as enjoyable as possible. In such short visits, it is often impossible to reach the more remote areas, frequently those with the most serious rural development problems. *See also* ROBERT CHAMBERS, 11; DEVELOPMENT METHODOLOGY, 319.

Significance The problem of rural development tourism reflects larger North-South issues. Planning their visits according to their own personal needs, the experts almost universally prefer to leave the North during the harsh winter months to spend time in the warm tropics. They similarly try to avoid going to tropical areas during the monsoon rains or periods of drought. The combination of limited time and lack of language ability minimizes their chances of spending time close to rural people in genuinely remote areas of developing countries. In many respects rural development tourism represents both wasteful foreign aid and miseducation. Despite the sensitivity and related embarrassment'of the topic, Chambers's courage in frankly addressing this issue is unfortunately uncommon in the development field.

Science and Development (304)

A term referring to the complex relationship between a nation's level of scientific capability and its development status. The study of this relationship represents an important interdisciplinary field of development studies with many controversial dimensions. The many complex questions addressed by scholars in this field include: Should developing countries spend limited resources on basic scientific research? How does a country grow scientific capability and expertise? How can scientific progress be measured? The measurement of scientific progress is becoming a field in itself with the growth of techniques, such as informetrics and bibliometrics, related to the measurement of the production of information and knowledge. Scientific development is directly related to the dependency debate. How can developing countries reduce their intellectual and technological dependence? Another related issue is the appropriateness of technology, including various elements of high technology. The extensive dimensions of this complex field have been aptly synthesized in a volume of the late Michael J. Moravcsik, *On the Road to Worldwide Science: Contributions to Science Development*. Ivan Illich in *Tools for*

Conviviality and Denis Goulet in *The Uncertain Promise: Value Conflicts in Technology Transfer* also provide critical assessments of the role of science in development. *See also* BRAIN DRAIN, 238; TECHNOLOGY TRANSFER, 308.

Significance   As measured by the number of scientists, scientific publications, and science students, a few advanced industrialized nations led by the United States, Western Europe, the Soviet Union, and Japan, account for 95 percent of world science. Their annual investment in science research is approximately $20–30 billion. As a result, the science gap between the industrialized countries and the LDCs has proven difficult to close. Most LDCs lack the educational facilities and scientific community to close the gap. Brain drain partly results from the understandable desire of Third World scientists to remain in the more dynamic, well-funded institutions of the North. Another factor militating against science development in the LDCs has been the failure of many LDC governments to support science, preferring instead to import technology. In July 1985, Thailand's minister of science and technology, Damrong Lathipipat, committed suicide, ostensibly because he felt that his country was giving inadequate attention to science and technology. Damrong's symbolic suicide reflects a perspective that probably has received too little attention. Some argue that a society's idea system derives more from scientific advancement than any other factor. Similarly, it can be argued that a substantial indigenous scientific infrastructure is essential for development. Those advocating such a perspective see science as the most powerful instrument in catalyzing the process of development (aided, of course, by social, economic, and political forces). Commitment to the development of science requires a long-term perspective since the gestation period for training quality scientists is lengthy, often a decade or more. Given the potentially vast resources of tropical rain forests and abundant sunlight in many LDC areas, the fields of biotechnology and solar photovoltaics would seem particularly relevant to developing countries. As Denis Goulet makes clear in his insightful writings, science and technology are two-edged swords. Despite the value of a such a warning, developing countries that fail to commit resources to scientific development will likely find themselves in perpetual intellectual and technological dependence.

Technical Assistance   (305)

The transfer of expertise and knowledge to developing countries as a dimension of foreign aid. Such transfers occur primarily through the provision of training and/or experts. These two approaches are sometimes referred to as the King of Siam versus Peter the Great approaches. The former emphasizes sending individuals abroad for training while the latter calls for use of foreign experts. The basic assumption underlying technical assistance is that it will help assure that aid funds are used effectively for development. Equipment or machines without the training to use them would be meaningless. Many aid projects have technical assistance built in as an integral part of the program of financial assistance. For example, in a major World Bank radio education project in Thailand, key Thai technicians and programmers received related training from the BBC in England and Thailand under the auspices of UNESCO. Drawing on contemporary computer jargon, some now refer to technical assistance as software in contrast to hardware such as dams, roads, machines, and other physical forms of aid. *See also* TECHNOLOGY TRANSFER, 308; INFRASTRUCTURE, 155.

Significance   Technical assistance has provoked considerable controversy. Since foreign experts are often highly paid and may live ostentatious life-styles, technical assistance can be resented. Another common criticism is the transfer of inappropriate expertise or techniques. There is also a lively debate as to whether technical assistance perpetuates or reduces long-term intellectual dependence. Ideally, technical assistance should lead to the building of local intellectual capacity, thus reducing future need for external technical assistance. Another important issue relates to the effectiveness of individuals in transmitting technical skills cross-culturally. Despite the popularity of overseas training, it represents an increasing burden on limited foreign exchange resources and, in countries such as China, Pakistan, and Taiwan, can lead to considerable brain drain. Given the rapid pace of technological change and innovation, technical assistance among nations is a natural phenomenon that has persisted for centuries and will continue.

Technical Cooperation among Developing Countries (306)
(TCDC)
The process of sharing expertise, knowledge, technology, experience, and ideas among the developing countries. TCDC is a means to enhance the self-reliance of the South and to foster more creative, cost-effective, and relevant technical assistance. Starting in 1972, a number of intergovernmental initiatives related to exploring the concept of TCDC began. In June 1977, senior consultants met in Kuwait to plan a major conference on TCDC. The result was the 1978 Buenos Aires Plan of Action for Promoting and Implementing Tech-

nical Cooperation among Developing Countries (BAPA). The UN Development Program established a special unit for TCDC to facilitate implementation of BAPA. This unit notes that more than 1,500 operational TCDC projects have been established among 87 developing countries. *See also* TECHNICAL ASSISTANCE, 305; APPROPRIATE TECHNOLOGY, 276.

Significance   The Buenos Aires meeting in 1978 was an important historical landmark indicating the formal birth of TCDC, even though such technical cooperation has existed for thousands of years. Implementation of TCDC is easier within the United Nations and multilateral framework than under bilateral technical assistance. The latter is still too often tied to providing expertise from the donor nation itself rather from than South countries. Major obstacles inhibiting the full implementation of TCDC are: (1) inadequate funding, (2) colonial legacies and mentalities insisting that Western expertise is generally superior, and (3) anxieties about not receiving the latest technologies or ideas. Despite these genuine problems, TCDC has the potential "to help release the latent creativity of two billion people, thus opening new horizons for mankind" (Seligman 1988:6). UNDP publishes a journal, *Cooperation South*, devoted exclusively to issues of TCDC.

Technical Fix   (307)
The notion that all global and development problems can be solved by technology, science, and innovation. The assumption underlying this concept is that science and progress not only can keep pace with emerging problems, but can virtually solve all current and future problems. Some would argue that the Green Revolution was a technical fix for the problem of world hunger.

Significance   The debate about technical fixes reflects a dramatic polarization between technocratic and ecological orientations toward development. Ecologists, deeply concerned about the need for early warning systems, are seriously skeptical about the ability of technical fixes to deal with long-term environmental problems such as the warming of the earth, ozone layer depletion, and hyperurbanization. Those believing in technical fixes are much more optimistic and project that future scientific breakthroughs will provide solutions to such global problems. The volume, *The God That Limps: Science and Technology in the Eighties* by Colin Norman, provides a thoughtful discussion of such issues, as do the late Michael J. Moravcsik, in *On the Road to Worldwide Science: Contributions to Science Development,* and other scholars such as Lewis Mumford and Buckminster Fuller.

Technology Transfer (308)
The international movement of technology as hardware, software, or related training. Technology transfer has been the center of considerable debate as it relates to closing the technology gap between rich and poor nations. Almost all of the world's scientific and technological research and development is conducted in the United States, Western Europe, the Soviet Union, and Japan. Most technological innovation is protected by international patent and intellectual property-rights agreements, without which major monetary incentives for innovation and investment would be lost. At the same time, few developing countries have seen fit to invest substantially in research and development of technology vital to their national development, and a situation of scientific dependency thus persists. In addition to private and bilateral agreements, the United Nations has served as a forum for negotiating terms of agreement for technology transfer from North to South. The Universal Convention of 1952 and its revised version of 1971, administered by UNESCO, provide for a less rigorous degree of protection on intellectual property rights, for example, by shortening the duration of protection before a patented item is passed into the public domain. The NIEO debate also raised the issue of technology transfer. Multinational corporations (MNCs) operating in developing countries were requested by the LDCs to make technology and training more readily available to host nations. Many developing countries, most notably the People's Republic of China, have not signed the international agreements, deeming them inappropriate and impractical for their purposes. However, this lack of agreement can prove a hindrance to international trade agreements and relations. Interest continues to grow in technical cooperation among developing countries (TCDC) as one solution to the problem of inadequate technology transfer to developing countries. *See also* TECHNICAL COOPERATION AMONG DEVELOPING COUNTRIES, 306; APPROPRIATE TECHNOLOGY, 276.

Significance Technology transfer is a vital tool for world development. Developing nations need not wait to build their own scientific and technological bases before reaping the benefits of technological advancement. Technological leaps, for example, may allow villagers to enjoy the benefits of technology developed in a quite different setting. Successful transfer involves far more than the physical movement of equipment and related documents. The Third World is strewn with transferred yet unused or useless technology, some donated by well-meaning organizations and some purchased at great cost. The applicability and sustaining power of a particular type of technology may vary widely among different locales and cultures. The discussion of appropriate technology is central to sound development practice. Technologically advanced nations and developing countries must continue to work toward fair and reasonable agreements regarding technology transfer if the majority of the world's population is to benefit, directly or indirectly, from rapid technological innovation.

Tied Aid (309)

Restrictions on development expenditures requiring that purchases of goods and services be made from the aid-giving country. This restriction is normally written into law as a political means to increase support for aid to developing countries. Private companies thus benefiting from development assistance become an active lobby on behalf of such expenditures. For example, an infrastructure-development project would be required to use U.S.-manufactured equipment. Similarly a student on an AID scholarship to the United States would need to fly on a U.S. air carrier. Approximately 70 percent of all U.S. bilateral aid and 80 percent of British aid goes to firms and individuals from the respective donor countries. *See also* FOREIGN AID, 285; BILATERAL AID, 277.

Significance Tied aid reduces the foreign exchange outflows associated with development assistance. It also contributes to both skepticism and resentment concerning the altruism of aid. When nearly all aid is tied, the choices of developing countries are highly limited and the most efficient procurement of goods and services is necessarily constrained. Tied aid also reduces the foreign exchange inflows associated with development assistance since local procurement of goods and services is restricted.

3. Analytical Concepts

Atkinson Index (310)

A measure of inequality based on the normative concept of a social welfare function. Mathematically the Atkinson Index is defined as: $A = 1 - (1/n) \ [\Sigma(x_{i/\mu})^{1-e}]^{1/1-e}$ where A = Atkinson Index of inequality; n = number of units in sample; x_i = the values of the inequality factor being measured (for example, income); μ = the average of x_i; and e = a special normative parameter to reflect preferences regarding the social welfare function (Allison 1978: 873). As e increases toward its limit of 1, A becomes more sensitive to transfers among lower incomes and less sensitive to transfers among the richest elements of a society. *See also* COEFFICIENT OF VARIATION, 314; GINI COEFFICIENT, 325; KUZNETS INDEX, 331; LOG VARIANCE, 334; THEIL'S INDEX, 350.

Significance   Though the Atkinson Index is mathematically more complex than other measures of inequality such as the coefficient of variation or log variance, it has a number of attractive features. It is scale-invariant (that is, it can be used to compare inequality of different factors or dimensions) and it satisfies the principle of transfers (that is, it always increases when funds shift from poorer to richer elements of society). Perhaps most importantly, the Atkinson Index includes both empirical values and a key normative parameter to reflect preferences related to the social welfare function. Thus, special concern for the poorest segments of society can be reflected by setting a higher e value. The measure also lends itself easily to the use of sensitivity analysis, where results can be compared for alternative values of e.

Borda Scores (311)

An extremely simple, old, but little used methodology for empirically comparing countries. This simple methodology dates from 1781. After countries are ranked on a set of criterion variables, their ranks are then summed. For example, if countries were being compared on 10 statistical indicators of the extent to which they are meeting the basic needs of their citizens, a top score of 10 would indicate that a country ranked first on all categories. If 20 countries were being ranked and compared, the lowest possible score would be 200, indicating that country was poorest in every category. These rankings could be based on such social indicators as the Physical Quality of Life Index (PQLI).

Significance   The Borda scores technique provides for the unambiguous ranking of countries with respect to development performance. The resulting performance index, however, is no better than the quality of the basic data underlying the rankings. The most relevant data for key criteria in some cases may be unavailable. Thus, proxy criteria and data must be used, reducing the overall reliability of the resulting Borda scores.

Capital-Output Ratio (312)

A key concept used in development theory and planning that shows the relationship between levels of investment and the related annual income resulting from such investments. The lower the capital-output ratio, the more productive that society is in converting investment into future income. With an average capital-output ratio of 5 to 1, a country that invests 15 percent of its national income would have an annual rate of income growth of 3 percent. A distinction must be made between the average and the marginal or incremental capital-output ratio (ICOR). The incremental ratio refers only to that which has been added to capital or income during a specific period. Using the example above, if the country in question has an ICOR of 3 to 1, an increase in investment of an additional 6 percent (from 15 to 21 percent) would result in a growth of additional income of 2 percent (from 3 to 5 percent). *See also* HARROD-DOMAR MODEL OF ECONOMIC GROWTH, 327.

Significance   The capital-output ratio concept is central to conventional development theory. Given this formulation, quantitative economic growth is simply a function of levels of savings and investment, and the capital-output ratio. The mathematical simplicity of this concept masks the basic complexities underlying the two key variables of the model. The level of savings and investment is affected by a wide range of factors such as fiscal and monetary policies, international capital inflows and outflows, and even cultural values related to savings and spending. The capital-output ratio is similarly affected by a wide range of factors related to applications of science and technology, levels of productivity, efficiency of government services, and status of relevant developmental infrastructure. An emphasis on the capital-output ratio is usually associated with an overly narrow definition of development as increases in per capita income.

Cluster Analysis (313)

A statistical technique for grouping cases with similar quantitative patterns or profiles. Since it works well with a small to moderate number of cases, it can be used to cluster countries with similar statistical profiles. The process yields a hierarchy of cluster solutions, ranging from one overall cluster to as many clusters as there are cases. For example, five clusters of countries might emerge from such an analysis. It is of special interest to see which developing countries are members of the same statistical cluster.

Significance   Cluster analysis relates to the ongoing debate about how the developing countries should be classified. It is increasingly recognized that it is overly simplistic to lump all developing countries together as part of the so-called Third World. Cluster analysis provides a rigorous procedure for grouping countries with similar statistical profiles. The clustering is based on the choice of variables or statistical indicators selected for comparing countries.

Coefficient of Variation (314)

An important statistic relevant to measuring levels of inequality. It can be easily calculated since it is simply the standard deviation divided by the mean. The higher the coefficient of variation, the greater the level of inequality with respect to the statistical measurement of any relevant phenomenon such as income, wealth, or educational attainment. A coefficient of variation of 0 represents perfect equality. If the average annual income per capita in a society is $2,000 and the standard deviation of income per capita is $1,000, the coefficient of variation (V) would be simply 0.50, or 50 percent. The range of V is from 0 to infinity. Since it is common for measures of inequality such as the Gini coefficient to be measured on a 0 to 1 scale, V can be converted to a similar scale by the simple formula, Transformed $V = V/(V+1)$. *See also* ATKINSON INDEX, 310; GINI

COEFFICIENT, 325; KUZNETS INDEX, 331; LOG VARIANCE, 334; THEIL'S INDEX, 350.

Significance   Though inequality is considered a major global and development issue, most standard statistical texts mention the coefficient of variation only briefly, with no hint at its potential use for measuring inequality. The coefficient of variation is also an extremely simple concept to understand mathematically, requiring only a knowledge of arithmetic and very elementary statistics. Its advantages and disadvantages compared to those of other measures of variation in inequality are much more complex and thoroughly discussed in an informative article by P. D. Allison titled "Measures of Inequality," in *American Sociological Review* 43 (1978):865–880.

Cost-Benefit Analysis   (315)
An analytical technique for evaluating development projects in terms of their economic returns. The cost-benefit analysis can be used either in preproject appraisal to inform decision makers with respect to project approval, or in postproject evaluation to ascertain a project's economic returns relative to its costs. This technique was first employed in assessing dam projects in the United States. In the postwar period it has been employed frequently in developmental contexts by such organizations as the World Bank and AID. It is easiest to use cost-benefit analysis when outcomes can be readily quantified in terms of monetary benefits. The assessment of future costs and benefits requires the use of a discount rate, reflecting time preference and the economic opportunity cost of financial resources committed to any project. Compound interest and annuity formulae are used in doing cost-benefit analysis. Sensitivity analysis is also frequently used to show how the benefit-cost ratios may vary with differing assumptions (e.g., the use of alternative discount rates). It is important to distinguish between social and private cost-benefit analysis. In social cost-benefit analysis *total* costs and benefits to society are estimated. For example, schooling has both social and private benefits. A more educated populace might contribute to lower crime rates, a social benefit of education. The basic formula of cost-benefit analysis is

$$NPV = \frac{\Sigma(B_t - C_t)}{(1+r)^t}$$

where NPV = net present value; t = time; B = total benefits; C = total costs; and r = the social rate of discount. The higher the value of NPV, the greater is the social return of a given development project. In private cost-benefit analysis only the costs and benefits to a particular individual or enterprise are calculated and a private rate of interest is used, such as the interest rates charged by private banks. *See also* TIME PREFERENCE, 351.

Significance   The cost-benefit analysis technique is controversial. Some argue that it can be used to favor projects for which outcomes can be readily measured in monetary terms. Some also object to the idea of attributing monetary value to human lives, which is often required in applying cost-benefit analysis to human resource projects in areas such as health and education. The major strength of the technique is that it requires policymakers and decision makers to make explicit various key assumptions and projections. The use of cost-benefit analysis can also lead to greater awareness of important external economies or diseconomies, and various unintended outcomes or costs. Decisions need not be made solely on the basis of a quantitative cost-benefit analysis, but can be supplemented by relevant qualitative data and considerations. For example, a project with a somewhat lower projected rate of return might still be selected because it would be located in an extremely poor region of a country. Cost-benefit analysis is one of many potential tools for use in project evaluation in development contexts.

Debt Service Ratio   (316)
A statistical indicator that shows the extent of a country's international debt and its ability to service such debt. The numerator of the ratio is debt service, which is the sum of repayments due in a year (both principal and interest). Total debt service includes both private and public debt, while public debt service includes only public and publicly guaranteed debt. Two different ratios are commonly used. In one ratio the denominator is GNP, while in the second, exports of goods and services is the denominator. If the latter total debt service ratio were 50 percent, that would mean that half of a nation's export earnings would be needed to pay its international debt. If the debt service to GNP ratio were 10 percent, then 10 percent of that nation's GNP would need to be used for paying off its international debt. *See also* DEBT CRISIS, 134.

Significance   Utilizing the debt service ratio, the two simply calculated measures noted above provide an excellent overview of a nation's international debt status. Some developing countries have specified maximum ratios to ensure that they do not accrue excessive future economic burdens. For countries with hard currencies, these ratios are less severe, since these nations can technically use their own printing presses to pay off international debt, although this approach is likely to create domestic inflation and weaken the nation's international exchange value. Countries with soft currencies never have this option as a means of reducing their external debt.

Demographic Transition (317)

The shift of a society from a pattern of high birth and death rates to one with low birth and death rates. During the middle stage of the transition, death rates fall more rapidly than birth rates, resulting in explosive population growth and an extremely young population structure. The introduction of modern health technologies in developing countries is generally considered the basis of the movement into the second phase of the transition. Successful family planning and population control lead to a completion of the transition and a movement into the third stage of a stable population. *See also* POPULATION PLANNING, 254.

Significance Countries vary considerably with regard to the duration of their demographic transition. For example, Japan underwent a rapid demographic transition and its population is thus aging rapidly. Other Asia-Pacific countries such as South Korea, Taiwan, Singapore, and Hong Kong have also experienced rapid demographic transitions. In the past decade, Thailand has had remarkable success in lowering fertility and moving toward the final stage of the demographic transition. As China vigorously pursues its one-child policy, its demographic transition is accelerating. In other parts of the Third World, however, the demographic transition has been much slower because of persisting health problems and cultural barriers to family planning. Generally, the speed with which a nation experiences the demographic transition is directly correlated with its level of economic development, rate of urbanization, level of education, and extent of female participation in the labor force.

Dependency Ratio or Burden (318)

A demographic concept referring to the percentage of a population that is under the age of 15 or over the age of 65. These individuals are considered too young or too old to be part of the labor force and thus are viewed as an economic burden. The higher the ratio, the more resources a society must devote to basic expenses for education and health, thus limiting other productive investment related to economic growth. *See also* DEMOGRAPHIC TRANSITION, 317.

Significance   Because of their young populations, most developing countries have high dependency ratios or burdens. In many developing countries, the dependency ratio may be 50 percent or higher. In most developed countries, it is less than 33 percent. The populations of both developed and developing countries will, however, be much older in the next century. Thus, as the dependency burden of LDCs falls from improved family planning and population control, their populations are aging considerably, partially offsetting the fall in the proportion of people under 15.

Development Methodology   (319)
Research, planning, and policy analysis used to analyze development issues and problems. These are the methods applied in the field of development studies. A number of these methods and tools are defined in this volume. Among such tools are cost-benefit analysis; manpower planning; input-output analysis; quantitative survey research (such as that done by Alex Inkeles, Daniel Lerner, Gabriel Almond, and Sidney Verba); ethnography (used primarily by development anthropologists); and social impact analysis. Over time considerable criticism of the conventional methodology of development has arisen. Radically oriented critical theorists say that conventional research ignores the important historical context of development and tends to legitimate the status quo of stratification, domination, and inequality. More mainstream scholar/doers such as Michael Edwards of Oxfam and Edward Heneveld (formerly of the Aga Khan Foundation) see the esoteric and oversophisticated nature of conventional methodology as an obstacle to development, limiting the access of ordinary citizens to power and influence. Robert Chambers at IDS (Sussex) has been highly critical of conventional rural development research and proposes the alternative of rapid rural appraisal, which facilitates the development of a genuine understanding of rural conditions.

Significance   Development methodology is clearly in a state of flux as appreciation and awareness grow of the need to recognize the importance and relevance of local knowledge and indigenous technical knowledge. What Denis Goulet calls one-eyed giants, that is, Westerners who have all the answers, are no longer acceptable. There is also growing concern for the need to link understanding and action (Michael Edwards). What Chris Argyris has called action science, studying real phenomena in their natural settings, is relevant to development studies. Other needs are for more participatory research and recognition of broader arrays of phenomena including emotion and myth. The future of development methodology rests with its openness to recognize the legitimacy of multiple ways of knowing. Integral to such a perspective is the need to listen to the people in developing societies and to "let the people speak their word," to use Paulo Freire's apt phrase.

Doubling Time (320)
The number of years it would take for the population of a country to double, assuming the maintenance of the current population growth rate. The doubling time is determined by the formula 70/n, wherein n = % annual growth rate. For example, Kenya with a growth rate of 4 percent has a doubling time of 28.5 years. The doubling time can also be computed using compound interest formulae and tables or logarithmic algebra. *See also* POPULATION PLANNING, 254.

Significance The concept of doubling time is useful in dramatizing how rapidly populations may grow. This may not be as apparent when considering annual percentage growth rates alone. Doubling time demonstrates that nations with rapid population growth must find ways of providing services and employment possibilities for vast numbers of new people in a matter of a few decades. Otherwise, population growth may undercut hard-fought development gains within a nation.

Energy/Efficiency Ratio (321)
An ecological approach to measuring nations' productivity in converting energy into economic goods and services. The energy/efficiency ratio is simply computed by dividing a nation's energy consumption by units of gross domestic product. The lower the ratio, the more efficient a country is in its energy utilization. Countries such as Japan with its emphasis on public transportation and the Netherlands with its emphasis on the use of bicycles reduce their energy consumption relative to their GNP and thus have lower ratios, reflecting greater efficiency. The U.S. ratio, for example, is 0.62 for 1984–1985, compared to 0.29 in Japan and 0.36 in the Netherlands. The less developed countries of Ivory Coast and Nigeria have ratios of only 0.13 and 0.18 respectively. Since the 1973 oil crisis the energy/efficiency ratio of nearly every OECD country has improved markedly with Japan having achieved the greatest efficiency. During the same period the ratio for developing countries has shown greater

inefficiency. The economies of the Eastern Bloc, until recently centrally planned, meanwhile remain the most inefficient users of energy in relationship to production. *See also* ENTROPY, 263; OVERDEVELOPMENT, 270; SUSTAINABLE DEVELOPMENT, 272.

Significance   The energy/efficiency ratio is a simple but powerful development indicator, but it is rarely used in evaluating national performance. By this criterion, many developing countries are actually more efficient than richer countries. The United States and Canada, for example, rank among the world's poorest performers by this measure, reflecting massive wastes of energy. However, this technique does not measure economic, human, or even ecological welfare. It simply measures how much energy a country consumes in producing its economic goods and services.

Ethnographic Futures Research   (322)

A methodology using anthropological qualitative interviewing to study alternative futures for nations undergoing rapid cultural and technological change. The goal of such research is to clarify value structures as they relate to anticipated futures. As part of the methodology, developed by Robert Textor at Stanford University, key informants are asked to project scenarios of most optimistic, most pessimistic, and most likely outcomes with respect to various domains such as technology and culture. Textor has employed this technique in studying the future of Austria and Thailand. A major example of the use of this methodology is Sippanondha Ketudat's East-West Center monograph, *The Middle Path for the Future of Thailand: Technology in Harmony with Culture and Environment* (1990).

Significance   Despite some references by scholars to ethnographic futures research, the horizons of policymakers and planners are often constrained by short-term problems and pressures. Too rarely do they have an opportunity to think about long-term (15 to 30 years) alternative futures. Ethnographic futures research can provide early warning signals of possible adverse or undesirable changes. The major problem with the methodology relates to choice of informants and their subjectivity in assessing alternative futures. This methodology does, however, provide a valuable addition to the pool of tools available for assessing long-term policy options for developing countries.

Ethnographic Residual Analysis   (323)

A technique that integrates the inquiry tools of econometrics and ethnography to develop a deeper understanding of cultural or social phenomena. In the first stage of this approach, econometric analyses are done in an attempt to explain a particular phenomenon. For example, a regression analysis, using the nation as the unit of analysis, could be undertaken of the determinants of quality of life in developing countries. Assuming a nonperfect relationship among the dependent variable, quality of life, and various explanatory variables such as income per capita, certain countries will be statistical outliers having much higher or lower quality of life than expected. For example, in such an analysis Sri Lanka might have a much higher quality of life than predicted by its per capita income and other conventional economic indicators. After anomalous cases are identified from the econometric analyses, the second stage is to use qualitative research such as ethnography to explore these unusual extreme cases in depth and help discover the unexplained variance. A similar technique could be used in developing countries, for example, to identify particularly effective rural schools or rural community-development programs. The same technique can be used for identifying extreme cases of failure or lack of success. This technique is described in the article, "Merging Quantitative and Qualitative Research Techniques," by G. Fry, S. Chantavanich, and A. Chantavanich, in *Anthropology and Education Quarterly*.

Significance   Research on developing countries tends to involve little communication between econometric-oriented researchers who often use the nation-state or rather large communities or regions as their units of analysis, and ethnographic researchers who often focus on relatively small rural settings. These researchers frequently appear to have relatively little respect for each other. The econometricians worry deeply about the $N = 1$ problem of small samples common in ethnographic research. Similarly, anthropologists and ethnographers worry about the superficiality of an overreliance on macrodata of often questionable quality. The technique of ethnographic residual analysis provides a mechanism for cooperative efforts between qualitative and quantitative researchers to gain a deeper understanding of development issues and phenomena.

Fiscal Neutrality   (324)
A concept derived from school-finance literature for assessing the equity of access to key public goods and services. Under conditions of fiscal neutrality, there should be no correlation between the economic wealth of a geographic or administrative division of a country and the quality of its public goods and services. Thus, the quality of

education should not vary with the socioeconomic conditions of various areas. The key assumption underlying fiscal neutrality is that all citizens should have equitable access to key public goods and services such as health and education. Obviously, complete fiscal neutrality is an ideal condition rarely achieved. *See also* GINI COEFFICIENT, 325.

Significance   The concept of fiscal neutrality provides a standard for measuring the extent to which public goods and services are distributed fairly without regard to socioeconomic status and geographic remoteness. This is important because developing countries face special problems in ensuring an equitable distribution of public goods and services across diverse geographic regions. As an example of relative success in achieving fiscal neutrality, the quality of Japanese public secondary schooling appears to be of reasonably uniform standard across prefectures. In developing countries, on the other hand, such educational uniformity is virtually unknown.

Gini Coefficient (325)

Developed by the Italian statistician and demographer Corrodo Gini, this statistic indicates the extent of equality in the distribution of some valued good or service. It is the most commonly used measure of equality of income distribution, though it can also be used to assess other dimensions of equality such as land concentration, wealth distribution, or resource utilization. The coefficient ranges from 0 to 1 in value. The lower the Gini coefficient, the greater the equality. A coefficient of 0 represents perfect equality and 1, perfect inequality. Technically, the Gini coefficient is directly related to the area between a 45-degree line of perfect equality and the Lorenz curve (named after Max Otto Lorenz, a U.S. government statistician), which shows the percentage share of the desired good possessed by a specific proportion of a population (see Figure 1). Shares are usually expressed in 10 percent deciles, though 20 percent quintiles may also be used. For example, the Lorenz curve will indicate the percent of income posssessed by the top 10 and bottom 10 percent of a population. Many procedures exist for calculating the Gini coefficient. The simplest method is to plot the Lorenz curve on mathematical graph paper and to calculate areas. The Gini coefficient is then equal to $A/(A + B)$ in Figure 1. For those with mathematical training, the Gini can be easily computed using integral calculus. Statistically, the Gini is equal to the mean difference of a distribution divided by twice the mean. Useful alternative methods for computing the Gini are provided by David M. Smith (1979: 364–365) and Herman P. Miller

Figure 1.

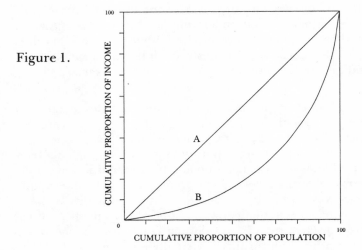

CUMULATIVE PROPORTION OF INCOME

CUMULATIVE PROPORTION OF POPULATION

(1971: 274–276). *See also* ATKINSON INDEX, 310; KUZNETS INDEX, 331; LORENZ DOMINANCE, 335.

Significance   Many development thinkers emphasize that inequality is the critical global issue. Thus, statistical measures such as the Gini coefficient and related Lorenz curve provide elegant tools for showing visually the extent of inequality in the world, a region, a nation, or a community. The major problem with respect to the Gini coefficient is the quality of the data underlying its calculation. Rigorous and reliable data on income and wealth distribution are often difficult to obtain. For those interested in the dynamics of income distribution, plotting the movement of the Gini coefficient for a society over time can provide considerable insight into the distributional impact of development policies.

Gross National Product   (326)
The total economic output of a country, including the output of residents working abroad less domestic income accruing to those abroad. It is mathematically defined as GNP = C + I + G + X − M, where GNP = gross national product; C = consumption expenditures; I = investment; G = government expenditures; X = exports; and M = imports. GNP is closely related to GDP, gross domestic product, which measures only products produced within a nation's territory, regardless of whether they are produced by local or foreign residents. Thus, Japanese firms producing in Indonesia contribute to

both Indonesia's GDP and Japan's GNP. *See also* NET DOMESTIC PRODUCT, 339.

Significance The gross national product is probably the most commonly used indicator of a country's economic progress. Despite its common use, the GNP is a rather limited economic indicator. It provides no information on the distribution of a nation's economic income or wealth, or on the resources and energy used in generating that level of output. GNP per capita data are often compared across countries in terms of U.S. dollars without adjusting for differences in costs of living. Despite these serious flaws, growth in GNP per capita is still the most commonly used measure of economic development and progress.

Harrod-Domar Model of Economic Growth (327)
A simple formula used in conventional development theory to explain economic growth. The formula is comprised of four variables: (1) ΔY, change in national income, the target or goal; (2) existing level of income, Y; (3) level of savings, S; and (4) capital-output ratio, K. The basic formula is

$$\text{Economic growth} = \frac{\Delta Y}{Y} = \frac{S}{K}$$

The level of savings, S, determines the amount of new investment that adds to a nation's productive capacity, for example, through new plants and equipment. See Michael Todaro, *Economic Development in the Third World* (1977: 52–53), for a derivation of the formula above. The higher the level of savings and investment, the higher the level of economic growth. A major reason for Japan's high postwar economic growth rate has been its consistently high national savings rate, encouraged by fiscal and monetary policies. The higher the value of K, the capital-output ratio, the lower the rate of economic growth. K shows the efficiency with which a nation can convert savings and investment into new output. The lower the K, the more efficiently the economy converts investment into new income. If a society has a poor developmental infrastructure, inefficient public and private organizations, and low-quality human resources, its capital-output ratio will tend to be high.

Significance Despite its simplicity, the Harrod-Domar formula reveals the basic mechanisms of the economic growth process. What it does not explain is the complex array of factors that impinge upon levels of savings and investment, and the efficiency with which these investments are converted into new income and growth. The Harrod-Domar formula also ignores distributional aspects of development. Though countries such as Brazil have achieved impressive growth in terms of the Harrod-Domar model, major distributional problems persist in that country.

Index of Social Progress (ISP) (328)
An index created by Richard J. Estes to measure changes in "the capacity of nations to provide for the basic social and material needs of their population" (Estes 1984:17). The ISP, as presented and applied in *The Social Progress of Nations* (1984), consists of 44 social indicators distributed among 11 subindexes: education, health, status of women, defense spending, economics, demography, geography, political stability, political participation, cultural diversity, and welfare effort. Revisions under consideration would add mental health, crime, and environmental pollution. *See also* DEVELOPMENT METHODOLOGY, 319; PHYSICAL QUALITY OF LIFE INDEX, 342; MEASURING AND COMPARING LEVELS OF POVERTY, 337.

Significance The index of social progress is one of the most comprehensive development indices yet devised and applied in social development studies. It reflects the multidimensional nature and complexities of development. The ISP is a powerful analytical tool for assessing differential development progress and comparing nation-states in their ability to improve the quality of life of their citizenry.

Infant Mortality Rate (329)
The number of deaths per 1,000 live births among children between birth and one year of age. It is one of the most important indicators of the welfare of a given population. The current average for all developed nations is 12–14, compared to 160–170 a century ago. In the developing nations the rate is about 70, a considerable improvement over the 1950 figure of 179. Much of this improvement can be attributed to worldwide use of antibiotics and immunization programs against infectious diseases. Almost 60 percent of the developing world's children now receive vaccinations. Recent promotion of oral rehydration therapy (ORT), accompanied by improved potable water sources, also contributes to lower infant mortality rates. ORT is used to combat the dehydration brought on by diarrhea, the greatest killer

of Third World children. Similar to the infant mortality rate is the child mortality rate, which indicates the probability of a child's dying before the age of five in a given population. *See also* ORAL REHYDRA-TION THERAPY, 297; LIFE TABLE, 332; NET REPRODUCTION RATE, 340.

Significance   The infant mortality rate is a key indicator of the health of children and their mothers. Throughout the Third World and even within regions of the richer nations, pregnancy and child-birth are leading causes of death for women and children, affecting the poorest of the poor within most societies. High infant mortality rates are associated with early marriage and childbearing and fre-quency of pregnancy. In addition, the rates are strongly correlated with levels of female literacy while only loosely related to economic indicators, especially GNP. Countries such as Costa Rica, Cuba, People's Republic of China, Jamaica, and Sri Lanka demonstrate that relatively low rates can be achieved without a high per capita GNP. Interestingly, lower infant mortality rates do not necessarily lead to higher population growth rates. In many instances, families have fewer children if they believe the living children are more likely to survive into adulthood.

Input-Output Analysis   (330)
A mathematically elegant tool of economic planning that shows in matrix format the economic interdependence among the basic sec-tors of an economy. All industries are assumed to be both producers of outputs and users of inputs from other industries. Such models vary in their complexity and comprehensiveness. Approximately 10 to 400 sectors are normally used, depending on the availability of economic data and mathematical modeling and computing capability. The basic ideal of this technique is to achieve internal consistency, and thereby avoid bottlenecks, shortages, and unnecessary or waste-ful surplusses. With such a system, production delays should be mini-mized. These techniques are most essential in planned economies. During Salvador Allende's Marxist regime in Chile, an attempt was made to computerize comprehensively the entire Chilean economy, using such techniques. The economist most frequently identified with this technique is Wassily Leontief. *See also* LINEAR PROGRAMMING, 333; NATIONAL PLANNING, 208.

Significance   Despite their mathematical elegance, there is little ev-idence to show that input-output models can adequately reflect the realities of complex economies, particularly in those countries where the quality and quantity of underlying economic data are seriously questionable or limited. These models also are based on economic assumptions that often are not adequately realistic. Perhaps the greatest utility of the technique of input-output analysis is more heuristic, as a means to identify key potential developmental bottlenecks or constraints. Such information could be valuable to policy-makers, who could then develop incentives or sanctions to minimize such constraints.

Kuznets Index (331)

A simple index for ascertaining extent of inequality. The index shows the extent of discrepancy between ideal and actual proportions. Mathematically it is expressed as

$$KI = \frac{\Sigma d_i}{n}$$

where KI = Kuznets Index; d_i = sum of absolute values of differences between the actual and ideal shares or proportions; and n = the number of groups or regions being compared. The index can, for example, conveniently be used to assess regional disparities in any country. Let us assume a country with five regions, each with 20 percent of the population. Let us further assume that one region has 50 percent of the nation's income, a second region has 20 percent of the income, and the poorest three regions each have 10 percent of the income. In this case the d_i or sum of disparities is equal to 0.30 + 0 + 0.10 + 0.10 + 0.10 or a total of 0.60. This is then divided by 5 to give an average discrepancy of 0.12. In this case the *maximal* possible sum of disparities would be 0.80 + 0.20 + 0.20 + 0.20 + 0.20 for a total of 1.60 divided by 5, or an average discrepancy of 0.32. A Kuznets Index of 0 would indicate perfect equality. The Kuznets Index can be converted to a 0-to-1 scale by dividing the average discrepancy (0.12) by the maximum possible discrepancy value (0.32). *See also* ATKINSON INDEX, 310; COEFFICIENT OF VARIATION, 314; GINI COEFFICIENT, 325; LOG VARIANCE, 334; THEIL'S INDEX, 350.

Significance   The Kuznets Index is one of a number of empirical measures of inequality. This statistic is particularly useful in comparing aggregate groups or regions to assess extent of departure from equal proportions or shares of desired goods or resources. A major advantage of the measure is its mathematical simplicity and conceptual clarity.

Life Table (332)

A mathematical model used by demographers to portray mortality conditions of a country and related prospects for longevity (Bogue 1969: 551). It is based upon a hypothetical cohort of 100,000 persons who are subject throughout their lifetimes to probabilities of dying observed in the actual population of that country during a specific time period, usually a particular year. A life table provides the following important demographic information:

1. The probability of dying within one year of persons at each age.
2. The average number of years a newborn infant can expect to live.
3. The average number of years of life remaining to a person of any age.
4. The probability of surviving from any given age to any other given age.
5. The probability of surviving for any given number of years, for persons at any age. (Bogue 1969: 551–552)

See also NET REPRODUCTION RATE, 340; TOTAL FERTILITY RATE, 352.

Significance   The life table provides important demographic data for assessing the quality of life in any country, since prospects for longevity are considered one of the most basic indicators of human well-being. From life table data, functions can be plotted showing major differences in demographic patterns between developed and developing nations. Like many other important demographic indicators, the predictions of a cross-sectional life table, based primarily on key demographic data for one year, may be quite inaccurate if major changes occur in future mortality patterns. It is also important to remember that the life table can be no better than the quality of the underlying demographic data upon which it is based. If these data are measured unreliably, the predictions derived from the life table, despite its mathematical and statistical sophistication, will be largely meaningless.

Linear Programming (333)

An applied mathematics tool highly useful in both planning and project implementation. Linear programming involves constraints and the need to optimize, maximize, or minimize certain factors such as costs. Though the tool is commonly used in industrial engineering in production or supply settings, it has also been used in educational and development planning. The key element in linear programming is an explicit objective function that states the outcome to be maximized or minimized. For example, in education, the outcome of an objective function might be to maximize school enrollments for a given geographic area. Complementing the objective function is a set of constraints that condition the objective function. For example, a budget constraint may specify that no more than a certain amount of funds can be spent. Using relatively simple principles from calculus and linear algebra, it is then possible to maximize or minimize the explicit outcome stated in the objective function, given the constraints indicated.

Significance Linear programming is a powerful mathematical tool that can facilitate improved efficiency in the use of limited and constrained resources. Its usefulness depends on the problem in question. For problems primarily technical in nature, it can be extremely valuable. For example, linear programming could be used to ascertain the least expensive way to train a large number of teachers, with respect to choices of place and size of training sites. The limitation of linear programming relates to those factors that cannot be expressed mathematically in the model. For example, teachers may be reluctant to serve in certain areas or seek quick transfers from such areas. Even more importantly, development projects often involve far more than a small number of specific outcomes. Important multidimensional outcomes are extremely difficult to quantify, such as human alienation or psychological trauma associated with loss of land resulting from large-scale irrigation projects.

Log Variance (334)

A popular measure of inequality often used by economists. Log variance can be simply computed by obtaining the logarithm of each income, for example, and then calculating the variance of those transformed values. The calculation can be made using a hand calculator with logarithmic and variance (the square of the standard deviation) functions. Using such a measure, differences in inequality in farm incomes between two villages could be compared. The higher the variance of the items, the greater the level of inequality, and the lower the variance, the lower the inequality level. A log variance of zero implies perfect equality. A problem arises if some value of a distribution of interest is equal to zero. In such cases the log variance is undefined. *See also* ATKINSON INDEX, 310; COEFFICIENT OF VARIATION, 314; GINI COEFFICIENT, 325; KUZNETS INDEX, 331; THEIL'S INDEX, 350.

Significance The log variance is an attractive measure of inequality from two perspectives. First, it is an easily understood concept that can be measured simply, independent of access to sophisticated computer technology. Second, it has the property of scale invariance, a critical criterion for measures of inequality. This means that the log variance could be used to compare the inequality of the distribution of agricultural land to the distribution of general wealth, or the distribution of the use of energy. Despite these attractive features, the log variance at high income levels (greater than 2.718 times the geometric mean) violates the principle of transfers. That is, at those higher levels of income, with a transfer of funds from a relatively poorer to a wealthier individual, the log variance would actually decrease, incorrectly suggesting a decrease in inequality (Allison 1978: 868). This drawback is not too serious since most income redistribution focuses on transfers to the poorer segments of society. The log variance has highly desirable inferential properties. Income and wealth data are usually not distributed normally, but are positively skewed and inherently nonnegative. By transforming such data into the log variance format a log-normal distribution results, making possible standard procedures of statistical inference.

Lorenz Dominance (335)

A methodology derived from the Lorenz curve for comparing income distribution across nations. To plot the Lorenz curve, data are presented on the percentage share of income held by various segments of a population. These segments are usually presented as deciles or quintiles (for example, the percentage of income held by the bottom 20 percent of the population). One country has Lorenz dominance over another if the percentage shares of its poorer segments are consistently superior to those of the other country. For example, data from the *World Development Report 1989* show that Sri Lanka has clear Lorenz dominance over Peru. The bottom 20 percent in Sri Lanka have 5.8 percent of household income, while in Peru this group has only 1.9 percent of income. The next poorest 20 percent in Sri Lanka have 10.1 percent of income, while in Peru, the next poorest 20 percent have only 5.1 percent of income. *See also* GINI COEFFICIENT, 325.

Significance With the use of the Lorenz dominance concept, it is possible to compare equality of income distributions across nations and to identify a hierarchy of countries arranged by the relative equity of their income distributions. Using such procedures, Amartya Sen of Oxford found that among Third World countries, Taiwan, Sri Lanka, South Korea, and India showed Lorenz dominance over countries such as Mexico, the Philippines, Venezuela, Peru, Honduras, and Brazil.

Marginal Analysis (336)

A commonly used method in economic analysis in which a change in one variable by a specific amount is associated with a change in another variable by a unit value. The change might be a change in one unit or one standard deviation. For example, if a country were to increase its rate of savings and investment by 10 percent, how much would its future rate of economic growth increase? The incremental capital-output ratio, a key variable in classical theories of economic growth, reflects marginal analysis. Regression analysis, a major quantitative tool used in economics and related social sciences, is basically a form of marginal analysis. An example in educational policy would be as follows. Suppose a developing country with a limited educational budget were to allow its student-teacher ratio to drift upward from 28 to 29. How much would the average educational achievement level drop as a result? This question is precisely what is meant by marginal analysis. Marginal analysis may be done with only two variables, or in a multiple-variable analysis with other variables introduced to control for factors that might influence the outcome variable. *See also* LINEAR PROGRAMMING, 333.

Significance Its simple mathematical elegance makes marginal analysis highly popular and widely used in the social sciences, particularly in economics. However, there are important drawbacks to marginal analysis. First, when only two variables are used, the marginal relations found may be spurious. Second, many models using marginal analysis are linear models. Some would argue that the world is not always linear, and thus such analyses may be overly simplistic. Third and most important, marginal analysis does not address the big questions of structure and major political, social, or economic transformation. Such changes clearly are not reflected at the margin. They are far more fundamental, and must be addressed from more macrohistorical and political-economy perspectives. Despite these limitations, marginal analysis and the techniques that utilize it such as regression analysis are useful quantitative tools for numerous policy analyses related to various development issues and problems. Such tools are also useful in economic and educational planning.

Measuring and Comparing Levels of Poverty (337)

A complex methodological problem central to the development field.

A key distinction in measuring and comparing levels of poverty is that between absolute and relative poverty. Absolute poverty can be defined as a condition in which individuals fall below basic minimal nutritional, health, or income levels. Relative poverty, in contrast, relates to low economic status in comparison with others nationally and internationally. Another important distinction is that between an inputs orientation and a results orientation toward measuring poverty. The input approach emphasizes nutritional or income levels, while the results approach focuses on outcome indicators such as life expectancy and literacy. The Morris physical quality of life index (PQLI) is an example of the latter. Stating the percentage of a population below a minimum threshold level of income essential for adequate nutrition is the conventional input-oriented approach. The recently formulated Human Development Index (HDI) used by the United Nations Development Programme (UNDP) in its *Human Development Report 1990* draws upon both types of indicators: life expectancy at birth, adult literacy, and purchasing power per capita (instead of traditional GNP per capita). *See also* DEVELOPMENT METHODOLOGY, 319.

Significance   With an increasing emphasis in the development field on giving priority to the poorest of the poor, it is critically important to be able to measure poverty rigorously and meaningfully. Valid international comparisons are important in determining priorities for development assistance. But numerous serious methodological problems arise with the definitions and measures suggested. For example, threshold statistical indicators provide no information on how far individuals are below the poverty line, or of the nature of the distribution of income and/or nutrition below that line. With respect to international comparisons, nutritional needs vary with climate, ethnicity, and physiology. International comparisons of income figures must be carefully adjusted for dramatic cost of living differentials across nations. A particularly interesting methodological approach is to rank countries with respect to both per capita income and success in poverty reduction. The empirical correlation found is far from perfect. Countries that have been particularly successful in reducing poverty relative to their income status include China, Sri Lanka, Cuba, Taiwan, and South Korea. In a World Bank paper titled *Levels of Poverty: Policy and Change* (1980), the Oxford scholar Amartya Sen has presented a thoughtful synthesis of alternative approaches to measuring and comparing poverty nationally and internationally.

Misplaced Precision   **(338)**
A common methodological error of reporting data to a ludicrously

precise level. This is a special problem in developmental contexts. Social science data in general and data from developing countries in particular are often measured with a certain degree of error. Peasant income, for example, is often underreported and school enrollments may be overstated. Thus, to present such data to five or six decimal points, such as in a correlation of 0.72513, or average income per capita of $1,514.35, is a clear example of misplaced precision.

Significance Social scientists have a natural tendency to try to emulate the approaches of physical scientists, who have powerful tools for measuring physical phenomena to a remarkable degree of accuracy. This tendency partially explains the reasons for misplaced precision. Much computer software also mechanically presents statistical results to great precision regardless of the quality of the original input data. Misplaced precision may lead policymakers and decision makers to place excessive trust in official statistics and data. Engaging in misplaced precision also may imply scientific arrogance.

Net Domestic Product (NDP) (339)
A refined measure of national economic product that reflects the environmental costs associated with development. Net domestic product is gross domestic product, that is, the total value of a country's national production (consumption plus government spending plus investment), less the natural-resource depletion associated with that production. Thus, the loss of natural resources such as petroleum, natural gas, forests, and soil is deducted from the gross domestic product. This modified form of "green" national accounting has been promoted by the World Resources Institute. Indonesia can be used as a concrete case to illustrate this refined form of national accounting. From 1971 to 1984, Indonesia's annual rate of growth averaged 6.9 percent. However, after deducting resource depletion during the period, the net growth drops to 4 percent a year. *See also* GROSS NATIONAL PRODUCT, 326.

Significance Since air, water, and forests are normally treated as free goods, they are undervalued economically and thus overutilized. The NDP approach to national accounting reflects a strong sustainable development perspective and an attempt to record the environmental costs associated with development. However, as described, the measure suffers from oversimplification, primarily in treating renewable and nonrenewable resources equally. If renewable resources such as forests are carefully replanted, then the environmental costs are less severe. Despite such problems, more refined measures of development such as NDP are important for making explicit the impact of development on environmental conditions and resources.

Net Reproduction Rate (NRR) (340)

A major demographic indicator that reflects a society's likely long-term population growth, based on fertility and mortality rates at a given time. Mathematically, the net reproduction rate is defined as ratio of infant females that will be born to a hypothetical cohort of 1,000 newborn females, based on the assumption that this cohort will be exposed to the empirical fertility and mortality rates of the given base year on which the analysis is based. If such a ratio is 1, then a population is exactly reproducing itself. If the ratio is greater than 1, the population is growing. If the ratio is less than 1, the population is not replacing itself. If a developing country has an NRR of 4.00, that means that in a generation the population would quadruple. The World Bank projects that countries such as China, Thailand, and Chile will reach an NRR of 1.00 by the year 2000. In contrast, it projects that Kenya and the Ivory Coast will not reach an NRR of 1.00 until 2050. *See also* LIFE TABLE, 332.

Significance There is one basic weakness in the net reproduction rate measure as a predictor of future population growth. Its calculation is based on an assumption of constant fertility and mortality rates as well as a stable age pattern of childbearing. In reality, the NRR tends to fluctuate widely over time within the same population. For example, during the past 15 years, the NRR for Thailand has gone steadily down because of dramatic decreases in the fertility rate and an increasing age of marriage. Increases in mortality caused by famine, disease, or war could also lead to a decline in the NRR. Despite these drawbacks, the NRR is a valuable demographic measure for providing an overview of a nation's likely demographic future.

Objectivity in Social Research (341)

The myth that social science research is objective and value-free. In an attempt to imitate the physical and natural sciences, social scientists, particularly those associated with the behavioral science movement and the philosophy of logical positivism, have attempted to create a value-free and objective social science. The impossibility of such an endeavor is clearly illustrated in the development field and was ably articulated in a neglected but important book, *Objectivity in Social Research* (1968) by the Nobel laureate from Sweden, Gunnar

Myrdal. Myrdal calls for all social scientists to state explicitly the value premises and assumptions underlying their research or policy work.

Significance   Researchers often pay homage to objectivity in social research, but its thorough implementation remains a myth. Many of the major discussions in the development field relate to highly normative and value-laden issues such as social justice, equality, poverty, basic human needs, and empowerment. A preoccupation with value-free social science could lead to avoidance of key normative questions in development and thus an implicit legitimization of the status quo and existing social systems and structures. Central to the development field and development thinking are the three critical domains of facts, values, and choices, which are part of an interactive complex.

Physical Quality of Life Index (PQLI)   (342)
Synthetic variable combining infant mortality, life expectancy at birth, and adult literacy rates to indicate the level of social development of nations. The index was devised by the Overseas Development Council under the direction of Morris D. Morris and presented in his book *Measuring the Condition of the World's Poor* (1979) as a non-income measure of well-being and a simple alternative to the more complex and comprehensive models devised by other international development organizations to determine nations of greatest need. Given the inadequacies of GNP as the primary indicator of development, Morris sought to devise an index independent of economic development, a "creative complement to the GNP" that focused on social accomplishments of nations. In fact, the correlation of PQLI with GNP is weak. He also wished to stress results as opposed to inputs and to utilize relatively value-free indicators. Each of the three indicators is indexed on a scale of 0 to 100 where 0 equals the worst national performance in 1950 and 100 represents the best expected performance by the end of the century. The PQLI of a nation is the average of the three indicators. Based on 1985 data, the scores range from 21 (Afghanistan) to 100 (Australia, France, and Iceland). *See also* INDEX OF SOCIAL PROGRESS, 328; INFANT MORTALITY RATE, 329; LITERACY, 249.

Significance   Use of the PQLI has become widespread in development circles, attesting to its appeal and usefulness. The PQLI can be a powerful tool for reassessing priorities in development planning and assistance, especially in regard to the performance of national health-care and educational services. For example, if a country achieves economic growth without subsequent improvements in the PQLI, it becomes clear that the benefits of development are not accruing to the general populace. However, the PQLI gives equal weight to each of two indicators of health status and to literacy, which is often based on questionable data. As such, the equal weighting is arbitrary and no rationale is given for it. Further, the index does not take into consideration other indicators of social welfare such as human rights and social justice. But its originators did not intend for it to be a measure of total welfare, which, being similar to development, cannot be adequately measured by any single indicator. The simplicity of the index reflects both its strength and its weakness.

Primate City (343)

A term that refers to a single urban area that dominates a society politically, economically, culturally, and intellectually. Several empirical measures exist to assess a city's primacy. The simplest measure is the index of primacy, which is equal to P^1 divided by P^2, where P^1 is the size of the country's largest city and P^2 is the size of its second largest city. A three-city index is computed by comparing the largest city with the combined populations of the next two largest cities. A four-city index is computed in an analogous fashion. The Nobel laureate Herbert Simon has developed a simple but elegant stochastic model for predicting the distribution of city sizes for any country. His model was published in an article in *Biometrika* in 1955. Among major primate cities of the world are Bangkok, Mexico City, Santiago, and Manila. Bangkok is the world's primate city par excellence with an index of primacy of approximately 40. *See also* URBAN INVOLUTION, 174.

Significance   The existence of primate cities reflects the problem of uneven development. Many developing countries have a tendency for major facilities and amenities to be concentrated in a primate city that dominates the society. Given the political power concentrated in primate cities, there is a vested interest in maintaining such dominance rather than adequately spreading development to more remote areas. Many transnational corporations prefer to locate in primate cities because of the amenities and the modern communications and transportation infrastructure, which are usually far superior than in regional towns or areas. Existing primate cities are likely to dominate their nations for decades to come.

Purchasing Power Parity Equivalent (344)

Adjustments made in comparing per capita income between

countries to account for important differences in costs of living. Countries' incomes per capita are usually compared by converting all figures into common U.S. dollar terms, but such comparisons can be highly misleading. Foreign exchange rates are based on goods traded internationally. But a haircut in India cannot be traded and thus has no effect on that nation's exchange rate. Without such adjustments, the income per capita of countries such as Switzerland and Japan tends to be somewhat exaggerated while the income per capita of countries such as India or China appears lower than in reality. The World Bank has developed data to compute purchasing power parity equivalents and to adjust conventional income per capita data.

Significance   The use of adjustments such as purchasing power parity equivalents provides a much more reliable guide to genuine differences in economic welfare and standards of living across countries. The resulting income disparities are somewhat less than they are normally thought to be. Even with such adjustments, it is important to keep in mind that income per capita figures reveal nothing about how income is distributed or whether basic needs are being met for an entire population.

Reductionism (345)

A logical fallacy associated with many discussions of development issues that attributes the lack of development to a single cause or factor. Perhaps the two most common reductionist development arguments are that poor countries are poor because of the climate or because the people are lazy and unmotivated. Some dependency theorists who argue that underdevelopment is caused solely by interconnections with the world capitalistic system are similarly reductionist.

Significance   Reductionism results from oversimplistic thinking that adversely affects social and policy discourse on the problems of developing countries. It is critically important for students and practitioners to recognize the multidimensional and complex interrelated array of factors impinging on development potential.

School Mapping (346)

An analytical technique to facilitate the rational and equitable location of primary and secondary schools in developing countries. The underlying assumption in school mapping, a technique developed at the International Institute for Educational Planning (IIEP) in Paris, is that decisions about school locations should be based primarily on empirical data such as differential demographic projections reflecting genuine need for additional schooling facilities. The school map is thus viewed as an integral part of educational planning and has four major purposes: (1) maximizing the opportunity for children of school age to receive basic educational services, (2) providing for equality of educational opportunity, (3) making educational systems more cost-effective, and (4) providing a data base to reform educational structures and systems. An excellent introduction to the technique of school mapping is provided in *Planning the Location of Schools: An Instrument of Educational Policy* (1977) by Jacques Hallak. *See also* EDUCATIONAL PLANNING, 244.

Significance   School mapping has been introduced in a number of developing countries, such as Sri Lanka, Morocco, Costa Rica, Nepal, Ivory Coast, Uganda, and Thailand. Its introduction has been supported by such international agencies as the World Bank and UNESCO. In the late 1970s Thailand introduced a nationwide school-mapping effort with financial assistance from the World Bank and technical assistance from the IIEP. There are three major obstacles to the implementation of school mapping: (1) the quality of relevant educational and demographic data is sometimes questionable, (2) local authorities may have limited political power over educational decisions in highly centralized educational systems, and (3) political forces and related interest groups may push for irrational decisions, inconsistent with school-mapping data. Despite these difficulties, school mapping encourages improved educational data collection, clearly documents educational disparities, and demonstrates the potential benefits of deconcentration of educational power and greater control in local areas.

Shadow Prices   (347)
Prices that reflect actual market conditions and the genuine opportunity costs of any factor or resource. In many developmental contexts existing prices are artificially too high or too low as a result of administrative rules or other market distortions. Official foreign exchange rates are frequently overvalued, thus making imports of foreign capital and consumer goods less expensive. Such distortions can lead to the use of overly capital-intensive processes and the overconsumption of Western luxury goods. Wage rates artificially higher than productivity can result in excessive unemployment or underemployment. The shadow prices used by development economists and planners are based on the best estimates of genuine supply and demand conditions without distortions.

Significance   The use of shadow prices in development planning and policy-making represents a refinement in economic analysis and a recognition that conventional economic data can be extremely misleading in certain developmental contexts. The major difficulty, however, is in determining proper and correct shadow prices. Public policies can be introduced to reduce market distortions and increase the convergence of shadow and actual prices. The realistic valuing of foreign exchange would be an example.

Social Impact Analysis (SIA)   (348)

The careful assessment of the effects of development projects on various groups in society. For example, the introduction of a new cash crop in an agricultural community might contribute to the foreign exchange earnings of a country, but have an adverse social impact in that the nutritional status of children might decline significantly as the result of a shift away from subsistence farming to the new cash crop. The systematic study of the impact of such a project on the nutritional status of rural children would be a SIA type of analysis. Similarly, new irrigation projects might lead to increased political and economic competition for new water resources and a decline in social harmony. Unfortunately, there are few well-documented longitudinal studies of the social impact of development projects. A volume edited by William Derman and Scott Whiteford of Michigan State University, *Social Impact Analysis and Development Planning in the Third World* (1985), provides examples of SIA in such countries as Costa Rica, Mexico, Nepal, Nigeria, Nicaragua, and Mozambique.

Significance   Social impact analysis implies a more participative approach to development in which those affected are provided an opportunity to express their views on projects being undertaken or proposed. Too often development projects are assessed only in terms of their macroeconomic aspects and their contribution to such outcomes as economic growth, export earnings, and shifts in economic structure. Their social impact is often ignored. With rapid changes in technology affecting many Third World nations the need increases to assess systematically and rigorously the social impact of these new technologies. To assess genuine social impact, interdisciplinary approaches are essential since development projects involve diverse dimensions. Applied anthropologists and cultural sociologists are often invited to participate in SIA. The actual amount of funds spent on SIA is minimal, relative to the aggregate costs of large-scale development projects.

Terms of Trade (349)

An analytical tool that uses the prices of a nation's imports relative to the prices it receives for its exports. Mathematically, this can be expressed simply as P^x/P^m, where P^x = an index for export prices and P^m = an index for import prices, for the same time period. If P^m increases relative to P^x, a country's terms of trade have deteriorated. Historically, the prices of manufactured goods have tended to increase relative to the prices of primary commodities such as sugar, rubber, and tin. Since many developing countries have traditionally exported for the most part primary commodities and imported manufactured goods such as cars and machines, over time many of these countries have experienced deteriorating terms of trade. The concept can also be applied internally to a developing country by comparing the prices of urban goods, P^u, relative to the prices of goods from rural areas, P^r. If P^u increases relative to P^r, the terms of trade are turning against the rural sector. Thus, trends in the P^u/P^r ratio often follow similar patterns to the P^x/P^m ratio since primary commodities are often produced in rural areas and urban areas tend to be the sites for most manufacturing operations. *See also* COMMODITY AGREEMENTS, 131.

Significance   Terms of trade is an important economic indicator. With a persisting deterioration of the terms of trade, a nation must export more and more to pay for a given amount of imports. Or alternatively, a rural sector must export more and more to pay for its imports from urban areas. There are several alternative approaches to dealing with the terms of trade problem. First, groups of countries producing certain commodities have organized to form international commodity agreements for such commodities as oil, tin, coffee, sugar, and tea. Such agreements, which may set specific production limits, help to stabilize commodity prices. Second, various developing countries are attempting to diversify their economies to reduce dependence on the export of only one or a few primary commodities. More diversified economies should generally be able to achieve better terms of trade, since the proportion of exports of primary commodities will decline.

Theil's Index (350)

A measure of inequality based on information theory. It is a measure of dispersion defined mathematically as $T = (1/N\Sigma x_i \log x_i \ \mu \log \mu)/\mu$ where T = Theil's Index; N = number of items in the sample; x_i equals the values of the items, the inequality of which is being measured; $\log x_i$ = the natural logarithm of those values; and μ = the mean of those values (Allison 1978: 867). The higher the value of Theil's Index, the greater the inequality. *See also* COEFFICIENT OF VARIATION, 314; GINI COEFFICIENT, 325; KUZNETS INDEX, 331; LOG VARIANCE, 334.

Significance Theil's Index is a scale-invariant measure. Thus, it can be used to compare the inequality of different types of factors such as energy consumption and land distribution. Unlike log variance, this measure can be used when values of zero occur in a distribution. Theil's Index also meets the criterion of transfers, that is, when funds are shifted from richer to poorer segments, T always decreases. In fact, the lower the level of incomes, the more sensitive T is to transfers. Thus, this is a highly desirable property with respect to measuring inequality of wealth or income that has diminishing marginal utility. Though Theil's Index is more complicated to calculate than either log variance or the coefficient of variation, it has several important advantages over those two measures when measuring the inequality of income or wealth.

Time Preference (351)
An orientation concerning the benefits or costs that may accrue in future time periods. Individuals and societies vary markedly in their time preferences. Time preference affects the social rate of discount used in computing the present value of future costs and benefits. Present-oriented individuals or societies discount the future highly, while future-oriented individuals or societies place a high value on such periods and show great concern for future generations. *See also* COST-BENEFIT ANALYSIS, 315.

Significance Though this is a technical economic concept relevant to cost-benefit analysis, time preference reflects important, basic values highly related to long-term development prospects. Individuals and societies concerned with the preservation of forests around the world, for example, have a strong future-oriented time preference, while those interested primarily in short-term financial gains from maximum cutting obviously have a time preference for the present. Longer-term time preferences are central to the notion of sustainable development and concerns for the quality of life of future generations.

Total Fertility Rate (TFR) (352)

A demographic measure that indicates the average number of children a woman in a given country will bear during her reproductive years. Its meaning is clear and simple. If the TFR is 6.3, an average female bears 6.3 children. If the TFR is 2.0, an average female bears 2.0 children, and such a society is basically reproducing itself. Actually a population with a TFR of 2.0 would eventually decline since not all females born survive to the end of their childbearing period and because slightly more than half of babies born are male (Bogue 1969: 659). In 1988, Kenya had a TFR of 8.1; India, 4.3; Mexico, 3.5; Indonesia, 3.2; and China, 2.4. *See also* LIFE TABLE, 332; NET REPRODUCTION RATE, 340.

Significance The TFR is considered the best single cross-sectional measure of fertility, that is, one based on a single year as compared to long-term data over time. Unlike the net reproduction rate, this measure is independent of mortality rates. Demographers generally argue that it is the most sensitive yet most meaningful way to measure fertility (Bogue 1969: 659).

Tracer Study (353)

An approach to educational evaluation that emphasizes the rigorous follow-up of school graduates. As a tool for use in educational planning, it is an alternative to more conventional rate-of-return analysis or the social demand requirements approach to educational planning. In tracer studies the basic objective is to ascertain how many graduates of an educational unit are employed, how long it took them to gain employment, whether they are under- or overemployed in terms of their educational background, and how their previous education relates to their current employment. Data from such tracer studies are then used to inform policy decisions concerning the allocation and distribution of limited educational resources. Tracer studies can lead to the closure of educational institutions whose graduates appear unneeded or underutilized. *See also* MANPOWER PLANNING, 251.

Significance Tracer studies may be considered highly threatening by some educational administrators. Without rigorous tracer studies, however, it is difficult to evaluate the relative quality of educational institutions and sectors. The Republic of Singapore has effectively utilized tracer studies to inform educational policy-making. Tracer studies are easiest to implement in such microstates since most graduates remain in close proximity to their training sites. In large countries such as Brazil or Indonesia, these studies are much more difficult to implement. Tracer studies represent a valuable tool for educational planners and policymakers who are open to major budget shifts and reallocations. Those opposed to tracer studies argue that educational policies and decision making should not be driven by labor market conditions, which are subject to change over time.

4. Development Movements, Projects, and Organizations

A. Movements and Projects

Asia-Pacific Program of Education for All (APPEAL) (354)
A basic education program adopted by the Fifth Regional Conference of Ministers of Education and those responsible for economic planning in Asia. Launched by the director general of UNESCO in February 1987, the program includes three principal components: (1) the eradication of illiteracy, (2) the universalization of primary education, and (3) provisions for developing continuing education programs. The first two goals are to be completed by the year 2000. Three key assumptions also underlie the program, namely: (1) democratization of educational opportunity, (2) interdependence between literacy and primary education, and (3) the importance of continuing education. By December 1987, 16 Asia-Pacific countries had started to implement APPEAL, among them India, China, Iran, the Philippines, Thailand, Pakistan, Bangladesh, and Indonesia. Among nongovernmental organizations (NGOs) involved in the program are the Bangladesh Council for Mass Education, the Chinese Peasant Association and Science and Technology Association, the National Youth Congress of Indonesia, and the National Farmers' Guide Movement of Pakistan.

Significance Despite the economic success of a number of Asia-Pacific countries, 75 percent of the world's illiterate population is in Asia. The goal of the 1960 Karachi Plan to provide free and compulsory primary education by the year 1980 has not been achieved. It is estimated that more than 125 million children in Asia fail to complete the minimal four years of primary education. Thus, APPEAL is a timely and needed program. Of special import is its emphasis on providing basic educational opportunities to women and

321

disadvantaged minorities. APPEAL's stress on the interdependence of formal and nonformal education is also highly appropriate. APPEAL recognizes the importance of literacy as a "potent form of consciousness." The successful completion of the APPEAL program would show the relevance of UNESCO and its international efforts as well as the potential for creative regional cooperation in the promotion of human resource development.

Aswan High Dam Project (355)

The physical centerpiece of Egypt's development program. The World Bank and U.S. aid agencies began discussion of the Nile dam project in the 1950s. By 1955, technical reviews and financial negotiations were begun. However, after the United States and Great Britain rebuffed Nasser by withdrawing offers of financial support in 1956, the Egyptian leader made plans to finance the construction with funds from the newly nationalized Suez Canal. When the United States and Egypt broke diplomatic relations in 1957, Nasser sought funding from the Soviet Union and construction was begun in 1960. The dam at Aswan was finished in 1967 and became the leading symbol of Soviet aid to the Third World. The high dam project was designed to increase agricultural production and electrical generating capacity to meet the needs of a nation whose population had doubled in the first half of this century. By 1950, Egypt had a population of 20 million, crowded in the delta region and along the banks of the Nile. The dam was to control flooding and increase the amount of irrigable land. In addition, the new source of electricity would be used in fertilizer production. All of these anticipated benefits were central to Egypt's national development plan.

Significance The high dam project met most of the basic goals as set forth by its planners, and it remains central to Egypt's economy and development. Unfortunately from a development perspective, no comprehensive study of the social and physical impacts of the dam was carried out. Further, it is difficult to speculate what conditions Egypt would be facing today had the dam not been built. While the benefits of the project were expected, a number of detrimental results did not seem to be anticipated, such as changes in water quality and the rate of silting in the reservoir, which threatens to render the dam dysfunctional within several decades. Ironically, the lack of silt downstream is the source of ongoing problems. For example, the brick-making industry suffers from a lack of silt. Agricultural land, once flooded and regenerated annually by the Nile, is now farmed more intensely, but productivity depends on artificial fertilizers and controlled irrigation. The result has been decreasing soil fertility and salinization. The once prosperous river-fishing industry is also now in shambles. In retrospect, the Aswan high dam project, along with similar major dam projects, raises serious questions of sustainability. The project illustrates the many environmental and development trade-offs involved in large-scale infrastructure projects and the difficulty of weighing immediate national needs against less well-defined future considerations. The Aswan dam symbolizes centralized planning on a massive scale and, some would say, a futile attempt to control nature. Partly as a result of the lessons of Aswan, large dam projects are meeting growing resistance throughout the developing world.

BRIDGES (Basic Research and Implementation in (356) Developing Education Systems)

A collaborative group project including educators, researchers, planners, and policymakers committed to improving opportunity and quality in Third World schools. "The goal of their collaborative effort is to identify policy options that will increase children's access to schooling, reduce the frequency of early school leaving and repetition, improve the amount and quality of what is learned, and optimize the use of fiscal and educational resources." This project is directed by the Harvard Institute for International Development (HIID) and the Harvard Graduate School of Education with major grant funding from the Office of Education, Bureau for Science and Technology, U.S. Agency for International Development (AID). Collaborating institutions are the Academy for Educational Planning and Management, Pakistan; Centre de Perfectionnement et de Formation en Cours d'Emploi; Institute for International Research (IIR); Michigan State University; the Open University, Indonesia; Research Triangle Institute in North Carolina; Texas Southern University; National Education Commission (NEC) of Thailand; National Institute of Education, Sri Lanka; and AID Missions and Ministries of Education in Burundi, Egypt, Indonesia, North Yemen, Pakistan, Sri Lanka, and Thailand. The project publishes *The BRIDGES Research Report Series*, which includes state-of-the-art reviews of key policy questions related to basic education in developing countries. The project also publishes education development discussion papers. The publications of the BRIDGES project often synthesize extensive international research related to a specific educational policy question such as access to basic schooling.

Significance   The BRIDGES project is an interesting example of collaborative policy research among U.S. and Third World institutions. Given its focus on basic education, it is responsive to concerns that AID should focus on the needs of the poorer segments of developing countries. Given that AID is no longer a major donor, its support of research projects of this type is designed to leverage massive sums spent on education by major donors such as the World Bank and Japan and by Third World governments themselves. The success of the BRIDGES project is dependent on two factors: the extent to which the various policy research studies are utilized, and the extent to which the project enhances and strengthens Third World capacities to carry out effective policy research related to basic education.

Caribbean Basin Initiative (CBI) (357)

A regional project initiated by the Reagan administration in 1983 to promote both free trade and free enterprise as mechanisms to enhance economic development in Caribbean nations. Among the 22 participating nations are Costa Rica, the Dominican Republic, Jamaica, Honduras, and Haiti. A central idea underlying the project is the proposal to provide duty-free access to U.S. markets as a way to raise incomes in the Caribbean region.

Significance This project is responsive to the call made several decades ago by the UN Conference on Trade and Development (UNCTAD) to emphasize trade, not aid, as the best way to promote indigenous economic development. Success of the project to date has been mixed. Many Caribbean economic leaders are disappointed that U.S. trade barriers persist, particularly in industries such as sugar and textiles that have strong U.S. political lobbies. Officials of AID are frustrated by the often too-protectionist acts passed by Congress that adversely affect this important initiative. Nevertheless, there are some tangible signs of success since CBI was launched. For example, nontraditional agricultural crops have quadrupled in Costa Rica, jobs in the Dominican Republic's free-trade zone have quadrupled, and U.S. nonoil imports have increased 27 percent since the program was initiated. However, it is impossible to state in definitive terms that these results were derived directly from the CBI.

Chipko Movement (358)

Literally meaning hugging, a grassroots environmental movement to foster preservation and conservation of India's forests. The Chipko movement is heavily influenced by Buddhist, Gandhian, and Sarvodayan thinking. Its major supporters and participants are rural women in the area of Uttarakhand in the Himalayan area of India. The term *Chipko* was popularized through the folk songs of Chipko activist Ghanshyam Sailani. The major demands of the movement were to replace the contract system of forest exploitation with forest-labor cooperatives, and to provide raw materials at concessional rates to local forest-based industries. Another demand was to ban the felling of trees in particularly sensitive areas. To push their demands, the movement used nonviolent marching on foot. Crucial to the spread of the movement was a 4,870-kilometer trans-Himalayan march in 1981–1983 by Sunderlal Bahuguna, a Gandhian activist and philosopher. Critics of the Chipko activists called them enemies of science, democracy, and development. As a reflection of their success in communicating their message, in a 1981 resolution the Indian Science Congress indicated support for the Chipko movement and recommended its expansion to all parts of India. In 1980, Prime Minister Indira Gandhi met with representatives of Chipko to discuss their demands. The movement ultimately led to a government-imposed ten-year ban on cutting trees in a sensitive area of 1,200 square kilometers. The Chipko movement emphasizes both sustainable development and decentralized production of soft energy paths, such as solar, wind, human and animal, biogas, and water. Dinesh Lakhanpaul's film *Chipko Andolan* (*Go and Hug a Tree*) provides an overview of the origins of the movement and its impact. *See also* APPROPRIATE TECHNOLOGY, 276; NONGOVERNMENTAL ORGANIZATIONS, 295; SUSTAINABLE DEVELOPMENT, 272.

Significance   Many consider Chipko to be one of the most effective grassroots environmental movements that has emerged in developing countries following the United Nations World Conference on the Human Environment held in Stockholm in 1972. Martin Haigh of Oxford Polytechnic considers the Chipko movement "the Third World's most celebrated indigenous non-government, non-urban environmental protection group" (Haigh 1988:99). The movement was instrumental in India's passing a Conservation of Forests Act in 1980 and has influenced India's Planning Commission's Working Group of Hill Areas Development for the Seventh Five-Year Plan. The philosophy of the movement emphasizes that global survival depends on the creative integration of Eastern wisdom and Western technology. The Canadian grand old man of trees, Richard St. Barbe Baker, was deeply impressed with the Chipko movement and stated:

> The only promising movement in the world is Chipko movement. These brave women say kill not our trees. These trees give us air to breathe, water to drink and food to eat. We need them for our survival.

325

Eastern Seaboard Project (359)

A Thai project designed to facilitate the spread of development away from the capital of Bangkok south and southeast to the eastern seaboard. The discovery of extensive natural gas and oil resources in the Gulf of Siam was the catalyst for this project. The infrastructure for developing and processing these resources has been established in the eastern seaboard area, where development is being financed by a combination of local and international resources. The eastern seaboard, where Pattaya, "the Acapulco of Southeast Asia," is located, has considerable tourist potential. A deep seaport has been built to facilitate development and commercial activities.

Significance Given that Bangkok is both sinking and hyperurbanized, the Eastern Seaboard Project is of special help in facilitating the spread of development beyond the capital. Despite the project, many new factories and companies continue to locate in the Bangkok metropolitan area because of its communications and government infrastructure and ready availability of migrant labor. The Eastern Seaboard Project has been criticized for being too capital-intensive and creating too little employment for the large investment sums involved. Despite these criticisms, the Eastern Seaboard Project reflects Thailand's role as an emerging newly industrialized country (NIC). The project is providing new technologies and training, and facilitating economic diversification through the production of many by-products made possible by the petrochemical industry. With this project in place, the Southeast of Thailand is certainly a major new pole of development that is likely to attract new capital and labor.

Food for Peace (360)

Also known as the P.L. (Public Law) 480 Program, a U.S. foreign aid program involving the dispensation of surplus agricultural commodities. The program, championed by the late Sen. Hubert Humphrey of Minnesota, was initiated by Congress in 1954 and soon became a central part of the U.S. aid program. The act authorized the purchase of massive quantities of foodstuffs, primarily surplus grain, and subsidized their sale to developing countries. The purposes of the program, which is still in existence, are to dispose of surplus U.S. agricultural commodities, to provide humanitarian food aid to needy Third World people, and to promote international economic development. It is assumed that cheaper grain frees money to be reinvested into the national economy of recipient countries. In addition, the program promotes the expansion of U.S. agricultural and commercial export markets and can be used to help stabilize commodity prices. In addition to direct sales of foodstuffs, Food for Peace is used for famine relief, school food programs, maternal and child health programs, and food-for-work programs. Often these distribution and related programs are administered by U.S. private voluntary agencies such as CARE. *See also* FOREIGN AID, 285.

Significance   In the early 1960s, at the height of the Food for Peace Program, P.L. 480 grains accounted for over 45 percent of total U.S. agricultural exports. Since that time U.S. agricultural exports have increased sevenfold in monetary value and P.L. 480 has diminished in importance. The program was clearly successful in achieving the objectives of export expansion and food surplus reduction. The agricultural commodities also helped feed millions of hungry people, most obviously when used in emergency relief which actually accounts for only a small percentage of Food for Peace. The program's long-term effects on development are mixed. In many cases the subsidized food undercut prices paid to local farmers, a strong disincentive for food production and a catalyst for rural-urban migration. Ironically, it was discovered that food aid could actually lead to food shortages by diminishing local incentives. Study of such unintended results has led to a growing sophistication in our understanding of the role of food aid as a tool for development.

Great Leap Forward   (361)

Mao Zedong's ambitious plan to speed the People's Republic of China along the path of economic development and socialism. The Great Leap Forward was initiated in 1958, lost most of its momentum the following year, and was officially ended in 1961. In economic terms, the Great Leap Forward aimed at an annual economic growth rate of 25 percent. The central feature of the plan was the creation of large rural communes comprised of existing cooperatives and involving 98 percent of the rural population. The communes, which were to function as political, social, and economic units, initially averaged 25,000 people. They in turn were divided into production brigades and smaller teams. When it soon became clear that the communes were too large, they were divided into 74,000 units. Premised on decentralization, the Great Leap Forward also involved similar reorganization in cities but to a lesser extent. The central government maintained direction over heavy industry, but even steel production was attempted, unsuccessfully, in small local units. In all, 80 percent of enterprises were decentralized. Mass participation was the cornerstone of what Mao envisioned as both a political and economic leap. He set aside the Soviet-style gradual five-year plan, believing that ideology could be the driving force behind unprecedented advances in production and economic development. *See also* DECENTRALIZATION, 199; MAO ZEDONG, 82.

Significance   In political terms, the Great Leap Forward more or less accomplished its goals. Mao's populist ideology took form as the masses were mobilized for change through a renewed revolutionary spirit. The movement also encouraged technological innovation at the local level which, though often unsuccessful, provided valuable lessons. The plan no doubt enhanced the nation's sense of self-reliance even though it could not be deemed an economic success by any means. The record in agricultural production was especially poor in comparison to the highly elevated expectations brought on by the campaign. Actual production figures were so overly inflated that by 1960 the government ceased keeping records. Eventually the disappointing economic results of the Great Leap Forward began to undermine some of Mao's support.

Greening of the Northeast   **(362)**
A major five-year development project launched in March 1987 by the Thai government to improve economic and environmental conditions in Thailand's impoverished Northeast. The project is formally known as the King's Royal Compassion Project for the Development of the Northeast. The Northeast is also plagued by uneven rainfall and long periods of drought. The project, suggested by Thailand's monarch, His Majesty King Bhumipol Adulyarej, calls for cooperation among the military, the universities, government development agencies, the private sector, and interested international donors to create programs to improve the quality of life in the Northeast. With peace in Southeast Asia, it was thought that the Thai military had underutilized manpower, matériel, and equipment that could be used for rural development purposes, such as the digging of fish ponds and small-scale irrigation ditches. General Chavalit Yongchaiyudh, former commander of the Thai army and former minister of defense, has been a major proponent and architect of the Greening of the Northeast project.

Significance   The Greening of the Northeast boldly attempts to deal directly with the problem of uneven development. Its consortial nature is also unusual and it will be interesting to see how effectively the military, universities, government agencies, private sector, and international donors can cooperate to achieve the goals of the project. Major concerns thus far seem to focus on the extent to which financial resources have been committed to the project and delays in implementing project plans. Some cynical critics argue that "green" refers not to forests but to military uniforms, implying that the military is dominating the project. It provides a fascinating laboratory to see to what extent the military can be used for genuine development purposes. There is also the question of whether five years is an adequate time frame to deal with the deep and serious problems of the Northeast. The extent to which this project succeeds may be of interest to other developing countries with similar serious problems of uneven development, such as Brazil with its arid and impoverished Northeast.

Harambee (363)

The self-help movement in Kenya. The word literally means "pull together" and is derived from a Swahili work chant used to rally workers in the coastal regions of Kenya. Its roots are in the Mau Mau uprising against the British when women formed groups to cope with the absence of the men. Jomo Kenyatta, first president of Kenya, introduced the work chant into the political arena to emphasize working together in the spirit of national unity. Later the word became a motto of African youth throughout the continent as nations fought for independence. *See also* ELVINA MUTUA, 88.

Significance Kenya today has a great number of grassroots self-help groups, many of them outgrowths of the Harambee movement. For example, estimates of the number of women's cooperatives range from 16,000 to 25,000. As was true during the struggle for independence, women are the major proponents and participants in harambee. The movement, which began in 1963, now contributes nearly one-third of all labor, materials, and finances invested in rural development in Kenya.

Information Network Referral Service (INRES-South) (364)

A special information-referral service mandated by the 1978 Buenos Aires Plan of Action for Promoting and Implementing Technical Cooperation among Developing Countries (TCDC). Its purpose is to match "specific developing country needs with developing country abilities to provide training and expertise" (Seligman 1988b:18). This information service is a special office within the Special Unit for TCDC at the UN Development Program (UNDP). Initially in 1978 INRES produced a trilingual (English, French, and Spanish) directory of relevant developing-country institutions. The system was computerized in 1985 and was renamed INRES-South in late 1987. To facilitate decentralization, microcomputer technology was utilized. Since 1986, there has been an emphasis on including information about actual work capabilities and related track records. INRES-South currently contains trilingual information on more than 40,000 training, expertise, and research and development capacities of institutions in developing countries. There are also descriptions of over 4,000 completed development projects. With the use of 22,000 key words and over 4,000 terms, various computer searches can be carried out.

Significance   The noble ideal of technical cooperation among developing countries is rather meaningless without information about the capabilities and expertise available in other developing countries. Thus, INRES-South is integral to the process of TCDC. As modern computer and telecommunications links among developing countries improve, the ease of accessing INRES-South will greatly improve. Though INRES-South is a necessary element in TCDC, it is not sufficient. Resources must be made available to be able to utilize the vast amount of existing expertise. INRES-South can also benefit developed nations that need expertise from the South. For example, in areas such as traditional medicine, new agricultural varieties, new vaccines, and special crystals related to laser technology, the South has important expertise to share.

"Look East"   (365)
A motto popularized in Malaysia and Singapore in the 1980s to stimulate a rethinking of development strategies and models. The underlying idea is that developing countries should look to countries of the East like Japan and South Korea as models for development rather than to the West. For example, Singapore has issued postage stamps extolling the virtues of quality control and quality control circles, popular concepts associated with Japanese economic dynamism. The preference for Eastern models of development is based on a Confucian philosophy frequently articulated by Singapore's leader, Lee Kwan Yew, which emphasizes a strong family, social and community solidarity, a drug-free environment, and the absence of social deviance as reflected in Western counterculture.

Significance   "Look East" attitudes toward the Japanese and their model of development tend to migrate over time from feelings of resentment for Japan's economic success to fashionable imitation of Japanese models and approaches. Those at higher levels of policy who promote a "Look East" philosophy fear the levels of discord and conflict associated with Western development and a highly open political process. Given the tragic events of June 1989 in China, the "Look East" motto has been tarnished, though from the beginning the focus has been on Japan and South Korea as exemplary cases of development. The "Look East" motto was not meant to imply that countries should merely imitate the past experiences of Japan and South Korea. Instead the notion was that these countries offered more relevant models of development that other nations could adapt for local use.

Mekong Project (366)

A project designed to develop the water and related resources of the Lower Mekong Basin in mainland Southeast Asia. Initiated in 1957 by ECAFE, the UN Economic Commission for Asia and the Far East (now known as ESCAP), the project is directed by the Committee for Coordination of Investigations of the Lower Mekong Basin (the Mekong Coordinating Committee), which has its headquarters in Bangkok, Thailand. The Lower Mekong Basin covers approximately 650,000 square kilometers of Thailand, Laos, Cambodia, and Vietnam. The Mekong River, flowing from its origins in China to the South China Sea in Vietnam, forms much of the political boundary between Laos and Thailand. As originally envisioned the Mekong Project was to provide improved flood control, a new and major source of hydroelectric power, and water for irrigating the relatively arid areas of the Lower Mekong Basin. The ideal outcome of this project is the greening of the Lower Mekong Basin.

Significance   The persistence of the Mekong Project despite the political turmoil in the Lower Mekong Basin demonstrates the power of international and mutlilateral cooperation for humanistic development. Because of the political turmoil that has affected Vietnam and Cambodia, and as a result of growing skepticism concerning the efficacy of large-scale dam projects, the goals of the Mekong Project have been only partially realized. Within the riparian countries of Southeast Asia, awareness has grown that large-scale and expensive dam projects would lead to the irrigation of only a small portion of the arid areas of the basin. The unanticipated costs of such projects in terms of relocation of farmers and water-borne diseases are also increasingly recognized. On the positive side, the tremendous hydroelectric potential of the Mekong may lessen the need for alternative sources of nonrenewable and harder energy sources such as nuclear power and oil. In March 1987, Thailand launched a Greening of the

Northeast Project, which covers the Thai portions of the Lower Mekong Basin. It will be interesting to follow the relationship between these two projects and to see to what extent the Thai project will learn from the experience of the international project.

Naam Movement (367)

A highly successful West African village or peasant cooperative movement. It was established in 1967 by Bernard Ledea Ouedraogo in Yatenga, Burkino Faso. Ouedraogo's philosophy, and the motto of the movement, is "to make the village responsible for its own development, developing without destroying, starting with the peasants." All programs are conceived, carried out, and managed by villagers. Projects build on traditional Mossi concepts and technology and use low-cost tools and materials. Technical experts are used only as trainers. Projects include the digging of wells, dam construction, aforestation, and gardening. Successful techniques and projects are promoted by visitation and exchanges. Practical training is carried out by workplace schools or on-site instruction. There are now over 2,500 Naam groups in seven federations in Senegal, Mauritania, Mali, Niger, and Togo. An outgrowth of the Naam movement, or a supplement to it, is the Six-S Association. The French name is *Se Servir de la Saison Seche en Savanne et au Sahel* (using of the dry season in the savanna and the Sahel). Set up by Ouedraogo in 1976 as an umbrella organization to provide technical and financial assistance to the Naam groups, Six-S raises international funds to purchase medicine, cement, pumps, and hand tools. The funds are also dispersed to groups as trust aid loans with the only stipulation that the loan be paid back with interest once the project pays off. *See also* BERNARD LEDEA OUEDRAOGO, 92; NONGOVERNMENTAL ORGANIZATIONS, 295.

Significance The Naam movement and the Six-S Association represent important models of development and development associations for Africa and other parts of the Third World. In this efficient and effective bottom-up program, much of what was once attempted by international development agencies and government programs is now being initiated and carried out by villagers. In this scenario, international agencies serve as liaisons and providers of technical and financial support. There has been a remarkable spontaneous growth of peasant organizations in Africa since the early 1970s, a result of persistent poverty and growing environmental problems (*see* Harrison, 1987). The Naam movement is one of the most successful and dynamic of such groups. It has helped raise the quality of life of thousands in Burkino Faso, ranked by most indicators as one of the poorest countries in the world, and become an excellent example of the possibilities of peasant initiatives for their own development. The Naam movement has expanded upon Oxfam's stone-contour conservation project by researching and promoting more efficient three-stone fires. Its integration of modern and traditional health care has influenced government health-care programs. The Naam movement has served as a model for similar organizations throughout West Africa. Most importantly, it serves thousands of citizens in their attempts to improve their quality of life.

National Bamboo Project (368)

A major development project with presidential priority in Costa Rica that emphasizes the use of bamboo as construction material for new housing. The idea underlying the project was developed in 1980 in a thesis by a Costa Rican architecture student, Ana Cecilia Chaves. Because of shortages of adequate housing and rapid deforestation, this project was particularly relevant to Costa Rica. Bamboo housing, common in countries such as Japan and China, has the advantage of costing only one-third the cost of a cement block house. Bamboo can be planted and harvested in five years with little work. *See also* APPROPRIATE TECHNOLOGY, 276.

Significance Since housing is one of mankind's basic human needs and since wooden housing ordinarily may contribute to deforestation, the National Bamboo Project has implications that extend well beyond Costa Rica. This project is an excellent example of both appropriate technology and technical cooperation among developing countries (TCDC). International consultants from Colombia have played an important role in the project. Its $7 million financing reflects creative cooperation among bilateral aid (the government of the Netherlands), a regional development bank (the Central American Bank for Economic Integration), and a multilateral international agency (UNDP). Central to the project is a critical training program organized by the Technological Institute of Costa Rica. This project has potential relevance to helping solve major housing crises in many developing areas.

Ngun Pan Project (369)

A development project introduced in Thailand following the student revolution of 1973. Ngun Pan literally means "to pass the money down." The project was developed by the Social Action party (SAP), which was particularly prominent in the period after the student uprising, which led to the restoration of democratic rule in Thailand. The project was a response to criticisms that Thailand's development program was overly centralized with too little decision making at the local level. Under the project, the tambol councils of Thailand were given lump sum grants to spend as they wished for local development projects. Considerable funds are spent for local labor to provide an income supplement to rural farmers during the dry season when they are unemployed or underemployed. The tambol in Thailand is a sub-district geographic-administrative designation that constitutes a group of villages. Members of the tambol council are elected by villagers in the region. Prior to the implementation of this project the tambol council had little power and primarily was a mechanism for providing top-down information and instructions from the government.

Significance Many developing countries have highly centralized administrative systems with relatively little delegation of authority to local communities. The Ngun Pan Project represents an experiment in the decentralization of power. Though the project appears to have disrupted social harmony at the village level by introducing opportunities for conflicts over the expenditure of grant funds, it gave local people an opportunity to participate in deciding upon development projects relevant to their genuine needs. Overall, it appears that many useful and valuable local projects resulted. Some were even named after Prime Minister M. R. Kukrit Pramoj, who was leader of the Social Action Party when this program was introduced. Subsequent governments have continued the project with some modifications. Now tambols with greater developmental needs are eligible to receive more funds. The current emphasis of the program is on the creation of rural jobs during the arid season. This program contrasts with the well-known Saemaul Undong project in South Korea in that Thailand's rural participants are not volunteers, but are actually paid for their development work.

Nicaraguan National Literacy Crusade (370)

The impressive basic literacy campaign of revolutionary Nicaragua. The crusade, known as *Cruzada Nacional de Alfabetizacion*, took place from March to August 1980, involved 100,000 volunteers, and brought literacy to nearly half a million citizens. The estimated cost of $25 million was covered entirely by international donations. The initial goal of the campaign, begun just seven months after the fall of Somoza, was to bring half the population to third-grade levels of literacy. In fact, Nicaragua's so-called second war of liberation reduced the national illiteracy rate from 50 percent (approximately 75 percent in rural areas) to under 15 percent. Literacy rates were determined and confirmed by the ability to pass a five-part test involving reading and writing exercises and a comprehension section. The majority (65,000) of the *brigadistas* were Nicaraguan youths who made up the Popular Literacy Army. They spread throughout the country, working alongside campesinos by day and holding classes at night. The remainder of the volunteers, the Popular Literacy Teachers, were literate workers and professionals who worked in barrios and areas near their homes. The volunteers were trained through a pyramid program that started with 80 trainees who in turn trained 560 instructors. Eventually 100,000 volunteers had been given pedagogical instruction based in part on the innovative and politically oriented methods of Paolo Freire. The Nicaraguans were joined by international volunteers including 1,200 from Cuba. The campaign was followed by adult classes given in education collectives by 10,000 instructors. *See also* LITERACY, 249; PAOLO FREIRE, 16.

Significance   The National Literacy Campaign was perhaps the most successful basic literacy campaign ever undertaken. It was unusual not only its scope and success, but in that it was carried out without any Nicaraguan government funds. Support was broad-based within Nicaragua, as demonstrated by the number of volunteers and the participation of all sectors of society. The campaign eventually became multilingual to meet the demands of speakers of English, Rama, Miskito, and Sumu on the Atlantic coast. International support was also broad-based. The crusade received financial and personnel assistance from private agencies such as Church World Service and from governments led by Sweden, Switzerland, the Netherlands, and the United States. An additional $10 million was raised through the sale of Patriotic Literacy Bonds. The success of the crusade cannot be fully expressed in quantitative terms alone. To the Nicaraguans, the crusade symbolized justice and equitable development. It helped create an immediate sense of accomplishment in the impoverished nation and undoubtedly a new sense of dignity and empowerment among previously illiterate campesinos. The experience of working with campesinos also had a profound effect on brigades of young volunteers, most of whom were of urban origins. Finally, the campaign clearly had political ramifications and helped solidify the position of the Sandinistas. The political content of the instructional material drew criticism locally and internationally. The crusaders responded that all education has political ramifications, whether to justify existing systems or to promote new ones.

Project Camelot (371)

A highly controversial applied social science research project launched in 1964 by the United States Army to determine the social and political factors underlying potential for internal war in developing countries. The objective of Project Camelot was "to determine the feasibility of developing a general social systems model which would make it possible to predict and influence politically significant aspects of social change in the developing nations of the world" (Galtung cited in Horowitz 1967:281). With a project budget of $6 million for three to four years, the army hoped to involve leading U.S. social scientists in the project. The contract was awarded to the Special Operations Research Office (SORO) of the American University. Dr. Hugo Nuttini, a professor at the University of Pittsburgh and an ex-Chilean, was asked to explore the possibility of Chile being a site for Project Camelot. Johan Galtung, a Norwegian social scientist teaching at the Latin American Faculty of Social Science (FLASCO) in Chile, was invited to participate in a conference to discuss the preliminary design of the project to assess internal war potential. Galtung not only refused to participate, but provided copies of project documents to Chilean colleagues who in turn shared the information with the Chilean Senate and the left-wing Chilean press. As a result, tremendous political pressure against the project developed, leading to its cancellation.

Significance Project Camelot has implications that extend far beyond Chile and the proposed social science research design involved. The project reflects major ethical dilemmas related to the role of the social scientist in relationship to government and the military. It raises fundamental issues regarding "hired guns" and "research prostitution." Another question is the relationship of the "pen to the sword" and "speaking truth to power" (Wildavsky, 1979). Project Camelot was cancelled in Chile, but was it implemented more quietly and secretively elsewhere in places such as Guatemala, Thailand, and the Philippines? Another complex question is whether such military-sponsored research contributes to or defuses potential for political violence. Given that the U.S. State Department in Chile had no prior knowledge of Project Camelot and found it a great embarrassment, the project also raises fundamental questions about the coordination of U.S. foreign policy in developing countries.

Saemaul Undong (372)

A Korean term meaning new community movement, referring to a rural development program initiated in 1970 by President Park

Chung-hee. Before 1970, Korea's national development plans had emphasized industrialization in urban areas. As a result the income gap between rural and urban areas widened. To redress such imbalances and achieve more balanced economic growth, Saemaul Undong was launched as a comprehensive rural community-development program. The spirit of self-help, diligence, and mutual cooperation were integral to the movement. Villagers provided free labor for projects, while the government provided materials and technical assistance. The poorest villages received the highest priority for such assistance. Thus, instead of allocating resources equally among rural areas, there was an attempt to distribute them equitably, based upon needs and performance in use of assistance received.

Significance   There are two unique aspects of the Saemaul Undong movement. First, unlike integrated rural development plans, Saemaul Undong began without a well-defined formal or theoretical framework. Second, the movement is purely Korean, with key principals and terms of Korean origin. This movement has achieved international recognition as an innovative program that had a significant impact in reducing urban-rural disparities. Development planners from around the world have visited Korea to observe the program. Korea's low levels of income inequality relative to other developing countries suggest the program's success. Apart from its direct economic impact, the program has also had substantial social benefits, leading to reductions in alcoholism, crime, and prostitution in rural areas. Despite its noted successes, the program is not without controversy. One common criticism is that it was initiated top-down, rather than originating from a rice-roots movement. Other critics argue that the top-down nature of the movement contributed to alleged elements of corruption, perhaps inevitable in a movement of this size and scope. Another allegation is that participation was not always totally voluntary and that social pressure necessitated active participation. Despite such controversies, Saemaul Undong represents a meaningful rural development model with relevance to nearly all developing areas with serious regional disparities and urban-rural income gaps.

Sarvodaya Shramadana   **(373)**
Founded in Sri Lanka in 1958, a nonpolitical, self-help people's movement and development organization based on Buddhist precepts. The literal meaning of Sarvodaya Shramadana is "the awakening of all society by the mutual sharing of one's time, thought and energy." Its activities range from local economic development

projects to the provision of basic services for women, children, and youth. The founders of the program were a group of students and teachers of Nalande College in Colombo, led by A. T. Ariyaratne, who organized holiday camps in remote villages in an effort to gain direct contact with the rural poor and extend their limited services and skills for development purposes. The movement has emerged as the largest nongovernmental organization in Sri Lanka and involves 3 million people in 8,000 villages. While remaining essentially a grassroots organization, it has established 52 extension centers, 5 development education centers, a research center, and a national and international headquarters. Ariyaratne continues to serve as president.

Significance   The Sarvodaya Shramadana movement's accomplishments are seen in its contributions to community development in Sri Lanka, a nation widely noted for a high quality of life relative to its income per capita. Further, the movement successfully draws on indigenous cultural and religious values to define appropriate development strategies. The movement views religion and tradition as resources rather than impediments to development. It stresses elements within Buddhist tradition that emphasize reverence for all life and the well-being of all. To achieve these goals at the village level, the movement provides volunteers, training, equipment, and capital for local initiatives. Sarvodaya is characterized by its promotion of the mutual sharing of labor, utilization of local resources, village mobilization by age groups, and the facilitation and development of local leadership. As such, it embodies the notion of participatory and sustainable development, as well as the local empowerment or awakening inherent in the movement's name.

South Commission (Independent Commission of the   (374) South on Development Issues)

A commission of prominent intellectuals and politicians from developing countries which was founded in May, 1986, in Kuala Lumpur, Malaysia, to assess the development progress of South countries and to propose new strategies to reduce global poverty, inequalities, and related economic stagnation. The commission is also called the South-South Commission. The Commission is totally independent of any formal governments or international organizations. Chaired by Julius K. Nyerere, former political leader of Tanzania, it has 28 members from countries in Asia, Latin America, the Middle East, Africa, the South Pacific, and southeastern Europe. Its list of members, which reads like a "who's who" of South development thinkers and policymakers, includes Ismail Sabri Abdalla (Egypt), Abdlatif Al-Hamad (Kuwait), Paulo Evaristo Arns (Brazil), Solita Collas-Monsod (Philippines), Eneas Da Conceicao Comiche (Mozambique), Gamani Corea (Sri Lanka), Aboubakar Diaby-Ouattara (Ivory Coast), Aldo Ferrer (Argentina), Celso Furtado (Brazil), Enrique Iglesias (Uruguay), Devaki Jain (India), Simba Makoni (Zimbabwe), Michael Manley (Jamaica), Jorge Eduardo Navarrete (Mexico), Pius Okigbo (Nigeria), Augustin Papic (Yugoslavia), Carlos Andres Pérez (Venezuela), Qian Jiadong (China), Shridath Ramphal (Guyana), Carlos Rafael Rodriguez (Cuba), Abdus Salam (Pakistan), Marie-Angelique Savane (Senegal), Tan Sri Ghazali Shafie (Malaysia), Upua Tamasese Tupuola Efi (Western Samoa), Nitisastro Widjojo (Indonesia), and Layachi Yaker (Algeria). Manmohan Singh of India serves as Secretary-General of the Commission. The work of the Commission has been summarized in a special report titled *The Challenge to the South: The Report of the South Commission* (1990), which represents a follow-up to the earlier Brandt Commission Report. Among topics covered in the report are 1) the current state of the South, 2) a self-reliant and people-centered approach to development, 3) the need for greater South-South cooperation, 4) the state of North-South relations and management of the international system, 5) the South and the 21st century, and 6) the work of the Commission itself. *See also* PARADIGMS OF DEVELOPMENT, 116; TECHNICAL CO-OPERATION AMONG DEVELOPING COUNTRIES, 306; CELSO FURTADO, 17; ABDUS SALAM, 93; MEASURING AND COMPARING LEVELS OF POVERTY, 337; BRANDT COMMISSION, 280; SUSTAINABLE DEVELOPMENT, 272.

Significance   The Commission and its work present a much needed South perspective on development issues, which have long been dominated by the "economism" perspective of North policymakers and scholars. The Commission has questioned conventional measures of development which inadequately reflect quality of life and other basic human conditions. It is working on the specification of alternative indicators related to environmental quality; democratic participation; income distribution; and progress in health, education, and shelter (Henderson 1989:18). It is also concerned with identifying the human costs of programs of "structural adjustment" prescribed by the IMF. The Commission's major impact may well be the creation of a new development paradigm to replace the "economism worldview" which has dominated the global debate about development. Given its nongovernmental status and the exclusion of North participation in its deliberations, the Commission's actual political influence may be limited, regardless of how compelling its intellectual arguments. The South Commission certainly represents an important "think tank" of the developing countries and its voice is critically needed to broaden the development debate as the 21st century approaches with its many challenges to both South and North nations.

Ujamaa (375)

Development concept originated by Tanzanian President Julius Nyerere in the mid–1960s. Roughly translatable as familyhood, the concept was embodied in the creation of communal village production units. Nyerere explained Ujamaa in a widely distributed pamphlet entitled "Socialism and Rural Development." He stressed respect for each member of the family, common property, and the obligation to work. The program was designed to stem rural-urban migration, achieve local and national self-sufficiency, and maintain human dignity and equality in the development process. The broader policy was adopted through the Arusha Declaration on February 5, 1967. At the national level it included the nationalization of major manufacturing and trade institutions. At the local level it involved collectivization and reorganization of village units. *See also* JULIUS NYERERE, 91.

Significance   The Ujamaa program was the first serious attempt to create an African version of socialism. Nyerere wished to avoid the two major imported models of development, international communism and capitalism. He argued that true development could only take place when local people participated in decision making. The ujamaa approach to development emphasizes the use of local resources and talent in building a new Tanzania. This has been particularly expedient in light of the unimpressive performance of the national economy. The ujamaa program partly explains the noteworthy success of Tanzania in meeting basic human needs requirements despite a weak national economy.

Vicos Project (Cornell-Peru Project) (376)

An applied rural development project initiated by Cornell University in collaboration with Peruvian anthropologists and scholars. The project was started in 1951 with the support of Carlos Monge, a Peruvian anthropologist and physician. Vicos refers to a hacienda of approximately 160 square kilometers located in a north-central Andes valley of Peru. The hacienda, mainly inhabited by indigenous Quechuas, was owned by outside landlords until Cornell took over the lease. The vision of those initiating the project was that it would represent an integration of applied research and political action to enable indigenous rural people to develop themselves and achieve a higher quality of life. Alan Holmberg, a professor from Cornell, became the de facto patron of the hacienda and was deeply involved with the project from its beginning until 1961. Numerous graduate students and scholars from Cornell as well as Peruvian scholars and students spent time at Vicos, using it as a laboratory to study problems of rural development. Cornell's involvement lasted until 1964 and the Peruvian government activity continued until 1974. In the early 1960s, the Peace Corps became involved in the project, which led to serious controversy and tensions between the indigenous people and the external volunteers. In 1962, following the intervention of Sen. Edward Kennedy, Vicos became a free community and the land was transferred to the indigenous people inhabiting it. Overall, the community of Vicos was able to enhance its standard of living more substantially than surrounding communities and areas.

Significance   The Vicos project is one of the most famous and most controversial rural development projects ever undertaken. Alan Holméberg, working with missionary-type zeal, envisioned Vicos as a universal model for community development. Holmberg showed remarkable commitment to the project, though clearly he was more interested in actions to improve the lives of the people of Vicos than in the research dimension. He still has not written "the book" about Vicos. However, Holmberg was extremely supportive and helpful to both Peruvian and U.S. researchers who used Vicos for data and as an applied laboratory. The Vicos project certainly facilitated the development of local research capacity, particularly in the areas of development and applied anthropology. Vicos has been the subject of considerable literature and written evaluation. Among major contributions have been the March 1965 issue of the *American Behavioral Scientist,* which represents the official description and evaluation of the project; an essay by William Mangin titled "Thoughts on Twenty-Four Years of Work in Peru: The Vicos Project and Me," in *Long-Term Field Research in Social Anthropology* (1979); and a book edited by Henry Dobyns, Paul Doughty, and Harold Lasswell, *Peasants, Power, and Applied Social Change: Vicos as a Model* (1971). As with so many model development projects, the key questions are: how special was Vicos and to what extent was its success due to the input of external funds and committed personnel, such as Holmberg himself? There is also the question of the role of the outsider. To what extent should outsiders become directly involved in the management of local projects? The extensive, rich Vicos case material provides a basis for continued debate about rural development strategies and the issues related to empowering indigenous minorities who may be severely exploited economically, socially, and culturally.

Villa El Salvador (377)

Peru's celebrated self-help urban development community. The community of more than 300,000, one of the many *pueblos jovenes* on the outskirts of Lima, is internationally recognized as a remarkable and exemplary organization. The original occupation of land by 200 homeless families that would lead to the creation of Villa El Salvador began in April 1971. They occupied a small plot of state land near the district of Pamplona. The police attempted to remove the families by force and stem the rapid expansion of the new settlement into the nearby hills and vacant lots. After intense negotiations between designated squatter leaders, sympathetic church representatives, and government officials, the government of Juan Velaso Alvarado decided to relocate 7,000 of the now 9,000 families to state land on the southern cone of Lima. In the next two years, the population rose rapidly as many families displaced by the 1970 earthquake settled in Villa El Salvador on their own accord. The residents soon designed their own government, designated the Self-Managed Urban Community of Villa El Salvador (CUAVES). Their model of urban development allows for free enterprises in a communally focused system as put forth in their Popular Integral Development Plan. The community, divided into 110 residential groups of 2,500 people, is highly participatory, organized, structured, and decentralized. The residential groups are made up of 16 blocks, each composed of 24 families. The blocks, each with its own elected leaders, form the basis of the bottom-up, democratic planning structure. Blocks communicate concerns and ideas to the secretary-generals of the residential groups who are responsible for implementing development planning and reporting to CUAVES. In Villa El Salvador, as throughout Lima, thousands of single-shop entrepreneurs operate as part of the unlicensed and unregistered informal sector. It is estimated that such operations produce nearly 40 percent of the nation's GDP. A small industrial park is being developed to support labor-intensive industries. CUAVES provides a means of mutual support for all sectors of the community. Lending schemes have been implemented. The residents of Villa El Salvador have created libraries and educational centers. They have begun farming nearby land and have planted a half million trees as well. The majority of the houses are brick and over 80 percent have running water.

Significance   While many of the problems associated with urban slums continue to face the residents of Villa El Salvador, the community stands as a remarkable example of dignity, creativity, and hope for the urban poor. As an ever-increasing percentage of the world's poorest take up residence in urban areas, viable models of urban community development are urgently needed. The creation of Villa El Salvador suggests that the most appropriate models may come from grassroots movements, not from centrally planned efforts. The lesson for governments may be not to impose upon the urban poor unnecessary regulations and unenforceable laws, but rather to show respect for the types of political and social systems that might emerge from the reality of the slums, shantytowns, or *pueblos jovenes.*

B. Organizations

Academy for Educational Development (AED)   **(378)**
A private, nonprofit organization actively responding to human development needs throughout the world. Its original goal, which has been greatly expanded, was to assist the long-range planning needs of U.S. universities and colleges. Established in 1961, AED is an example of the growing number of nongovernmental organizations actively involved in the international development field. The AED has four major purposes: (1) meeting basic human needs for health, education, and employment; (2) increasing access to learning; (3) transferring technology and improving the flow of information; and (4) enhancing institutional development. Among diverse services provided by AED are needs assessment, research and policy studies, program evaluation, student placement, and conference planning. Examples of the hundreds of clients served by AED since 1961 are U.S. Agency for International Development (AID), the Asian Development Bank, the World Bank, United Nations Development Program (UNDP), U.S. Information Agency (USIA), the Ford Foundation, and many universities and large transnational corporations. In 1987, AED's annual income was $55 million. AED currently has 23 project offices in such developing countries as Nepal, Pakistan, Tunisia, Egypt, Indonesia, Ecuador, and Peru. Its U.S. headquarters, like that of many nongovernmental organizations (NGOs) involved in international development, is located in Washington, D.C.

Significance   The Academy for Educational Development is one of the prominent nongovernmental organizations active in the area of human resource development. Like the Ford Foundation, AED has both domestic and international programs. The growth in AED programs and funding since 1984 reflects implementation of the privatization of development assistance and perhaps increasing concern about the need to give greater priority to human resource development. Data on the relative effectiveness of AED compared to other agencies in the human resource development field are not available. The relative effectiveness of such organizations as AED is reflected in their reputations among key decision makers in development agencies. Their success is also related to the quality of their core staff and the external consultants they utilize in various projects.

Aga Khan Network (379)

The largest development organization in the Third World, one that emphasizes bottom-up development. With headquarters in Geneva and Paris, it is headed by Prince Karim Aga Khan, the spiritual leader of the Ismaili Muslims. Its projects and group of companies are active in 25 countries. It is particularly noted for cost-effective, low-cost development models. Among noteworthy Aga Khan projects are the Industrial Promotion Services (IPS) of Nairobi, Kenya, and the Rural Support Program in northern Pakistan. The latter project has helped improve living standards for approximately 400,000 people living in the remote mountainous areas of Chitral and Gilgit. The project in Kenya has led to a healthy leather export industry that is expected to bring in $12 million of foreign exchange each year.

Significance The Aga Khan Network shows the potential of Third World philanthropy and related leadership in promoting bottom-up and self-sustaining development. Though considerable wealth exists in most developing countries, there has been no strong tradition of philanthrophy, particularly with a development and transnational outlook. Many projects supported by the Aga Khan Network have potential for replication in other developing countries.

American Council for Voluntary International Action (380)
(InterAction)

A coalition of more than 100 U.S. private voluntary organizations (PVOs) engaged in international humanitarian efforts in relief and development. Formed in 1984, the organization seeks to enhance the recognition and effectiveness of a diverse membership through interaction with the U.S. Congress, government agencies, funding sources, and the general public. Its stated goal is "to foster partnership, collaboration, leadership, and the power of the PVO community to speak as one voice as it strives to achieve a world of self-reliance, justice and peace." In working toward these goals, InterAction sponsors an annual forum for PVOs, engages in publication, and serves as a clearinghouse for information regarding development and development education. It also works to promote high ethical standards within the PVO community, both in fund-raising and fieldwork. InterAction is itself a member of two broader coalitions, the International Council of Voluntary Agencies (ICVA) and the Independent Sector. *See also* PRIVATE VOLUNTARY ORGANIZATIONS, 300.

Significance   InterAction is an effective and valuable tool for coordinating and enhancing the work of a diverse group of organizations that have come under criticism for their lack of cooperation and maverick styles of operation. The organization plays a key role not only in coordinating the efforts of PVOs, but also in communicating the importance and effectiveness of their work. This has resulted in improved recognition and support for PVOs. InterAction has also played an important role in encouraging PVOs to act as key resources for educating the American public about development issues.

American Friends Service Committee (AFSC)   (381)
The primary peace and humanitarian service organization of the Religious Society of Friends (Quakers). AFSC was founded in 1917 to carry out a massive child-feeding program in Europe following World War I. It is one of the oldest and most respected of the many North American PVOs working in international relief and development. AFSC's activities are broad-ranging both in the United States and overseas. In 1947 AFSC, along with the Friends Service Council of London, was awarded the Nobel Peace Prize, primarily for its refugee work during and after World War II. AFSC also engages in development work and conflict resolution throughout the world. The Friends' peace tradition has allowed them to work where other organizations have not been welcome or allowed to operate by the ruling government. For example, AFSC helped alleviate suffering on both sides of the Nigerian civil war and was one of the few groups to remain in Vietnam after 1975. But while AFSC's programs transcend political differences, the organization is not apolitical. It maintains an effective presence at the United Nations and in Washington, D.C., advocating policy changes to address the root causes of hunger, maldevelopment, displacement, and war. AFSC supports numerous efforts in peace education, development education, and conflict

345

resolution, for example, in regard to arms control, race relations, the Arab-Israeli conflict, and the North-South dialogue. The organization is supported almost entirely by private donations. *See also* PRIVATE VOLUNTARY ORGANIZATIONS, 300.

Significance   For more than seven decades AFSC has demonstrated its commitment to relieving human suffering in its many forms throughout the world. The organization's approaches to bringing about greater social justice through creative, nonviolent action serve as models and inspiration for other relief and development agencies. AFSC has always understood the close linkages between peace and development issues, and advocated a holistic approach to development work long before its present popularity. The organization's effectiveness is greatly enhanced by its mutually reinforcing work in the development field, policy issues, and peace education. In this regard, AFSC serves as a model for other organizations. Most importantly, this relatively small group has effectively responded to human need in the United States and throughout the world by striving to redress the root causes of suffering and conflict.

Asia Foundation   (382)

A foundation that provides assistance to the developing countries of Asia in a wide range of areas. It supports programs in social welfare, health, medicine, law and human rights, religion and development, economic affairs, technical and industrial development, modernization of agriculture, education, and conservation of natural resources, among other areas. Established in 1954, with headquarters in San Francisco, the Asia Foundation seeks to foster cooperation and understanding among the peoples and countries of Asia as well as to enhance U.S. understanding of Asian countries and cultures. The foundation is unusual in that most of its funding comes from the U.S. Congress. *See also* DEVELOPMENT FOUNDATIONS, 281; WILLIAM P. FULLER, 72.

Significance   Because of alleged involvement with the CIA during the Vietnam War era, the Asia Foundation has a history of controversy, particularly with respect to academic scholars who questioned the appropriateness of such relations. In the postwar period, such controversies have all but disappeared, and some scholars argue that it is better to take funds from a congressionally supported agency than from one funded by the administration. Unlike the larger foundations, the Asia Foundation has not specialized but has maintained broad-ranging interests. It has always been open to funding innovative ideas and projects that are extremely small in financial terms; these projects would never receive serious attention from other major donors because of the economies of scale factor. Despite its reliance on funding from the Congress, the Asia Foundation operates autonomously and is thus considered a nongovernmental organization. Its staffing patterns and procedures mirror those of other private development foundations. Most of its funds go directly to the developing countries of Asia. Over the years the foundation has had a major project to recycle scholarly books from the United States to libraries and schools in Asia. Given the growing importance of the Asia-Pacific region and the dynamic leadership of William Fuller as president, the Asia Foundation's development influence is likely to grow in the 1990s and the next century.

Asian Development Bank (ADB)   (383)

A regional development bank for Asia and the Pacific, opened in December 1966 with headquarters in Manila. The charter of the bank stipulates that 60 percent of its capital must be from the region. Australia and New Zealand are considered part of the Asia-Pacific region covered by the ADB. The bank is jointly sponsored by almost 50 governments in Asia, the Pacific, and Europe. Over its 20 years of existence, the ADB has loaned approximately $20 billion to less developed countries (LDCs) in the Asia-Pacific region. Normally for every dollar loaned, the borrowing country itself matches with approximately $1.50, or cofinancing enables the bank to leverage its loans effectively. By 1987, its original capital had grown from $1,223 million to $19,476 million. The ADB's first president was Takeshi Watanabe, a committed internationalist. Its other three presidents have also been Japanese. From the beginning, they followed the principle that the Asian Development Bank should not be dominated by Anglo-Saxons. Some 36 nationalities are represented on the bank's staff of approximately 600.

Significance   Many development specialists consider the Asian Development Bank to be the most successful regional organization in Asia. Though the ADB is only about one-tenth as big as the World Bank, it is likely to grow, given the increasing economic power of the Japanese, the bank's major capital contributor. The economic dynamism of many of the ADB's key members will provide it with new sources of capital funds in the decades ahead. The People's Republic of China joined the bank in 1986. Reflecting its skills in diplomacy, Taiwan remains in the bank as Taipei, China. Dick Wilson has recently written a detailed history of the ABD titled *A Bank for Half the*

World: The Story of the Asian Development Bank 1966–1986, which provides extensive details on its economic and political evolution. Takeshi Watanabe's autobiographical volume, *Towards a New Asia* (1977), also offers valuable reflections on the bank's origins, philosophy, and operating procedures.

Asian Institute of Technology (AIT)   (384)

A South-based international university that trains students and conducts research in a variety of scientific and technical areas related to development. Established in 1959 and having become autonomous in 1967, AIT is located about 40 kilometers north of Bangkok in Thailand. Students from approximately 30 countries, mostly Asian, attend AIT, which is often referred to as the MIT of Asia. Countries with the largest numbers of students at AIT are Thailand, the Republic of China, Sri Lanka, the Philippines, and Bangladesh. Faculty are from 29 different countries. Funding for AIT also comes from diverse international sources, with the greatest support from the United States, Thailand, and Japan.

Significance   The Asian Institute of Technology is noted for its applied, interdisciplinary focus and emphasis on appropriate technology. Brain drain from AIT to the West is extremely low (only 3.5 percent), a remarkable achievement. Students at AIT receive high-quality training in a realistic development context. AIT represents an exemplary model of combined North-South and South-South cooperation to train applied scientific and technological personnel for developing countries in Asia.

Australian International Development Assistance   (385)
Bureau (AIDAB)

The agency responsible for administering Australia's annual budget of approximately $1 billion for development assistance. Prior to 1973, Australia's aid was handled by a number of governmental departments. The Australian Development Assistance Agency (ADAA) was established in 1974 to unify the country's various aid programs. Then in 1976, the activities of ADAA were subsumed within the Department of Foreign Affairs, and the Australian Development Assistance Bureau (ADAB) was formed. In 1983, the Australian government asked Sir Gordon Jackson to chair the Committee to Review the Australian Overseas Aid Program. The committee's report, known as the Jackson Report, identified a number of administrative and managerial shortcomings in the Australian aid program.

As of 1988, a number of the Jackson recommendations had been implemented. In September 1987, ADAB changed its name to AIDAB, to reflect its greater international and global orientation. AIDAB is now part of the Ministry of Foreign Affairs and Trade. Despite the change in name, most of Australia's aid remains bilateral. In fact, approximately one-third goes to Papua New Guinea. Another 36 percent goes to other developing countries, primarily in the Asia-Pacific region; eight percent goes to international financial institutions, namely the World Bank and Asian Development Bank; and 19 percent to other global programs such as the World Food Program (WFP), UNDP, and the International Fund for Agricultural Development (IFAD). After Papua New Guinea, the major recipients of Australian aid, in order of funds received, are Indonesia, Malaysia, China, the Philippines, and Thailand. The major aid sectors of AIDAB are agriculture and environment, infrastructure and industry, food aid, education and training, emergency relief and refugees, health, women in development, and aid and trade. AIDAB also provides annual funds for Australia's peace corps, called the Australia Volunteers Abroad Scheme, and for the Australian Council for Overseas Aid (ACFOA), the coordinating body for approximately 80 Australian NGOs involved in development assistance. *See also* BILATERAL AID, 277; BILATERAL AID AGENCIES, 278.

Significance   In 1988, Australia's foreign aid represented 0.37 percent of its gross national product (GNP), down from 0.56 in 1982 and below the UN target of 0.70. Australia's current level of aid is about average for members of the Development Assistance Committee (DAC) of the Organization for Economic Cooperation and Development (OECD). The geographic focus of Australian aid is the developing countries of Southeast Asia and the South Pacific. Australia's ten largest aid projects in 1989 were all in Southeast Asia, primarily in Indonesia and the Philippines. Australia does provide some assistance to African countries, such as Tanzania and Mozambique. Excluding direct assistance in support of the government budget of Papua New Guinea, 78 percent of AIDAB's program expenditures were on goods and services sourced in Australia, showing that much of its aid program economically benefits various Australian business and commercial interests.

Cairns Group of Free Traders   (386)

A group of 14 farming nations that advocate agricultural trade reform. Named after a small coastal community in northeast Queensland, Australia, where the organization was formed, this group consists of Argentina, Australia, Brazil, Canada, Chile, Colombia, Fiji, Hungary, Indonesia, Malaysia, the Philippines, New Zealand, Thailand, and Uruguay. Its particular goal is the elimination of agricultural subsidies, particularly in the European Economic Community and the United States, because these large subsidies adversely affect agriculturally oriented economies with minimal subsidies, such as the members of the Cairns group.

Significance   This is a highly unusual international coalition in that it transcends ideological and North-South barriers. The group includes one Eastern Bloc country, three North countries, and ten South countries from three geographic areas—Southeast Asia, Latin America, and the South Pacific. The group reflects the notion introduced several decades ago by the Argentine development theorist Raúl Prebisch of trade, not aid, and his aggressive criticism of protectionism among nations at the center against those in the periphery. This coalition also hints of a possible long-term emergence of an OGEC (organization of grain-exporting countries) type of cartel if excessive protectionism persists in Europe and the United States. If the Cairns group were to achieve its goals, this would alleviate the global debt crisis by enabling key developing countries to export more effectively. This coalition also places Australia, Canada, and New Zealand at the forefront as spokespersons for key South agricultural economies.

Canadian International Development Agency (CIDA)   (387)
Canada's bilateral aid agency, established in 1968 to replace the External Aid Office. CIDA administers 75 percent of all Canadian official development assistance (ODA), the remainder being disbursed through multilateral agencies such as the World Bank. CIDA reports to the Parliament through the secretary of state for external affairs. Canada has an international reputation for strong support of development assistance. Former Prime Minister Lester Pearson, while serving as chairman of the UN Committee on International Development in 1969, urged industrialized nations to commit at least 0.7 percent of their GNP to development assistance by 1980. Until recently, Canada's commitment has been near 0.5 percent, short of the stated goal, but sixth among OECD countries. This amounts to more than $2.6 billion in aid administered by CIDA, the world's seventh largest development assistance program. The government's foreign aid charter, new in 1988, *Sharing Our Future*, reaffirmed Canada's commitment to developing countries, especially those in Africa. Recent efforts to address Canada's deficit spending, however, have

resulted in reduced allocations to CIDA and a government emphasis on quality not quantity in its aid programs. *See also* BILATERAL AID AGENCIES, 278.

Significance   In addition to administering conventional bilateral aid programs, the Canadian International Development Agency has established a number of innovative specialized programs that have served as models for other donor countries. For example, CIDA was the first bilateral agency to recognize the importance and potential of NGOs as partners with government programs. CIDA's Nongovernmental Organization Program has supported Canadian-based NGOs in the form of matching grants since 1968. Over 200 organizations now receive funding. In a similar vein, CIDA sponsors the Institutional Cooperation and Development Services Program (ICDS) to encourage Canadian initiatives that contribute to the human resource capacities of developing countries. Canadian universities, cooperatives, unions, and professional associations have created ties with their counterparts in developing countries. CIDA also supports over 100 international NGOs through the INGO Program created in 1974. Another innovation is the Public Participation Program, which supports efforts to inform Canadians about development issues. As a result, Canada has been at the forefront of development education. Citizen support for development cooperation is unusually strong. Other special programs include the Industrial Cooperation Program, Management for Change, and the Voluntary Agriculture Development Aid Program. Together these programs represent CIDA's unique contributions to development assistance.

CARE (Cooperative for American Relief Everywhere)   **(388)**
The world's largest private, nonsectarian, nonprofit relief and development organization. CARE was founded in November 1945 as the Cooperative for American Relief to Europe to serve as a conduit for private relief material, including the famous CARE packages, to the devastated continent. Following this effort, rather than disbanding, the organization turned its attention to the developing nations. In the early 1950s, CARE shifted its emphasis from relief to development and self-help projects, and soon became the largest distributor of Food for Peace commodities. Though a private agency, the organization has a history of close cooperation with and support from the U.S. government and, more recently, from governments of the LDCs. Today CARE employs an international staff of more than 7,000 based at the headquarters in New York City, in the 50-plus regional offices throughout the United States, and in 39 recipient countries. The

organization has international members and associates in ten OECD countries. CARE operates with an annual budget of over $300 million, two-thirds of which is comprised of agricultural commodities and freight donated by the U.S. government. *See also* PRIVATE VOLUNTARY ORGANIZATIONS, 300; FOOD FOR PEACE, 360.

Significance As it did after World War II, CARE continues its extensive work in food assistance and emergency relief. Along with Catholic Relief Service, it remains the primary distributor of Food for Peace commodities. It has established excellent working relations with governments throughout the developing world. CARE apparently has made a successful transition to development work. Two-thirds of its operating budget now supports programs in food production, small-business support, and health and nutrition. With an impressively low overhead of 5 percent, CARE continues to serve as an important focus for, and symbol of, nonsectarian private concern for the world's poor and hungry.

Center for Development Communications (CDC) (389)
An innovative group located in Cairo, Egypt, that utilizes popular broadcast media to promote preventive health care, health education, and family planning. The center was established in 1984 and is directed by Dr. Farag Elkamel. The basic assumption underlying the center's work is that popular electronic media can be a powerful mechanism for providing health education to the poor and illiterate, who often are unable to use printed media. CDC's first major production was a television program to promote oral rehydration therapy (ORT). Despite initial skepticism of the professional medical community, the program proved extremely effective. Currently the center is developing a series of 45-minute soap opera type programs about a Cairo-based doctor who returns to his village each week. The CDC's major programming to date has been a series titled *Sehettak Biddonia* (meaning *Your Health in Your World*), which provides practical health information in a popular format. CDC has been a major recipient of external Ford Foundation funding.

Significance Despite having only 14 full-time professionals on its staff, CDC has had a major impact in Egypt. Its example has already had a significant influence on the radio and TV programming of the Egyptian Ministry of Health. Given the success of its initial programming on ORT, CDC developed a national medical education program that resulted in 25,000 doctors and 18,000 nurses receiving training in the latest ORT techniques. CDC's approach is extremely interdisciplinary and it utilizes popular actors, singers, and comedians to share its important health messages. CDC's programming also emphasizes the need to use simple human language rather than esoteric technical jargon in communicating with ordinary citizens. It also has demonstrated the importance of making educational television entertaining. CDC's efforts to date show the potential impact of small but creative nongovernmental developmental groups. The work of CDC also shows the potential power of the popular media in promoting broad-based health education and family planning. Its success is relevant to many other LDCs with serious health problems, high levels of illiteracy, and a substantial radio and/or television infrastructure.

Club of Rome (390)

An international informal association of scientists, educators, and leaders that seeks to foster international understanding of issues with global implications. The studies of the club, formed by Aurelio Peccei and Alexander King in 1968, have centered on the issues of population growth, food supplies, energy and related resources, and environmental pollution. Results of its commissioned studies are distributed to decision makers in the private and public sectors throughout the world. Its first major study, *The Limits to Growth* (1972), was a landmark presentation of global trends in population, resource consumption, industrial output, and pollution to the year 2010. This study was followed by the Reshaping the Global Order (RIO) project, coordinated by Nobel laureate Jan Tinbergen. The RIO Report (1976) was commissioned in response to the proposals of the Charter of Economic Rights and Duties of States, adopted by the Sixth Special Session of the UN General Assembly. The report attempts to examine and clarify the issues raised by the proponents of a new international economic order (NIEO). In addition to its publishing program, the organization sponsors conferences and symposia on global issues. The Club of Rome has five current goals: continued study of the effects of population growth, study of the potential and implications of new scientific knowledge, research on innovative means of managing human affairs, creation of a nonviolent world, and development of human resources on a global scale. Membership consists of groups in 11 countries and a core group of 100 individuals from 40 countries. *See also* SUSTAINABLE DEVELOPMENT, 272.

Significance   The Club of Rome is still best known for *The Limits to Growth,* which is available in more than 30 languages. In it, the club challenged the notion of unlimited industrial growth and resource consumption, the basis of many development approaches. It helped alert the world to the dangers of exponential growth in population, resource consumption, and subsequent levels of pollution. The club's research continues to serve as a catalyst for discussion and policy initiatives concerning alternative futures, global environmental issues, and development strategies. It emphasizes the global and interdisciplinary nature of many current problems confronting decision makers, consumers, and planners.

Colombo Plan   **(391)**
A regional economic and social development plan and organization created in 1950 by the ministers of foreign affairs of the British Commonwealth of nations meeting in Colombo, Ceylon (Sri Lanka). They established the Colombo Plan for Cooperative Economic Development in South and Southeast Asia, which was launched in 1951. The plan is administered by the Colombo Plan Council for Technical Cooperation in South and Southeast Asia. The council was originally made up of representatives of seven commonwealth nations who developed a six-year agreement. The organization now involves 24 countries including Afghanistan, Australia, Burma, Bhutan, Cambodia, Canada, India, Indonesia, Iran, Japan, Republic of Korea, Laos, Malaysia, Maldives, Nepal, New Zealand, Pakistan, Papua New Guinea, the Philippines, Singapore, Sri Lanka, Thailand, the United Kingdom, and the United States. The headquarters remains in Colombo. The council meets several times a year to identify pertinent issues for consideration by the Consultative Committee, the principal review and deliberative body of the plan. It reviews the progress of projects and member nations and discusses resource allocation for development cooperation among members. The Colombo Plan Bureau, the permanent organ of the plan, carries out research, maintains records of assistance programs, and publishes reports. In 1975 the plan established the Staff College for Technician Education in Singapore to assist member countries in developing technical education.

Significance   The Colombo Plan was the first major regional development organization involving primarily Third World nations. For four decades it has promoted development cooperation among a diverse set of nations. It has been particularly effective in promoting technical cooperation among developing countries (TCDC) as well as facilitating development assistance to and within the region.

Commonwealth Fund for Technical Cooperation (392)
(CFTC)
A donor agency established in 1971 as part of the Commonwealth
Secretariat "to assist developing member countries by providing experts, advisers, and consultancy services and arranging training
abroad for their nationals" (Commonwealth Secretariat 1987:1). The
CFTC also has programs to help export promotion (begun in
1972) and industrial advance (1980). The Commonwealth Secretariat, established in 1965 with headquarters in London at the Marlborough House, is an organization of 49 countries, all of which are
former British colonies. CFTC's total budget for 1986–1987 was
£19,308,923, supplemented by contributions from specific projects in
member countries. About 30 percent of CFTC's basic budget is provided by Great Britain. *See also* TECHNICAL ASSISTANCE, 305.

Significance   Though it is quite a small donor agency, CFTC has an
excellent reputation based on the quality of its work, its
cost-effectiveness, and the innovative character of many of its programs. CFTC fosters both North-South and South-South technical
cooperation, and uses a higher percentage of experts from South
countries than do most development agencies. CFTC faces financial
problems because the rise in the value of the British pound has adversely affected the size of many members' contributions. Each year
the commonwealth secretary-general publishes a report that provides
details on the activities and budget of the CFTC. CFTC also publishes
important development studies that are readily available in commonwealth countries.

Community Colleges for International Development (393)
(CCID)
A consortium of 40 U.S. and Canadian community colleges established in 1976 to implement international programs and projects.
CCID has three basic objectives: (1) to assist other countries, particularly in developing areas, in midlevel manpower development with a
special focus on technical/vocational education; (2) to enhance opportunities for the students and staff members of community colleges
and associated institutions overseas for professional development
through international study and exchange; and (3) to provide leadership and service in facilitating the international dimensions of

community colleges. Major activities of CCID are technical training, consulting, implementation of bilateral agreements, providing education for international students, hosting of international visitors, and the hosting of two annual conferences on international education and the community college. CCID also publishes a quarterly newsletter titled *International News* with editorial offices at Bunker Hill Community College in Boston.

Significance   Traditionally, the most prestigious universities in the United States and the land grant universities, with their emphasis on applied agriculture, have been most commonly associated with international development. Many assume that the less prestigious community colleges would have little or nothing to offer developing countries. Strongly rejecting such a notion, the CCID emphasizes that the community colleges offer high-quality technical training and have many well-qualified and committed teachers. The CCID also stresses the flexibility of the community colleges in being able to respond to diverse training needs and to offer such programs at a much lower cost than colleges or universities. The relevance of the community college is shown in the interest of the People's Republic of China in drawing upon Western experience in developing a community college system. The PRC's interest in community colleges probably derived from their open commitment to serving all students regardless of their socioeconomic background and their emphasis on teaching and practical training. With member colleges having over 500,000 students and offering more than 300 courses of study, the CCID and its members must be recognized for their potential role in facilitating human resource development in LDCs.

Consultative Group on International Agricultural   **(394)**
Research (CGIAR)
An organization that promotes Third World agriculture by coordinating and supporting a network of research facilities known as International Agriculture Research Centers (IARCs). Founded in 1971 with the support of the Rockefeller Foundation, the Ford Foundation, the World Bank, and UNDP, CGIAR serves as an umbrella organization for the following agencies: International Rice Research Institute (IRRI, Philippines); International Center for Improvement of Maize and Wheat (CIMMYT, Mexico); International Center for Tropical Agriculture (CIAT, Colombia); International Institute of Tropical Agriculture (IITA, Nigeria); International Potato Center (CIP, Peru); International Crops Research Institute for the Semi-Arid Tropics (ICRISAT, India); International Laboratory for

Research on Animal Diseases (ILRAD, Kenya); International Center for Agriculture Research in Dry Areas (ICARDA, Syria); International Livestock Centre for Africa (ILCA, Ethiopia); International Food Policy Research Institute (IFPRI, United States); West African Rice Development Association (WARDA, Liberia); International Board for Plant Genetic Resources (IBPGR, Italy); and the International Service for National Agriculture Research (ISNAR, Netherlands). The group has headquarters in Washington, D.C., and operates with an annual budget of about $180 million, one-quarter of which comes from the United States. *See also* GREEN REVOLUTION, 180; INTERNATIONAL UNDERTAKING ON PLANT GENETIC RESOURCES, 288; SUSTAINABLE AGRICULTURE, 188; BIOTECHNOLOGY, 279; INTERNATIONAL RICE RESEARCH INSTITUTE, 423.

Significance   CGIAR supports a network of organizations that have been and will continue to be vital to improving world food production. CIMMYT and IRRI served as catalysts for the Green Revolution, and they and their partner institutions continue to seek breakthroughs that will allow food production to keep pace with or exceed population growth. By supporting a variety of organizations, CGIAR promotes diversity in food production through the improvement of a number of traditional staple crops in addition to wheat and rice. Foods such as potatoes, yams, sorghum, and cassava were virtually ignored by Green Revolution research and development. In addition, CGIAR supports the important task of improving livestock. Recently the group modified its goal statements to reflect its new emphasis on support for research leading to more sustainable food production systems. As a coordinating body, CGIAR is effective in promoting technology transfer related to food production and curbing redundant efforts among the numerous agriculture research institutes. M. S. Swaminathan, director general of IRRI, calls CGIAR "the most meaningful affirming flame shining in our spaceship world today."

Cultural Survival   (395)
An activist organization that works to promote the welfare and preserve the cultures of ethnic minorities around the world. Its office is in the Peabody Museum of Ethnography at Harvard in Cambridge, Massachusetts. The organization has a modest annual budget of approximately $800,000 and receives funding from organizations such as AID and the Ford Foundation. With these funds, Cultural Survival supports approximately 40 projects around the world, many of which focus on the land rights of ethnic minorities. The organization also

publishes a popular quarterly journal, *Cultural Survival Quarterly,* and occasional reports documenting conditions and the status of various minorities. The organization's philosophy is echoed in these words by its director of research, Jason Clay:

> What we're really talking about is people taking control of their own lives, having more say about the extent to which they want to take part in the national society and the speed with which they want to become part of it.

See also CULTURAL DEVELOPMENT, 219.

Significance Despite its modest budget and limited resources, Cultural Survival is making an impressive effort to help ethnic minorities to maintain the richness of their traditions and cultures. The preservation and persistence of these cultures is often threatened by internal nationalistic forces and external international forces. The organization's publications help to publicize the problems of and threats to indigenous minority cultures in various nations. In its overall approach, Cultural Survival is basically conciliatory and willing to engage in dialogue with institutions such as the World Bank. It is considered less confrontational in style than Survival International.

Dag Hammarskjöld Foundation (396)

A Swedish foundation established in 1962 as a living memorial to Dag Hammarskjöld for his work as secretary-general of the United Nations from 1953 to 1961. Reflecting Hammarskjöld's concern for the poorer nations of the world, the foundation has a strong development orientation. It is located in Uppsala, Sweden. During the past 25 years, it has organized over 90 conferences and produced approximately 75 publications. It places a special emphasis on the distribution of materials to Third World individuals and organizations. The foundation's major publication is an excellent biannual journal, *Development Dialogue: A Journal of International Development Cooperation.*

Significance The Dag Hammarskjöld Foundation attempts to provide an alternative perspective on development issues. Since 1975, it has emphasized the theme of "Another Development." In that year, it published a volume titled *What Now: Another Development,* which represents the intellectual basis for its work. During the past decade the foundation has focused on key sectoral aspects of an alternative development strategy. Sectors stressed include rural development; health; education; science and technology (particularly plant genetic resources and biotechnology); international monetary policy; information and communications; and participation.

Development Alternatives with Women for a New Era   (397)
(DAWN)

Known as DAWN, this group functions as a women's research and policy organization. DAWN was founded in 1984 in Bangladesh and now has its headquarters in Rio de Janeiro. The group operates on the premise that the development process may be most clearly understood through the experiences of women as they struggle to meet their basic needs and those of their families. DAWN has members from 12 developing countries. The group describes itself as

> a network of activists, researchers, and policymakers...committed to developing alternative frameworks and methods to attain the goals of economic and social justice, peace, and development free from all forms of oppression by gender, race, and nation.

See also WOMEN IN DEVELOPMENT, 256; NONGOVERNMENTAL ORGANIZATIONS, 295.

Significance   DAWN is representative of a number of new and dynamic women's research and policy organizations based in the Third World. They contribute an important and often overlooked perspective on development and social change. DAWN functions as a valuable resource for policy formulation. DAWN has established working groups engaged in research, publications, advocacy, training, international relations, and communications. The group's focus is on food, energy, and the debt crisis as they relate to women and women's movements in the developing countries.

Development Assistance Committee (DAC)   (398)

A coordinating and consultative body established in 1961 as part of the Organization for Economic Cooperation and Development (OECD) to provide a forum among various donors for the open and critical discussion of development assistance. Original members of the DAC were Belgium, Canada, France, the Federal Republic of Germany, Italy, United Kingdom, United States, the Netherlands, and Japan. Joining later were Denmark (1963), Sweden (1965), Austria (1965), Australia (1966), and Switzerland (1968). The DAC superseded the Development Assistance Group (DAG) which was established with similar purposes in 1960. Basic goals of the DAC are to improve coordination among the donor nations, to promote the growth of aid volume, and to encourage an equitable sharing of the aid burden. Its annual aid review provides a wealth of information on the quantity and quality of assistance and the relative performance of the members. The DAC sets targets, for example, for an amount of aid as a percentage of GNP. DAC also concerns itself with problems of aid implementation. Each year the OECD publishes a valuable annual report titled *Development Co-operation* providing details on each member's development assistance profile. *See also* BILATERAL AID, 277; BILATERAL AID AGENCIES, 278; ORGANIZATION FOR ECONOMIC COOPERATION AND DEVELOPMENT, 427.

Significance The DAC has been a success as a forum to discuss common problems in providing development assistance and in pressuring some nations to increase the quantity of their overseas development assistance. Nevertheless, the DAC has clearly failed to achieve an equitable sharing of the aid burden. In terms of percentage of GNP, Norway, for example, provides five times more assistance than does the United States. Such disparities among the industrial countries in percentage of GNP given to official development assistance have persisted despite the goals and proddings of the DAC. To meet the development challenges of the next century, even greater coordination and collaboration among the donor nations will be essential. The DAC provides an efficient and open mechanism for such creative cooperation.

Equal Media (399)
A new film production company in London that aims to give a global voice to Third World filmmakers. The founders, Sarah Hobson from England and Parminder Vir from India, are deeply concerned about the images of the Third World conveyed by conventional media. They are committed to providing alternative images by providing Third World peoples a voice through media. Equal Media will organize a biannual Third Eye Festival of Third World Cinema. Currently Hobson is coproducing a feature film, sponsored by Equal Media, on how inappropriate aid has adversely affected peasants in the Senegal River Valley. The film is directed by Gabriel Auer, noted for a political film on Uruguay.

Significance Popular Western media such as James Bond movies and musicals like *The King and I* grossly distort images of the Third World. Unfortunately, there is relatively little awareness in the Western world of the growth in creative and important films from the Third World. If Equal Media can survive financially, it can play a major role in acquainting the West with the rich diversity of film in the Third World and provide Westerners with more balanced images of the cultures and peoples of developing countries.

Ex-Volunteers International (EVI) (400)

An umbrella organization consisting of representatives from associations of ex-development volunteers in Europe and Japan. EVI normally meets twice a year in a European city, with each association sending a delegation of one to four persons. Countries included in the organization are Belgium, Denmark, Germany, France, Britain, Ireland, Italy, Japan, the Netherlands, Norway, Sweden, and Switzerland. The EVI secretariat intends to involve associations from the developing countries, such as the ACIVA (Association for African Voluntariate). The organization places special emphasis on development education. *See also* PEACE CORPS, 433; JAPAN OVERSEAS COOPERATION VOLUNTEERS, 425.

Significance   Former development volunteers in Europe and Japan represent a growing and potentially powerful political force that can affect the development policies of various industrial nations. EVI provides a forum for individuals from these 12 countries to share their development experiences and insights, and represents a potentially powerful force for facilitating improved education in Europe and Japan about developing countries. Its counterpart in the United States is the National Council of Returned Peace Corps Volunteers.

Food and Agriculture Organization (FAO) (401)

Established in 1945 as a specialized agency of the United Nations, the FAO fosters international cooperation in food production and distribution of agricultural products. FAO aims to help raise nutrition levels and standards of living, especially for rural populations, throughout the developing world. To this end, the organization sponsors research and compiles data related to nutrition, agriculture, forestry, and fisheries, including an agroclimatic data base, a computerized system that calculates the growing periods, temperature, and moisture conditions throughout the Third World. It compiles and makes available forecasts and appraisals regarding the worldwide production, distribution, and consumption of agricultural products. In addition, it helps member states, nearly every nation in the world, obtain information on agricultural investment and commodities. The FAO operates with a budget of more than $500 million. With a staff of over 10,000 working at the organization's headquarters in Rome, and in regional and country offices throughout the developing world, the organization is considered by many to be excessively top-heavy. Edouard Saouma of Lebanon has held the office of director-general of the FAO since 1975. *See also* INTERNATIONAL UNDERTAKING ON PLANT GENETIC RESOURCES, 288; MULTILATERAL AID AGENCIES, 291.

Significance   The FAO is the world's leading organization dealing with international food production and distribution. Its activities span a broad range of issues and concerns including food policy, famine relief, nutrition, education, and technical assistance. For example, the FAO is the key party in the International Undertaking on Plant Genetic Resources. It recently approved an "agreed interpretation" of the controversial undertaking aimed at ensuring unrestricted availability of germ plasm to research firms and organizations while giving parallel recognition to the economic rights of Third World farmers who have preserved plant genetic resources. The FAO also administers the World Food Program, established in 1963 by the UN to collect food in areas of plenty and distribute it to areas of high need. The program uses food for emergency relief and as a resource for development projects and nutrition programs. In its broader work, the FAO serves as a resource for developing countries seeking to improve agricultural production systems. As the gap between world food production and population closes, the work in which the FAO is involved becomes even more crucial to international development.

Ford Foundation   (402)
The largest foundation in the international development field. Established in Michigan in 1936 by Henry Ford and Edsel Ford with a modest gift of $25,000, the foundation's initial focus was on local philanthrophy in Detroit and Michigan. With Henry Ford's death in 1947, the foundation inherited about 90 percent of the Ford Motor Company assets. By 1951, its endowment was a vast $417 million. In that year the foundation moved its headquarters to Pasadena, California, and then to New York City in 1953. Increasingly, the foundation directed its attention to international issues. Under the leadership of McGeorge Bundy (1966–1979), the Ford Foundation's international development activities boomed. It maintained major offices around the world in key cities such as Mexico City, Bogota, Cairo, New Delhi, Dacca, Jakarta, Nairobi, Bangkok, and Manila. Unfortunately, the foundation's assets were invested almost entirely in blue-chip U.S. stocks. This led to a serious erosion of its financial base in the early and mid–1970s, and a reduction in its international pro-

gramming. In 1979, the board of trustees, comprised of prominent corporate and international figures, appointed Franklin A. Thomas as the foundation's new president. Thomas is a brilliant lawyer associated with the late Robert Kennedy and famous for his community development efforts in Bedford-Stuyvesant in New York City. To reduce costs, Thomas took the decisive but controversial action of closing several overseas offices and releasing a number of high-ranking foundation administrators. He has stressed provision of funds to facilitate opportunities for minorities and women and a more systematic integration of the foundation's international and domestic programming. The monthly *Ford Foundation Letter* provides detailed information on the foundation's grants and programs. *See also* DEVELOPMENT FOUNDATIONS, 281.

Significance   The Ford Foundation, with current assets of approximately $3.5 billion, is clearly the largest organization of its type in the international development field. Unlike the Rockefeller Foundation, which has focused on science, medicine, and agriculture, the Ford Foundation has provided support internationally on a broader basis in a wide range of areas, such as development administration, human rights, education at all levels, law, the social sciences, agriculture, population and health, community development, arms control, women in development, natural resource management and environment, and culture. Thousands of nationals from developing countries have studied abroad under foundation grants in a variety of fields. Capacity and institution building have been major features of the foundation's international development programing. It has also provided leadership in coordinating the activities of international donor agencies by helping support a series of meetings of such organizations in Bellagio, Italy. Though a U.S.-based foundation, its approach has been international. Its staff and consultants are international in character, and it has provided fellowships to enable nationals from LDCs to study in a variety of geographic and political locales, including even the Soviet Union. A large professional and international network of former Ford grantees and staff members is one of the many legacies of the foundation's impact on international development.

German Foundation for International Development   (403)
(Deutsche Stiftung für Internationale Entwicklung)
(DSE)

An important German development agency established in 1959 that emphasizes dialogue and training. With headquarters in Berlin, the DSE was established by the Feder and Land governments at the initiative of the political parties represented in the *Bundestag* "to foster the relations between the Federal Republic of Germany and the developing countries on the basis of a mutual exchange of experience." Since 1959, through its various training and seminar programs DSE has enabled approximately 75,000 specialists and executive personnel from over 100 countries to discuss international development issues or undertake advanced professional training. From 1980 to 1988, DSE's annual expenditures have grown from DM 45 million to DM 88.9 million. Since 1960, the greatest number of participants in DSE programs have been from Brazil, Thailand, Kenya, the Philippines, and Indonesia. Approximately 55 percent of the DSE's programs are conducted in the Federal Republic of Germany. The DSE maintains a Documentation Centre (ZD) in Bonn and a Development Information Centre (EPIZ) in Berlin. These are valuable resources for the German public and for trainees from developing countries. The DSE also publishes five development-oriented magazines, including *D + C Development and Cooperation* (editions are available in German, French, and Spanish; *Echo aus Deutschland;* and *Entwicklung + Ländlicher Raum. See also* DEVELOPMENT FOUNDATIONS, 281.

Significance Development agencies like DSE are increasingly recognizing the importance of the human resource aspect of development. A sign of this trend is the UN's recent adoption in Djakarta of a plan for human resource development. The DSE also emphasizes training and dialogue related to the global ecological crisis and recognizes the essential need for interdisciplinary and international solutions. The DSE has recognized the growing role of women in development, and has shown a strong interest in culture. For example, the president of its board of trustees, Hans-Gunter Hope MP, has proposed the creation of the House of the Cultures of the World in former Congress Hall in Berlin as an important step in acquainting the German public with the variety in Third World cultures. Germany, with the world's largest volume of exports and a strong international currency, has vast financial resources that can contribute to human resource development in Third World countries.

German Volunteer Service (Deutscher   **(404)**
Entwicklungsdienst) (DED)
The national overseas voluntary service organization of the Federal Republic of Germany. DED operates under the mandate and financial support of the federal government in bilateral cooperation with governments of 26 developing countries, to whose requests it re-

sponds. Project agreements are determined by DED and local authorities in the host country. DED provides approximately 800 volunteers in the fields of technical programs, agriculture, health, education, and community development, with emphasis placed on technical assistance. Volunteers, with an average age of 33, are selected on the basis of vocational and personal qualifications. They are assigned to two-year terms but may extend up to five years at the request of the partner agency. DED is a nonprofit organization controlled jointly by the minister for economic cooperation and the association Lernen und Helfen Übersee (Learning and Helping Overseas), which coordinates German NGOs active in development assistance and youth work.

Significance DED's unique strategy for development assistance formally joins government and NGO efforts for local development projects. It provides a small, but well-trained corps of professionals engaged in technical assistance throughout the Third World. Its most notable contributions to development have been achieved in math and science instruction, fresh water supply, soil and forest conservation, rural health services, self-help initiatives in urban slums, and social and vocational rehabilitation programs.

Grameen Bank of Bangladesh (405)

A unique lending organization that offers capital to small-scale borrowers who are shut out of the conventional banking system. This practice has since been dubbed microenterprise lending. The bank was established in 1979 by economist Muhammed Yunis while he was teaching at Chittagong University. He guaranteed the original loans himself, finding no support from a banking community not accustomed to working with small transactions. The Grameen (village) Bank operates by forming small groups designed for mutual support and supervision. A borrower must appear with four cosigners to secure a loan, which may be as small as $1, averages $67, and seldom exceeds $300. These groups of five are combined into units of fifty that meet regularly with bank officials to discuss their projects. Most of the participants have been more than half a million landless women, many of whom have become self-employed entrepreneurs. In its first ten years, the bank established more than 350 branches, which made loans in 6,000 villages. It has lent more than $60 million to nearly 300,000 borrowers at 16 percent interest. The repayment rate on loans is a remarkable 98 percent. Currently the bank has a reserve of $11 million with 75 percent of shares owned by the poor.

Significance   The Grameen Bank of Bangladesh represents appropriate technology in the field of finance. Its growth and level of participation attest to the profound need for small-scale credit for the poor of developing nations, a need that has long been recognized. Although much has been written about appropriate scale, participation, and the need to reach the poorest of the poor in the development process, few, if any, financial institutions have geared themselves to working with the poor majority. The success of the Grameen Bank also attests to the integrity and creativity of the poor. Conventional banks can no longer argue that the poor are bad credit risks, though some caution would be advised in drawing generalized conclusions, given the diversity of conditions and cultures of the Third World. In India, for example, the Grameen system has not yet met with great success due to leadership failures. Nevertheless, the system may well prove a viable model for microenterprise lending throughout the world, including the more developed countries. It is now being implemented by other institutions such as Indonesia's Baden Kredit Kecamatan, the Rural Bank of Ghana, and a number of development agencies, including the newly created Southern Development Bancorporation, a network of financial institutions designed to provide loans to small-scale borrowers in the United States.

Group of 77   (406)

A loose affiliation of developing countries concerned with international economic issues. The group was formed during the first UN Conference on Trade and Development (UNCTAD) in 1964 through the "Joint Declaration of the 77 Developing Countries" in attendance. The declaration helped set the agenda for what emerged a decade later as the call of the LDCs for a new international economic order (NIEO). It attempts to bring about fundamental and systematic changes in trade and development relationships between North and South, using the United Nations as its forum. With no formal structure or permanent office or staff, the group includes developing countries in Africa, Asia, and Latin America that share similar positions in the world economy. These countries now total almost 130 (127 in 1986), but the original designation persists. While the term *Group of 77* is often used interchangeably with *nonaligned nations*, the designation does not include the Eastern Bloc countries. *See also* NEW INTERNATIONAL ECONOMIC ORDER, 161; THIRD WORLD, 122.

Significance   As it did at UNCTAD I, the Group of 77 continues to represent the general trade and development concerns of the LDCs and serves as a symbol of Third World solidarity. Admittedly the

NIEO reforms envisioned by the group have not been realized, but it persists in providing new frameworks for international trade nego- tiations and development cooperation, and functions as the voice of the largest voting block at the United Nations. The members meet as a major caucus before sessions of the General Assembly and at in- ternational conferences dealing with economic and development matters to plan a Third World strategy on critical issues. Thus, on most economic-related issues, Third World voting prevails. In some cases, however, unity gives way to diversity. At the UN Law of the Sea Conference in the 1980s, for example, Group of 77 members were frequently divided on questions relating to their positions as land- locked versus coastal states, and as importers versus exporters of cer- tain minerals.

Gulf Cooperation Council (GCC) (407)

An organization of six Arab gulf states that together hold half of the world's oil reserves. The council, composed of Kuwait, Bahrain, Qatar, Oman, United Arab Emirates, and Saudi Arabia, aims to coor- dinate and integrate the economic policies of the member states and to strengthen the group's position within the world economy. Of im- mediate concern for the GCC is the diversification of the region's economy to reduce dependence on crude oil production, following the example of Saudi Arabia which has managed to sustain economic growth with steady or reduced oil production. The group plans to di- versify through production of refined oil products such as plastics and petrochemicals. As a group the six states generate considerable bar- gaining power with the United States and the European Economic Community, which have resisted their diversification efforts through the imposition of high tariffs on refined oil and oil-based products. As a market for U.S. and EEC goods, the six states are quite limited given their combined population of only 12 million.

Significance   Because of its members' strategic location and vast oil reserves, the GCC is potentially one of the most economically influen- tial organizations in the world. Its importance will depend on the extent and speed with which the oil-importing nations can lessen their dependence on oil imports. Currently, fuel payments account for the bulk of many developing countries' national budgets. The United States imports nearly half of its oil, well above the amount im- ported before the oil crisis of 1973. To date, the oil-importing na- tions have gained much from the GCC's orientation, which exerts a powerful influence within OPEC to keep oil prices and supply from fluctuating significantly, thus preventing economic crises in many nations. Among its member states, the GCC will likely continue to serve as a tool for sustained economic growth and development and even political stability within a region of high volatility.

Harvard Institute for International Development (408) (HIID)

An integral part of Harvard University that is actively engaged in development projects around the world. Established in 1962, this institute was known as the Development Advisory Service until 1974. Because of the HIID, hundreds of Harvard professors, research associates, and graduate students have been able to gain hands-on experience in working on development projects around the world. Currently the institute has 83 research professionals and 38 supporting professionals.

Significance   The presence of HIID on the campus reflects Harvard's commitment to share its expertise and technical knowledge with developing countries. Individuals returning from HIID projects overseas in turn contribute to internationalizing and enriching the Harvard undergraduate and graduate curriculum. HIID also provides a mechanism for development scholars/doers to engage in both academic and practical development work on a long-term continuing basis. The presence of HIID contributes to Harvard's role in training professionals and students from developing countries. In his book, *Beyond the Ivory Tower: The Social Responsibilities of the Modern University* (1982), Harvard's president, Derek Bok, argues that universities have an obligation to engage in technical assistance work in developing countries. HIID represents a highly successful model and mechanism for links between universities and developing countries.

Improving the Efficiency of Educational Systems (IIES) (409)

A consortium of U.S. organizations involved in educational development. Made up of Florida State University, Howard University, the Institute of International Research, and the State University of New York at Albany, IIES has as its principal goals helping developing countries improve the performance of their educational systems and strengthen their capabilities for educational planning, management, and research. IIES is funded through a 1984 initiative of AID. Countries collaborating with the IIES initiative to improve educational efficiency are Botswana, Haiti, Indonesia, Liberia, Nepal, Somalia, and the Yemen Arab Republic. The consortium regularly publishes *IIES Communiqué*, which provides details on its activities. In 1988, Douglas

Windham, an economist of education at SUNY-Albany, published *IIES Project Summary,* which assesses the rationale for IIES, its structure, the nature of its activities, and its accomplishments to date. *See also* EDUCATIONAL PLANNING, 244.

Significance   Large-scale development projects of the IIES type represent a laboratory of interactions between Western professionals and indigenous development personnel and institutions. Projects of this type generally reflect a philosophy of building human resource capacity and institution building. The cooperation among three universities and a private development agency (IIR) is another special dimension of this project. Evaluation of such efforts involving substantial AID funding represents a formidable challenge. Because seven countries in five regions are involved, there is an unusual opportunity to assess how varying cultural and political contexts impinge on the potential effectiveness of a major development project. This project also represents so-called soft development, which focuses on human capacity building rather than material equipment and physical construction.

Institute for Natural Resources in Africa (INRA)   (410)

The second United Nations University (UNU) research and training center approved in 1986. The main center of INRA will be located at Yamoussoukro, the capital of the Côte d'Ivoire, and its mineral resources unit will be in Lusaka at the School of Mines of the University of Zambia. The governments of Côte d'Ivoire and Zambia have pledged $5 million and $2 million respectively to the UNU's Endowed Fund for INRA. France, Ghana, Nigeria, and the OPEC Fund will also provide support to INRA. INRA is designed to

strengthen national institutions in Africa, help scientists throughout the continent attract others back to Africa, and, in general, help provide the African scientific community with the necessary management framework to ensure that the results of high quality research are applied rapidly and on a sustained basis in areas where they are urgently needed.

Significance   Given Africa's serious environmental problems, natural resource potential, and relative lack of scientific and technological capacity, INRA is a critically important institution. As with the UNU itself, initial funding support for INRA has been disappointing, though once it begins operating it will be able to make its case more persuasively. With substantial funding, INRA has the potential to make a major impact on Africa's ability to achieve sustainable development and better meet the basic needs of its people.

Institute of Development Studies (IDS)   **(411)**
A leading academic center for the study of development issues. Established in 1966 at the University of Sussex in England, its basic mandate is to serve as the national center concerned with Third World development and the relationships between rich and poor countries. IDS's three basic activities are research, teaching, and operational assignments in developing countries. The institute has eight thematic research groups in the following areas: rural development; gender; health; education; role of the state; international, that is, foreign trade strategies of LDCs; structural adjustment and international finance; and industrialization. IDS's teaching program has five dimensions: (1) 4- to 6-week study seminars; (2) 13-week short courses on selected development policy issues; (3) an interdisciplinary master's degree program in development studies; (4) a master's program on gender and development; and (5) extensive supervision for doctorates in development studies. Its annual budget of approximately £3 million derives primarily from a grant from the British Overseas Development Administration and the institute's direct income from various fees, projects, and other grants. Among the current IDS staff of 45 fellows are such noted scholars as Robert Chambers, Hans Singer, Richard Jolly, and Stephany Griffith-Jones. IDS has its own development library with over 200,000 nonserial holdings and is a depository for UN material. Its extensive publication program includes *IDS Bulletin*, a quarterly with each issue devoted to a specific development theme; *IDS Discussion Papers; IDS Research Reports;* and *IDS Development Bibliography*, a new series. IDS has just negotiated a book series to be published by Oxford University Press. *See also* ROBERT CHAMBERS, 11; H. W. SINGER, 50.

Significance   Much current international development policy and thinking are dominated by the World Bank and the International Monetary Fund. Thus, it is important to have independent study centers like IDS that can provide alternative perspectives on development issues. The staff of the IDS is also actively involved in various ongoing projects around the world. These frequent field encounters enable the staff to keep current on development issues and thus to enrich the institute's teaching and training programs. IDS studies that have had the greatest impact include Michael Lipton's *Why Poor People Stay Poor* (1976) and Robert Chambers's *Rural Development:*

Putting the Last First (1983). IDS is a leading and cutting-edge center for the study of development issues.

Inter-American Development Bank (IDB) (412)

The major international public lending institution for Latin America. The bank was established in 1959 by the Organization of American States (OAS). Members' contributions provide the source for all loans. The IDB operates with ordinary and interregional capital resources and has established a Fund of Special Operations (FSO), from which low-interest loans repayable in the currency of the borrower are made. Voting is weighted by the amount of capital stock held by each member state. As a result, the United States holds 35 percent of the votes. Brazil, Argentina, Mexico, and Venezuela have received the major share, over 40 percent, of all loans administered by the IDB. Initially, the bank placed heavy emphasis on social development projects that were largely supported by the United States's Social Progress Trust Fund. By the mid–1960s the focus had shifted to the more restrictive FSO and the support of production and infrastructure sectors. These changes paralleled the shifts in policy occurring within the Alliance for Progress. Major areas of activity supported by the IDB since then include agriculture and fisheries, industry and mining, and physical infrastructure (energy, transportation, and communication). Along with tourism, these areas account for about 80 percent of all activities supported by IDB loans. The bank also provides technical assistance to borrowers. *See also* DEBT CRISIS, 134; ALLIANCE FOR PROGRESS, 275.

Significance   IDB's policies since its inception reflect the politics, dilemmas, and contradictions of inter-American financial aid that have contributed to the current debt crisis. With the containment of Fidel Castro in Cuba, emphasis shifted from social development to production and infrastructure. Even though the majority of soft loans intended for the poorest countries actually went to the most developed countries of Latin America, by the early 1980s Brazil and Mexico had become the largest debtor nations and could not meet repayment schedules. Since 1982, inter-American trade has declined as the IDB searches for new ways to meet the needs of the major contributor to the bank, the United States, and those of the Latin American states.

Inter Governmental Group on Indonesia (IGGI) (413)

A group of 16 donor nations formed in 1967 to coordinate financial aid to Indonesia. The IGGI is actually not a formal organization, but instead a series of meetings and discussions concerning development assistance to Indonesia. An abortive communist coup attempt in September 1985 led to the eventual overthrow of Sukarno and a major restructuring of the Indonesian economy away from his undisciplined inflationary and debt-producing policies. In general, the IGGI discussions led to pressure for the donor nations to improve the terms for new financial aid to Indonesia. The IGGI also enabled Indonesia to renegotiate its debt accrued during the Sukarno years. In 1967 the IGGI coordinated approximately $167 million of financial assistance to Indonesia.

Significance   The IGGI provided an open forum to discuss Indonesian development policies and related foreign aid policies of the donor nations. This group is an impressive example of country-oriented aid coordination. While the coordination among donor agencies is highly commendable, in the 1990s and the twenty-first century, a mechanism such as the IGGI would likely be resented as impinging too much on the economic sovereignty of LDCs. In the late 1960s, however, Indonesia was attempting to restore its international economic reputation and legitimacy, and the IGGI provided a valuable forum for that process. G. A. Posthumus, a Dutch adviser to Indonesia from 1969 to 1971, has written a thoughtful overview of the IGGI, *The Inter Governmental Group on Indonesia (I.G.G.I.)* (1971).

Intermediate Technology Development Group, Ltd. (414)
(ITDG)

The world's pioneer organization in the development and promotion of appropriate or intermediate technology for Third World development. ITDG was founded in 1965 by E. F. Schumacher, Julia Porter, and George McRobie, who continues to direct the organization. The group's activities focus on meeting the technological needs of the rural poor, which are often bypassed by conventional development programs or provided with ill-suited technology. The stated aim of ITDG is "to act as a technical advising resource for development organizations, field personnel, and the public, serving to promote an awareness of the importance of the choice of technology in development." In the group's work in such areas as building construction, water provision, agriculture, transportation, health, energy, and female employment, great emphasis is placed on appropriateness and affordability in low-income areas. ITDG contends that "rural areas will continue to grow unless self-help technologies are made available to the poor countries with assistance in their use." ITDG of North

America, Inc., is a sister organization with shared goals. *See also* APPROPRIATE TECHNOLOGY, 276; E. F. SCHUMACHER, 45.

Significance   Since its founding, ITDG has served as the leading organization in the appropriate technology movement. Its goals and activities embody the vision of E. F. Schumacher, who popularized the notion of industrialization and development through intermediate technology. The group continues as one of the best known and best established organizations in the field of appropriate technology.

International Development Research Centre (IDRC)   (415)
A highly respected research organization with broad-ranging development interests. Also known as the Canadian International Development Research Centre, it was established in 1970 by an act of the Canadian Parliament and is funded by the same body. The purpose of the center is to initiate, support, and conduct research into the problems of developing regions and into the means of applying and adapting scientific, technical, and other knowledge in those regions. IDRC cooperates with the Canadian International Development Agency (CIDA) and numerous intergovernmental and nongovernmental organizations.

Significance   IDRC, one of the world's leading development research institutions in the world, is a vital element of Canadian international assistance and an invaluable source of information for other development agencies. The center conducts and supports research in a broad range of areas including food production, processing, and storage; silvaculture and aquaculture; water and energy supply; health services; population studies and family planning; science and technology policy; and communication and information sciences. IDRC also helps developing countries to enhance their own development research. Projects supported by the center are usually identified, designed, and managed by LDC researchers in their own countries. In North America, IDRC is well known for its influence on policy formulation and analysis related to international development assistance, and its promotion of development education.

International Executive Service Corps (IESC)   (416)
A volunteer corps initiated in 1964 by President Lyndon Johnson to provide experienced U.S. executives as consultants to projects in developing countries. IESC has 80 offices around the world and since 1965 it has placed more than 10,000 volunteers in assignments in 82

countries. These retired American executives share their knowledge by spending three to four months in a country and usually by helping small firms. Volunteer executives receive no salary or consultants' fees. Their basic living expenses are provided by IESC and/or the host government. IESC receives substantial funding from AID and approximately 200 corporations. IESC headquarters in Stamford, Connecticut, maintains a registry of approximately 10,000 volunteers covering 200 categories of expertise. In each country in which IESC is present, a local advisory board articulates the nation's special needs. It is estimated that 59 percent of the projects in which IESC volunteers are involved are related to basic human needs. *See also* PEACE CORPS, 433; TECHNICAL ASSISTANCE, 305.

Significance Retired executives represent a group of individuals with considerable expertise relevant to many developing countries. IESC may have been initiated in part as a response to the criticism that U.S. Peace Corps volunteers tended to be young with little or no practical experience. Questions have been raised about the success of IESC volunteers in adapting their expertise to local conditions and their limited cross-cultural or language abilities. Despite these possible limitations, IESC represents an impressive effort to freely share knowledge, technology, and other expertise to developing countries. It provides a useful complement to the Peace Corps, which would rarely attract individuals with the experience represented by IESC volunteers.

International Foundation for the Survival and (417) Development of Humanity

The first international private foundation to be based in the Soviet Union. The foundation was formed on January 14, 1988, in Moscow. Though its legal seat will be in Stockholm, the organization will be located in Moscow with a branch office in Washington, D.C. The foundation "calls for new cooperative efforts for harnessing humankind's ingenuity, knowledge, skills, and resources across all national and ideological boundaries to meet global threats and challenges"(*see* The International Foundation 1990). A tentative list of priority funding areas includes disarmament; development, including education, medicine, culture, religion, economy, and organization; environment; and human rights. The foundation has an elected governing board of directors, comprised of 30 prominent individuals from 12 countries. Ideas for the foundation grew out of the International Peace Forum for a Nuclear-Free World and Human Survival held in Moscow in February 1987. Subsequent preparatory meetings for establishing the foundation were held in 1987 in Trieste, Moscow, and New York. *See also* DEVELOPMENT FOUNDATIONS, 281.

Significance　　This new private foundation was formally announced in the presence of Mikhail Gorbachev in the Kremlin on January 15, 1988. Its location in the Soviet Union reflects Gorbachev's various reform initiatives. It will be interesting to follow the development of this new foundation and observe the extent of its autonomy and its possible use by the Soviet Union as a foreign policy tool. Of special importance will be the nature of the foundation's funding and the obstacles posed by the ruble's not being a hard currency. This organization promises to be a fascinating new actor in the international development field.

International Fund for Agricultural Development　　　　**(418)**
(IFAD)

A specialized UN agency with headquarters in Rome to help small farmers and the landless poor in developing countries. Founded in 1977, it has a 143-nation governing council. The fund has provided about $2.3 billion for loans and grants for 221 projects in 89 developing countries. Funding for the IFAD comes primarily from the Western nations and major oil producers. IFAD is the only development agency in which OPEC participates as a bloc. IFAD funding is based on voluntary contributions rather than annual fixed assessments.

Significance　　The IFAD is considered one of the most successful and efficient specialized agencies of the United Nations. It has the reputation of being the only UN organization whose primary goal is to help the rural poor to help themselves. Its relatively small size enables it to avoid the excessive bureaucratization associated with much larger development agencies. In 1988 it faced something of a financial crisis because of a drop in donations from oil-rich countries, resulting from the slump in the global oil market. The IFAD then attempted to persuade middle-income developing countries such as South Korea and Brazil to provide more support for its activities. The IFAD's need to rely continually on donations for its operating expenses makes it much less financially secure than other UN agencies that are funded through regularized annual assessments. IFAD's 1990 goal is $750 million. Overall, its size and its emphasis on assisting the landless make it part of the new "barefoot" approach to development.

International Labor Organization (ILO)   **(419)**

An organization associated with the UN that works to promote social justice for working people everywhere. Founded in 1919 under the Treaty of Versailles, ILO was an autonomous institution associated with the League of Nations. An agreement approved on December 14, 1946, made the ILO the first agency associated with the United Nations. It formulates international policies and programs to help improve working and living conditions; creates international labor standards to serve as guidelines for national authorities in putting labor policies into action; and carries out an extensive program of technical cooperation to help governments make these policies effective in practice. The organization also engages in training, education, and research to help advance these efforts. For example, in 1969, the ILO launched the World Employment Programme (WEP) as its main contribution to the International Development Strategy for the UN's Second Development Decade. The program included short-term advisory missions, the formation of national and regional employment teams, and a wide-ranging research program. Workers' and employers' representatives have equal voices with those of governments in formulating ILO policies. Politicization contrary to U.S. objectives led to the United States's withdrawal in 1977, weakening the ILO by the loss of 25 percent of its revenue base. In 1980, the United States rejoined the organization.

Significance   The ILO has been instrumental in setting international labor standards in such areas as freedom of association, working conditions, and wages and compensation. This is especially important considering the ability of international corporations to move to countries of least resistance. The member states who ratify the conventions are obliged to implement their provisions, while recommendations provide guidance for national policy, legislation, and practice. Through its technical cooperation program, ILO experts assist member countries in such fields as vocational training, management, employment policies, occupational safety and health, cooperatives, and small-scale handicraft industries. The ILO operates the International Institute for Labor Studies in Geneva, and the International Center for Advanced Technical and Vocational Training in Turin, Italy.

International Monetary Fund (IMF)   **(420)**

International lending and finance regulatory body established in 1945. Its charter is contained within the articles of agreement adopted by the UN Monetary and Financial Conference held at Bretton Woods, Massachusetts, in 1944. Headquartered in Washington, D.C., the IMF became a specialized agency of the United Nations in 1947. It is closely affiliated with the World Bank. The boards of governors meet jointly on an annual basis, the two organizations engage in numerous parallel and overlapping missions, and membership in the World Bank is contingent upon membership in the IMF. The fund was established as a tool for international monetary cooperation, to promote stable foreign currency exchange markets and international trade. Its role as an instrument for correcting balance-of-payment deficits of member countries has recently cast the IMF as a central figure in the international debt crisis. Each of its 150 member nations is represented by a governor on the board of governors, and a 21-member executive board determines rules and procedures of operation. The fund relies upon members' contributions and borrowing arrangements to finance its own operations. Voting power is set by a complex quota system determined by each member's national income, monetary reserves, export/income ratios, and other economic indicators. As a result the United States controls about 20 percent of the votes, and decision making is dominated by the Group of Ten, composed of representatives from the major industrial powers: Belgium, Canada, France, the Federal Republic of Germany, Italy, Japan, the Netherlands, Sweden, the United Kingdom, and the United States, along with Switzerland, an associate member. The quota also determines the amount of financial reserves a country must make available to the fund as well as its rights to draw on the general fund. Drawings are generally limited to 200 percent of a member's quota with repayments at 7 percent interest over a three-to-five-year period. The IMF pays creditors at the current dominant interest rate. In 1969 the IMF created a scheme of special drawing rights (SDRs) to supplement the general fund. The SDR, sometimes referred to as paper gold, is an accounting creation without any backing that debtor nations may use to settle debts. Debtors run down their drawing rights while creditors' balances increase. The value of the SDR is determined by a basket of major currencies.

With the collapse of the Bretton Woods system in the early 1970s the role and operations of the IMF underwent a major transition. The Jamaica Agreement of 1976 reduced the role of gold, acknowledged the system of floating currencies introduced by the EEC in 1973, revised the SDR system, and authorized the sale of the fund's gold reserves. In 1983 and 1984 the IMF increased quotas and availability of funds in light of the debt crisis and began playing a crucial role in the creation of rescue packages for highly indebted nations. In 1990, after three years of negotiations, the members of the IMF agreed to increase the resources of the fund from $120 billion to

$180 billion to meet the growing demands of the Third World and Eastern Europe. *See also* DEBT CRISIS, 134; WORLD BANK, 454; AUSTERITY PROGRAM, 124.

Significance   The International Monetary Fund was established as a vital link in helping stabilize the international finance system after World War II. It has generally been successful in promoting flexible but stable currency exchange markets. Much of the fund's work involves annual meetings with member countries to ensure that their financial policies are soundly promoting economic growth and price stability. In addition, the IMF exercises surveillance over the exchange rate policies of member nations. As an outgrowth of these functions, the IMF has become a key institution relevant to the international debt crisis. It now works closely with the World Bank to assist indebted nations in avoiding default on loans from the bank and private commercial institutions. The IMF has emerged as the lender of last resort for many developing countries. Without a good credit rating from the IMF, it is virtually impossible for countries to receive credit from any other institution. Loans are most often made under the conditions of structural adjustment or austerity programs as required by the IMF. This usually involves the devaluation of currency, export expansion, and reduced government spending on social services and subsidies. The fund's adjustment programs have been broadly criticized for being overly draconian and unduly burdensome on the poorest sectors of society. Nevertheless, IMF funds are in high demand by debtor governments, which have little other recourse. Ironically, IMF lending to developing countries has dropped dramatically from its peak of 12 billion SDRs in 1983, partially as a result of the growing indebtedness of the United States, now the world's largest debtor. Currently, the IMF draws in more funds from LDCs than it lends. Nearly half of recent funds have gone to highly indebted Latin American countries. The IMF will no doubt continue to play a major role in the international finance system.

International Planned Parenthood Federation (IPPF)   (421)
A leading international family planning organization. IPPF was founded in 1952 in Bombay and originated from the International Committee on Planned Parenthood, first gathered in 1948. It has member agencies in 114 countries with an annual budget of over $55 million. The organization's activities are widespread, as reflected in its statement of purpose:

to promote the formation of family planning associations in all countries; assist the integration of family planning into the development effort; further the training of physicians, nurses, health visitors and social workers in the practical implementation of family planning services; assist governments, through member family associations and in cooperation with other NGOs in implementing the World Population Plan of Action and the recommendations of the 1984 International Conference on Population.

IPPF supports family planning services throughout the world as well as scientific research on the biological, sociological implications of human fertility and its regulation. The organization holds consultative status with ECOSOC and UNESCO. It also works in cooperation with UNFPA, the FAO, and UNICEF. Its publications include two quarterlies, *People* and *Research in Reproduction,* as well as the bimonthly *IPPF Bulletin. See also* POPULATION PLANNING, 254.

Significance IPPF is the major private body promoting family planning in developing countries. Its activities have helped create highly successful and model programs in places such as Korea, Taiwan, Singapore, and Hong Kong. These cases illustrate the potentially powerful links between successful family planning and related economic and educational development.

International Potato Center (CIP) (422)

One of 13 international applied agricultural research centers under the umbrella of the Consultative Group on International Agriculture Research (CGIAR). Established in the early 1970s with Rockefeller Foundation support in Peru, CIP collects and maintains a world germ plasm pool of wild and cultivated native South American potatoes. This bank of germ plasm contains natural resistances valuable for potato breeders in a variety of developmental settings. The World Potato Collection at CIP contains all known existing wild and domesticated potato species. More than 10,000 varieties grown by Andean farmers have been preserved. The center also supports experimental research to improve potato farming. CIP produces the extremely valuable *Potato Atlas,* which provides an overview of potato agriculture in developing countries. CIP has also developed the International Potato Reference files containing data on potato production in 80 developing countries in the Americas, Africa, Asia, and the South Pacific. *See also* CONSULTATIVE GROUP ON INTERNATIONAL AGRICULTURAL RESEARCH, 394.

Significance   Along with rice, wheat, and corn, the potato is one of the world's key nutritional staples. Thus, the applied research on potatoes and their cultivation at CIP is particularly important. Along with CIMMYT in Mexico, CIP is noted for utilization of applied anthropologists in its research program. Unfortunately, such applied work is not always fully appreciated in academia despite its important implications for global welfare. The CIP does research in different agroecological zones of Peru to make its work more relevant to other developing countries. Applied research centers like CIP are making important contributions to preserving global biological diversity and reducing hunger. The irony of CIP is that Peru itself is still facing such serious development problems related to poverty and inequality.

International Rice Research Institute (IRRI)   **(423)**
An applied agricultural research and training center established in 1960 at Los Baños by the Ford and Rockefeller foundations with the help and approval of the government of the Philippines. IRRI is one of 13 applied agricultural research centers supported by the Consultative Group on International Agriculture Research (CGIAR), which consists of 50 donor agencies or countries. Among research projects it supports: genetic evaluation and utilization, control and management of rice pests, irrigation water management, constraints on rice yields, soil and crop management, and consequences of new technology. IRRI's professional staff includes 63 agricultural economists, 48 entomologists, 62 agronomists, and 37 plant pathologists. The institute maintains an international rice germ plasm center. In one of its cooperative programs with other countries, IRRI helped China to set up a national rice research institute. IRRI's total budget for 1986 was $32,625,586 U.S. with the largest support coming, in decreasing order, from AID, the Japanese government, and the European Economic Community. *See also* ROBERT CHANDLER, 64; GREEN REVOLUTION, 180; CONSULTATIVE GROUP ON INTERNATIONAL AGRICULTURE RESEARCH, 394.

Significance   Given the importance of rice as a major world food resource, the research work of IRRI is particularly crucial. Research at IRRI resulted in the influential but controversial Green Revolution. A key question is whether the type of research supported at IRRI increases the world's genetic diversity of rice varieties, or whether it leads to greater homogeneity of varieties in use and thus to greater vulnerability. As with the CIP in Peru, an irony of IRRI is that the Philippines continues to face serious problems of poverty and inequality.

Japan International Cooperation Agency (JICA) (424)

Japan's organization responsible for the provision of development assistance. In the 1980s Japan emerged as a *foreign aid superpower*, to use Robert Orr's apt term, and it became the world's largest donor agency in 1988, making JICA a powerful actor on the world development scene. Actually, Japan's overseas development assistance is implemented by both JICA and the Overseas Economic Cooperation Fund (OECF). The latter disburses yen loans, while JICA administers grants and technical assistance. Compared to the other members of the DAC or OECD, Japan provides the smallest percentage of outright grants, based on the philosophy that loans encourage the development of economic self-reliance and provide a recycling of development funds. In Southeast Asia, there is a common view that Japan offers better terms on its loans than the World Bank, for example. The aid programs of JICA have tended to emphasize large-scale infrastructure projects. Once a debtor nation, Japan has evolved its aid program through four distinct phases: (1) reparation payments to Asian countries damaged by Japanese militarism during World War II; (2) promotion of Japanese exports to developing countries; (3) securing areas and strategic supply lines of natural resources; and (4) a current attempt to be responsive to international pressures for "economic citizenship" and to reduce Japan's huge trade surpluses. These stages are articulated in Robert M. Orr's book, *The Emergence of Japan's Foreign Aid Power* (1990). *See also* BILATERAL AID, 277; BILATERAL AID AGENCIES, 278.

Significance Though Japan's level of overseas development assistance in 1987 was only 0.31 percent of its GNP, lagging behind the DAC average of 0.34, its foreign aid has been growing dramatically, primarily because of the overall strength of the Japanese economy and the strong value of the yen. Despite its image, Japanese aid is now less tied than commonly thought. The private sector also plays a major role in Japanese aid. Keidanren, Japan's formal business association, recently established the Japan International Development Organization (JAIDO) which may become larger than the government's aid program. Some 63 percent of Japan's aid goes to Asian countries and 34 percent to Southeast Asian nations. Thus, Japan's aid is an important element in the economies of a number of Asian countries. As a foreign aid superpower and the world's largest donor agency, Japan and JICA will have increasing political and economic influence in the decade of the 1990s and the century ahead.

Japan Overseas Cooperation Volunteers (JOCV) (425)

The Japanese equivalent of the U.S. Peace Corps. In its 25 years of operation since being established in 1965, this organization has sent approximately 10,000 volunteers to work in developing countries. Currently about 2,000 Japanese volunteers are serving in 38 countries. JOCV is known for its selectivity. Only one in six applicants is accepted, and the Japanese volunteers have stronger technical skills than the average Peace Corps volunteer. JOCV is also noted for the rigor of its training program for volunteers. The size of JOCV has steadily increased and the agency is currently trying to triple the number of its volunteers. *See also* PEACE CORPS, 433.

Significance   With its vast trade surplus and foreign exchange reserves, Japan is now the world's largest donor agency. Given the extent of Japan's financial capability, the size of JOCV is surprisingly small, particularly compared to the Peace Corps which has placed over 125,000 volunteers overseas during its three decades of existence. A major expansion of JOCV might provide greater balance in Japanese foreign assistance, which has been traditionally oriented toward large capital projects. Service abroad can greatly facilitate Japan's process of internationalization, as returned JOCV personnel play an important role in development education in Japan and internationally. With a significant increase in size JOVC could become a substantial lobbying force for greater Japanese foreign assistance and less tied aid.

Mennonite Central Committee (MCC)   (426)

The international service organization of the Mennonite and Brethren in Christ churches of North America. MCC supports nearly 1,000 volunteers working primarily at the village level in over 50 countries. The organization was founded in 1920 to aid Russian Mennonite refugees but has since evolved into a well-known international development organization. Volunteers offer services in a variety of sectors including agriculture, education, health and nutrition, appropriate technology, disaster/refuge relief, community development, material and food aid, income/employment generation, and conflict resolution. In addition, MCC operates a number of specialized programs. These include: SELFHELP Crafts, which supports cottage industry and distributes the products, primarily through MCC-related shops; Mennonite Disaster Service, which coordinates work crews and relief efforts following natural disasters; and Peace Section, which concerns itself with the broad issues of justice, militarism, and reconciliation in North America and abroad. MCC also sponsors an international visitors program, youth exchange, and development education. *See also* PRIVATE VOLUNTARY ORGANIZATIONS, 300.

Significance   The work and dedication of Mennonite Central Committee volunteers is highly regarded throughout the development community and the Third World. MCC has developed a reputation for devising and carrying out effective small-scale and low-cost development projects. The three-year commitment required of most overseas volunteers no doubt contributes to their unusual ability to work in concert with local people. In this regard, MCC serves as a model for other development agencies often criticized for carrying out preconceived "quick and dirty" projects. The range of concerns and activities of MCC also signifies that the organization conceives of "development" in broad terms. As a church-related organization, MCC enjoys the advantages of a steady and built-in constituency which not only provides the majority of volunteers, but also enables it to expend fewer resources, relative to other private agencies, in garnering financial support. MCC also maintains a deliberate distance from United States foreign aid and frequently voices its opposition to official foreign policy, particularly as it relates to developing nations. The organization's presence in countries with widely varying political systems reflects its commitment to "people to people" partnerships irrespective of ideological differences between governments.

Organization for Economic Cooperation and Development (OECD)   (427)

Organization of 24 industrialized market economy nations formed in 1961. It replaced and extended the work of the Organization for European Economic Cooperation, which coordinated efforts under the Marshall Plan for European economic recovery following World War II. The OECD coordinates and promotes policies designed to enhance economic growth, financial stability, and trade in and among member nations. In addition it attempts to harmonize international development assistance directed toward the LDCs. The organization is governed by a council comprised of representatives from all member states. Activities are carried out by more than 200 committees and a secretariat, which deal with a variety of topics and issues including economic policy coordination, consumer affairs, science, labor, insurance, trade, technical assistance, industry, and environment. The most important semiautonomous agencies are the International Energy Agency, the Development Center, the Educational Research and Innovation Center, and the Interfutures Project, a long-range study and analysis group. Member nations include 19 Western European nations and Australia, Canada, Japan, New Zealand, and the United States. Yugoslavia holds special status as an associate member. Bilateral aid levels and policies of OECD members are discussed, debated, coordinated, and monitored by the Development Assistance Committee (DAC). *See also* BILATERAL AID, 277; DEVELOPMENT ASSISTANCE COMMITTEE, 398.

Significance   The OECD coordinates the activities and policies of the most economically powerful nations of the world. Decisions relating to aid for development and other matters are usually initiated by the Group of 7 largest members: Canada, France, Germany, Great Britain, Italy, Japan, and the United States. Cooperation among these nations is vital for the health of the broader world economy. In addition, the organization collects and disseminates extensive statistical information and studies. OECD has an extensive publication program, including an annual volume on the development assistance efforts of member states titled *Development Co-operation.* In 1985 the OECD published a valuable review of 25 years of development cooperation by its members.

Organization of African Unity (OAU)   (428)
An organization that supports African development, including the role of liberation movements. The OAU was established on May 25, 1963, in Addis Ababa, Ethiopia, with its charter signed by representatives of 32 governments. Today 51 governments and two liberation movements (the African National Congress and POLISARIO) are members of OAU. It has been instrumental in persuading the United Nations to accept liberation movements as legitimate and to grant them observer status. OAU also has been involved in settling, or at least influencing, the resolution of a number of boundary conflicts and interstate civil uprisings on the continent. The economic committee of OAU studies in depth the causes for the small share of developing countries in world trade, the persistent deterioration of terms of trade associated with the export of primary products, and related problems. OAU has also made plans for continental telecommunication networks, efficient air and road transport, and standardized and coordinated postal procedures and practices on the African continent. *See also* DECOLONIZATION, 200; NEW INTERNATIONAL ECONOMIC ORDER, 161.

Significance   Since its founding, the OAU's activities and efforts have extended well beyond those of a political consortium. In addition to its promotion of the unity and solidarity of African states, the OAU has helped coordinate and intensify the cooperation and efforts of African states to achieve a better life for their peoples. The OAU has attempted, often with limited success, to coordinate and harmonize members' political, diplomatic, educational, cultural, health, welfare, scientific, technical, and defense policies. This has proven to be no easy task given the size, diversity, and relative impoverishment of the continent. In 1980 the heads of state of the OAU countries adopted the Lagos Plan of Action, the first of its kind since the establishment of the OAU. It is an African development strategy for the two decades spanning 1980–2000. The plan begins by outlining the disappointing results of the development strategies implemented in the previous development decades. In addition to reiterating the need for greater cooperation in development efforts, the plan calls for the establishment of an African Common Market and an African Economic Community by the year 2000. If this is to come about, no doubt the OAU must play a key role.

Organization of Petroleum Export Countries (OPEC)   (429)

Organization of 13 oil exporters, which functions as the best known and most successful of Third World–based commodity cartels. Members include Algeria, Ecuador, Gabon, Indonesia, Iran, Iraq, Kuwait, Libya, Nigeria, Qatar, Saudi Arabia, United Arab Emirates, and Venezuela. Together these countries account for one-third of current world oil production and two-thirds of proven reserves. OPEC was founded in 1960 with headquarters based in Vienna. During its first decade, the organization faced a buyer's market, and attempts at price control were only modestly successful. Much of the decision-making power regarding production and pricing rested with the major transnational oil companies. In 1965, OPEC nations began coordinating levels of production and, subsequently, prices. OPEC began to assert itself more effectively in the early 1970s. In 1970, OPEC raised prices 30 percent and moved to obtain greater shares of control in the oil industry. By 1973, the beginning of the energy crisis, OPEC nations accounted for 55 percent of the world's production of crude oil. At that time, OPEC ceased to negotiate price increases with the seven major transnationals that controlled 90 percent of world oil trade. These moves coincided with the Arab oil embargo, a response by a subblock of OPEC nations to the Arab-Israeli War of 1972. It should be noted that the non-Arab members actually increased production during the embargo. The new assertiveness of OPEC in a period of rapid growth in demand for petroleum led to the dramatic rise in world oil prices from $3 a barrel in 1970 to a peak of $40 in 1979. Over the next decade the Western industrialized nations, which consume most of the OPEC oil by far, responded by supporting production and purchases from non-OPEC countries such as Mexico, Canada, and Norway; increasing domestic production; and encouraging conservation and efficiency in energy use. As a result, by the early 1980s, OPEC faced a soft market, even after the second oil shock brought on by the Iran-Iraq War. Meanwhile, its share of world production dropped to 30 percent by 1983. However, OPEC countries still account for two-thirds of the world's known reserves, a figure that is likely to increase. OPEC countries are currently producing at half capacity while other producers are maximizing output. *See also* NEW INTERNATIONAL ECONOMIC ORDER, 161; COMMODITY AGREEMENTS, 131.

Significance　　While the Organization of Petroleum Export Countries has been only moderately effective in controlling market prices, it stands alone as the most successful and important of commodity cartels. The dramatic price hikes in the early 1970s were primarily attributable to OPEC policies, but OPEC currently plays a bigger role in moderating and stabilizing world prices than in raising them. OPEC also stands as an important symbol for the Third World. It is not coincidental that the call for a new international economic order was issued on the heels of OPEC's assertiveness in the early 1970s and the success of the Arab oil embargo. OPEC was the first Third World–based organization to gain any effective leverage over the Western industrialized nations. OPEC recognized that higher prices could also have detrimental effects on oil-importing developing nations. In a measure of solidarity, in 1974 OPEC established a compensation fund for LDCs affected by the rising prices of petroleum. In 1976 this became the OPEC Special Fund for International Development. OPEC's role in the world oil market and the world economy is now diminished. However, its long-term policies, coupled with diminishing supplies of non-OPEC oil, assure its continued importance well into the future.

Overseas Development Council (ODC)　　　　　　　　　　(430)

A private, nonprofit organization whose purpose is to foster understanding of "the economic and social problems confronting the developing countries and of the interests of the United States in their development progress." The council functions as a policy research center focusing on four key areas of U.S. relations with developing countries: trade and industrial policy, international finance and investment, development cooperation, and U.S. foreign policy. Through staff and commissioned research, it seeks to establish an agenda for development cooperation, stressing interdependence and mutual interests of the United States and developing nations. The ODC, located in Washington, D.C., was established in 1969 and is

funded by private foundations, corporations, and individuals. *See also*
FOREIGN AID, 285.

Significance   The Overseas Development Council has been instrumental in bringing needed attention to a vital, but often overlooked
area of U.S. foreign relations and is recognized as the major forum
for related discussions. The findings of its highly informed and comprehensive analysis of U.S.–Third World relations are a vital resource for policymakers, academics, business, NGOs, and special
interest and advocacy groups focusing on development issues. Praise
from a wide range of professionals and politicians attests to the broad
base of support and respect for the work of the council. Its work takes
on even greater importance with the growing recognition of the need
for informed decision making in North-South relations.

Oxfam   (431)
Originally the Oxford Committee for Famine Relief (1942), a respected international nonprofit relief and development organization.
Oxfam consists of six autonomous organizations based in Montreal
and Ottawa, Canada; Great Britain; Australia (Community Aid
Abroad); Belgium; and the United States. The agencies fund
self-help development projects and disaster relief and carry out a progressive public-education program on development and hunger
issues. Oxfam may be best known for its ability to mobilize resources
for famine relief, but it is also committed to support of longer-term
projects, committing two-thirds of its annual budget to small-scale,
self-help development programs. The six constituent organizations
neither seek nor accept government funds. *See also* PRIVATE VOLUN-
TARY ORGANIZATIONS, 300; DISASTER RELIEF, 283.

Significance   Oxfam is a model agency in many respects. It has developed an international reputation for integrity and efficiency of
operation, creativity in meeting the needs of the poor, and responsiveness to disasters—as in Bangladesh, Cambodia, and Ethiopia.
Oxfam seeks to minimize the role of expatriates and technical advisers, instead placing emphasis on providing opportunities for local creative enterprise. It has been a pioneer in establishing a partnership
relationship between PVOs and local groups. It has also demonstrated its commitment to follow-up work, moving from disaster
relief to development projects. In addition, Oxfam continues to play
a key role in development education for its immediate constituency
and the broader public. Its broad range of activities, including publications and involvement in public policy decisions in the developed

countries, attests to its holistic approach to development and development assistance.

Pan African Institute for Development (PAID) (432)

An institute that trains senior officials in management and organizational development through technical seminars and symposiums. The institute was founded on January 20, 1964, following an initiative from the Inter-African Colloquium of May 1962. Members of PAID include national sections and individuals from 33 countries. PAID provides consultants to assist in the preparation and implementation of operational development projects. The study of rural development problems and their solution through small-scale intensive case studies is an emphasis of PAID's activities. It also assists in setting up subregional education and research networks. *See also* TECHNICAL ASSISTANCE, 305.

Significance PAID's contributions lie in its assistance of economic, social, and cultural development of African nations by means of change at individual and institutional levels. It promotes the training of Africans to take responsibility at various levels to promote the local improvement of living standards. It maintains a dual role as both an international association and a training institute.

Peace Corps (433)

A new U.S. foreign policy initiative to enable youth to do grassroots development work overseas, established in 1961 by President John F. Kennedy. Though the idea originated with Sen. Hubert Humphrey, Kennedy quickly made it a part of his political campaign. The Peace Corps, now operating in 64 countries, has three basic objectives: (1) to help developing countries meet critical manpower needs, (2) to enhance cultural understanding between the United States and developing countries, and (3) to improve U.S. understanding and knowledge of developing countries. As of 1990, more than 125,000 Americans had served in the Peace Corps, the world's largest international volunteer organization. Over time the Peace Corps's popularity has fluctuated. Initially, it was greeted with considerable enthusiasm by U.S. youth and it attracted many of the country's "best and brightest." In later years, particularly in the days of Vietnam and Watergate, many young people became disillusioned with government and were reluctant to join the Peace Corps. Though it provides specialized training for its volunteers, it has been criticized for sending abroad individuals with inadequate skills and experience. Many radicals also criticize the Peace Corps as a public relations front for U.S. governmental and business interests. Abroad there is a commonly expressed view that the Central Intelligence Agency (CIA) utilizes volunteers as agents to obtain information about developing countries. Empirical evidence for such a view is weak; as part of the Peace Corps legislation, Kennedy postulated that the CIA not be allowed to hire former volunteers in the years immediately following their Peace Corps service. Currently, the Peace Corps is enjoying renewed popularity with new opportunities and needs developing in Eastern Europe and Central America. Twenty-six additional countries have requested Peace Corps volunteers, and the corps plans to serve 15 of them by 1992. Within 20 months, the Peace Corps will have expanded its range of countries as much as in the previous 20 years (Broder 1990). With increased interest in the Peace Corps, the agency currently accepts approximately one out of four applicants. *See also* JAPAN OVERSEAS COOPERATION VOLUNTEERS, 425.

Significance   The U.S. Peace Corps has inspired the establishment of similar bodies in many other industrialized countries such as Japan, Australia, New Zealand, Canada, and the United Kingdom. Nigeria has also established a similar program to serve West Africa. There is considerable controversy concerning the impact of the Peace Corps, but few argue that it has made a major developmental impact in any particular country. The impact of the Peace Corps varies by region. In Latin America, for example, perhaps the Peace Corps's greatest influence has been to increase political consciousness of persisting structural problems of inequality and inequity, in the minds of both volunteers and villagers. In contrast, in certain African countries that have serious shortages of trained personnel in fields such as public health, volunteers have provided critically needed personnel. In Asia, volunteers have often become exposed to powerful alternative value systems such as Buddhism, Hinduism, and Islam, which have had strong influences on their subsequent lives. In this regard, Peace Corps service in almost any region has taught Americans how to live cheaply and has contributed significantly to the growing voluntary simplicity movement in the United States. Returned volunteers have enriched and enhanced the work of other development organizations, bringing a grassroots perspective to agencies such as AID. The Peace Corps has also had an important impact in improving the foreign language skills of Americans, who are noted for usually being monolingual. As a result of Peace Corps service, a substantial number of Americans know uncommonly taught languages such as Arabic, Swahili, Korean, Hindi, and Thai. Finally, perhaps the greatest impact of the Peace Corps has been the creation of a potentially powerful political lobby in the United States that may influence general foreign policy and particularly foreign aid policy to be more responsive to the needs of the poor in developing countries. Returned volunteers are also valuable resources for development education.

Population Council (PC) (434)

A leading international population planning agency founded in 1952. The Population Council maintains the Center for Biomedical Research which works to enhance human welfare via improved and more available birth-control methods. Through publications, workshops, the awarding of fellowships, and sponsorship of postdoctoral training, the agency works to enhance institutional capacity for family planning at the local, national, and regional levels. Part of the council's effort involves study of women's roles in the development process. PC maintains regional offices in Mexico, Thailand, and Egypt. Its headquarters are in New York City with a liaison office in Tokyo. In addition to periodic briefing papers on population issues and a newsletter, PC publishes the quarterly journal, *Population and Development Review,* and the bimonthly journal, *Studies in Family Planning. See also* POPULATION PLANNING, 254.

Significance   The Population Council has been a major sponsor of research and development related to family planning and contraception. It has also actively supported training in the population field for nationals from developing countries. With domestic U.S. political factors adversely affecting funding for international population planning activities in the 1990s, the role of the Population Council is particularly valuable.

Red de Información y Documentación en Educación (435)
para América Latina y el Caribe (REDUC)

A bibliographic data bank whose Spanish title translates as Information, Documentation, and Education Network for Latin America and the Caribbean. REDUC was formed cooperatively by 27 associated centers in 19 countries of the Latin American and Caribbean regions. The products of REDUC provide access to the most important research being done on education in the region. The network's activities are coordinated by the Research and Educational Development Center (CIDE) in Santiago, Chile. Among REDUC's products are analytic abstracts on education in Latin America and the Caribbean, an index of these abstracts, various research studies and reports, national bibliographies, bibliographies of newspaper articles on education, abstracts of meetings and symposia, and state-of-the-knowledge reports on a number of subjects. REDUC has primarily used microfiche technology for information storage and retrieval, but in the summer of 1987, a project was launched to computerize this information system using a participant computer conferencing system. The computerization of the system is being assisted by the Ontario Institute for Studies in Education (OISE) in Toronto. *See also* TECHNICAL COOPERATION AMONG DEVELOPING NATIONS, 306.

Significance   REDUC is a fascinating example of South-South cooperation in responding to the challenges of the new information era and of the potential for developing countries to learn from each other's experiences. Since information flow traditionally has been primarily between North and South countries, little information exchange has occurred among South nations. It is important to note that REDUC was an indigenous idea developed in Chile, not a program imposed on Latin America by external donor agencies. Although the Canadian government now supports this effort, its origin was with Latin American intellectuals. Questions are raised about the appropriateness of technologies such as this sophisticated information network when many more basic needs are not being met in Latin America. The amount of money spent on REDUC could have little direct impact on meeting basic needs in Latin America. However, as Latin American governments spend larger sums on education, the REDUC network can potentially influence the efficiency and equity of such expenditures by drawing on various regional experiences and expertise. To the extent that REDUC is successful, it could become a model for other regions such as Southeast Asia, West Africa, and the Middle East.

Research Centre for Cooperation with Developing   **(436)**
Countries (RCCDC)
A development studies research center located in Ljubljana, Yugoslavia, emphasizing South-South cooperation. Established in 1967, the center is located at the University of Ljubljana, but has operated independently since 1973. RCCDC's fields of activity include applied and fundamental research, information-documentation services, training, consulting, and publishing in the development area. As a major actor in Yugoslavia's economic cooperation with developing countries, RCCDC works closely with the Yugoslav Bank for International Economic Cooperation. The center also cooperates with similar institutes throughout the developing world and with UN agencies

such as UNCTAD, UNIDO, FAO, the World Bank, and various regional development banks. RCCDC has an extensive program of publications, including the journal *Development and South-South Cooperation*; "Developing Countries," a loose-leaf information system on 122 developing countries and results of all major research projects of RCCDC; *News on Developing Countries,* a weekly bulletin; and a "Development and Cooperation" monograph series. *See also* INTERNATIONAL DEVELOPMENT RESEARCH CENTRE, 415; SWEDISH AGENCY FOR RESEARCH COOPERATION WITH DEVELOPING COUNTRIES, 442.

Significance   Among the socialist countries, Yugoslavia has been most active in the development field and RCCDC represents the major center of the country's thought on development. Yugoslavia has also been extremely supportive of the concepts of technical and economic cooperation among developing countries, and RCCDC is a major center focusing its research on such an approach to development.

Rockefeller Foundation (RF) (437)

The world's premier private philanthropic organization with a history of commitment to international development. The Rockefeller Foundation was incorporated by the New York state legislature in 1913 to "promote the well-being of mankind throughout the world." Its initial efforts were in the field of public health and medicine, building on the work of the Rockefeller Sanitary Commission in hookworm control. Wickliffe Rose, who had directed the commission's work in the southern United States, conceived of an international effort to control the disease, and was named head of the foundation's International Health Board. The first international project involved RF actively in 52 countries. The foundation also established schools of health throughout the world, including the School of Hygiene and Public Health at the Johns Hopkins University and the famous Peking Union Medical College. China was also the site of Dr. John Grant's pioneering efforts in establishing a community-based health-care system. Health care in prerevolutionary China represented RF's single largest investment. Elsewhere, particularly in the United States, RF was instrumental in the fight against a number of once common diseases such as typhus, influenza, rabies, yaws, and tuberculosis. It also sponsored major campaigns in the United States and Brazil to control malaria in the Western Hemisphere. A great effort also went into the development of a vaccine for yellow fever. RF continues as a major supporter of medical research.

In 1942, the foundation began its cooperation with the Mexican government. The Mexican program, under the direction of J. George Harrar, later to be president of RF, worked to improve basic food crops, particularly wheat and corn, through the breeding of improved strains. Harrar brought in Norman Borlaug, whose work in Mexico under RF sponsorship gave rise to the Green Revolution. In 1956, the foundation extended its crop-improvement initiative to Asia in response to an invitation from the Indian government. RF and the Ford Foundation together established the International Rice Research Institute in 1960 in Los Baños, the Philippines. The IRRI quickly produced hybrid rice strains that helped extend the Green Revolution to the rice producers of Asia. IRRI was the first in a network of international crop research institutes established throughout the world that receive continued support from RF.

In 1963 the foundation's trustees focused its efforts in five areas, some as continuations of past efforts. These activities are now carried out in the following programs: arts, humanities, and contemporary values; conquest of hunger; equal opportunity; international relations; and population and health. *See also* GREEN REVOLUTION, 180; DEVELOPMENT FOUNDATIONS, 281.

Significance   The Rockefeller Foundation has demonstrated a long-standing commitment to economic and social development of the less developed countries as well as to poor and minority groups in the United States. The foundation's most notable and dramatic international achievements have been in the areas of health care, agriculture, and education. In developing countries, RF has been primarily involved in promoting improved higher education programs in medicine, the sciences, agriculture, and economics. With its emphasis on creating academic programs of excellence, it has been criticized for promoting elitism and overly sophisticated technologies and thus contributing to inequality and uneven development. Despite such controversies, there is a consensus that the Rockefeller Foundation has had a major impact on the research development capacity of LDCs, particularly in the areas of health, population, agriculture, science, and economics.

Society for International Development (SID)   (438)

A private organization established in 1957 as a forum for exchange of ideas and information regarding international development. Today it has the largest membership of any international development organization with over 9,000 members in 132 countries. The members are organized into 87 SID chapters, 43 in the North and 44 in the South, each with autonomy in defining its goals and interests. The society's stated purpose is to promote international understanding of an interdependent world, facilitate cooperation and communication among international development groups, and to advance development education. The organization boasts a diverse membership and keeps close contact with development organizations, practitioners, and thinkers throughout the world. The secretariat is located in Rome and has official UN representation in New York, Geneva, Paris, and Vienna. SID, financed by membership dues and grants, holds an international conference every three years. Marie Angelique Savane of Senegal is the current chairperson, having succeeded Barbara Ward.

Significance   Because of its broad-spanning network of information, SID has been at the forefront of development thinking and action. For example, its advocacy of basic human needs in the early 1970s was followed by considerable attention to women in development and sustainable development strategies. Its informative quarterly journal, *Development,* presents a diversity of perspectives, opinion, and development experience. Accessible to all, SID brings together a variety of development professionals, academics, and citizens, reflecting its broad-based, multicultural, and multidisciplinary approach. The society anticipated the current growing recognition of the importance of development education in the North and citizen participation in the South as essential elements in international development.

Southeast Asian Ministers of Education Organization   (439) (SEAMEO)

An international organization focusing on the development of human resources. Established by ministers of education in Southeast Asia in 1965, SEAMEO is not a political organization but instead focuses on human resources with a strong emphasis on regional training programs. Its charter states its purpose as being to

> promote cooperation among the Southeast Asian nations through education, science and culture in order to further respect for justice, for the rule of law, and for the human rights and fundamental freedoms which are the birthrights of the peoples of the world (SEAMEO Charter)

SEAMEO has seven regional centers and projects: (1) SEAMEO Regional Centre for Tropical Biology (BIOTROP) in Bogor, Indonesia; (2) SEAMEO Regional Centre for Educational Innovation and Technology (INNOTECH) in Quezon City, Philippines; (3) SEAMEO Regional Centre for Education in Science and Mathematics (RECSAM) in Penang, Malaysia; (4) SEAMEO Regional Language Centre (RELC) in Singapore; (5) Southeast Asian Regional Centre for Graduate Study and Research in Agriculture (SEARCA) in Los Baños, Philippines; (6) SEAMEO Project in Archaeology and Fine Arts (SPAFA), a network of subcenters with the coordinating office in Bangkok, Thailand; and (7) SEAMEO Tropical Medicine and Public Health (TROPMED), a network of national centers with a central office in Bangkok. SEAMEO's governing and policy-making body is the Southeast Asian Ministers of Education Council (SEAMEC). The executive arm of the council, the SEAMEO Secretariat (SEAMES), has headquarters in Bangkok. SEAMEO's member countries are Indonesia, Cambodia, Lao People's Democratic Republic, Malaysia, the Philippines, Singapore, Thailand, and Brunei Darussalam, which joined in 1984 as the eighth member. France, Australia, and New Zealand are associate members, and the Association of Canadian Community Colleges is an affiliated member. In addition to its support from member nations, SEAMEO receives considerable financial support from governments and organizations such as Canada, Denmark, Japan, Germany, the United States, the United Kingdom, the Netherlands, IDRC, the Ford Foundation, and the Luce Foundation. *See also* MULTILATERAL AID AGENCIES, 291.

Significance   SEAMEO represents an example of successful South-South cooperation to enhance human resource development. Over 15,000 individuals have participated in various SEAMEO seminars and training workshops. An excellent example of apolitical regional cooperation, SEAMEO shows how development assistance can be provided through indigenous regional organizations. Its apolitical nature is attested by the continuing membership of Laos and Cambodia despite dramatic political changes in those countries in the 1970s. SEAMEO's workshops and seminars have contributed to the development of a regional identity as Southeast Asians from various nations worked together creatively on common problems.

Stanley Foundation   **(440)**
A private institution concerned with international development, with headquarters in Muscatine, Iowa. Its goal is to work toward "a secure peace with freedom and justice by encouraging study, research, and discussion of international issues." Though the foundation is

interested in international affairs in general, it has a special concern for development issues and sponsors international conferences, citizen education programs, and related publications. It sponsors the monthly magazine, *World Press Review,* which covers numerous Third World newspapers and magazines. The foundation is not a grant-making institution. *See also* DEVELOPMENT FOUNDATIONS, 281.

Significance   The Stanley Foundation is deeply concerned about enhancing the effectiveness of various international agencies such as the United Nations that are important for resolving global development problems. It is interested in many key global development issues, such as human rights, cultural preservation, promotion of educational opportunity, resource depletion, global warming, international pollution, power of nonstate economic actors such as transnational corporations (TNCs), and the technological revolution and its developmental impacts.

Survival International   **(441)**
An international organization committed to publicizing the problems of ethnic minorities around the world. Its headquarters are in London and its special branch in the old Quaker complex in downtown Washington, D.C., houses Survival International USA. Survival International has a similar approach to Amnesty International and several of its staff members were formerly with Amnesty. Survival International frequently criticizes conventional development projects of agencies such as the World Bank and offers alternative development projects. *See also* CULTURAL DEVELOPMENT, 219.

Significance   As ethnic nationalism continues to grow, organizations such as Survival International play an important role in enhancing consciousness of ethnic minorities and their status worldwide. Survival International tends to be more confrontational than Cultural Survival. Many political "greens," particularly in Europe, see the ethnic groups with which Survival International is concerned as a source of inspiration and ideas for the "green" movement. Survival International emphasizes a nonconventional perspective on development that reflects the needs and insights of indigenous minorities. The organization argues that many traditional values are highly relevant in the modern era and that certain ways that have been lost need to be revitalized. Organizations such as Survival International contribute to the preservation of the world's rich cultural diversity.

**Swedish Agency for Research Cooperation with   (442)
Developing Countries (SAREC)**
A Swedish government agency that aims to strengthen the endogenous research capacities of developing countries. Established in 1975,
its purpose is to promote research that supports the developing countries' efforts to achieve self-reliance and economic and social justice.
Since 1979, SAREC has functioned as an independent agency under
the Swedish Ministry of Foreign Affairs. In recommending the establishment of SAREC, the Committee on Development Research of the
Swedish Riksdag (Parliament) envisioned it as promoting all types of
research concerned with the problems and development of South nations. Among priority research areas of SAREC are desertification
and deforestation, AIDS, reproductive health, research infrastructure including libraries, women's research, and social science in
Africa. The agency gives special priority to Africa with 53 percent of
its funds allocated for this region. Another 35 percent is allocated for
Latin America and 12 percent for Asia. SAREC also supports development research by Swedish nationals, with approximately 10 percent of its total budget used for such research. With respect to
development fields, SAREC allocates approximately 33 percent of its
budget for agriculture and rural development, 23 percent for health
and nutrition, 18 percent for technology and industrialization, 6 percent for culture and education, 6 percent for the social sciences, and
14 percent for general support. Its total annual budget for
1988–1989 was projected to be $48 million. Since its inception its
budget has steadily increased. SAREC has one regional overseas
office located in Harare, Zimbabwe. It also provides annual support
to 11 of the applied agricultural research centers of the Consultative
Group on International Agriculture Research (CGIAR) such as IRRI,
CIP, and ICRISAT. *See also* CONSULTATIVE GROUP ON INTERNATIONAL
AGRICULTURE RESEARCH, 394; INTERNATIONAL RICE RESEARCH
INSTITUTE, 423.

Significance   SAREC's contributions address the frequent neglect
of the research dimension of the development process. Most development agencies focus their assistance on the hardware or physical aspects of development such as dams, factories, roads, condoms,
medical supplies, and equipment, supplemented by technical assistance related to the utilization of the hardware. Research has often
been ignored or neglected as a luxury. However, without the building of indigenous research capacity, developing nations will remain
forever intellectually and technologically dependent. Thus, the work

397

of agencies such as SAREC and IDRC (in Canada) is particularly important. Also noteworthy is SAREC's willingness to help build research capacity in socialist developing countries such as Ethiopia, Vietnam, and Cuba. While SAREC's budget has been growing, it is still disappointingly small in comparison to the amount of funds spent by various countries on military activities.

Third World Network (443)

An alternative to conventional information sources on the Third World. Established in 1984 in Penang, Malaysia, the network provides a more effective mechanism for the articulation of the needs and rights of Third World peoples around the world. It includes groups and individuals particularly concerned about the needs for a fairer distribution of world resources and forms of development that fulfill human needs and are "ecologically and humanly harmonious." One activity is the Third World Network Features Service, an alternative to conventional news sources such as AP, UPI, and Tass. Releasing features written by Third World journalists, the service is based and managed in the Third World. Among topics covered are economics, finance, basic needs, environment and resources, science and technology, culture, and political developments. These features are translated into Spanish, Portuguese, Bahasa Indonesia, and various languages of the Indian subcontinent. Global newspapers that draw upon the Third World Network Features Service include *The Voice of Germany, Canberra Times, International Herald Tribune, Japan Times,* and the *Indonesian Observer.* The Third World Network's publications program encourages research studies in areas of concern to Third World peoples. Among books published have been *Third World: Development or Crisis?, Damming the Narmada, Merchants of Drink,* and *Forestry Crisis and Forestry Myths.* Another program, Alert for Action, informs Third World groups of important events or issues requiring immediate action. A recent example concerned the adverse social and ecological impacts of large-scale eucalyptus planting. The network also prepares extensive dossiers on special topics and issues. As suggested by its title, a critically important dimension of this organization is Third World networking, accomplished through international conferences and the establishment of formal links and networks. Among those formed thus far are the World Science Movement, the Third World Rainforest Movement, the Third World Concerned Lawyers, and Program for People's Economics. The Third World Network has established secretariats in Indonesia, Thailand, India, Brazil, and Uruguay. Its headquarters is in Penang,

Malaysia. *See also* NEW WORLD INFORMATION AND COMMUNICATION ORDER, 252.

Significance　The establishment of the Third World Network directly reflects the concerns of those calling for a new international information order and for better balance in providing information about developments in the Third World. Western media coverage of Third World issues and events tends to focus on the sensational and the violent, thus often distorting current conditions in developing countries. The Third World Network is an alternative information source. A key question is how broadly the network's features and publications are disseminated. With a geographically and culturally diffuse membership, the question arises of how effective the network can be in mobilizing resources on key policy issues affecting Third World peoples. However, the dramatic and growing impact of the information revolution and related technologies enhances the feasibility of movements such as the Third World Network.

Trickle Up Program (TUP) (444)

A unique and highly successful support program for small-scale enterprise, also refered to as microenterprise, in the Third World. The program was started in 1979 by Mildred and Glenn Leet, whose years of experience in developing countries convinced them of the abilities and creativity shown by the poor when given the opportunity. TUP is designed to provide that opportunity to those in the informal sector who otherwise have no access to investment capital, even in the small amounts they require. TUP gives grants of $100 in two installments to groups of five or more people who need only fill out a one-page business plan. The recipients must agree to invest 1,000 hours of unemployed time over a maximum three-month period and to reinvest at least 20 percent of profits. They also agree to file reports on their operations and results with TUP. The entrepreneurs start labor-intensive operations using locally available materials and equipment, and existing skills. The most common type of enterprise undertaken involves production, processing, or marketing of food. Businesses involving clothing and household goods are also common. The program operates with low overhead owing to the volunteer work of the over 2,000 in-country coordinators, comprised of professional personnel of local and international development agencies. Over 900 organizations have participated in the program. By the end of its first decade of operation, the TUP had supported nearly 75,000 people involved in more than 10,000 enterprises in 83 countries. The

Leets estimate that two-thirds of TUP-supported enterprises have been sustained, resulting in total profits of $10 million. From its headquarters in New York, TUP maintains a computerized data bank on projects throughout the world.

Significance Like the Grameen Bank of Bangladesh, the Working Women's Forum of India, and the savings clubs of Zimbabwe, the Trickle Up Program demonstrates both the widespread need for support of small-scale enterprise and the creativity and reliability of the poor entrepreneur in utilizing even modest support. As the name suggests, the program is designed to assist the poor who often did not benefit from the approaches of the past development decades, which focused on providing aid for infrastructure and other capital-intensive projects with the assumption that the benefits of these efforts would trickle down to the poor. With TUP, as with the Grameen Bank, the majority of participants are women. With rapid Third World urbanization, creative means of income generation are vital to the well-being of the many who no longer have the means to grow their own food. The TUP is an example of a low-cost, highly participatory, and replicable program that directly benefits the poor in many countries. Its success calls for reassessment of the informal sector, as suggested by Peruvian Hernando de Soto.

United Nations Children's Fund (UNICEF) (445)

A United Nations agency established in 1946 to advance children's welfare, primarily in Asia, Africa, and Latin America. Its original mandate was to provide relief to children suffering the effects of a Europe devastated by war, thus its original name, UN International Children's Emergency Fund. When the UN General Assembly gave it permanent status, it deleted "International" and "Emergency" but retained the agency's well-known acronym, UNICEF. UNICEF reports to the General Assembly through the Economic and Social Council (ECOSOC). It has headquarters in New York, regional offices in 119 countries of the developing world, and 34 national UNICEF committees, primarily in developed countries, that assist in fund-raising activities, such as the sale of greeting cards. A major current thrust of UNICEF is to reduce infant mortality rates around the world through community-based health care and the promotion of oral rehydration therapy (ORT). Another special emphasis is dissemination of knowledge on nutrition and sanitation. Much of UNICEF's aid is given in the form of technical assistance to improve the design, administration, and evaluation of projects that aid children. Other UNICEF assistance, as part of its basic services strategy, includes the direct provision of commodities such as textbooks, water pipes, and faucets, and donation of funds to strengthen administrative services. Support for primary and nonformal education is also within the agency's mandate. UNICEF's total budget for 1986 was $325.9 million, of which 36.6 percent was spent to provide basic health care, including family planning. Among publications of the agency are *State of the World's Children, UNICEF Annual Report,* and *Facts about UNICEF. See also* MULTILATERAL AID AGENCIES, 291; ORAL REHYDRATION THERAPY, 297.

Significance   Recipient of the 1965 Nobel Peace Prize, UNICEF is considered by many to be one of the UN's most effective agencies. UNICEF is noted for emphasizing appropriate and intermediate technologies and for drawing upon important local knowledge. Its work relates to basic needs. UNICEF has also given special priority to helping children in the poorest of the poor developing nations, such as Afghanistan, Bhutan, and Nepal. In 1979, UNICEF headed UN activities related to the International Year of the Child, which marked the twentieth anniversary of the Declaration of the Rights of the Child. UNICEF's current executive director, James P. Grant, has an excellent reputation in the international development field. In a number of respects, UNICEF is an exemplary development agency.

United Nations Conference on Trade and Development   (446) (UNCTAD)

The central UN body concerned with trade and related issues. Following the initiative of the Group of 77, UNCTAD was established in 1964 as a permanent organ of the UN General Assembly and in 1968 was designated as a participating and executing agency of UNDP. Raúl Prebisch was instrumental in the organization's founding and served as its first secretary-general. UNCTAD's main purposes are

> to promote international trade with a view to accelerating economic development, to formulate principles and policies on international trade, to initiate action for the adoption of multilateral trade agreements, and to act as a center for harmonizing trade and development policies of Governments and regional economic groups.

With 168 members, UNCTAD is not only concerned with increasing trade, but especially with negotiating better terms of trade and finance for the LDCs. To this end, UNCTAD sponsors research and programs concerning debt, shipping, commodities, market access, trade preferences and tariffs, and technology transfer to LDCs and

South-South cooperation. Meeting every four years the conference functions as an important instrument of assessment of the world trade situation. The Trade and Development Board carries out follow-up work related to conference decisions. It reports to the General Assembly through ECOSOC. *See also* RAÚL PREBISCH, 40; TERMS OF TRADE, 349; NEW INTERNATIONAL ECONOMIC ORDER, 161.

Significance　By serving as a focal point for the formulation of international trade and finance policies, UNCTAD is an important mouthpiece for the LDCs. Most of the issues and ideas related to the NIEO have been promoted and taken under serious consideration by the body. Some of UNCTAD's notable accomplishments include: the creation of the General System of Preferences in 1970 to enhance the trading position of developing nations; the establishment of the Convention on the Code of Conduct for Liner Conferences to improve the working arrangements of shipping conferences; and the initiation and subsequent adoption of an Integrated Program for Commodities. UNCTAD has been instrumental in helping to change national laws and international agreements concerning the transfer of technology so as to make it more accessible and affordable for LDCs. Further, UNCTAD continues to seek new arrangements for relieving the external debt of many LDCs. In regard to real decision-making power, many argue that UNCTAD can only act in the shadow of the General Agreement on Trade and Tariffs (GATT) where voting reflects actual economic power of individual nations. It is no coincidence that UNCTAD schedules its meetings to follow immediately the GATT gatherings. The objectives of the GATT emphasize reduction of all trade barriers and have often been at odds with UNCTAD's call for preferential treatment of the LDCs. Not surprisingly, the Northern countries prefer the GATT as the primary instrument of North-South dialogue regarding international trade and finance. UNCTAD continues to foster constructive dialogue regarding international trade and finance policy but, unlike GATT, it serves only as a forum, not a decision maker. Nevertheless, it can and often does make recommendations to the UN General Assembly for the adoption of trade and development policies.

United Nations Development Program (UNDP)　　　(447)
The central funding, planning, and coordinating agency for technical assistance in the UN system. The establishment of the UNDP in 1965 merged the United Nations Expanded Program of Technical Assistance and the United Nations Special Fund of the Economic and Social Council. The secretariat of the UNDP and its four regional bu-

reaus (namely Africa, Asia and the Pacific, the Arab States, and Latin America and the Caribbean) have their headquarters in New York. The UNDP has field offices in 115 countries, each headed by a resident representative who serves as the coordinator for all agency projects in that country. Unlike the World Bank and bilateral aid agencies, the UNDP's major activity is not the provision of direct financial resources, but the promotion of international technical cooperation. Its funds are used primarily for technical assistance, equipment, and fellowships for study and training in other countries. UNDP also assists countries in designing, administering, and evaluating programs and projects that will attract international and local development capital. UNDP supports over 5,000 projects annually, placing highest priority on assistance to the poorest countries. More than 80 percent of its funds are directed to countries with a per capita annual income of $750 or less. Funding for the UNDP derives from the voluntary contributions of the member nations of the United Nations. Of its budget of $1 billion, nearly 75 percent is spent for field programs. The UNDP publishes a number of journals that are reflective of its various developmental efforts. Examples are the *Mini-Report, Development in Action, Co-operation South,* and *Decade Watch. See also* MULTILATERAL AID AGENCIES, 291.

Significance   The work of the UNDP provides an excellent complement to the financial assistance of the World Bank and the various bilateral aid agencies. The overall budget of the UNDP is small compared to the World Bank or JICA, Japan's bilateral development agency. But UNDP activity influences the way in which the larger development sums are utilized and spent. It supports a broad range of development activities in over 150 countries through cooperation with 36 UN organizations, numerous research institutes, and development experts. UNDP activities are designed to enhance the absorptive capacity of developing nations and their potential for economic development and growth. Another attractive feature of UNDP technical assistance and support for human resource training is that it is untied. UNDP fellowships can be utilized in the country that can provide the best or most relevant training. Similarly, experts engaged by the UNDP may come from any country. Thus, the UNDP can support South-South cooperation without the political constraints associated with tied aid.

United Nations Economic Commission for Latin   **(448)**
America and the Caribbean (ECLAC)
Regional research and program agency dealing with a range of

internal development matters. Established in 1948 by Resolution 166 of the UN Economic and Social Council, as the UN Economic Commission for Latin America, it is known as CEPAL in Spanish. Its present title was adopted in 1985. As one of the regional economic commissions of the United Nations, ECLAC is an agency of ECOSOC, to which it reports periodically on its economic and social development activities in the Latin American and Caribbean regions. Governments of 40 nations are members of ECLAC. Its basic activities are based on the concept that dynamic development policies and programs are required to accelerate Latin America's growth from within. ECLAC carries out studies and programs in collaboration with the governments of the region in the fields of foreign trade, agricultural production, industrial development, transport and communications, regional integration, statistics, natural resources, and environment. These programs are supplemented by social development activities related to demography, information media, and child and youth development.

Significance   ECLAC initiates and participates in measures for facilitating concerted action for dealing with urgent economic problems and for improving economic performance in Latin America and the Caribbean countries, both among themselves and with other countries in the world. It conducts or sponsors investigations and studies of regional economic and technological problems and developments. It also undertakes and sponsors the collection, evaluation, and dissemination of economic, technological, and statistical information. Giving special attention to the problems of economic development, ECLAC assists in the formulation and development of coordinated policies as a basis for practical action promoting economic development in the region. It also assists the Economic and Social Council in discharging its functions with respect to the United Nations technical assistance program, in particular by assisting in ECOSOC's appraisal of these activities in the Latin American and Caribbean regions. In carrying out these functions, ECLAC encourages analyses of the social aspects of economic development and the complex interrelationship between economic and social factors.

United Nations Industrial Development Organization   (449) (UNIDO)
The arm that initiates and coordinates all UN activities relating to industrial development. Established in 1967 by the UN General Assembly to promote and accelerate the industrialization of developing countries through direct assistance and mobilization of national and

international resources, UNIDO serves as a resource for countries seeking to expand and modernize their industries and acts as a liaison between developing and industrialized countries. UNIDO also initiates its own studies and gathers considerable data related to world industry, including technological and marketing information. It offers advisory and planning services upon request and sponsors training programs, study tours, fellowships, seminars, and specialized meetings. Related to these activities, UNIDO operates a special industrial services program to supplement other UN industrial development activities by providing short-term and emergency aid to help solve urgent technical problems. UNIDO is headquartered in Vienna and operates with a staff of 2,500 and a budget approaching $100 million. *See also* INDUSTRIALIZATION, 111.

Significance UNIDO serves as an important resource for industrializing nations. It may provide information and assistance usually inaccessible to developing countries, and it brings industrialized and developing nations together in a spirit of cooperation. In effect, it supplements the efforts of the LDCs to bring their industries into more efficient and competitive positions vis-à-vis the industrialized nations. UNIDO also supports efforts to give developing countries more direct and affordable access to current industrial and technical information, much of which is protected by international intellectual property rights agreements.

United Nations University (UNU) **(450)**
An international community of scholars, engaged in research, postgraduate training, and dissemination of knowledge in support of the principles of the United Nations. The UN University was proposed by Secretary-General U Thant in 1969 and began formal operations in 1975, with headquarters at the University Centre in Tokyo. The university, without walls or a student body, supports an international network of scholars working in five key areas: (1) peace, security, conflict resolution, and global transformation; (2) the global economy; (3) hunger, poverty, resources, and the environment; (4) human and social development and the coexistence of peoples, cultures, and social systems; and (5) science and technology and their social and ethical implications. Unlike most UN organizations, the UNU is not financed by annual funds from the General Assembly, but by interest from an endowment fund, initiated with a pledge of $100 million U.S. from Japan, which had grown to $192.2 million as of January 1988. Thirty-nine universities around the world are associated with the UNU. It is creating research and training centers in various parts

of the world to help solve well-defined, long-term problems. Two such centers have already been approved: the United Nations University World Institute for Development Economics Research (WIDER) operating in Helsinki and the United Nations Institute for Natural Resources in Africa (INRA) being established in Côte d'Ivoire, supported financially by that nation and by Zambia. An Institute for New Technologies (INTECH) was approved in 1988 and will be located in Maastricht, Netherlands. Feasibility studies are being conducted on the possibility of an Institute of Advanced Studies in Japan, an Institute for Outer Space and Society in Austria, and a Centre for Computer Software Development in Macau. *See also* WORLD INSTITUTE FOR DEVELOPMENT ECONOMICS RESEARCH, 456.

Significance   The long-term impact of the UNU will depend on the quality and relevance of research it supports to facilitate the resolution of global development problems. With an annual operating budget of only $43,507,000 U.S., its leverage is limited. Unfortunately, member nations of the UN such as the United States have not generously added to the initial endowment fund. The importance of the UN University lies in its bringing together scholars from various developing nations to cooperate creatively in trying to resolve pressing global development problems.

U.S. Agency for International Development (AID)　　　　(451)
The world's largest bilateral development agency. The agency is the major component of the International Development Cooperation Agency (IDCA), established in 1979 to oversee all U.S. development assistance. AID was established in 1961 to administer the bulk of U.S. foreign aid funds, programs, and projects, as a result of the Foreign Assistance Act. The agency replaced the International Cooperation Agency and the Development Loan Fund. The Foreign Assistance Act of 1961 has been amended on numerous occasions and now states 33 separate objectives of U.S. foreign aid. The three major objectives have to do with national security, the provision of humanitarian aid, and U.S. commercial interests. AID's activities are carried out within four major programs: Development Assistance, Economic Support Fund, Food for Peace, and Disaster Assistance. Foreign aid accounts for about 1 percent of U.S. tax revenues. The $15 billion proposed for U.S. foreign aid in 1991 includes $7.1 billion for bilateral economic development aid, $5.6 billion for military aid, $0.8 billion for food aid, and $1.9 billion for multilateral assistance. Of this amount, only $2.4 billion is categorized as development assistance (DA). Typi-

cally DA accounts for less than 40 percent of AID's funds and less than 10 percent of all U.S. foreign aid, including military assistance.

The development assistance programs include work in: education and human resources; agriculture and rural development; health; family planning; and energy, environment, and natural resources. In addition to its own development projects, AID works jointly with U.S. private voluntary organizations (PVOs) and multilateral organizations such as WHO, FAO, and UNICEF. Through the Office of International Training, over 260,000 people have received specialized training. AID is also a strong supporter of development research, and its results and findings are broadly distributed. The 1973 New Directions legislation instructed the agency to develop more poverty-focused programs with special consideration for the poorest countries and withdrawal of support for countries with inadequate human rights records. The effect of this policy change was somewhat mitigated by the exclusion of the Economic Support Fund (ESF) from its jurisdiction.

The ESF is part of the U.S. Security Assistance Program. Accounting for 20 percent of nonmilitary foreign aid, it is directed toward countries considered of strategic interest to the United States. Since 1977 Israel and Egypt have received the largest share of ESF allocations; in fact these two countries have received 47 percent of all U.S. foreign aid in that time. Other major recipients of Economic Support Funds are the Philippines, Pakistan, El Salvador, and Turkey.

AID also administers the Food for Peace Program established by Public Law (P.L.) 480 in 1954. More than 320 billion tons of food, most of it wheat, have been sent abroad through the program. Food aid generally accounts for 10 percent of U.S. foreign aid. This has been a highly controversial practice since food donations can undermine local markets and incentives while creating dependency on food from U.S. markets.

The fourth major AID activity is directed by the Office of Foreign Disaster Assistance (OFDA), which has responded to more than 1,000 disasters in 135 countries. *See also* FOREIGN AID, 285; BILATERAL AID, 277; NEW DIRECTIONS, 294; FOOD FOR PEACE, 360.

Significance   Any assessment of AID must consider its plurality of purposes. Because of its multiple and sometimes contradictory mandates, AID comes under scrutiny from several directions. Much of the criticism of AID stems from disagreements regarding the purpose of foreign aid in general. Many contend that AID's effectiveness as a development agency is greatly hampered by its close ties to U.S. military and economic interests, which direct funds and efforts away from areas of greatest need. Despite the New Directions mandates, low-income countries receive less than 10 percent of all U.S. bilateral assistance. Further, Food for Peace and other programs have often been more effective as tools for creating and expanding U.S. markets than as development programs benefiting the LDCs. Over 70 percent of AID allocations go directly to U.S. organizations and individuals, nearly half to 21 corporations. Interestingly, this figure is often quoted to justify foreign aid spending to those who question its benefit to the United States. AID is also called to task for its inefficiency as a development agency. A common criticism is that AID projects too often take the form of large, capital-intensive programs that are overly dependent on U.S. firms and products. Further, a directly hired, foreign-based AID employee costs about $200,000, well above the average for nongovernmental employees. Partly in response to this criticism, AID has increasingly subcontracted projects to already established U.S.-based PVOs. The other major trend within AID is increased support for the private entrepreneurial sector of developing countries. In an effort to enhance its own efficiency and effectiveness, AID is also working to increase its cooperation with multilateral development organizations.

Volkswagen-Stiftung (Volkswagen Foundation) (452)

The Federal Republic of Germany's major philanthropic foundation supporting academic and scientific research. Until March 1989, the foundation's name was Stiftung Volkswagenwerk. Established in 1961 and operating since 1962, the foundation has its headquarters in Hannover. Like its U.S. counterpart, the Ford Foundation, the Volkswagen Foundation has been a major supporter of both German and foreign scholars working in areas deemed to be of high priority. At the end of 1987, the foundation's assets were approximately 1,838 billion DM. The Volkswagen Foundation has three major programs related to international development. The first, in existence since 1981, focuses on basic development in Latin America, Asia, and Africa. A Southeast Asia program initiated in 1976 is now included as part of the basic development program. A second program, started in 1979, fosters partnerships between German and foreign engineering and natural science institutions. The third and most recent program, started in 1986, fosters scientific cooperation between German and Chinese academic institutions. In 1987, 57 such China-related projects were funded. The foundation provides support for both the humanities and the sciences. In 1987, 48.9 percent of projects were in the humanities and the social sciences, 36.4 percent in the natural sciences and medicine, and 14.6 percent in engineering-related fields. Reflecting the human capacity–building orientation of the foundation, 54.9 percent of grants in 1987 were for personnel costs. With respect to geographical distribution of direct grants, in 1987, 47 projects were funded in Asia, 16 in Central and South America, 11 in the Middle East, and 5 in Africa. The foundation's overall philosophy emphasizes interdisciplinary research, the internationalization of science, and the openness of information. *See also* DEVELOPMENT FOUNDATIONS, 281.

Significance While the international dimensions of the Volkswagen Foundation are modest in scope, they do provide key scholars in developing countries opportunities to develop linkages with major academic and scientific institutes in the Federal Republic of Germany. Given Germany's reputation for quality and precision in the scientific and technological areas, such linkages have valuable implications for countries seeking to enhance their scientific and technological capacities. The foundation seems to emphasize less political scientific research collaborations. For example, its projects in China are all science-oriented, and thus should be less adversely affected by the political turmoil of June 1989 than the social science projects of other development organizations. In most cases, foundation assistance appears to be tied in the sense that funding is provided to foster collaboration between German and foreign academic institutions. The foundation does not appear to make block grants to institutions in developing countries to utilize wherever they desire. Overall, the organization seems to recognize Germany's special comparative advantages in the science and technology areas that have made Germany the world's leading exporter. Through grants from the Volkswagen Foundation, scientists and scholars in developing countries can receive support for their research and develop important linkages with German academics working in key scientific fields relevant to both industry and development.

Winrock International Institute for Agricultural   **(453)**
Development
A world leader in providing technical assistance and support for sustainable agricultural development. Created in 1985 with the merger of the Agricultural Development Council (ADC), the International Agricultural Development Service (IADS), and the Winrock International Livestock Research and Training Center, the institute is commonly known as Winrock International. It has headquarters at Petit Jean Mountain near Morrilton, Arkansas, and regional offices in Washington, D.C., and Bangkok, Thailand. Its international staff of

225 represents 20 countries, and staff in 16 developing countries are working on approximately 100 major projects, programs, and consulting assignments. The institute's 1989 budget was approximately $35 million. Among its distinguished governing board members are the Nobel laureate Norman Borlaug; Garret Hardin, author of *Tragedy of the Commons*; Walter Falcon, director of the Food Research Institute at Stanford; and Winthrop P. Rockefeller. With respect to organizational structure, Winrock International has four regional divisions (Asia, Africa and the Middle East, Latin America and the Caribbean, and United States); a Development Studies Center; and a Public Affairs and Communications Division that emphasizes the dissemination of research and project findings. *See also* SUSTAINABLE AGRICULTURE, 188.

Significance Noted for its concerns for sustainable agricultural development and environmentally sound agricultural practice, Winrock is also known for an emphasis on training and human resource development to facilitate the development of indigenous agricultural research capacity. With its important and prestigious links with the Rockefeller and Ford foundations, Winrock is associated with the system of international agricultural research centers that fostered the global Green Revolution in wheat and rice production in the 1960s. To disseminate the results of its extensive agricultural technical assistance work, Winrock has an extensive publications program that includes a development-oriented literature series, agricultural development indicators, various books, occasional papers, a development education series, an African rural social science series, and a regular newsletter, *WinWorld*.

World Bank (454)

The world's foremost development financing institution, comprised of the International Bank for Reconstruction and Development (IBRD) and the International Development Association (IDA). The bank is closely affiliated with two other agencies, the International Finance Corporation (IFC), established in 1956 to promote private investment in developing countries, and the Multilateral Investment Guarantee Agency (MIGA), established in 1988 to encourage equity investment and other direct investment flows to developing countries. Together these four agencies are known as the World Bank Group. The World Bank also works closely with the International Monetary Fund (IMF). The IBRD and the IMF were established together at the Bretton Woods International Finance Conference in 1945. Membership in the World Bank is contingent upon membership in the IMF. The IBRD was established as a source of funds for the reconstruction and development of 151 member states. The bank loans to governments deemed creditworthy by MIGA. Operating funds are acquired through member contributions, the size of which determine the voting power of the members. The United States usually controls about 20 percent of the votes. Further funds are gained from interest payments and borrowing through commercial channels. The bank maintains preferred-creditor status because until quite recently it had never taken a loss or rescheduled a loan. Debtor countries unable to repay loans through economic growth must borrow from commercial sources or from the IMF. IBRD loans are typically made over a 5-to-15-year period, recently at around 8 percent interest. In 1989, the IBRD approved loans totalling over $16 billion, more than twice the amount loaned at the beginning of the decade. At the same time, the bank's soft loan branch, the IDA, authorized nearly $4.9 billion in low-interest and no-interest loans, $4.3 billion of which went to countries with per capita incomes of less than $480. The IDA was established in 1960 to assist the poorest countries. More than 40 countries are eligible for IDA funds.

The World Bank has a history of favoring medium to large-scale infrastructure projects. In its first twenty years, 70 percent of bank loans financed such projects. The biggest sectoral shares go to agriculture and rural development (one-quarter) and energy (one-fifth). In response to the international debt crisis, the bank has recently adopted terms of conditionality involving structural adjustments on the part of recipient countries. About 25 percent of current loans are now made under the condition that the government will make recommended policy changes similar to those advocated by the IMF in its structural adjustment programs. *See also* INTERNATIONAL MONETARY FUND, 420; DEBT CRISIS, 134; INFRASTRUCTURE, 155.

Significance   Without question the World Bank has functioned successfully as an international bank. However, critics question how effective it has been as a development institution. Though its records are not open to public scrutiny, the bank itself comes under considerable review from the development field. The strongest critique comes from those who question whether bank-funded projects ever benefit the poor, a charge that is often leveled against large-scale, capital-intensive projects regardless of the sponsor. They further point out that less than 10 percent of the loans are allocated for humanitarian improvements in the areas of health and education. Such projects seldom generate an immediate monetary return. The bank contends that it is effective in helping to meet the needs of the poor, both directly through poverty-focused programs and indirectly through the creation of infrastructure and the fostering of national economic growth with trickle-down impact. The bank has also been criticized by environmentalists who object to its support of projects that have proven to be detrimental to the environment. Ranching projects that encourage deforestation of rain forests and large dam and irrigation projects have been particularly controversial. Despite its many detractors, the bank's funds remain in high demand and it currently remains the world's second largest donor agency, after the Japanese government.

World Health Organization (WHO) (455)

The world's predominant international, nonprofit health organization. WHO is a specialized agency of the United Nations, linked to the Economic and Social Council (ECOSOC). WHO was established in 1946, taking over the responsibilities of the International Office for Public Health, which operated in Paris after World War II, and the peacetime functions of the Health Division for the UN Relief and Rehabilitation Administration (UNRRA). Article 1 of WHO's constitution states its objective to be "the attainment by all peoples of the highest possible level of health." Health, as defined by WHO, is "a state of complete physical, mental, and social well-being and not merely the absence of disease or infirmity." In response to this broad mandate, the organization supports a wide range of activities, acting as the directing and coordinating authority on international health work. Headquartered in Geneva, WHO employs a staff of 4,400. In addition to its direct operating budget of over $650,000,000 projected for 1990–1991, WHO's direct and indirect budget exceeds $1.5 billion including contributions from 166 member states, funding from the United Nations Development Program (UNDP) for health projects, and support for mutual interest projects carried out in cooperation with UN and other international organizations involved in health issues.

Significance Since its founding, the World Health Organization has assisted nearly every country in the world in strengthening health services. This service is especially important for the many developing countries with severely limited resources for health care. WHO also promotes cooperation among governments and various international health organizations in their attempts to eradicate and control epidemic and endemic diseases. WHO conducts and promotes considerable research as well as health education and training. It publishes numerous periodicals in every major language including *Weekly Epidemiological Record, Bulletin of the World Health Organization,* and *World*

Health Statistics Annual. Since 1987 WHO has emerged as the world's leading organization in combating spread of the AIDS virus. WHO estimates that 5 million to 10 million people may be infected by the virus, the majority in the Central Africa "AIDS belt." WHO is working with other UN agencies to provide an integrated, global approach to address the many aspects of this and other major health problems.

World Institute for Development Economics Research (456) (WIDER)

A research and training center of the United Nations University. The center was established in 1983 and began operations in 1985 in Helsinki, Finland. WIDER is financed by a UNU endowed fund, with the major contribution from the government of Finland, supplemented by donations from the governments of Sweden and India and the James S. McDonnell Foundation. The principal purpose of the institute is to help identify and meet the need for policy-oriented research on pressing global economic problems, particularly those with the most direct impact in the developing countries. Scholars working at WIDER come from diverse national backgrounds. Among specific policy questions being studied at WIDER are the U.S. deficit, the crisis in commodity trade, and Japan's balance-of-payment surplus. WIDER's research projects are grouped into three main themes: (1) hunger and poverty, the poorest billion; (2) money, finance, and trade—reform for world development; and (3) development and technological change—the management of change. WIDER has thus far published 56 working papers and 17 developing country studies. Its newsletter, *WIDER News,* reports on current developments at the institute. *See also* UNITED NATIONS UNIVERSITY, 450.

Significance WIDER's policy-oriented development research is already attracting attention and having noticeable impact. For example, its ideas on recycling the Japanese surplus were widely acclaimed by the international financial press. Through meetings WIDER has organized in countries such as Egypt, it fosters cooperation among South researchers and research institutes. WIDER also organized a meeting in Mexico to consider future strategies in light of Mexico's debt reconstruction. WIDER's work goes beyond conventional economic boundaries, as in its study of the link between violence and knowledge domination, and an examination of the philosophical implications for feminists of upholding cultural integrity. WIDER is likely to become an increasingly important actor in conducting research related to the global economy and development.

World Resources Institute (WRI) (457)

An independent, nonpartisan research and policy center dealing with issues of environment and development. WRI's 85-member interdisciplinary staff based in Washington, D.C., cooperates with advisors and institutions in more than 50 countries. The research and policy studies of the institute aim to provide accurate and current information about global resources and environmental conditions to aid governments, international organizations, and the private sector in efforts to foster development while preserving natural resources and environmental integrity. WRI has four research programs: conservation of forests and biological diversity; climate, energy, and pollution; economics and institutions; and resource and environmental information. The institute's Center for International Development and Environment provides policy advice and technical assistance to developing countries. *See also* SUSTAINABLE DEVELOPMENT, 272.

Significance   WRI provides vital information for understanding the complex relationships between development and environment. Of special importance is its biennial edition of *World Resources*, published in cooperation with the International Institute for Environment and Development and United Nations Environment Program. It is an excellent, authoritative assessment of the world's natural resources, the most complete reference on global resources currently available. WRI's timely and thorough research provides an empirical, statistical background for assessing the state of development and the environment around the globe.

Worldwatch Institute (458)

A leading research and policy organization focusing on emerging global environmental, development, and social trends and issues. Founded in 1974 by Lester Brown, its current president, the organization encourages a reflective approach to global problem solving. Worldwatch takes a creative, international approach to problems that do not adequately fit conventional frameworks. The institute conducts work on a wide range of issues including population trends and policy, local initiatives in problem solving, renewable energy, and food and agriculture. *See also* SUSTAINABLE DEVELOPMENT, 272.

Significance   Since its inception, Worldwatch Institute has been on the leading edge of sustainable development issues, especially as they are considered on a global scale. The institute's publications are valuable resources for information on a wide variety of current environment and development issues. In fact, Worldwatch is best known for its annual edition of *State of the World,* an updated "assessment of the earth's health." The annual suggests policies needed to reduce poverty while correcting global environmental damage. *State of the World* is translated into the world's major languages and more than 100,000 copies are sold in English alone. It is an important reference for governments, international organizations, and academics. Primarily owing to this publication, Worldwatch Institute, with a staff of only 18, has a relatively large impact on many policy decisions related to sustainable development.

BIBLIOGRAPHY

Achebe, Chinua. 1959. *Things fall apart.* New York: Astor-honor, Inc.

Achebe, Chinua. 1960. *No longer at ease.* New York: Fawcett Premier.

Achebe, Chinua. 1964. *Arrow of God.* London: Heinemann.

Achebe, Chinua. 1966. *A man of the people: A novel.* New York: John Day Co.

Achebe, Chinua. 1973. *Christmas in Biafra, and other poems.* Garden City, N.Y.: Anchor Books.

Achebe, Chinua. 1984. *The Trouble with Nigeria.* London: Heinemann Eductional Books.

Achebe, Chinua. 1987. *Anthills of the Savannah.* London: Heinemann.

Adelman, Irma, and Cynthia Taft Monis. 1967. *Society, politics, and economic development: A quantitative approach.* Baltimore: Johns Hopkins Press.

Adelman, Irma, and Cynthia Taft Monis. 1973. *Economic growth and social equity in developing countries.* Stanford, Cal.: Stanford University Press.

Ahmad, Feroz. 1981. "The political economy of Kemalism," pp. 145-163 in Ali Kazancigil and Ergun Özbudun, eds. *Atatürk: Founder of a modern state.* Hamden, Connecticut: Archon Books.

Alexandrides, Costas G., and Barbara Bowers. 1987. *Countertrade: Practices, strategies and tactics.* New York: Wiley.

Allison, Paul D. 1978. "Measures of inequality." *American Sociological Review.* Vol. 43. December. pp. 865-880.

Alvares, Claude Alphonso, and Ramesh Billorey. 1988. *Damming the Narmada.* Penang, Malaysia: Third World Network.

Amin, Samir. 1974. *Accumulation on a world scale: A critique of the theory of underdevelopment.* Translated by Brian Pearce. New York: Monthly Review Press.

Amin, Samir. 1976. *Unequal development: An essay on the social formations of peripheral capitalism.* Translated by Brian Pearce. New York: Monthly Review Press.

Amin, Samir. 1978. *The law of value and historical materialism.* Translated by Brian Pearce. New York: Monthly Review Press.

Amin, Samir. 1984. "Self-reliance and the new international economic order," pp. 204-219 in Herb Addo, ed. 1984. *Transforming the world economy?:*

Nine critical essays on the new international order. London: Hodder and Stoughton in association with the United Nations University.

Amin, Samir. 1989. *La faillité du developpement en Afrique et dans le tiers monde: Une analyse politique.* Paris: L'Harmattan.

Amin, Samir. 1989. *Eurocentrism.* New York: Monthly Review Press.

Arevalo, Juan José. 1961. *The shark and the sardines.* Translated by June Cobb and Raul Osegueda. New York: L. Stuart.

Arevalo, Juan José. 1963. *Anti-kommunism in Latin America: An x-ray of the process leading to new colonialism.* Translated by Carleton Beals. New York: L. Stuart.

Arevalo, Juan José. 1946. *Escrito políticos y filosoficas.* Guatemala: Tip. Nacional.

Arnove, Robert F., ed. 1980. *Philanthropy and cultural imperialism.* Bloomington: Indiana University Press.

Ball, Nicole. 1981. *The military in the development process: A guide to issues.* Claremont, Cal.: Regina Books.

Banfield, Edward C. 1958. *The moral basis of a backward society.* Glencoe, Ill.: Free Press.

Baran, Paul A. 1957. *The political economy of growth.* New York: Monthly Review Press.

Baran, Paul A. 1970. *The longer view: Essays towards a critique of political economy.* New York: Monthly Review Press.

Baran, Paul A. and Paul M. Sweezy. 1966. *Monopoly capital: An essay on the American economic and social order.* New York: Monthly Review Press.

Barnet, Richard, and Ronald E. Müller. 1974. *Global reach: The power of the multinational corporations.* New York: Simon and Schuster.

Bauer, P. T. 1972. *Dissent on development: Studies and debates in development economics.* Cambridge, Mass.: Harvard University Press.

Bauer, P. T. 1984a. *Reality and rhetoric: Studies in the economics of development.* Cambridge, Mass.: Harvard University Press.

Bauer, P. T. 1984b. "Remembrances of studies past: Retracing first steps," pp. 27-43 in Gerald M. Meier and Dudley Seers, eds. *Pioneers in Development.* New York: Oxford University Press.

Bauer, P. T., and Basil S. Yamey. 1957. *The economics of under-developed countries.* Chicago: University of Chicago Press.

Becker, Gary Stanley. 1975. *Human capital: A theoretical and empirical analysis, with special reference to education.* New York: National Bureau of Economic Research.

Benería, Lourdes, ed. 1982. *Women and development: The sexual division of labour in rural societies.* New York: Praeger.

Berger, Peter. 1967. *The sacred canopy: Elements of a sociological theory of religion.* New York: Doubleday.

Berger, Peter 1974. *Pyramids of sacrifice: Political ethics and social change.* New York: Basic Books.

Berger, Peter. 1986. *The capitalist revolution: Fifty propositions about prosperity, equality, and liberty.* New York: Basic Books.

418

Berger, Peter, ed. 1987. *Capitalism and equality in the Third World.* New York: Institute for Educational Affairs.

Berger, Peter, Brigitte Berger, and Hansfried Kellner. 1973. *The homeless mind: Modernization and consciousness.* New York: Vintage.

Bloom, Allan. 1987. *The closing of the American mind.* New York: Simon and Schuster.

Bobbio, Norberto. 1977. "Preface," pp. viii-xi in Alastair Davidson, *Antonio Gramsci: Towards an intellectual biography.* London: Merlin Press.

Bogue, Donald J. 1969. *Principles of demography.* New York: Wiley.

Bok, Derek Curtis. 1982. *Beyond the ivory tower: Social responsibilities of the modern university.* Cambridge, Mass.: Harvard University Press.

Boserup, Ester Talke. 1965. *The conditions of agricultural growth: The economics of agrarian change under population pressure.* New York: Aldine Publications Co.

Boserup, Ester Talke. 1970. *Woman's role in economic development.* London: George Allen and Unwin Ltd.

Boserup, Ester Talke. 1981. *Population and technological change: A study of long term trends.* Chicago: University of Chicago Press.

Boulding, Elise. 1988. *Building a global civic culture: Education for an interdependent world.* New York: Teachers College Press.

Boulding, Kenneth. 1941. *Economic analysis.* New York: Harper.

Boulding, Kenneth. 1945. *The economics of peace.* New York: Prentice-Hall Inc.

Boulding, Kenneth. 1964. *The meaning of the twentieth century: The great transition.* New York: Harper & Row.

Boulding, Kenneth. 1968. *Beyond economics: Essays on society, religion, and ethics.* Ann Arbor: University of Michigan Press.

Boulding, Kenneth. 1978. *Ecodynamics: A new theory of societal evolution.* Beverly Hills: Sage Publications.

Boulding, Kenneth. 1985. *Human betterment.* Beverly Hills: Sage Publications.

Boulding, Kenneth. 1985. *The world as a total system.* Beverly Hills: Sage Publications.

Braudel, Fernand. 1982. *Civilization and capitalism, 15th-18th century.* New York: Harper & Row.

Brock, Colin. 1985. "Culture and identity in Grenadian education," pp. 69-91 in Colin Brock and Witold Tulasiewicz, eds. *Cultural identity & educational policy.* New York: St. Martin's Press.

Broder, David. 1990. *Washington Post.* April 25, A, p. 27.

Buchanan, Keith. 1967. *The Southeast Asian world: An introductory essay.* New York: Taplinger.

Bullock, Mary Brown. 1980. *An American transplant: The Rockefeller Foundation and Peking Union Medical College.* Berkeley: University of California Press.

Burgess, Anthony. 1961,1983. *Devil of a state.* London: Hutchinson.

Burgess, Anthony. 1972,1984. *Malayan trilogy.* London: Heinemann.

Carnoy, Martin. 1974. *Education as cultural imperialism.* New York: P. McKay Company.

Carnoy, Martin. 1984. *The state and political theory.* Princeton, N.J.: Princeton University Press.

Carnoy, Martin, and Henry M. Levin. 1985. *Schooling and work in the democratic state.* Stanford, Cal.: Stanford University Press.

Carnoy, Martin, and Derek Shearer. 1980. *Economic democracy: The challenge of the 1980s.* White Plains, N.Y.: M.E. Sharpe. Distributed by Pantheon Books.

Carson, Rachel. 1962. *Silent spring.* New York: Fawcett Crest.

Castaneda, Afredo, Manuel Ramirez III, and P. Leslie Harold. 1973. *A new philosophy of education.* Riverside, Cal.: Systems and Evaluations in Education.

Chambers, Robert. 1980. *Rapid rural appraisal: Rationale and reportoire.* England: Institute of Development Studies at the University of Sussex.

Chambers, Robert. 1980. *Rural poverty unperceived: Problem and remedies.* Washington, D.C.: World Bank.

Chambers, Robert. 1983. *Rural development: Putting the last first.* London: Longman.

Chambers, Robert. 1985. *Managing rural development: Ideas and experience from East Africa.* West Hartford, Conn.: Kumarian Press.

Chambers, Robert. 1989. *Farmer first: Farmer innovation and agricultural research.* New York: Bootstrap Press.

Chambers, Robert, Richard Lonhurst, and Arnold Pacey, eds. 1981. *Seasonal dimensions to rural poverty.* Totowa, N.J.: Allanheld, Osmun; London: F. Pinter.

Chantavanich, Amrung, Supany Chantavanich, and Gerald Fry. 1990. *Evaluating primary education: qualitative and quantitative policy studies in Thailand.* Ottawa: International Development Research Centre.

Chenery, Hollis B. 1974. *Redistribution with growth: Policies to improve income distribution in developing countries in the context of economic growth.* London: University of Sussex by Oxford University Press.

Chenery, Hollis B., and Moises Syrquin. 1975. *Patterns of development 1950-1970.* London: Oxford University Press.

Chenery, Hollis B., Samuel Bowles, and others, eds. 1971. *Studies in development planning.* Cambridge: Harvard University Press.

Chinweizu, Onwuchekwa Jemie, and Ihechukwu Madubuike. 1983. *Toward the decolonization of African literature.* Washington, D.C.: Howard University Press.

Christaller, Walter. 1933. *Die zentralen Orte in Süddeutschland.* Jena: Gustav Fischer.

Christaller, Walter. 1966. *Central places in southern Germany.* Translated from *Die zentralen Orte in Süddeutschland* by Carlisle W. Baskin. Englewood Cliffs, N.J.: Prentice-Hall.

Clairmonte, Frederick, and John Cavanagh. 1988. *Merchants of drink: Transnational control of world beverages.* Penang, Malaysia: Third World Network.

Bibliography

Clark, Colin. 1957. *The conditions of economic progress.* Third edition. New York: St. Martin's Press.

Clark, Colin. 1977. *Population growth and land use.* Second edition. New York: St. Martin's Press.

Clark, Colin. 1977. *Poverty before politics: A proposal for a reverse income tax.* London: Institute of Economic Affairs.

Club of Rome. See Donella H. Meadows.

Coates, Austin. 1968,1975. *Myself a Mandarin.* Hong Kong: Heinemann Asia.

Commonwealth Secretariat. 1987. *Report of the Commonwealth Secretary-General.* London: Commonwealth Secretariat Marlborough House.

Cornia, Giovanni, Richard Jolly, and Frances Stewart, eds. 1987. *Adjustment with a human face: Protecting the vulnerable and promoting growth.* New York: Oxford University Press.

Crawford, John G., Sir. 1987. *Policy & practice: Essays in honor of Sir John Crawford.* Australia: National University Press.

Critchfield, Richard. 1973. *The golden bowl be broken: Peasant life in four cultures.* Bloomington: Indiana University Press.

Critchfield, Richard. 1981. *Villages.* Garden City, N.Y.: Anchor Press/Doubleday.

Cuny, Frederick C. 1983. *Disasters and development.* Edited by Susan Abrams for Oxfam America. New York: Oxford University Press.

Curle, Adam. 1966. *Planning for education in Pakistan: A personal case study.* Cambridge: Harvard University Press.

Currie, Lauchlin B. 1961. *"Operation Colombia"- A national economic and social program.* Bogotá, Colombia.

Currie, Lauchlin B. 1981. *The role of economic advisers in developing countries.* Westport, Conn.: Greenwood Press.

Dekker, Eduard D. (Multatuli, pseud.). 1974. *Max Havelaar.* Amsterdam: Van Oorschot.

Deming, W. Edwards. 1982. *Quality, productivity, and competitive position.* Cambridge, Mass.: Center for Advanced Engineering Study, MIT.

Derman, William, and Scott Whiteford, eds. 1985. *Social impact analysis and development planning in the Third World.* Boulder: Westview.

Dobyns, Henry F., Paul L. Doughty and Harold D. Lasswell, eds. 1971. *Peasants, power, and applied social change: Vicos as a model.* Beverly Hills, Cal.: Sage Publications.

Easterlin, Richard A., and Eileen M. Crimmins. 1985. *The fertility revolution: A supply-demand analysis.* Chicago: University of Chicago Press.

Education and World Affairs. Committee on the International Migration of Talent. 1970. *The international migration of high-level manpower: Its impact on the development process.* New York: Praeger.

Ehrlich, Paul R. 1968. *The population bomb.* New York: Ballantine Books.

Elgin, Duane. 1982. *Voluntary simplicity: An ecological lifestyle that promotes personal and social renewal.* Toronto: Bantam Books.

Emmanuel, Arghiri. 1972. *Unequal exchange: A study of the imperialism of trade.* Translated from French by Brian Pearce. New York: Monthly Review Press.

Estes, Richard J. 1984. *The social progress of nations.* New York: Praeger.

Fanon, Frantz. 1968. *The wretched of the earth.* Translated by Constance Farrington. New York: Grove Press.

Frank, Andre Gunder. 1966. "The development of underdevelopment" *Monthly Review.* Vol.18. September. pp.17-31.

Franz, Uli. 1988. *Deng Xiaoping.* Translated from German by Tom Artin. Boston: Harcourt Brace Jovanovich.

Freire, Paulo. 1967. *Educação como prática da liberdade.* Rio de Janeiro: Paz e Terra.

Freire, Paulo. 1972. *Pedagogy of the oppressed.* Translated by Myra Bergman Ramos. New York: Herder and Herder.

Fromm, Erich. 1976. *To have or to be?* New York: Harper & Row.

Fry, Gerald, Supang Chantavanich, and Amrung Chantavanich. 1981. "Merging quantitative and qualitative research techniques: Toward a new research paradigm," *Anthropology and Education Quarterly.* Vol. 12, No. 2. pp. 145-158.

Fry, Gerald, and Clarence Thurber. 1989. *The international education of the development consultant: Communicating with peasants and princes.* Oxford: Pergamon Press.

Furtado, Celso. 1963,1984. *The economic growth of Brazil: A survey from colonial to modern times.* Westport, Conn.: Greenwood Press.

Furtado, Celso. 1976. *Economic development of Latin America: Historical background and contemporary problems.* Translated by Suzette Macedo. New York: Cambridge University Press.

Furtado, Celso. 1982. *A nova dependencia.* Rio de Janeiro: Paz e Terra.

Furtado, Celso. 1983. *Accumulation and development: The logic of industrial civilization.* Translated by Suzette Macedo. New York: St. Martin's Press.

Galtung, Johan. 1982. *Environment, development, and military activity: Towards alternative security doctrines.* Oslo: Universitetsforluget.

Gant, George F. 1979. *Development administration: Concepts, goals, methods.* Madison: University of Wisconsin Press.

Geertz, Clifford. 1963. *Agricultural involution: The process of ecological change in Indonesia.* Berkeley: University of California Press.

Geertz, Clifford. 1963. *Peddlers and princes: Social change and economic modernization in two Indonesian towns.* Chicago: University of Chicago Press.

Geertz, Clifford. 1968. *Islam observed: Religious development in Morocco and Indonesia.* New Haven: Yale University Press.

Geertz, Clifford. 1988. *Works and lives: The anthropologist as author.* Stanford, Cal.: Stanford University Press.

George, Henry. 1879. *Progress and poverty.* New York: H. George & Co.

George, Henry. 1881,1982. *The land question, and related writings: Viewpoint and counterviewpoint on the need for land reform.* New York: R. Schalkenbach Foundation.

George, Henry. 1897. *The science of political economy.* New York: Continental Publishing Co.

Gillis, Malcolm, et al. 1987. *Economics of development.* 2nd ed. New York: W. W. Norton.

Bibliography

Gorman, Robert F., ed. 1984. *Private voluntary organizations as agents of development.* Boulder: Westview Press.

Goulet, Denis. 1971. *The cruel choice: A new concept in the theory of development.* New York: Atheneum.

Goulet, Denis. 1977. *The uncertain promise: Value conflicts in technology transfer.* New York: IDOC/North America.

Graham, Edward M. 1982. "General Agreement on Tariffs and Trade," pp. 442-444 in Douglas Greenwald, ed. *Encyclopedia of Economics.* New York: McGraw-Hill.

Gramsci, Antonio. 1975. *Quaderni del carcere.* Torino: G. Ginandi.

Gramsci, Antonio. 1988. *Gramsci's prison letters.* Translated by Hamish Henderson. London: Awan in association with the Edinburgh Review.

Gran, Guy. 1983. *Development by people: Citizen construction of a just world.* New York: Praeger Publishers.

Gutierrez, Gustavo. 1973. *A theology of liberation: History, politics, and salvation.* Translated and edited by Sister Caridad Inda and John Eagleson. Maryknoll, N.Y.: Orbis Books.

Hagen, Everett E. 1962. *On the theory of social change: How economic growth begins.* Homewood, Ill.: Porsey Press.

Haigh, Martin J. 1988. "Understanding Chipko': The Himalayan people's movement for forest conservation," *International Journal of Environmental Studies.* Vol. 31. pp. 99-110.

Hallak, Jacques. 1977. *Planning the location of schools: An instrument of educational policy.* Paris: UNESCO, International Institute for Educational Planning.

Harbison, Frederick Harris. 1973. *Human resources as the wealth of nations.* New York: Oxford University Press.

Harbison, Frederick Harris, and Charles A. Myers. 1964. *Education, manpower, and economic growth: Strategies of human resource development.* New York: McGraw-Hill.

Hargreaves, John D. 1988. *Decolonization in Africa.* London: Longman.

Harrington, Michael. 1962. *The other America: Poverty in the United States.* Baltimore: Penguin.

Harrington, Michael. 1977. *The vast majority: A journey to the world's poor.* New York: Simon and Schuster.

Harrison, Paul. 1987. *The Greening of Africa: Breaking through in the battle for land and food.* Great Britain: Paladin.

Hassan, Z., and C. H. Lai, eds. 1984. *Ideas and realities: Selected essays of Abdus Salam.* Singapore: World Scientific.

Haya de la Torre, Victor Raúl. 1936. *A donde va Indoamérica?* Santiago, Chile: Editorial Ercilla, 3rd ed.

Haya de la Torre, Victor Raúl. 1956. *Treinta años de aprismo.* México: Fondo de Cultura Económica.

Hellbank, J. H., et al. 1982. *John Rawls and his critics: An annotated bibliograghy.* New York: Garland Pub.

Henderson, Hazel. 1989. "National economic indexes are not enough," *Christian Science Monitor.* August 17,18.

Bibliography

Hill, Polly. 1986. *Development economics on trial: The anthropological case for a prosecution*. New York: Cambridge University Press.

Hirsch, E. D. 1987. *Cultural literacy: What every American needs to know*. Boston: Houghton Mifflin.

Hirschman, Albert O. 1958. *The strategy of economic development*. New Haven: Yale University Press.

Hirschman, Albert O. 1963. *Journeys toward progress: Studies of economic policy-making in Latin America*. New York: Twentieth C. Fund.

Hirschman, Albert O. 1967. *Development projects observed*. Washington: Brookings Institution.

Hirschman, Albert O. 1971. *A bias for hope: Essays on development and Latin America*. New Haven: Yale University Press.

Hirschman, Albert O. 1981. *Essays in trespassing: Economics to politics and beyond*. Cambridge: Cambridge University Press.

Hirschman, Albert O. 1984. *Getting ahead collectively: Grassroots experiences in Latin America*. New York: Pergamon Press.

Hla Myint, U. 1965,1980. *The economics of the developing countries*. New York: F.A. Praeger.

Hla Myint, U. 1971. *Economic theory and the underdeveloped economy*. New York: Oxford University Press.

Hla Myint, U. 1971. *Southeast Asia's economic development policies in the 1970s*. New York: Praeger Publishers.

Horowitz, Irving Lewis. 1966. *Three worlds of development: The theory and practice of international stratification*. New York: Oxford University Press.

Horowitz, Irving Lewis. 1967. *Rise and fall of project Camelot: Studies in the relationship between social science and practical politics*. Cambridge, Mass: MIT Press.

Horowitz, Irving Lewis. 1970. *Masses in Latin America*. New York: Oxford University Press.

Horowitz, Irving Lewis. 1982. *Beyond empire and revolution: Militarization and consolidation in the Third World*. New York: Oxford University Press.

Horowitz, Irving Lewis. 1982. *Taking lives: Genocide and state power*. Third edition. New Brunswick, N.J.: Transaction Books.

Horowitz, Irving Lewis, José de Castro, and John Gerassi. 1969. *Latin America Radicalism: A documentary report on left and nationalist movements*. New York: Random House.

Huntington, Samuel P. 1968. *Political order in changing societies*. New Haven: Yale University Press.

Illich, Ivan. 1971. *Deschooling society*. New York: Harper & Row.

Illich, Ivan. 1973. *Tools for conviviality*. New York: Harper & Row.

Independent Commission on International Development Issues. 1980. *North-south: A programme for survival*. A report of the Independent Commission on International Development Issues under the chairmanship of Willy Brandt. London: Pan Books.

The International Foundation. 1990. *Protection of the environment: A call for global leadership*. Moscow: The International Foundation for the Survival and Development of Humanity.

Jacobs, Norman. 1971. *Modernization without development: Thailand as an Asian case study.* New York: Praeger.

Johnson, Edgar. 1970. *The organization of space in developing countries.* Cambridge: Harvard University Press.

Kahl, Joseph. 1968. *The measurement of modernization: A study of values in Brazil and Mexico.* Austin: the University of Texas Press.

Kawasaki, Ichiro. 1969. *Japan unmasked.* Tokyo: C.E. Tuttle.

Kazancigil, Ali, and Ergun Özbudun, eds. 1981. *Atatürk: Founder of a modern state.* Hamden, Connecticut: Archon Books.

Khammaan Khonkai. 1982. *The Teachers of Mad Dog Swamp.* Translated by Gehan Wijeywardene. St. Lucia, New York: University of Queensland Press.

Kidder, Rushworth M. 1988. "U.S. foreign aid goals focus on literacy and global poverty," *Christian Science Monitor.* August 17, 22.

Klare, Michael T., and Peter Kornbluh, eds. 1988. *Low intensity warfare: Counterinsurgency, proinsurgency, and antiterrorism in the eighties.* New York: Pantheon Books.

Kloppenburg, Jack R., ed. 1988. *Seeds and sovereignty: The use and control of plant genetic resources.* Durham, N.C.: Duke University Press.

Korsmeyer, Pamela, and George Ropes, eds. 1988. *The development directory: A guide to the U.S. international development community.* Madison, CT: Editorial PKG.

Korten, David C. 1990. *Getting to the 21st Century: Voluntary action and the global agenda.* West Hartford, Conn.: Kumarian Press.

Kuznets, Simon S. 1941. *National income and its composition 1919-38.* New York: National Bureau of Economic Research.

Kuznets, Simon S. 1971. *Economic growth of nations: Total output and production structure.* Cambridge, Mass.: Belknap Press of Harvard University Press.

Langoni, Carlos Geraldo. 1987. *The development crisis: Blueprint for change.* San Francisco: International Center for Economic Growth.

Lapierre, Dominique. 1985. *The City of Joy.* Translated from the French by Kathryn Spink. Garden City, N.Y.: Doubleday.

Lappé, Frances Moore. 1971,1982. *Diet for a small planet.* New York: Ballentine Books.

Lappé, Frances Moore, and Joseph Collins. 1979. *World hunger: Ten myths.* San Francisco: Institute for Food and Development Policy.

Lappé, Frances Moore, Joseph Collins, and Carry Fowler. 1977. *Food first: Beyond the myth of scarcity.* Boston: Houghton-Mifflin.

Lappé, Frances Moore, Joseph Collins, and David Kinley. 1980. *Aid as obstacle: Twenty questions about our foreign aid and the hungry.* San Francisco: Institute for Food and Development Policy.

Lederer, William J., and Eugene Burdick. 1958. *The Ugly American.* New York: Norton.

Lee, O-Young. 1984. *Smaller is better: Japan's mastery of the miniature.* Tokyo: Kodansha.

Lenin, V. I. 1917,1939. *Imperialism as the highest state of capitalism.* New York: International Publishers.

Bibliography

Lenin, V. I. 1899,1960. *Development of capitalism in Russia.* Moscow: Foreign Languages Publication House.

Lerner, Daniel. 1958. *The passing of traditional society: Modernizing the Middle East.* Glencoe, Ill.: Free Press.

Levy, Marion J. 1966. *Modernization and the structures of societies: A setting for international affairs.* Princeton: Princeton University Press. 2 vols.

Levy, Marion F. 1988. *Each in her own way: Five women leaders of the developing world.* Boulder: Lynne Riener Publishers.

Lewis, Sir W. Arthur. 1954. "Economic development with unlimited supplies of labor." *Manchester School of Economics and Social Studies.* Vol. XXII. No. 2. May 1954. pp.139-191.

Lewis, Sir W. Arthur. 1955,1978. *The theory of economic growth.* London: Allen & Unwin.

Linder, Staffan Burenstam. 1986. *The Pacific century: Economic and political consequences of Asian-Pacific dynamism.* Stanford, Cal.: Stanford University Press.

Lipton, Michael. 1976. *Why poor people stay poor: Urban bias in world development.* Cambridge, Mass.: Harvard University Press.

Lovins, Amory B. 1977. *Soft energy paths: Toward a durable peace.* New York: Harper & Row.

Lubis, Mochtar. 1982. *A road with no end.* Singapore: Graham Brash.

Lubis, Mochtar. 1963,1983. *Twilight in Djakarta.* New York: Oxford University Press.

Lubis, Mochtar. 1983. *The Indonesian dilemma.* Singapore: Graham Brash.

Main, Jeremy. 1989. "The informal route to prosperity." *Health & Development.* Vol. 1, March/April.

Mangin. William. 1979. "Thoughts on twenty-four years of work in Peru: The Vicos project and me," pp. 65-84 in George M. Foster, et al., eds., *Long-term field research in social anthropology.* New York: Academic Press.

McClelland, David Clarence. 1961. *The achieving society.* Princeton, N.J.: Van Nostrand.

McNamara, Robert. 1981. *The McNamara years at the World Bank: Major policy addresses of Robert S. McNamara, 1968-1981.* Baltimore: Johns Hopkins University Press.

McNeely, Jeffrey A., and Paul Spencer Wachtel. 1988. *Soul of the tiger: Searching for nature's answers in exotic Southeast Asia.* New York: Doubleday.

Marshall, Alfred. 1961. *Principles of economics.* London: Macmillan.

Meadows, Donella H., et al. 1972. *The limits to growth: A report for the Club of Rome's project on the predicament of mankind.* New York: Universe Books.

Meier, Gerald, and Dudley Seers, eds. 1984. *Pioneers in development.* New York: Oxford University Press.

Memmi, Albert. 1957,1965,1967. *The colonizer and the colonized.* Translated by Howard Greenfeld. Boston: Beacon Press.

Memmi, Albert. 1968. *Dominated man: Notes towards a portrait.* New York: Orion Press.

Mendes Filho, Francisco. 1989. *Fight for the forest.* London: Latin American Bureau.

Migdal, Joel. 1975. *Peasants, politics and revolution: Pressures toward political and social change in the Third World.* Princeton: Princeton University Press.

Miller, Herman P. 1971. *Rich man, poor man.* New York: Crowell.

Moorehead, Alan. 1987. *The fatal impact: the invasion of the South Pacific 1767-1840.* London: Hamilton.

Moravcsik, Michael J. 1988. *On the road to worldwide science: Contributions to science development.* Singapore: World Scientific.

Morris, Morris David. 1979. *Measuring the condition of the world's poor: The physical quality of life index.* New York: Pergamon Press.

Myrdal, Gunnar. 1957,1958. *Rich lands and poor: The road to world prosperity.* New York: Harper.

Myrdal, Gunnar. 1968,1971,1972. *Asian drama: An inquiry into the poverty of nations.* New York: Pantheon Books.

Myrdal, Gunnar. 1969. *Objectivity in social research.* New York: Pantheon Books.

Myrdal, Gunnar. 1970. *The challenge of world poverty: A world anti-poverty program in outline.* New York: Pantheon Books.

Nasser, Gamal Abdel. 1954. *The philosophy of the revolution.* Cairo: Information Department.

Norman, Colin. 1981. *The God that limps: Science and technology in the eighties.* New York: Norton.

Nyerere, Julius K. 1960. *Freedom and development.* Dar Es Salaam, Tanzania: The Gat Printer.

Nyerere, Julius K. 1968,1981. *Ujamaa, essays on socialism.* New York: Oxford University Press.

Nyerere, Julius K. 1969. *Nyerere on socialism.* Dar Es Salaam, Tanzania: Oxford University Press.

Nyerere, Julius K., et al. 1990. *The challenge to the South: The report of the South Commission.* New York: Oxford University Press.

O'Donnell, Gillermo A. 1979. *Modernization and bureaucratic authoritarianism: Studies in South American politics.* Berkeley: Institute of International Studies.

Olson, Mancur, Jr. 1965. *The logic of collective action: Public goods and the theory of groups.* Cambridge, Mass: Harvard University Press.

Olson, Mancur, Jr. 1982. *The rise and decline of nations: Economic growth, stagflation, and social rigidities.* New Haven: Yale University Press.

Orr, Robert M. 1990. *The emergence of Japan's foreign aid power.* New York: Columbia University Press.

Osmánczyk, Edmund Jan. 1985. *Encyclopedia of the United Nations and International Agreements.* Philadelphia: Taylor and Francis.

La Palombara, Joseph, and Stephen Blank. 1979. *Multinational corporations and developing countries.* New York: The Conference Board.

Pearson, Lester. 1969. *Partners in development: Report.* New York: Praeger.

Popkin, Samuel. 1979. *The rational peasant: The political economy of rural society in Vietnam.* Berkeley: University of California Press.

Posthumus, G. A. 1971. *The Inter Governmental Group on Indonesia (I.G.G.I.).* Rotterdam: Rotterdam University Press.

Prebisch, Raúl. 1981. *Capitalismo, periférico: Crisis y transformación.* Mexico: Fondonde Cultura Económica.

Pyatt, Graham. 1984. "Comment," pp. 78-83 in Gerald M. Meier and Dudley Seers, eds. *Pioneers in development.* New York: Oxford University Press.

Raucher, Alan R. 1985. *Paul G. Hoffman: Architect of foreign aid.* Lexington, Kentucky: University Press of Kentucky.

Rawls, John. 1971. *A theory of justice.* Cambridge, Mass.: Belknap Press of Harvard University Press.

Redclift, Michael. 1987. *Sustainable development: Exploring the contradictions.* London: Methuen.

Redfield, Robert. 1956. *Peasant society and culture: An anthropological approach to civilization.* Chicago: University of Chicago Press.

Reid, Anthony. 1988. *Southeast Asia in the age of commerce, 1450-1680.* New Haven: Yale University Press.

Rifkin, Jeremy. 1980. *Entropy: A new world view.* New York: Viking Press.

Riggs, Fred Warren. 1964. *Administration in developing countries: The theory of prismatic society.* Boston: Houghton Mifflin.

Rogers, Barbara. 1979. *The domestication of women: discrimination in developing societies.* New York: St. Martin's Press.

Rosenstein-Roden, Paul W. 1943. "Problems of industrialization of Eastern and South-eastern Europe." *Economic Journal.* Vol. 53. June-September. pp. 202-211.

Rosenstein-Roden, Paul W. 1981. *The new international economic order.* Boston, Mass.: Boston University.

Rostow, Walt W. 1971. *The stages of economic growth: a non-communist manifesto.* England: Cambridge University Press.

Rostow, Walt W. 1978. *The world economy: History and prospect.* Austin: University of Texas Press.

Said, Edward W. 1973. *The Arabs today: Alternatives for the future.* Columbus, Ohio: Forum Associates.

Said, Edward W. 1978. *Orientalism.* New York: Pantheon Books.

Said, Edward W. 1979. *The Question of Palestine.* New York: Time Books.

Schmidt, Manfred. 1982. "Does corporatism matter?" pp. 237-258 in Gerhard Lembruch and Philippe C. Schmitter, eds. *Patterns of corporatist policy-making.* Beverly Hills, Cal.: Sage Publications.

Schneider, Bertrand. 1988. *The barefoot revolution: A report to the Club of Rome.* Translated by A. F. Villon. London: IT Publications.

Schultz, Theodore W. 1964. *Transforming traditional agriculture.* New Haven: Yale University Press.

Schultz, Theodore W. 1981. *Investing in people: The economics of population quality.* Berkeley: University of California Press.

Schultz, Theodore W. 1986. pp. 762-763 in Mark Blaug, ed. *Who's who in economics: A biographical dictionary of major economists 1700-1986.* Cambridge: The MIT Press.

Schumacher, Ernst Friedrich. 1973. *Small is beautiful: Economics as if people mattered.* New York: Harper & Row.

Schumacher, Ernst Friedrich. 1977. *A guide for the perplexed.* New York: Harper & Row.

Schumacher, Ernst Friedrich. 1979. *Good work.* New York: Harper & Row.

Schumpeter, Joseph A. 1950. *Capitalism, socialism, and democracy.* New York: Harper.

Schumpeter, Joseph A. 1951,1989. *Imperialism and social classes.* Fairfield, N.J.: A. M. Kelly.

Schumpeter, Joseph A. 1954,1986. *History of economic analysis.* New York: Oxford University Press.

Schumpeter, Joseph A. 1961,1983. *Theory of economic development: An inquiry into profits, capital, credit, interest, and the business cycle.* New Brunswick, N.J.: Transaction Books.

Schweitzer, Albert. 1948. *On the edge of the primeval forest: Experiences and observations of a doctor in equatorial Africa.* Translated by C.T. Campion. London: A&C Black.

Scott, James. 1972. *The Moral economy of the peasant: Rebellion and subsistence in Southeast Asia.* New Haven: Yale University Press.

Scott, James. 1985. *Weapons of the weak: Everyday forms of peasant resistance.* New Haven: Yale University Press.

Seligman, Ruth. 1988a. "The Buenos Aires plan of action for promoting and implementing technical co-operation among developing countries: Ten years after." *Cooperation South.* No. 2. September. pp. 6-17.

Seligman, Ruth. 1988b. "INRES-South: At the cutting edge of computer technology to speed information to developing countries." *Cooperation South.* No. 2. September. pp. 18-21.

Sen, Amartya Kumar. 1973. *On economic inequality.* Oxford: Clarendon Press.

Sen, Amartya Kumar. 1981. *Poverty and famine: An essay on entitlement and deprivation.* New York: Oxford University Press.

Sen, Amartya Kumar. 1984. *Resources, values and development.* Cambridge, Mass.: Harvard University Press.

Sen, Amartya Kumar. 1987. *On ethics and economics.* New York: B. Blackwell.

Servan-Schreiber, Jean Jacques. 1981. *The world challenge.* New York: Simon and Schuster.

Shiva, Vandana. 1988. *Staying alive: Women, ecology, and development.* London: Zed Books.

Sigmund, Paul. 1972. *The Ideologies of the developing nations.* New York: Praeger, 2nd ed.

Simon, Julian L., and Herman Kahn, eds. 1984. *The resourceful earth: A response to Global 2000.* Oxford: B. Blackwell.

Simonson, Rick, and Scott Walker, eds. 1988. *Multicultural literacy: Opening the American mind.* St. Paul: Graywolf Press.

Sinai, I. R. 1964. *The challenge of modernization: The West's impact on the non-Western World.* London: Chatto & Windus.

Singer, Hans W. 1950. "Distribution of gains between investing and developing countries," *American Economic Review.* Vol. 40. May. pp. 473-485.

Singer, Hans W. 1964. *International development: growth and change.* New York: McGraw Hill.

Singhal, Ish K. 1990. "The GATT and agriculture in the developing world," paper presented at the 4th Annual Conference of the Northwest Regional Consortium for Southeast Asian Studies, University of Washington, October 19-21.

Sippanondha Ketudat with Robert B. Textor, collaborator and ed. 1990. *The Middle Path for the future of Thailand: Technology in harmony with culture and environment.* Honolulu: East-West Center.

Smith, David Marshall. 1979. *Where the grass is greener: Living in an unequal world.* Baltimore, Md.: Johns Hopkins University Press.

Soedjatmoko. 1985. *The primacy of freedom in development.* Lanham, Md.: University Press of America.

Soedjatmoko. 1988. *Policymaking for long-term global issues.* Washington, D.C.: Institute for the Study of Diplomacy, Edmund A. Walsh School of Foreign Service, Georgetown University.

Soto, Hernando De. 1989. *The other path: The invisible revolution in the Third World.* New York: Harper & Row.

Stavrianos, L. S. 1981. *Global rift: The Third World comes of age.* New York: Morrow.

Streeten, Paul. 1959. "Unbalanced growth." *Oxford Economic Papers.* Vol.11. No. 2. June. pp.167-190.

Strong, Maurice F. 1985. *Beyond the famine: New hope for Africa.* London: Oxford Davies Memorial Institute for International Studies.

Sulak Sivaraksa. 1980. *Siam in crisis: Collected articles.* Bangkok: Suksit Siam.

Sulak Sivaraksa. 1985. *Siamese resurgence: A Thai Buddhist voice on Asia and a world of change.* Bangkok: Suksit Siam.

Sunkel, Osvaldo, and Stephany Griffith-Jones. 1986. *Debt and development crisis in Latin America: The end of an illusion.* New York: Oxford University Press.

Thornberry, Patrick. 1990. *Rights of minorities in international law.* Fair Lawn, N.J.: Oxford University Press.

Thurber, Clarence E., and Lawrence S. Graham, eds. 1973. *Development administration in Latin America.* Durham, N.C.: Duke University Press.

Thurow, Lester C. 1975. *Generating inequality: Mechanisms of distribution in the U.S. economy.* New York: Basic Books.

Tinbergen, Jan. 1958. *The design of development.* Baltimore: International Bank for Reconstruction and Development by Johns Hopkins University Press.

Tinbergen, Jan. 1964. *Central planning.* New Haven: Yale University Press.

Tinbergen, Jan. 1967. *Development planning.* Translated by N. D. Smith. New York: McGraw Hill.

Tinker, Irene. 1982. *Energy needs of poor households.* East Lansing, MI.: Michigan State University Press.

Tinker, Irene, and Michele Bo Bramsen, eds. 1975. *Women and world development.* Washington, D.C.: Overseas Development Council.

Tinker, Irene, and Priscilla Reining, eds. 1975. *Population: dynamics, ethics and policy.* Washington, D.C.: American Association of the Advancement of Science.

430

Tinker, Irene, and Richard L. Park, eds. 1959. *Leadership and political institutions in India.* Princeton, N.J.: Princeton University Press.

Todaro, Michael P. 1971. *Development planning: Models and methods.* Nairobi: Oxford University Press.

Todaro, Michael P. 1985. *Economic development in the Third World.* New York: Longman.

Todaro, Michael P., ed. 1983. *The struggle for economic development: Readings in problems and policies.* New York: Longman.

United Nations Development Programme. 1990. *Human Development Report.* New York: Oxford University Press.

Walinsky, Louis, eds. 1977. *Agrarian reform as unfinished business: The selected papers of Wolf Ladejinsky.* New York: Oxford University Press for the World Bank.

Wallerstein, Immanuel. 1974. *The modern world system.* New York: Academic Press, 3 vols.

Wallerstein, Immanuel Maurice. 1979. *The capitalist world economy: Essays.* Cambridge: Cambridge University Press.

Ward, Barbara. 1962. *The rich nations and the poor nations.* New York: W. W. Norton & Co.

Ward, Barbara. 1979,1981. *Progress for a small planet.* New York: W. W. Norton & Co.

Ward, Barbara, and B. T. Bauer. 1966,1968. *Two views on aid to underdeveloped countries.* Bombay: Vora.

Ward, Barbara, J. D. Runalls, and Lenore D'Anjou, eds. 1971. *The widening gap: development in the 1970s.* A report on the Columbia Conference in International Economic Development, Williamsburg, Virginia and New York, Feb. 15-21, 1970.

Watanabe, Takeshi. 1977. *Towards a new Asia: Memoirs of the first president of the Asian Development Bank.* Manila: Asian Development Bank.

Weeramantry, C. G. 1976. *Equality and freedom: Some Third World perspectives.* Colombo, Sri Lanka: Hansa Publishers.

Werner, David. 1977. *Where there is no doctor: A village health care handbook.* Palo Alto, Cal.: Hesperian Foundation.

Werner, David. 1987. *Disabled village children: A guide for community health workers, rehabilitation workers, and families.* Palo Alto, Cal.: Hesperian Foundation.

Werner, David, and Bill Bower. 1982. *Helping health workers learn.* Palo Alto, Cal.: Hesperian Foundation.

Wilber, Charles K., ed. 1988. *The political economy of development and underdevelopment,* 4th ed. New York: Random House, Business Division.

Williamson, Peter J. 1985. *Varieties of corporatism: A conceptual discussion.* Cambridge: Cambridge University Press.

Willis, B. 1948. *A Yanqui in Patagonia.* Stanford, Cal.: Stanford University Press.

Wilson, Dick. 1987. *A bank for half the world: The story of the Asian Development Bank, 1966-1986.* Manila: Asian Development Bank.

Wood, Geof. 1985. *Labelling in development policy: Essays in honor of Bernard Schaffer.* London: Sage Publications.

Wood, W.A.R. 1965. *Consul in paradise: Sixty-nine years in Siam.* London: Souvenir Press.

World Commission on Environment and Development. 1987. *Our common future: The report of the World Commission on Environment and Development.* New York: Oxford University Press; Oxford: Oxford University Press.

Worsley, Peter. 1984. *The three worlds: Culture and world development.* Chicago: University of Chicago Press.

Yemma, John. 1988. "More investors venture into Third World," *Christian Science Monitor,* August 11,12

Zeigler, L. Harmon. 1988. *Pluralism, corporatism, and Confucianism: Political association and conflict regulation in the United States, Europe, and Taiwan.* Philadelphia: Temple University Press.

INDEX

References are to entry numbers. A reference in **bold** type indicates the entry number where a particular term is defined within the text. Numbers in roman type refer to entries the reader may wish to consult for further information about a term.

433